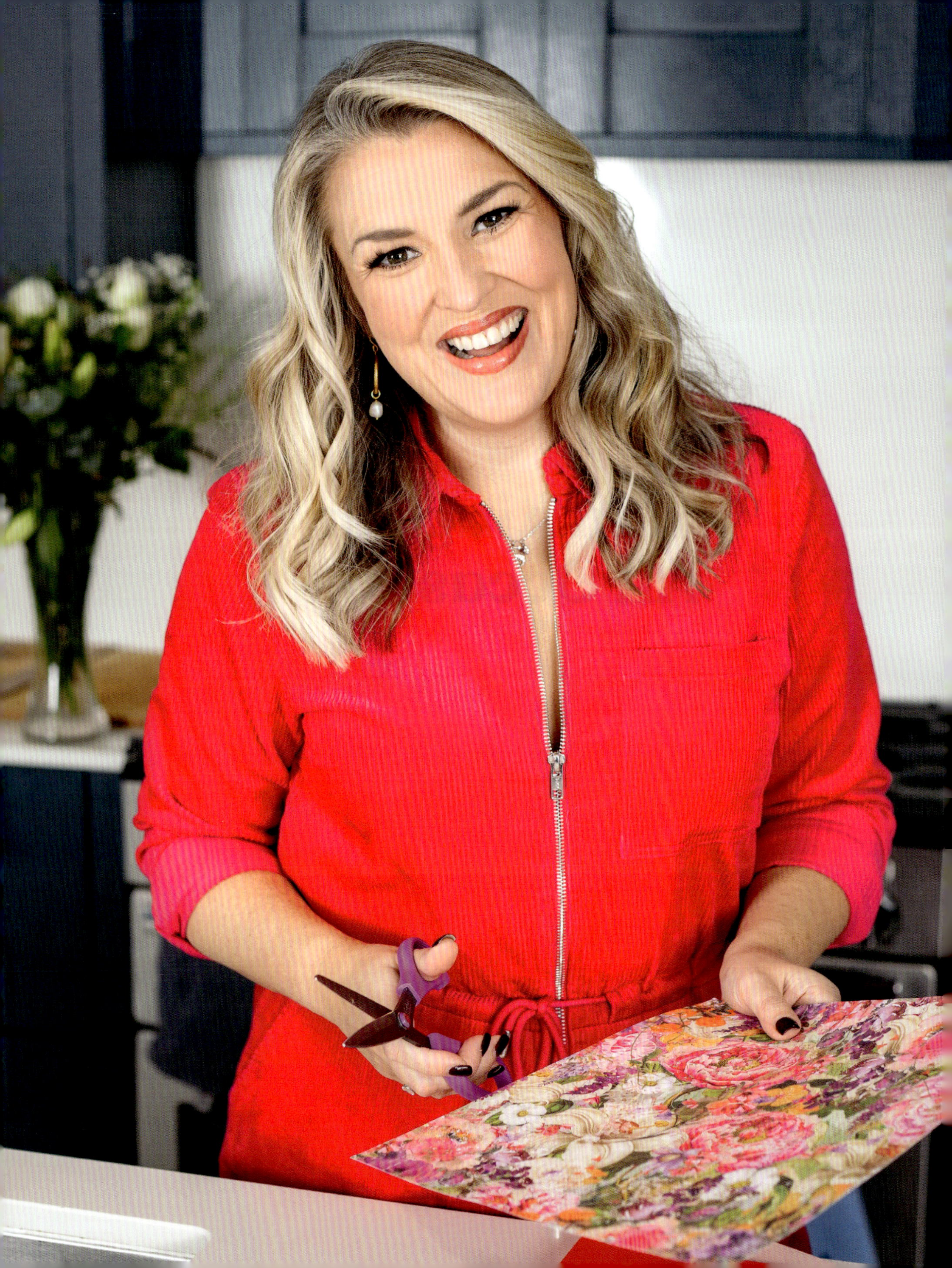

Crafting for All Occasions

70 PAPERCRAFT
AND GIFT IDEA PROJECTS

SARA DAVIES

bantam

TRANSWORLD PUBLISHERS

UK | USA | Canada | Ireland | Australia
India | New Zealand | South Africa

Transworld is part of the Penguin Random House group of companies whose addresses can be found at global.penguinrandomhouse.com.

Penguin Random House UK, One Embassy Gardens, 8 Viaduct Gardens, London SW11 7BW

penguin.co.uk

Penguin Random House UK

First published in Great Britain in 2026 by Bantam
an imprint of Transworld Publishers

001

Designed and typeset in Mark Pro and Recoletta by Bobby Birchall, Bobby&Co Design.
Printed and bound in China by C&C Offset Printing Co., Ltd.

The authorized representative in the EEA is Penguin Random House Ireland, Morrison Chambers, 32 Nassau Street, Dublin D02 YH68

A CIP catalogue record for this book is available from the British Library.
ISBN: 9780857509574

Penguin Random House is committed to a sustainable future for our business, our readers and our planet. This book is made from Forest Stewardship Council® certified paper.

FSC www.fsc.org MIX Paper FSC® C018179

**To Oliver and Charlie,
my best ever creations,
with all my love**

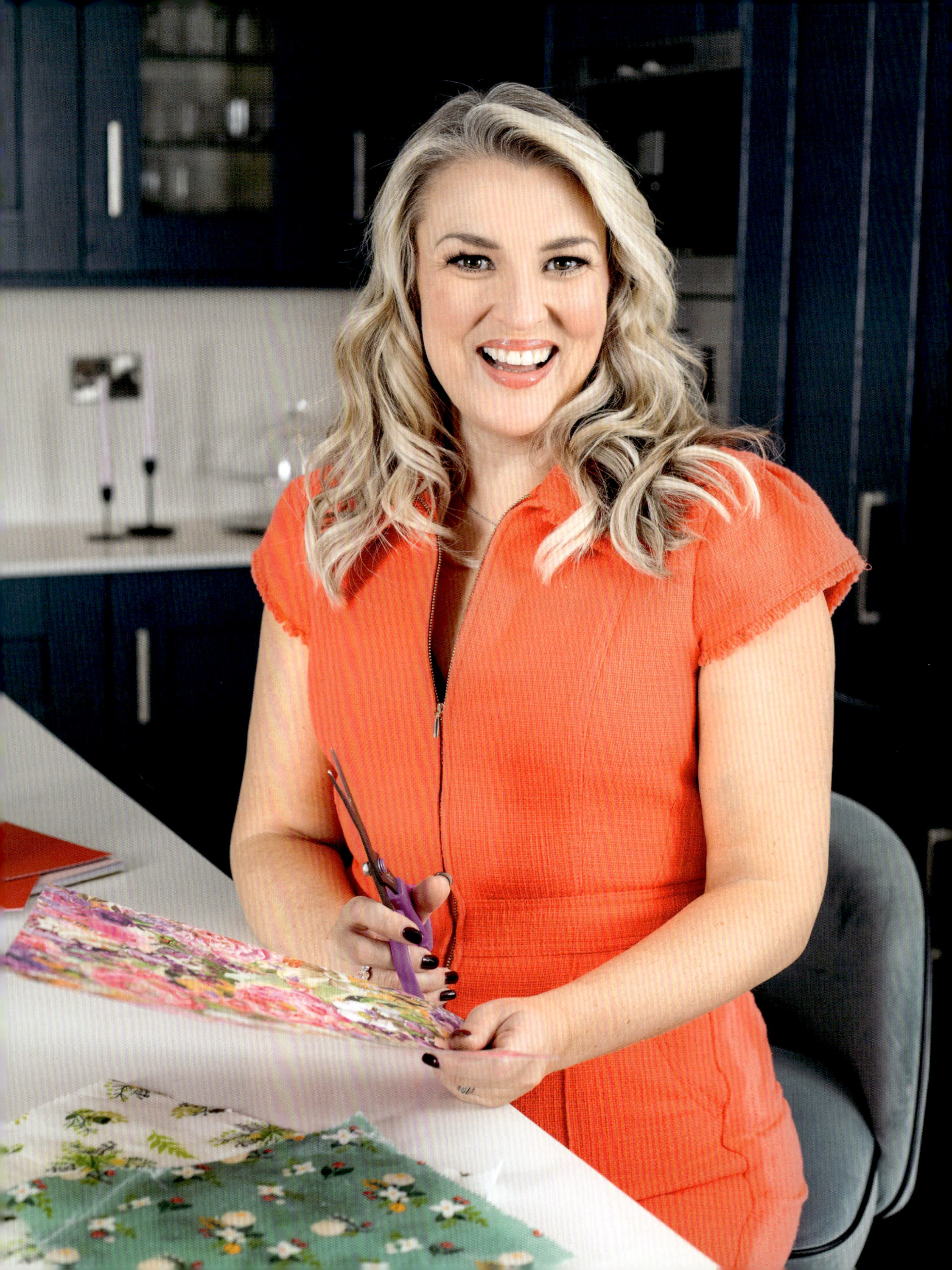

Contents

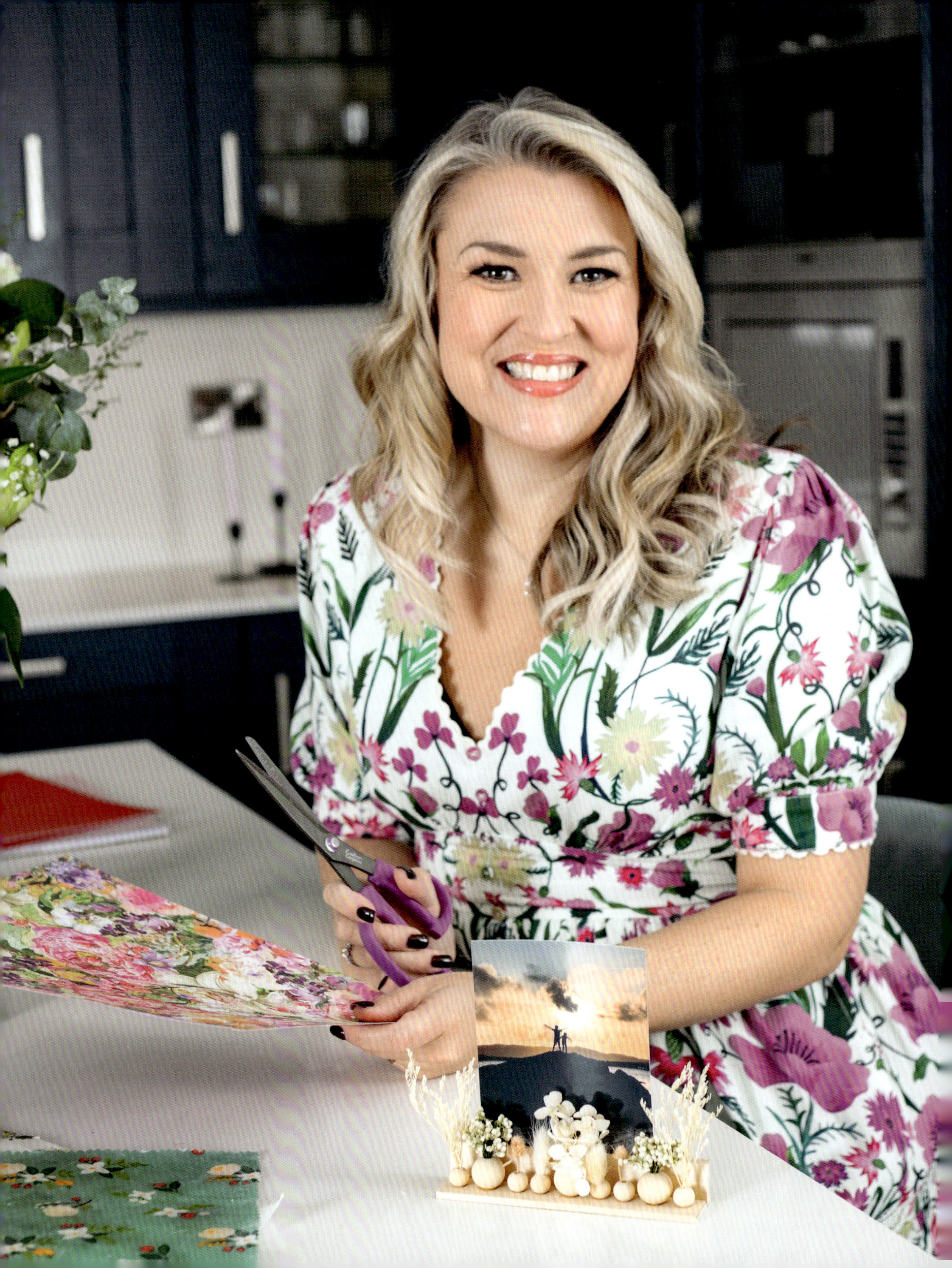

Introduction

If there's one thing I've learned over the years, it's that crafting isn't just a hobby – it's a lifeline. It's a pocket of peace we carve out for ourselves, a moment to slow down, breathe and let our hands take the lead to give our minds a break.

I've always believed that getting stuck into a good craft project can work wonders for your mental health and wellbeing. But, if I'm being completely honest, do you know what brings me the most joy? Crafting for other people.

Whether it's making a handmade card to celebrate my mam or dad, or creating a thoughtful little gift for a friend just because, I've always felt that crafting becomes even more meaningful when it's shared with someone else. The joy begins the moment you sit down with the intention of making something, then it's the rhythm of cutting and sticking, choosing colours, adding those personal touches. It's in those quiet moments, when you're completely immersed in making something with your own hands, that real contentment takes root.

And then comes the best bit: gifting it! That feeling when you pass on something you made with love, and you see the look on someone's face. It's just priceless, and there's nothing quite like it. That connection, the thought, the time, the care – all reminders of why crafting can be such a special part of life.

In this book, I'm bringing you a whole year's worth of crafty inspiration with a particular focus on papercraft and small gift ideas. From Easter delights and Mother's Day treasures to birthday surprises, wedding favours, new home wishes, Father's Day treats, new baby celebrations, congratulations, Halloween fun and, of course, a bit of Christmas magic, there's something to make for every season and every special moment. I know how tricky it is to have endless amounts of time to sit and create, so there's a real mix of things that you can do in 30 minutes as well as projects that need a bit more time and attention.

In my experience, the world of crafting continues to use traditional measurements such as inches and cups, so I've used them where appropriate in this book. However, some projects use metric measurements for accuracy. If you prefer to work in metric, most tape measures and weighing scales display both units, or you can use Google for quick conversions.

I'm so glad to have you on this journey with me. So grab your tools, gather your papers and supplies, and dive into the joy of crafting for every occasion.

I hope you enjoy it – let's get making!

Love,

Sara x.

Acknowledgements

Well, here we are again! I can't believe that I've been blessed with the task of writing another craft book, and I have absolutely loved pulling together each and every project across these pages.

When *Craft Your Year* came out a few years ago, it had the most incredible response. I noticed that more than a few people were asking for another challenge, something that could really stretch the crafty muscles! And that's exactly what *Crafting for All Occasions* is: something that I know my craft community will absolutely love while still offering plenty of projects for people who are just starting their foray into crafting, so I hope you enjoy it.

As always, I want to give my amazing family a huge thank you for their support because none of this would be possible without them and they have made me the person I am today. Mam, Dad, Helen, Matt, Val, John, Simon, Oliver and Charlie – thank you.

Thank you to my incredible team – Ash, Bianca and Jodie – who have helped make my vision for this book a reality.

To my publisher, Steph, and the ever-amazing team at Transworld. Jack Storey on jacket design, Rachel Aird on production, Oliver Martin on publicity and Elle Brown on marketing, not forgetting Bobby Birchall who designed the book and Rebecca Wright on copy-editing. Thank you for doing such a phenomenal job with this book!

Thank you to my agents, Paul Stevens and Laura Hill, and the team at Independent Talent.

And lastly, a huge thank you for picking up a copy of this book – I hope you enjoy these special projects as much as I did.

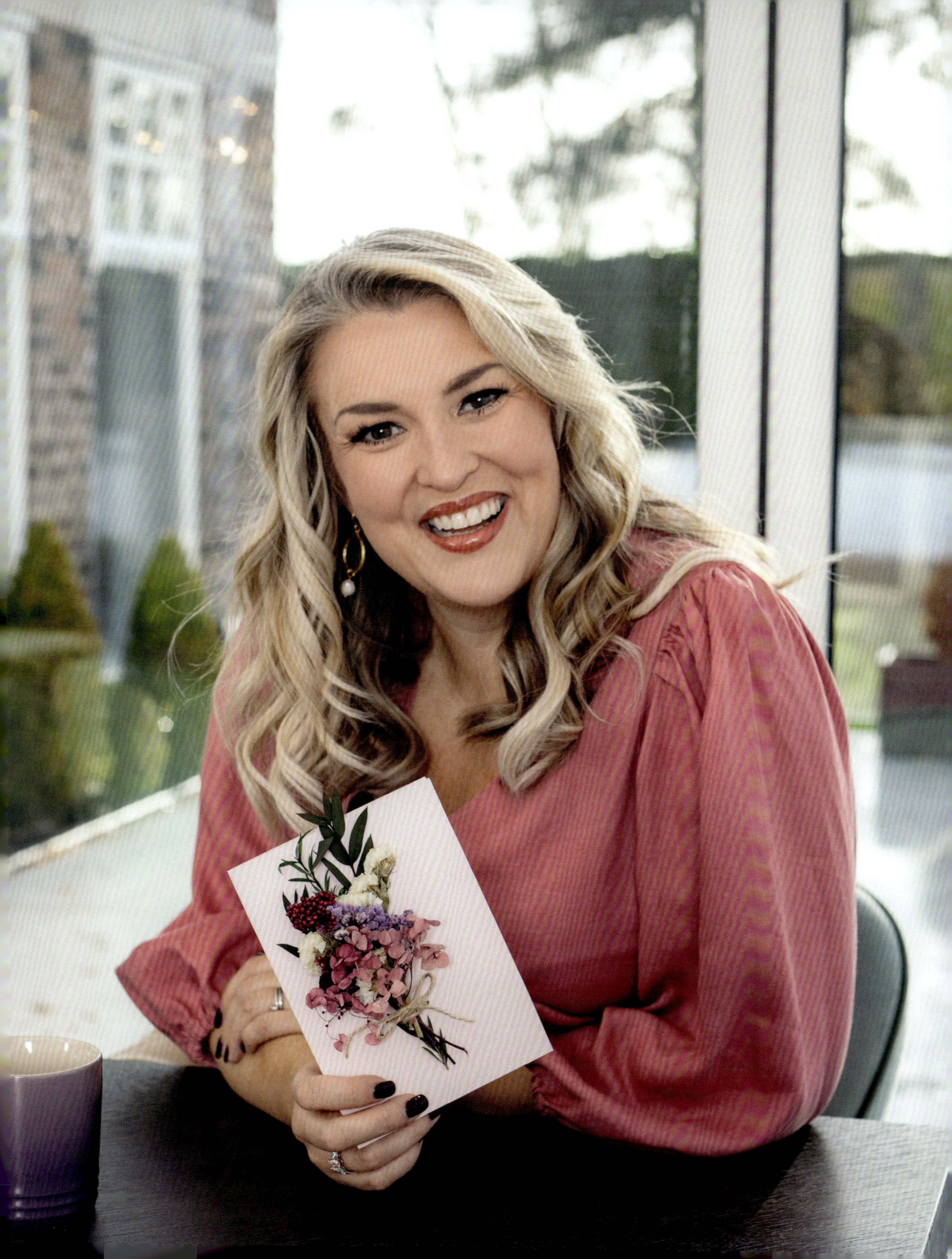

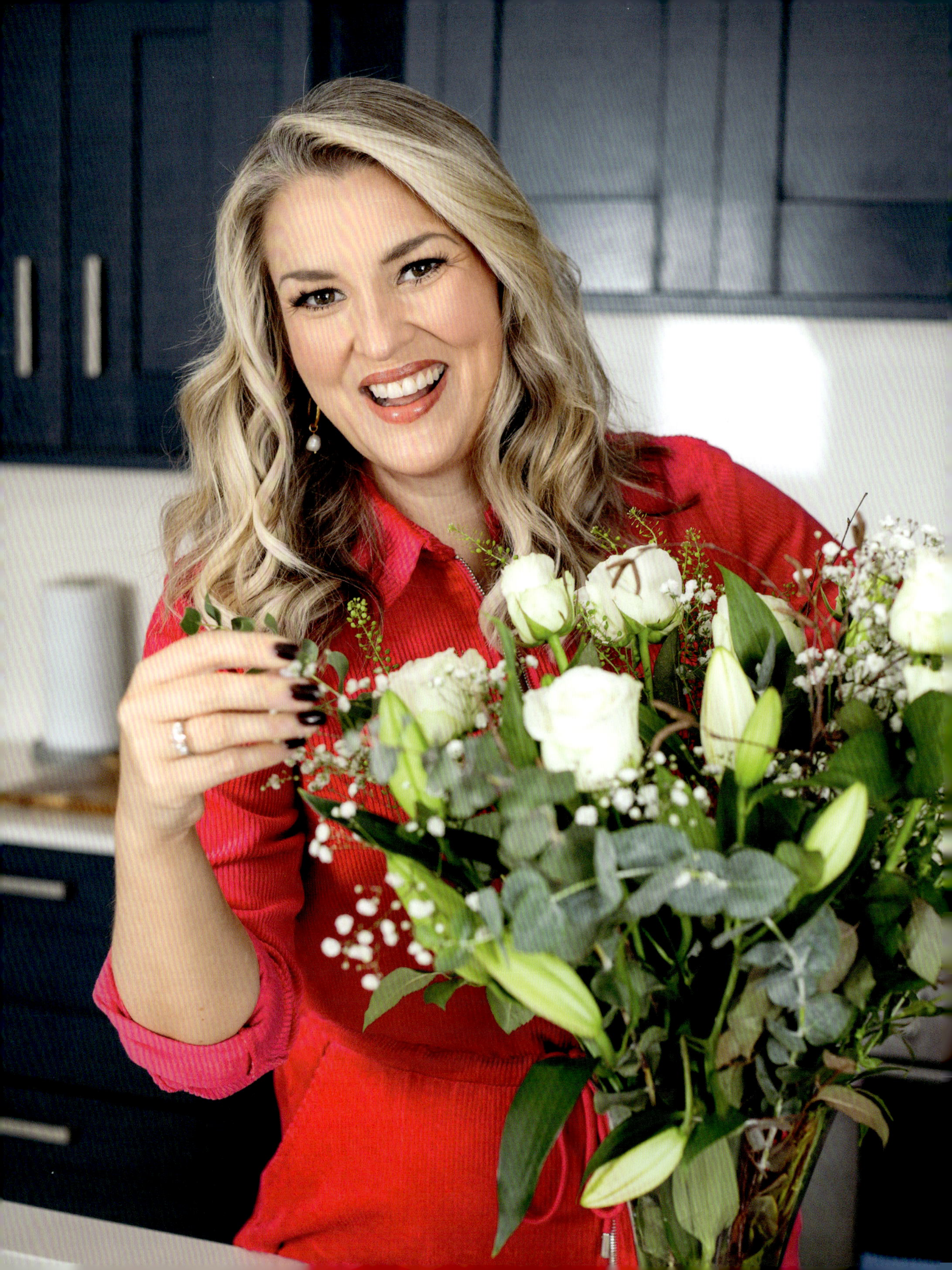

Dates to Remember

Birthday

Anniversary

Easy

Clay Book Page Holder

This gorgeous clay book page holder is the perfect project for bookworms of all ages, and it's one of those makes that looks really impressive but is so simple to create.

What I love most about this project is how easy it is to personalize. You can add different colours, patterns, textures or even initials to make it completely unique for the person you're gifting it to. Whether it's for a birthday, Christmas, a teacher, or just a thoughtful surprise for a fellow book-lover, this is a heartfelt keepsake they'll reach for every time they curl up with a good book!

You will need:

- Air-dry clay
- Clay tools or household items such as cookie cutters and pencils
- Acrylic paints or paint pens
- Small paintbrushes
- Mod Podge

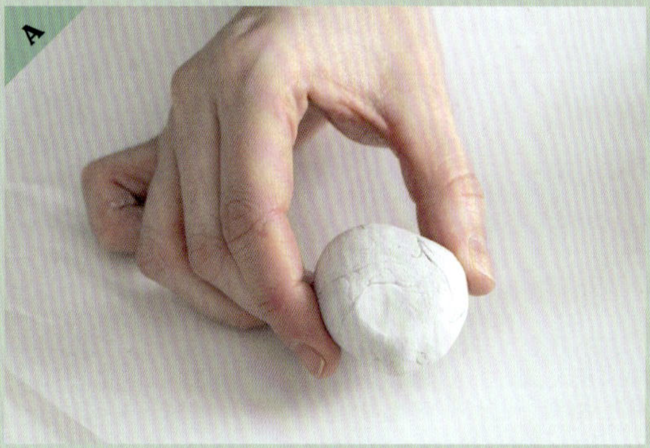

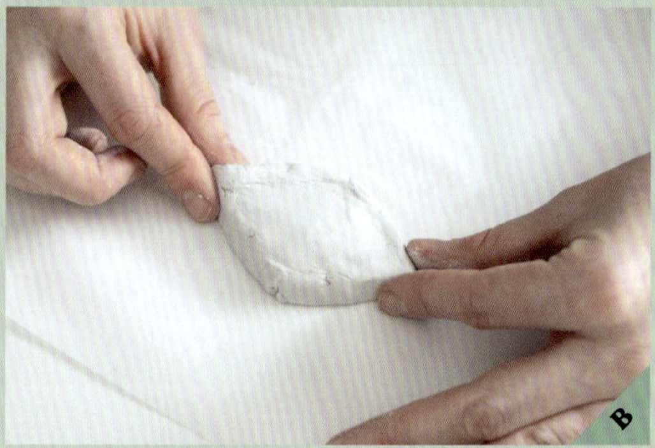

1 Take a small piece of clay and knead until pliable. **(A)**

2 Roll into a ball then pinch into an almond shape around ½" thick. **(B)**

3 Carefully press a knife or circular object into the clay to form a thumb hole. Make sure the hole is large enough for a comfortable grip but not large enough to weaken the structure. **(C)**

4 Smooth the edges. **(D)**

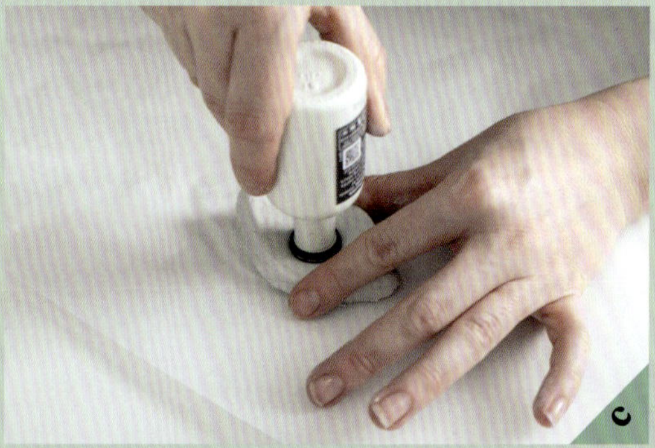

5 At this point, add any details, such as stamps or texture, to the page holder.

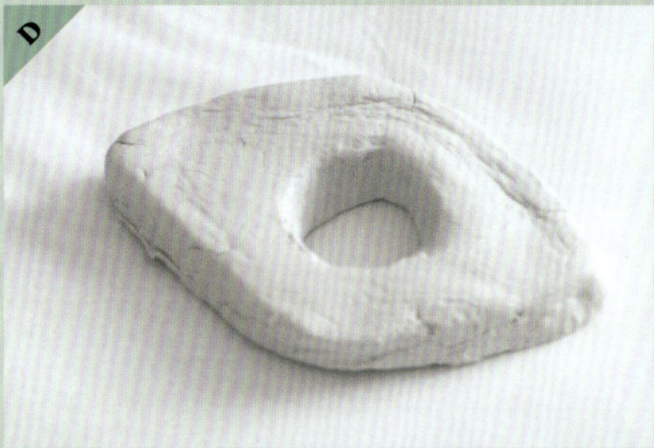

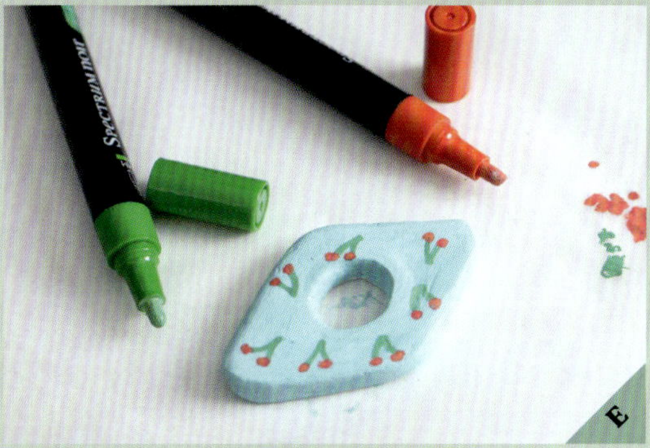

6 Set aside to dry for around 24–48 hours.

7 Once fully dry, paint your page holder using acrylic paints or paint pens. Allow each layer of paint to dry fully before adding additional details or colours. **(E)**

8 Finally, seal with a layer of Mod Podge for durability and shine, then set aside to dry. **(F)**

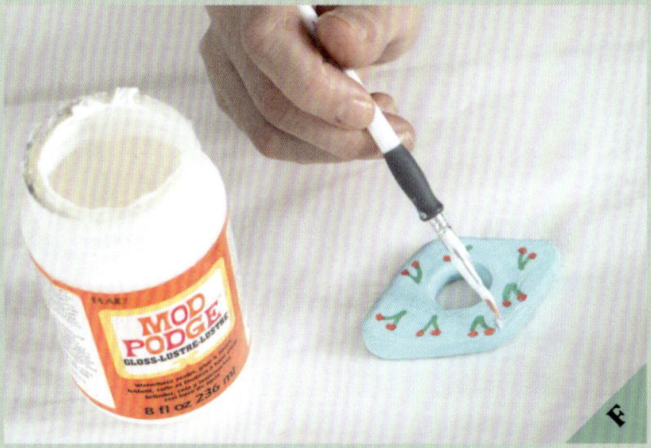

9 Your page holder is ready to gift!

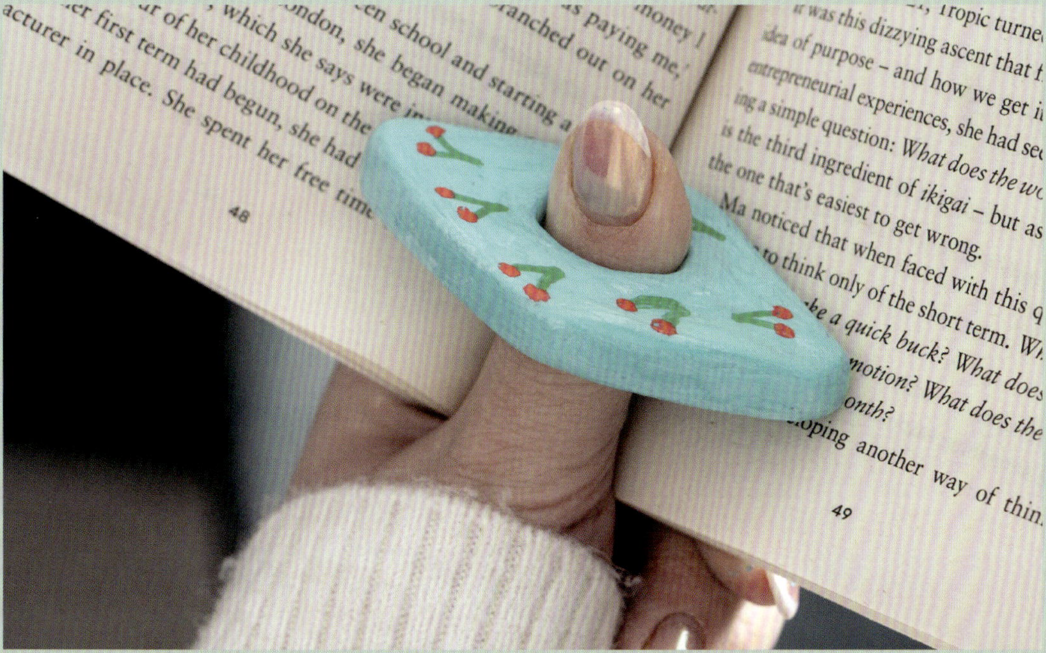

Advanced

Gift Card Envelope

If you're looking for a lovely way to present a gift card and make it feel that little bit more special, you're going to love this project. Using just a single sheet of paper and a few simple folds, you can create a stylish gift-card wallet that looks far more complicated than it actually is.

This is a brilliant make for anyone who enjoys paper crafting and wants to try something a bit different. It's quick to put together, wonderfully satisfying, and easy to personalize with your favourite papers. Once you've mastered the folds, you'll find yourself coming back to this design time and time again. It's perfect for birthdays, celebrations, or just because.

You will need:

- 8″ × 8″ paper
- Scoring board or ruler
- Scoring tool
- Scissors
- Standard-size gift card

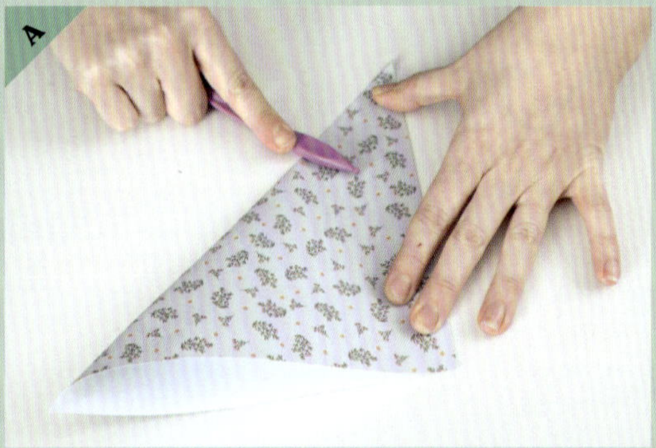

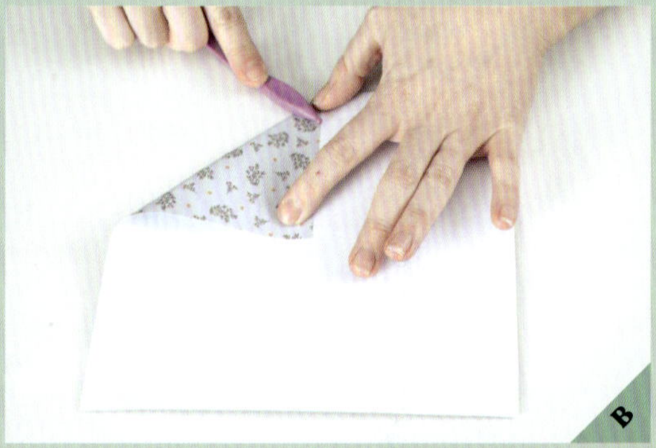

1 Fold the 8″ × 8″ piece of paper in half diagonally, then unfold. **(A)**

2 Fold one corner in towards the centre fold line. **(B)**

3 Repeat on the opposite corner and unfold. **(C)**

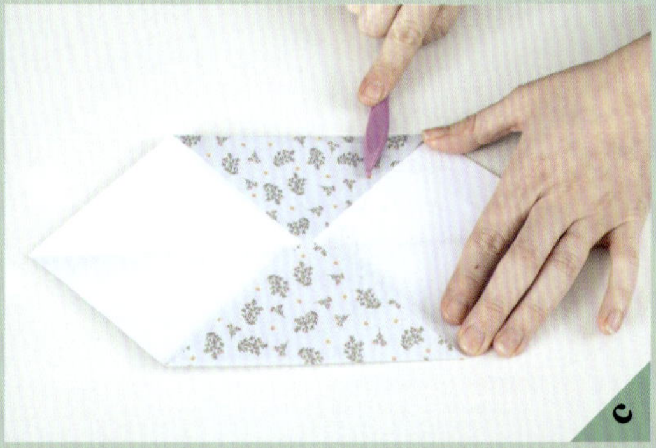

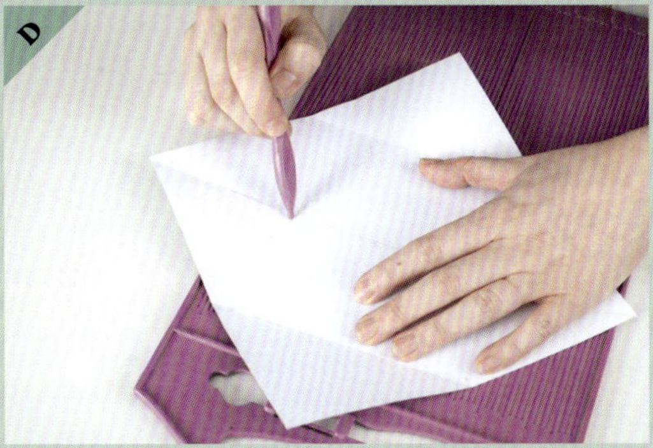
D

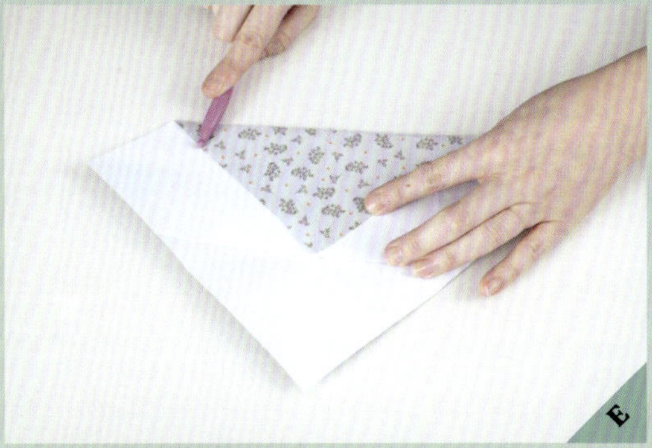
E

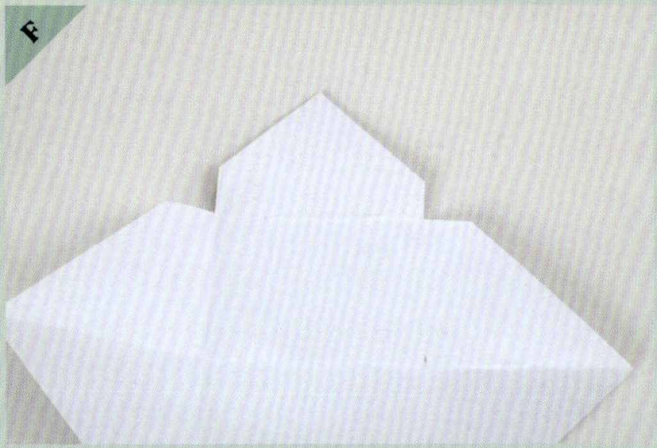
F

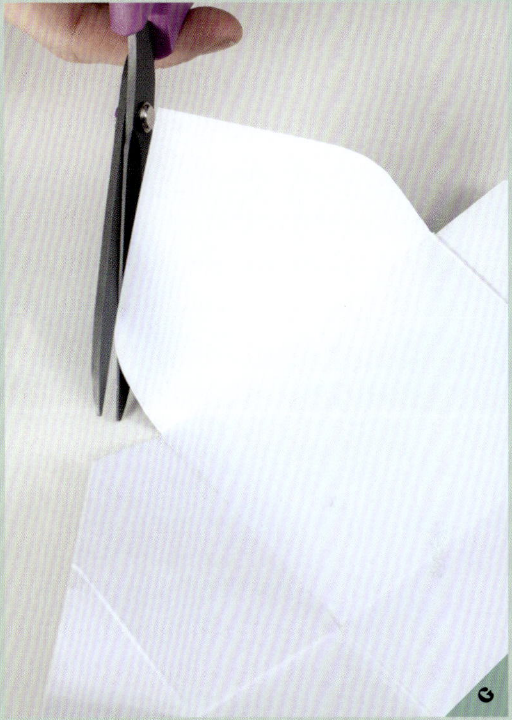
G

4 Measure 7⅜" in from the left-hand unfolded corner and score vertically along that line. **(D)**

5 Fold the left-hand corner across to meet the latest score line, taking care to burnish all the folds well. **(E)**

6 To neaten the wallet, cut away the two small triangles you've created, then round off the points. **(F and G)**

7 Now, fold the bottom section up so you're left with the rounded edges at the top of the piece. **(H)**

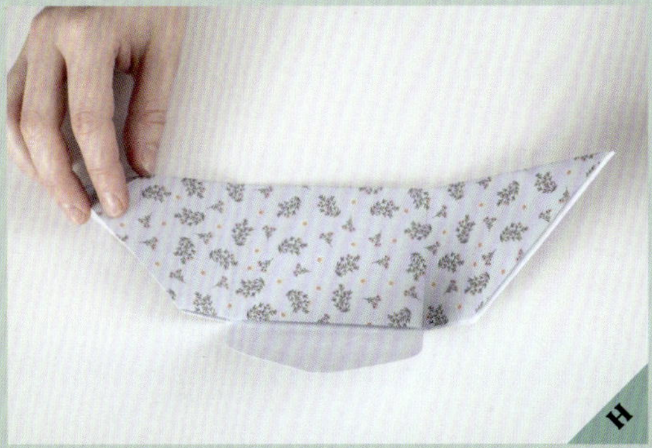
H

TOP TIP **Using double-sided paper for this project means that your wallet will look just as lovely on the inside as it does on the outside.**

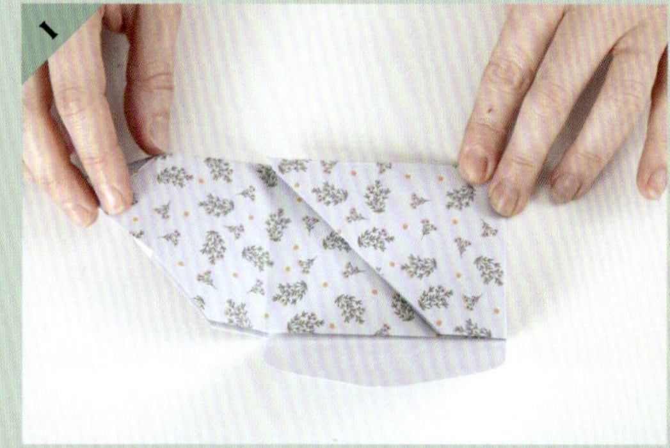

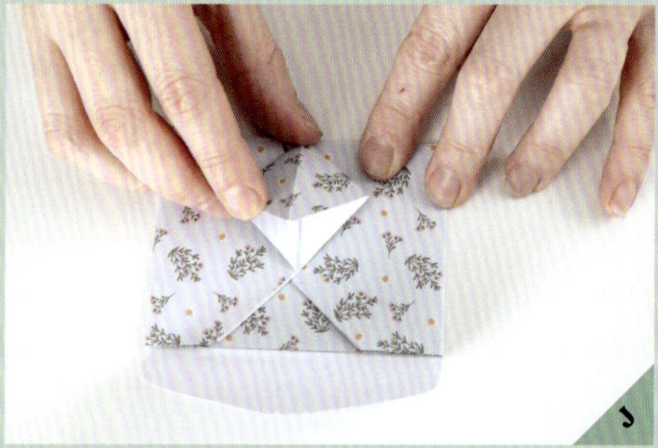

8 Fold in the left-hand side, then the right. Fold the right-hand side back on itself so its point meets the right edge. Let this flap stand upright, then gently push the triangle down and away from you to form a diamond.

9 Insert the gift card into the wallet, fold the top down, and tuck it into the diamond shape to secure. **(J)**

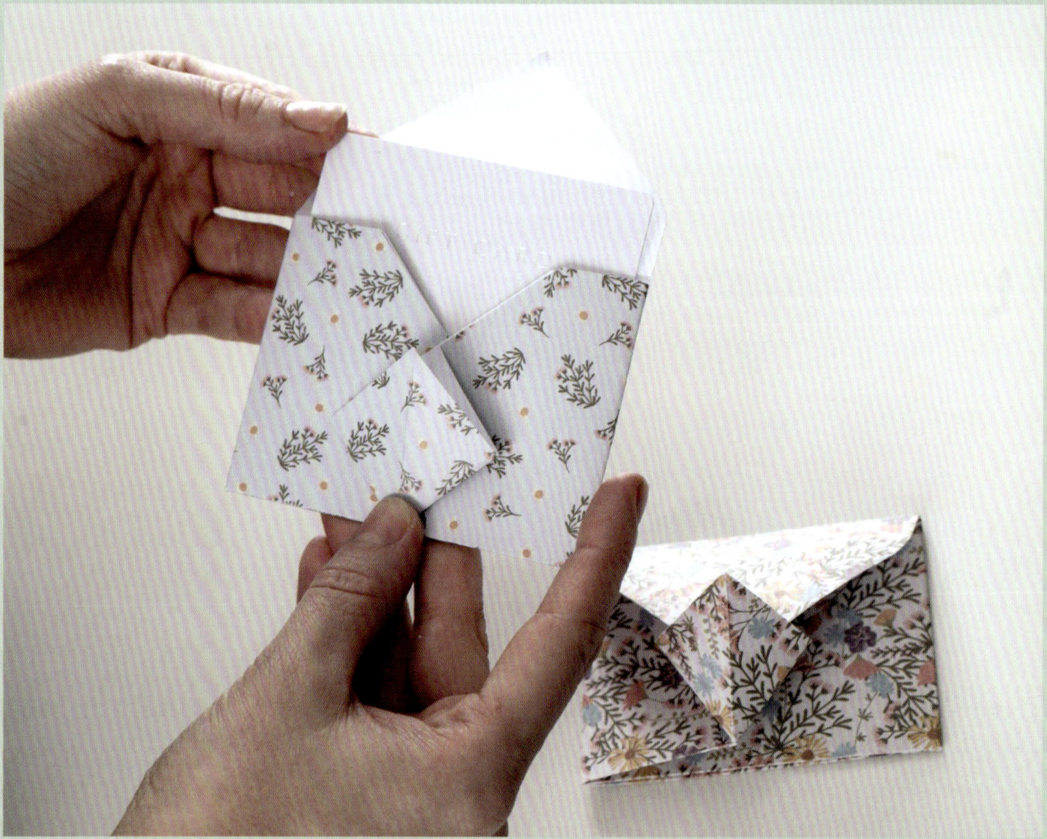

Intermediate

Paper Bow

I love crafts that create a big impact without needing lots of materials, and this paper bow is a perfect example. It's incredibly versatile too. You can use it as a striking topper for a wrapped present, add it to a gift bag for an extra handmade touch, or even decorate the front of a card. The best part is seeing a simple square of paper transformed into a pretty, professional-looking bow that instantly elevates any gift.

You will need:

- 6″ × 6″ paper
- Scoring tool
- Scissors
- Glue gun

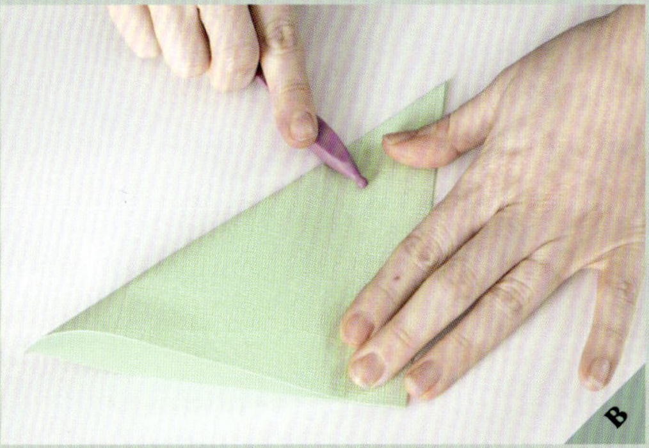

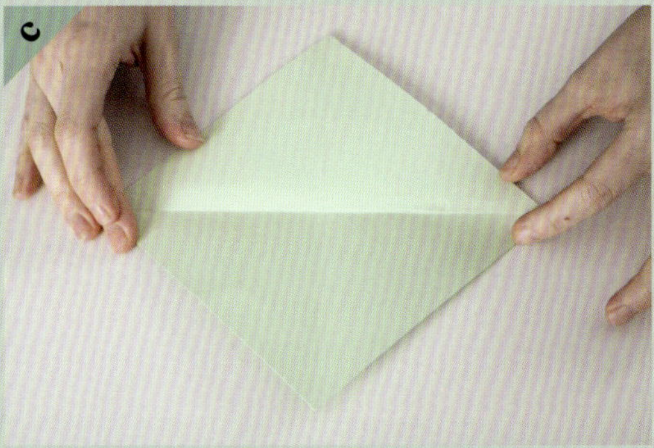

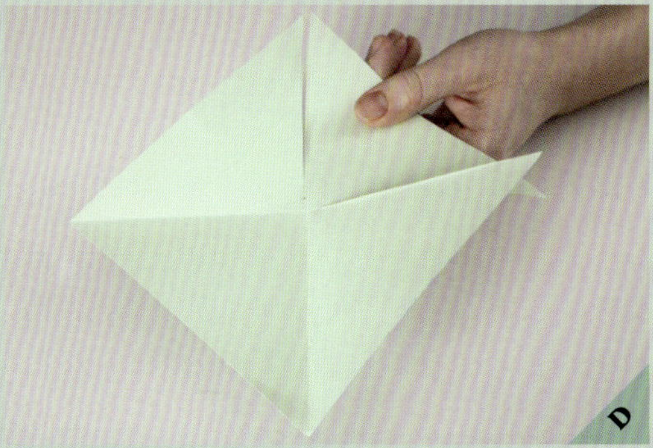

1 Take the 6″ × 6″ piece of paper and fold in half diagonally. **(A and B)**

2 Open it out, then fold it in half diagonally in the opposite direction. **(C)**

3 Cut along each fold line, stopping about ¼″ from the centre so the sections remain connected. **(D)**

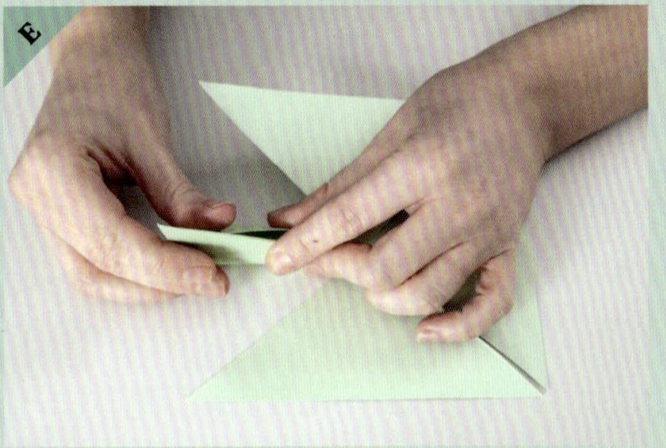

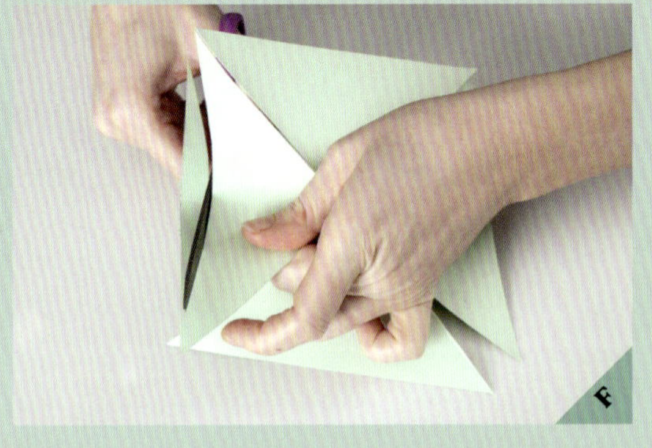

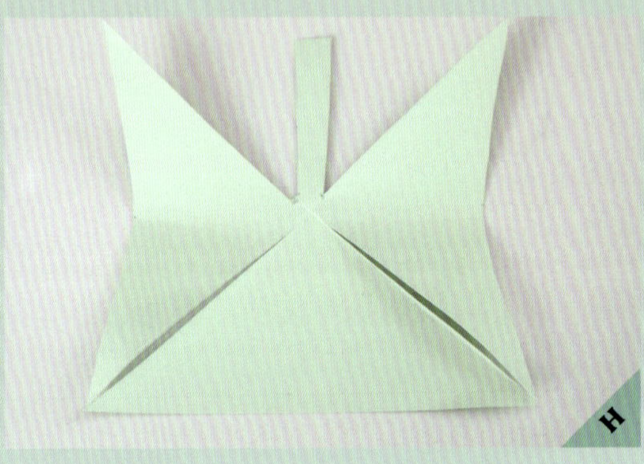

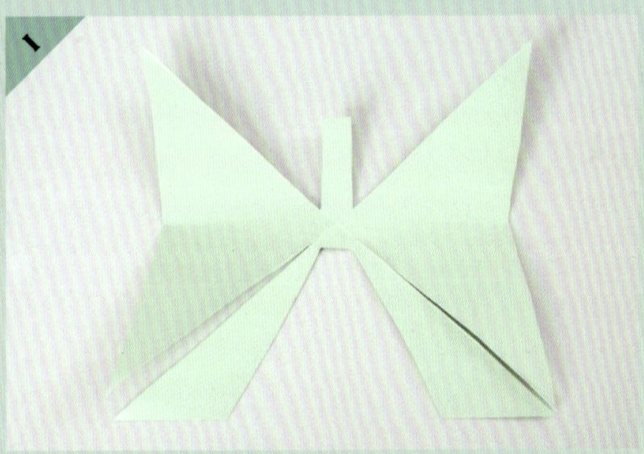

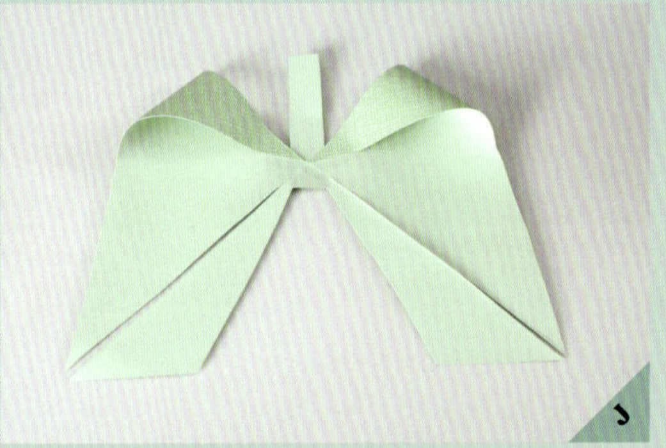

4 Take one of the four triangular sections and gently fold the points together to meet. **(E)**

5 Trim about ½" from the fold across to where the points meet, to shape the bow. **(F)**

6 Repeat this folding and trimming on the opposite triangular section. **(G)**

7 From one of the remaining sections, trim away two triangles so you're left with a narrow strip approximately ¼" wide. **(H)**

8 On the final section, cut away a triangle from the centre to create the bow tails. **(I)**

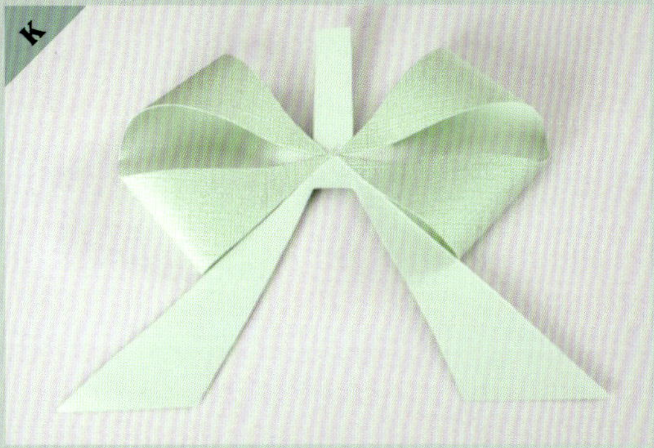

9 Fold the four points into the centre and glue them securely in place. **(J and K)**.

10 Take the narrow strip, fold it over the front of the bow, and glue it neatly at the back.

11 Trim away any excess paper to complete your bow.

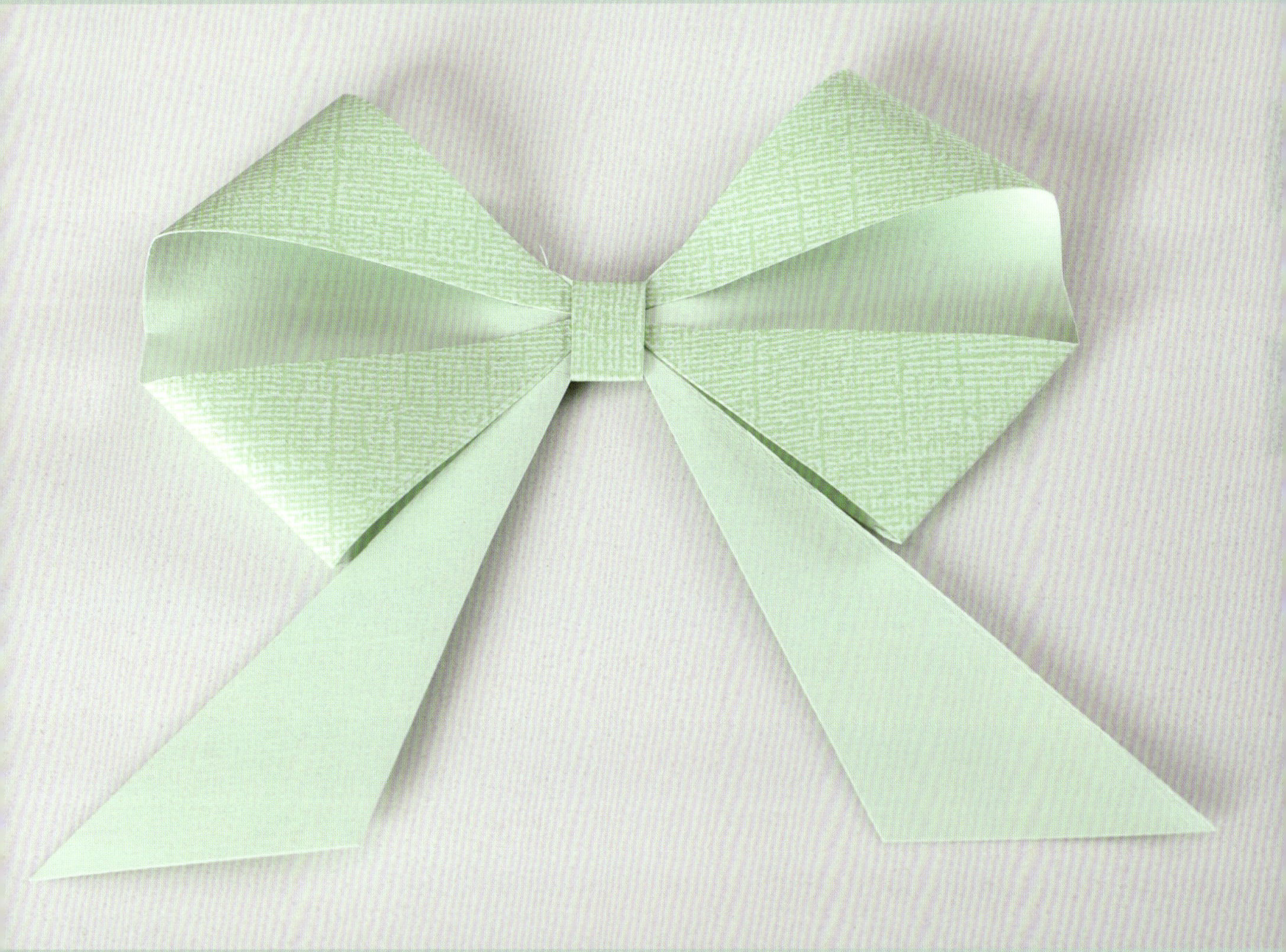

Advanced

Tulip Card

There's something truly magical about handmade cards – they carry a personal touch and can brighten someone's day. In this project, you'll create a beautiful 3D floral card that combines the delicate art of watercolour with layered paper techniques.

Each step is simple to follow, and the results are well worth every minute of effort. This project is not only an opportunity to create something striking but also a wonderfully relaxing and rewarding creative experience. So gather your supplies and let your creativity flourish.

You will need:

- 6″ × 6″ card base (or cut from your own cardstock)
- Kraft card
- Coloured paper (for petals)
- Pencil
- Scissors
- Glue
- Bone folder or ruler
- Watercolour card
- Watercolour paints
- Water
- Small and medium-sized paintbrushes
- Green pen
- Ribbon or bow
- Gemstones

1 If you don't have a pre-cut 6″ × 6″ card base, cut one from some cardstock.

2 Create a mat for the card from some Kraft card measuring 5¾″ × 5¾″. **(A)**

3 On scrap paper, draw an oval shape approximately ¼″ wide by ¾″ tall, then cut it out carefully. This is your petal template. **(B)**

TOP TIP Use a bone folder or the edge of a ruler to gently crease each petal before stacking. This helps create a realistic 3D effect and allows the flowers to pop off the card without flattening.

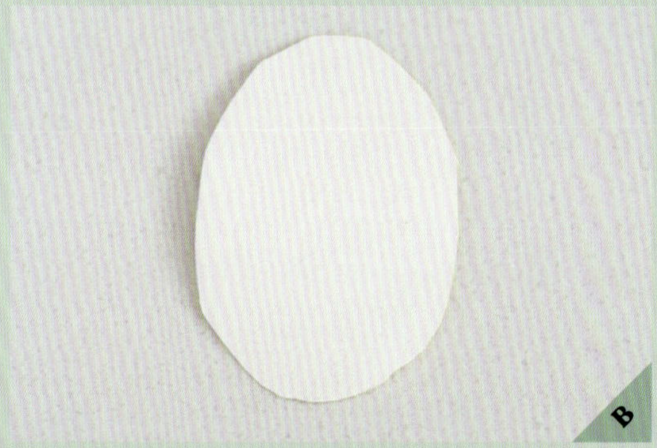

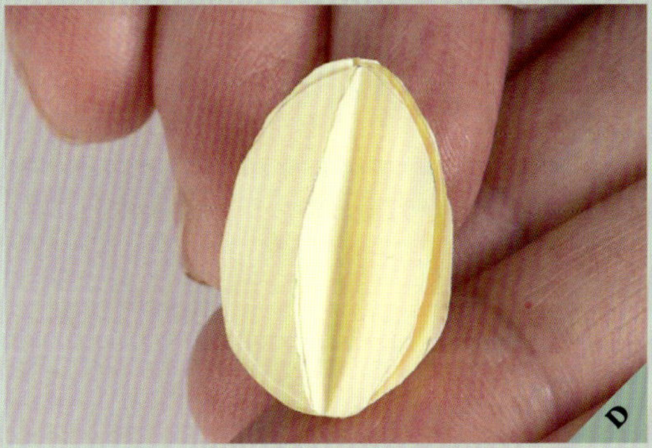

4 Cut a strip of coloured paper wide enough to comfortably fit the petal template. Draw around the template eight times and cut out the petals. **(C)**

5 Fold each petal gently in half lengthways to add dimension. Stack the folded petals on top of each other, aligning the bases, and secure with glue to form a flower head. **(D)**

6 Repeat steps 4–5 to create seven flower heads in total.

7 Cut a piece of watercolour card measuring slightly smaller than the piece of Kraft card – approximately 5⅝" × 5⅝" or wide enough that a border of the Kraft card is visible. **(E)**

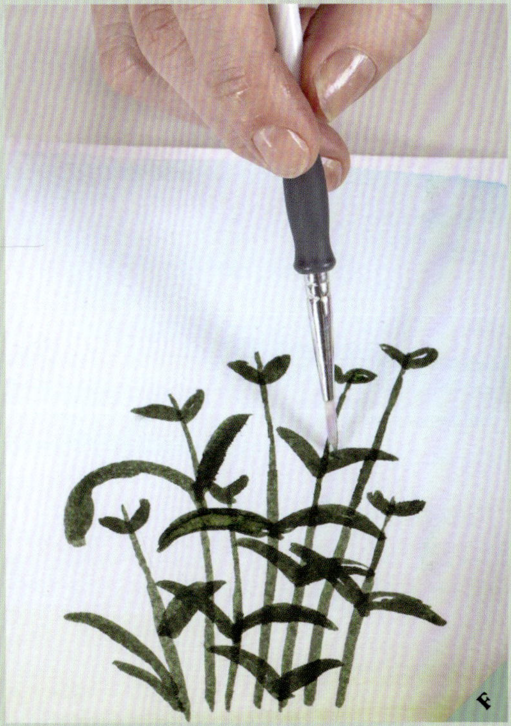

8 Using watercolour paints, create a soft blue and green wash to suggest sky and grass, then set aside to dry fully.

9 Lightly pencil in stems for each flower, then trace over the lines with watercolour paint or a green pen and add leaves. **(F)**

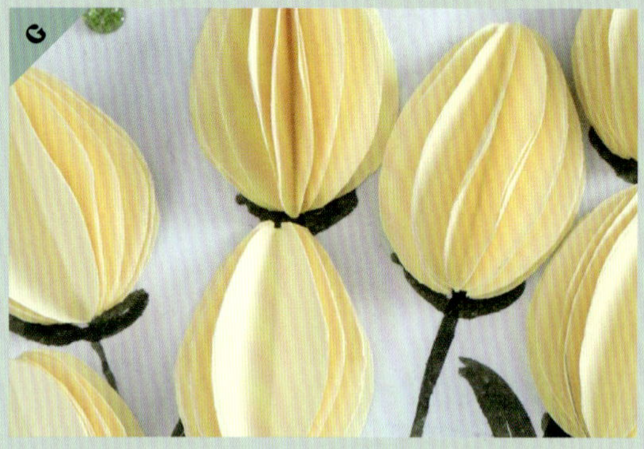

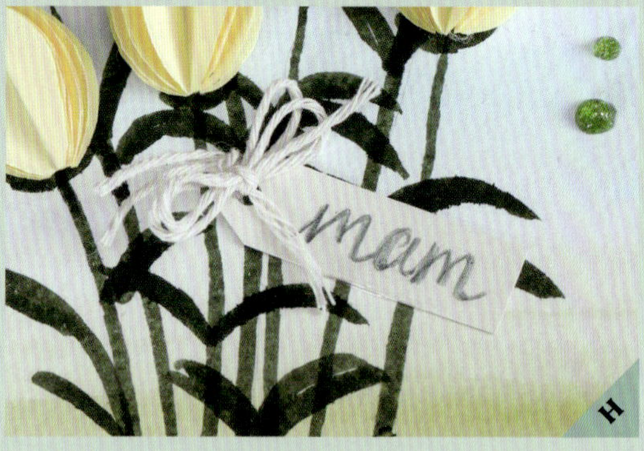

10 Glue each flower head in place over its drawn stem, then attach the watercolour panel to the Kraft layer. **(G)**

11 Add a sentiment, finish with a ribbon or bow, and glue a few gemstones in place as a final touch. **(H)**

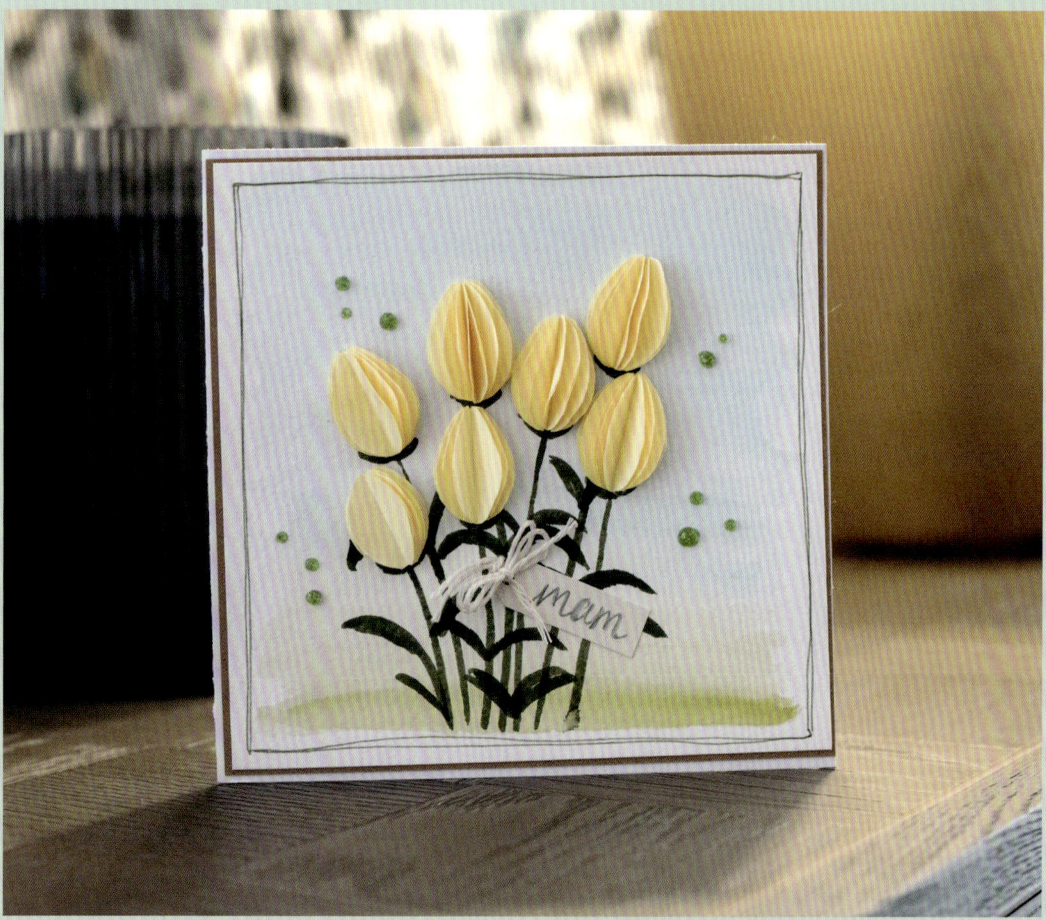

Easy

Floral Photo Frame

In my humble opinion, the best kind of gifts are both beautiful and personal, and this DIY floral frame is exactly that. The combination of natural wooden beads and dried flowers gives it a rustic, handmade charm. It's satisfying to create and a lovely way to display a favourite photo.

You will need:

- Three wooden paint paddles (or another soft wood alternative measuring roughly 5⅞" × ¼")
- Glue gun
- Wooden beads in two different sizes (NB beads with holes, not solid balls)
- Dried flowers
- Photograph

TOP TIP Personalize your frame using your recipient's favourite colours.

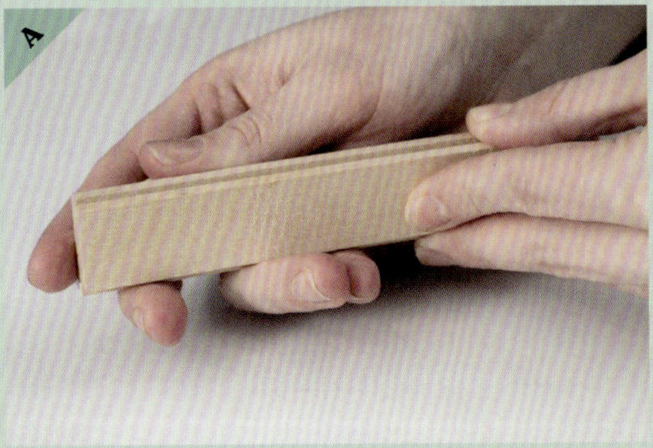

A

1 Take two of the wooden paint paddles and apply hot glue along both long edges of one piece but leaving a clear gap in the centre for your photograph. Press the second paddle on top so the two pieces are stacked, forming the back of the frame. You can make the frame as big or as small as you like – just use lengths of wood to match the size of frame you wish to make. **(A)**

2 Set the stacked paddles aside to dry completely.

3 Next, take the third wooden paddle and run a line of hot glue along one of the long, thin edges.

B

4 Fix this piece to the front of the stacked paddles along one edge, so the stacked pieces stand upright and the third piece lies flat at the front. This creates the base and front support of the frame. **(B)**

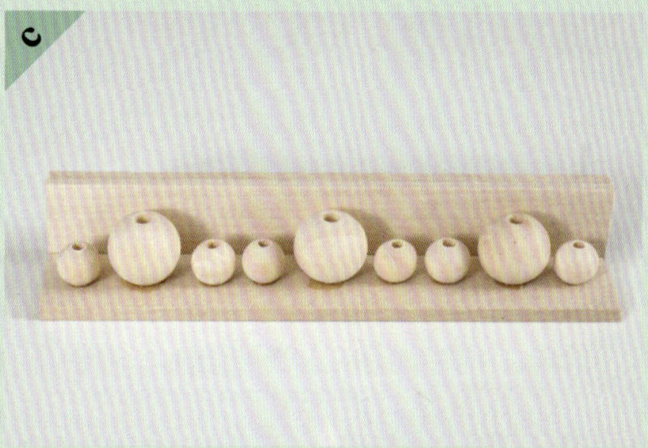

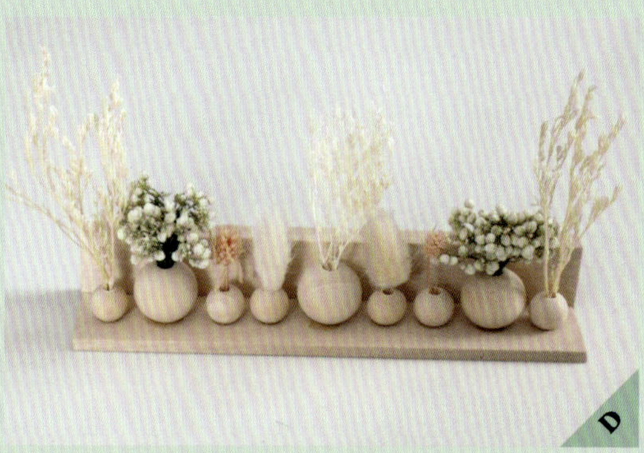

5 Allow the glue to dry fully before continuing.

6 Position the wooden beads on the front face of the frame with the holes facing upwards, then secure them in place using hot glue. **(C)**

7 Insert dried flowers in to the holes in the beads, mixing colours and textures to create a natural arrangement. **(D)**

8 Finally, slide your chosen photograph into the gap between the two wooden paddles created in step 1.

9 And that's it – a gorgeous, handmade floral frame, all ready to be wrapped and gifted!

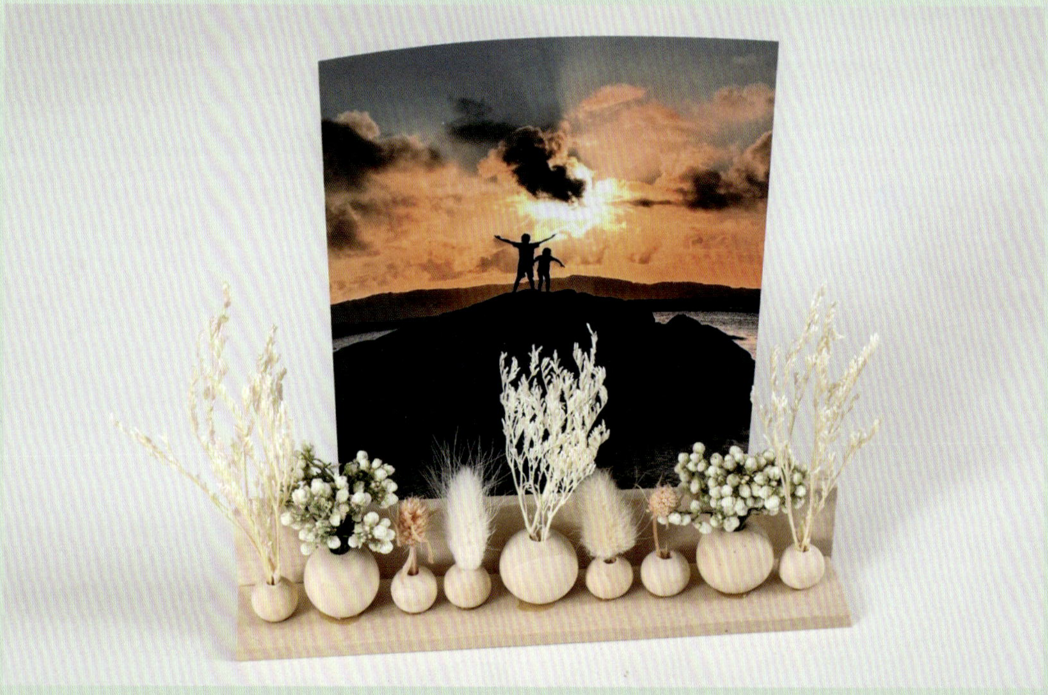

Intermediate

Bouquet Magnet Card

This dried floral bouquet card is a thoughtful way to celebrate special occasions such as anniversaries or birthdays. The miniature bouquet isn't just a beautiful decorative touch, it doubles as a removable fridge magnet, so the recipient can enjoy a small reminder of the celebration all year round!

You will need:

- White card
- Patterned paper
- Scissors
- Glue tape pen
- Dried flowers
- Thin twine
- Kraft card
- Craft knife
- Craft mat
- Magnetic sheet
- Glue gun
- Card
- String
- Pen

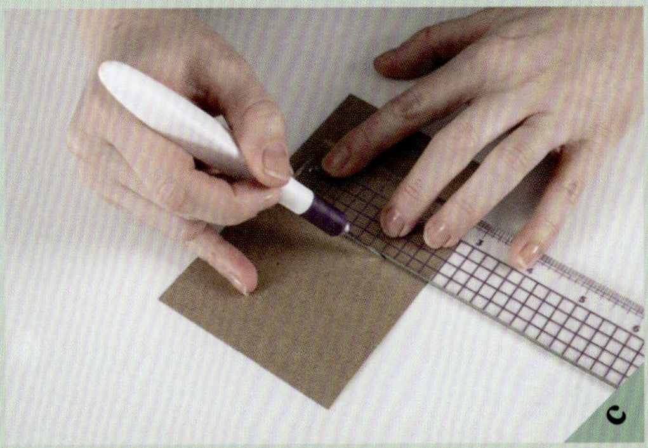

1 Create a 5″ x 7″ card base. **(A)**

2 Cover the front of the card with patterned paper using a tape pen. **(B)**

3 Select a small bunch of dried flowers and tie them together with thin twine to create a miniature bouquet.

4 Cut a rectangle of Kraft card measuring 5½″ x 3½″. Using a craft knife and mat, make two horizontal lines to create a slot approximately 1″ wide. **(C and D)**

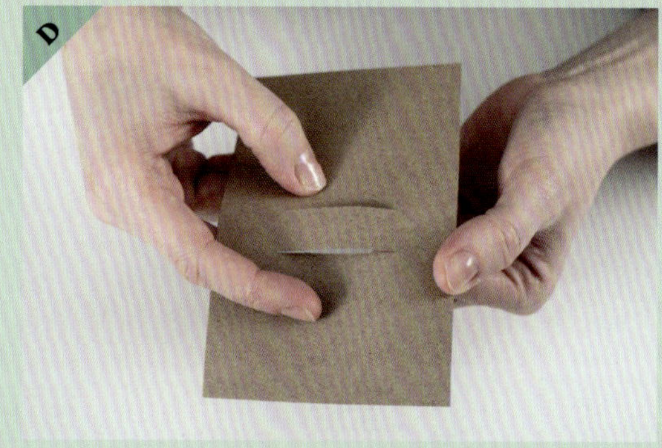

D

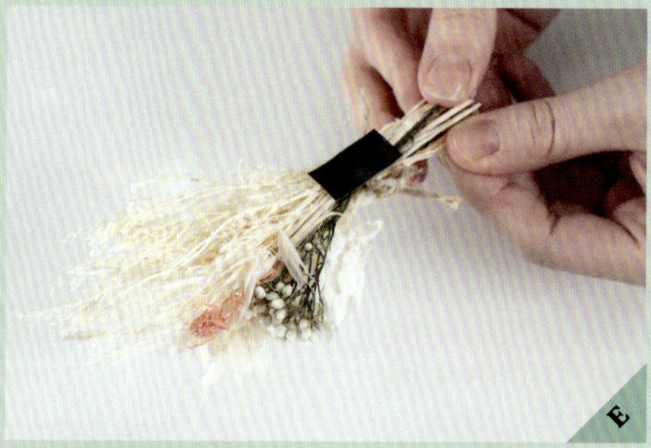

E

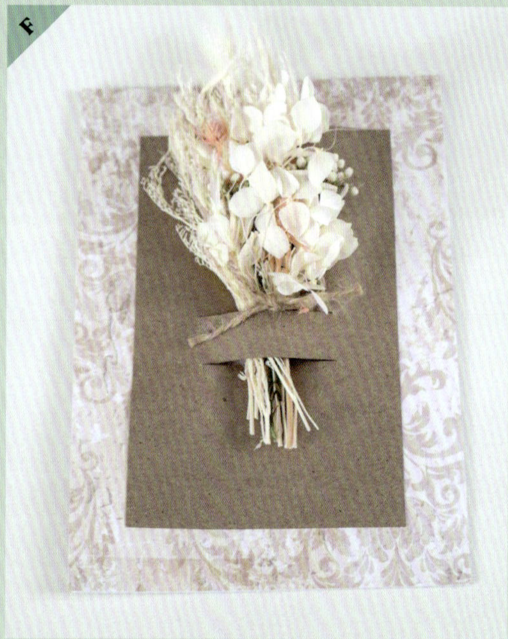

F

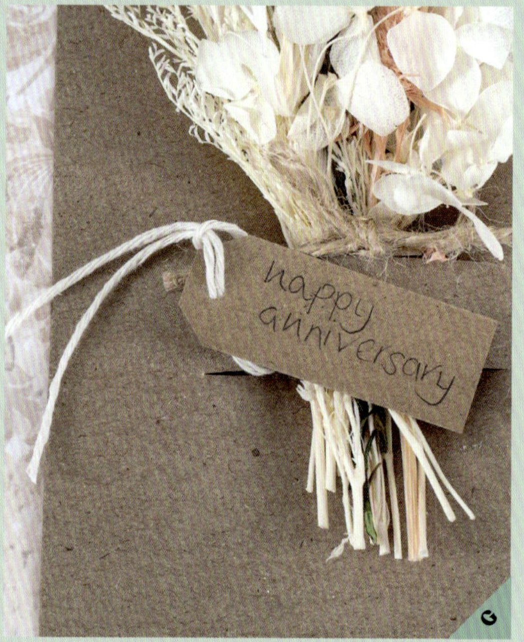

G

5 Attach a small strip of magnetic sheet to the back of the dried bouquet using hot glue. **(E)**

6 Tuck the bouquet into the slot on the Kraft card.

7 Apply adhesive along the back edges of the Kraft panel and fix it to the front of the 5″ × 7″ card base. **(F)**

8 Cut a piece of card measuring 1¾″ × ¾″ and create a tag using a short length of string. Write out a sentiment and attach it to the front of the card to finish. **(G)**

TOP TIP **Personalize this card with your partner's or special someone's favourite flowers.**

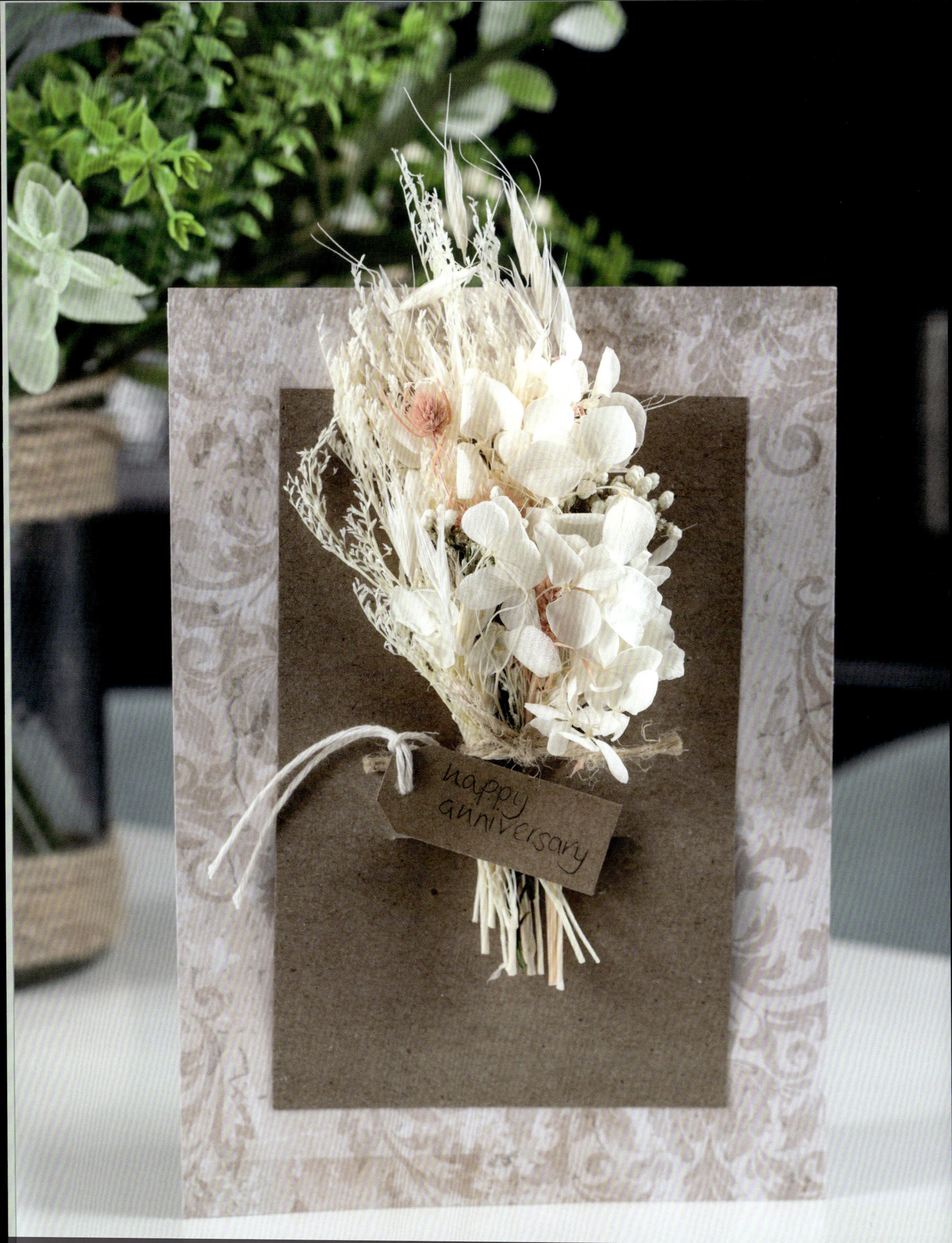
happy
anniversary

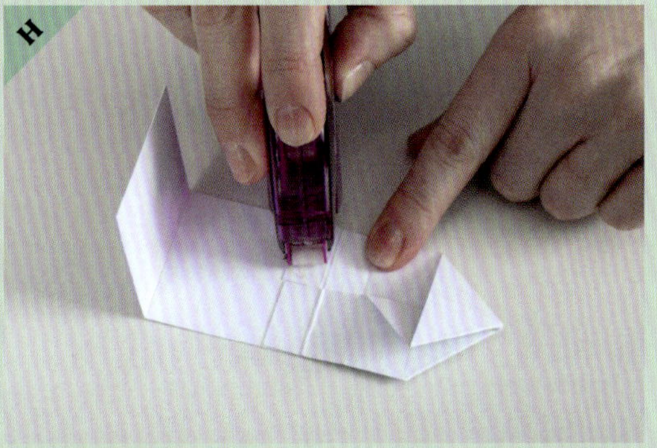

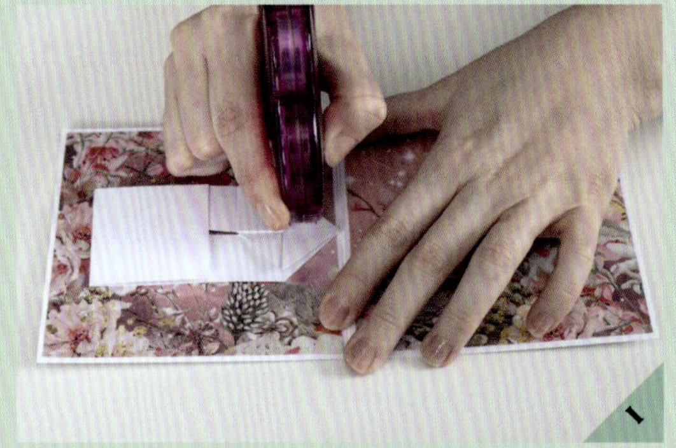

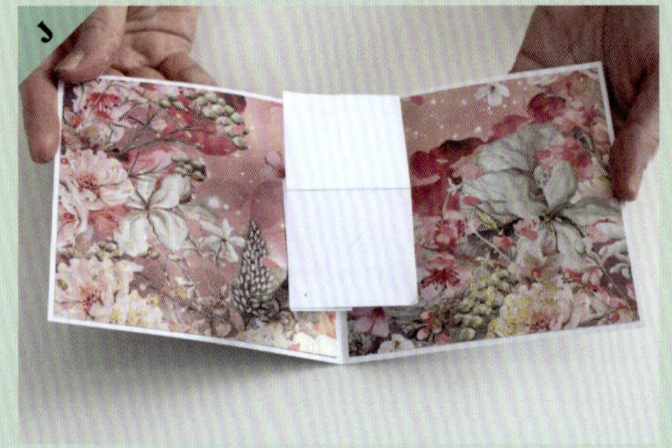

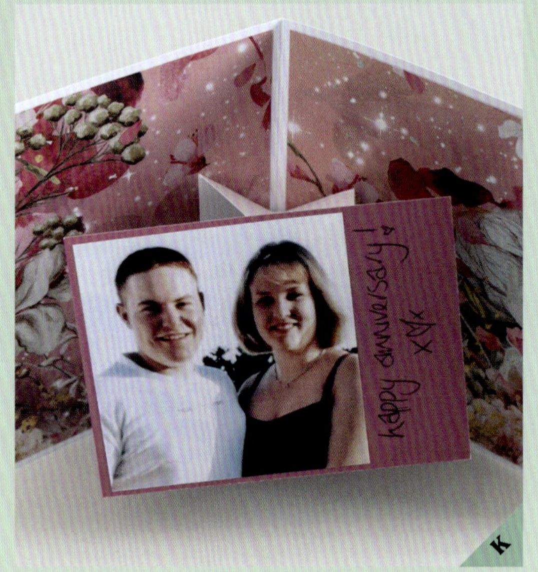

12 Apply glue to the second ½" tab on the opposite side and secure it to the other half of the folded piece. **(H)**

13 Decorate the inside of the 5" × 5" card base with patterned paper.

14 Apply glue to one pointed section of the mechanism and adhere it to one inside of the card. Repeat on the opposite side so the mechanism is centred. **(I)**

15 Open the card to check that the mechanism twists and unfolds smoothly. **(J)**

16 Add a photo and handwritten message to a similarly sized piece of pink card and adhere it to the top of the mechanism to finish. **(K)**

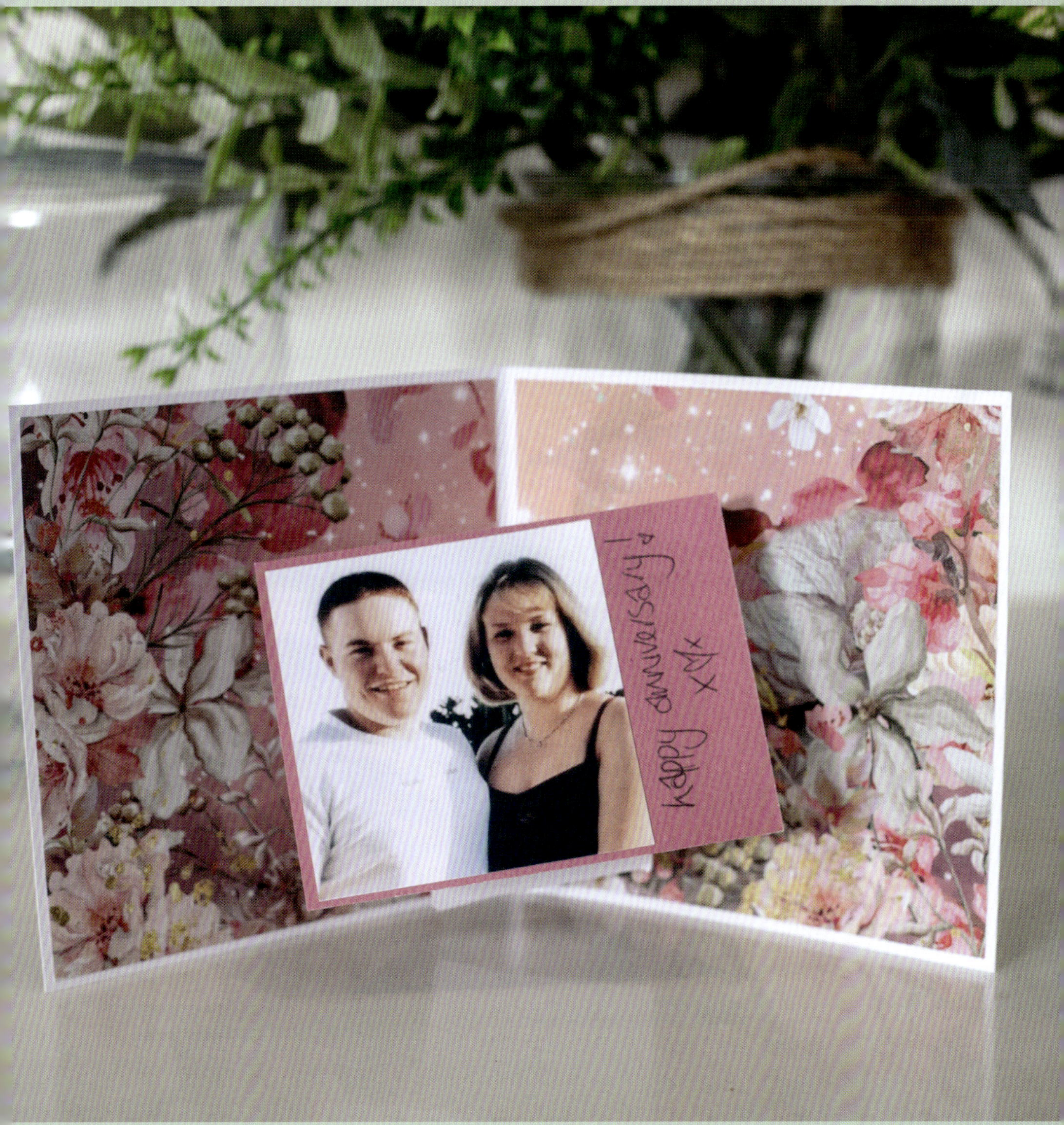
happy anniversary!
xxx

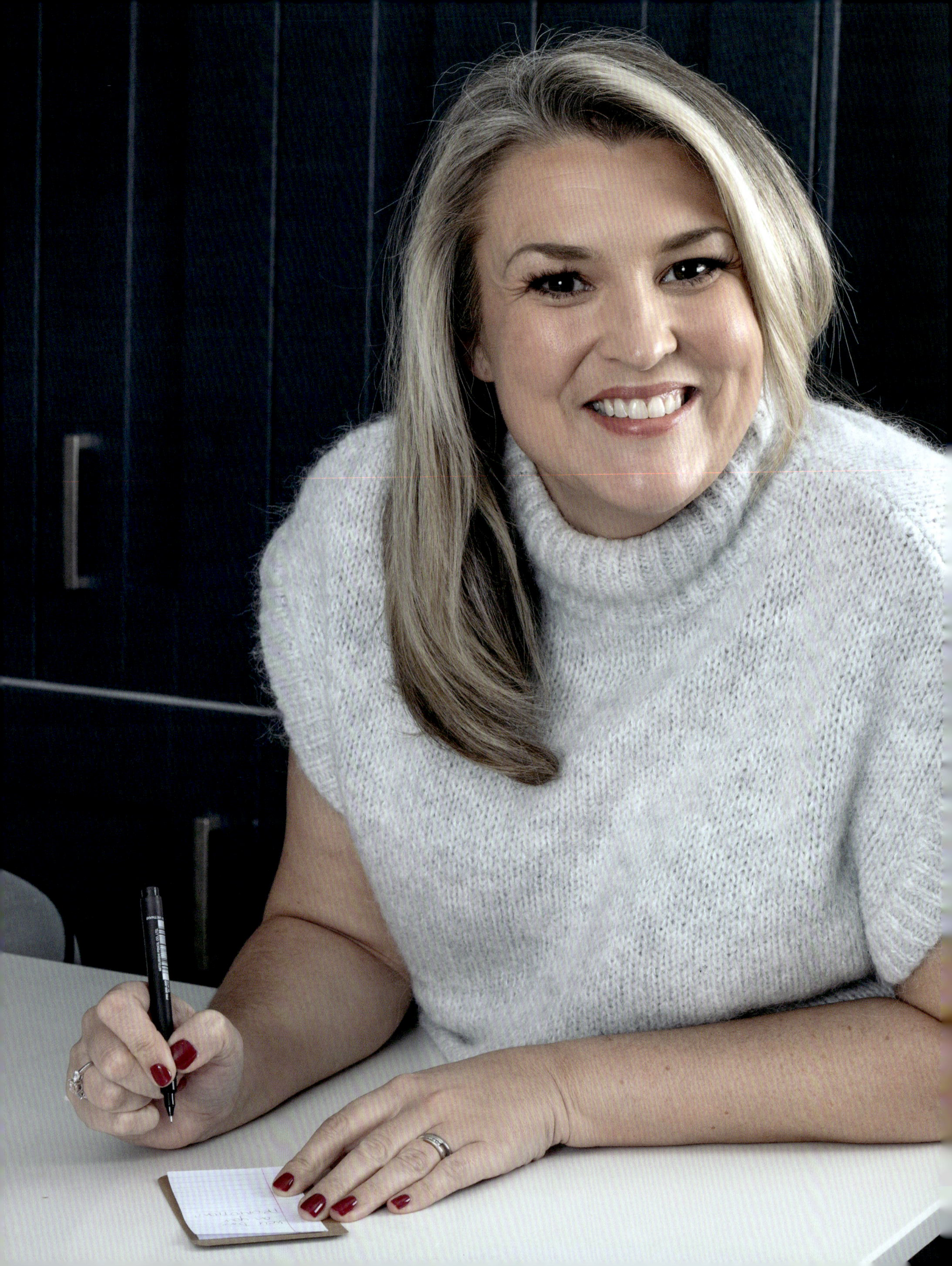

Year-Round Occasions

Wedding

Get Well Soon

Retirement

Teacher Gifts

Easy

Découpage Wine Bottle

The most meaningful gifts are the ones made with love, and this découpage wine bottle is a beautiful way to turn a bottle of bubbly into a keepsake – perfect as a thank-you for your bridesmaids or a thoughtful, personal wedding gift. It's simple to create, but it looks so elegant and considered – exactly what you want for the big occasion!

You will need:

- Champagne or prosecco bottle (or bubbles of your choice)
- White acrylic paint or white gesso
- Two medium or large paintbrushes
- Cloth (for cleaning up any mistakes)
- Decorative napkins
- Scissors (NB smaller elements are easier to cut out with smaller scissors)
- Mod Podge
- Ribbon (optional)

1 Ensure the surface of the bottle is clean and dry.

2 Apply an even coat of white paint or gesso over the glass surface of the bottle, then set it aside to dry fully. **(A)**

3 Apply a second coat of paint if needed for an opaque finish, and allow it to dry completely. **(B)**

4 While the paint is drying, cut out the napkin elements you'd like to use. Carefully separate the layers of each napkin so you're left with the single patterned layer. **(C and D)**

5 Using a clean paintbrush, apply a thin layer of Mod Podge to a small area of the bottle. Gently place a napkin piece on to the glued area and smooth it carefully to remove any creases or air bubbles. **(E)**

TOP TIP Smooth the napkin pieces gently from the centre outwards to avoid creases.

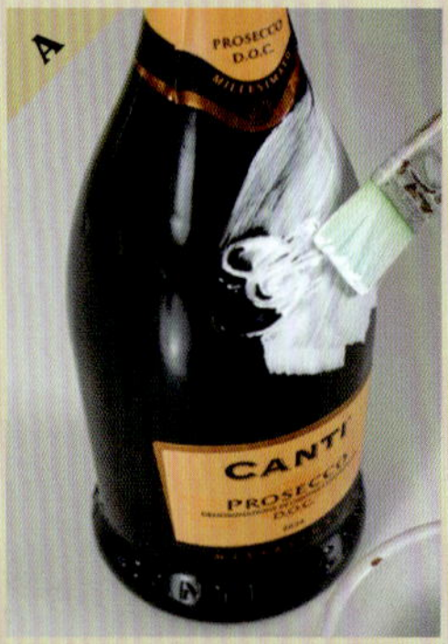

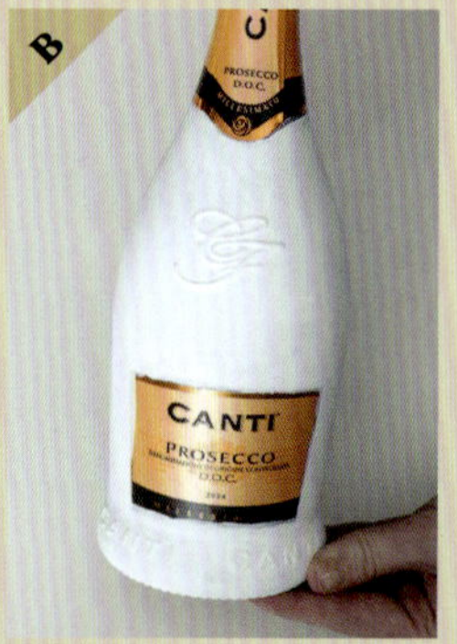

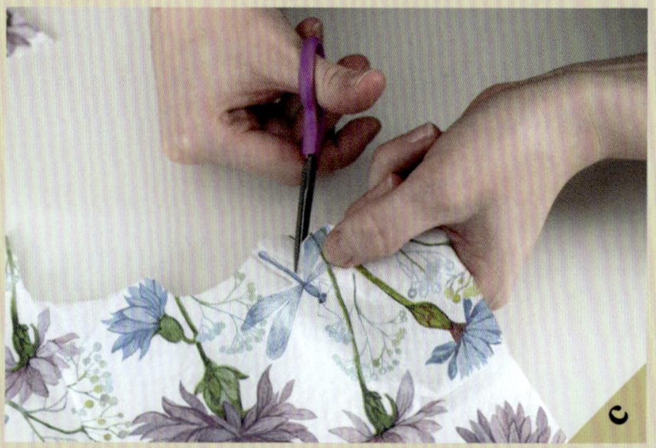

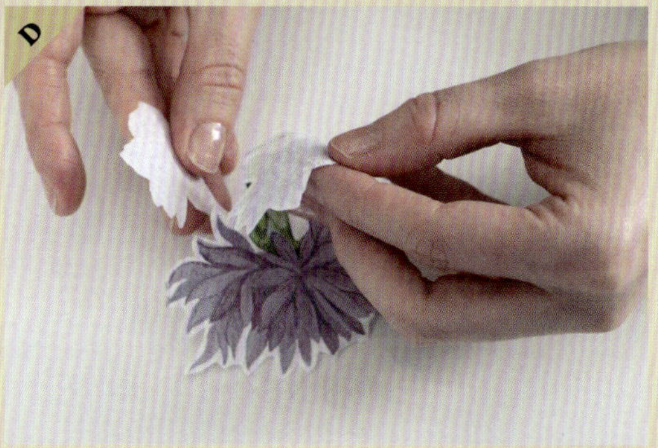

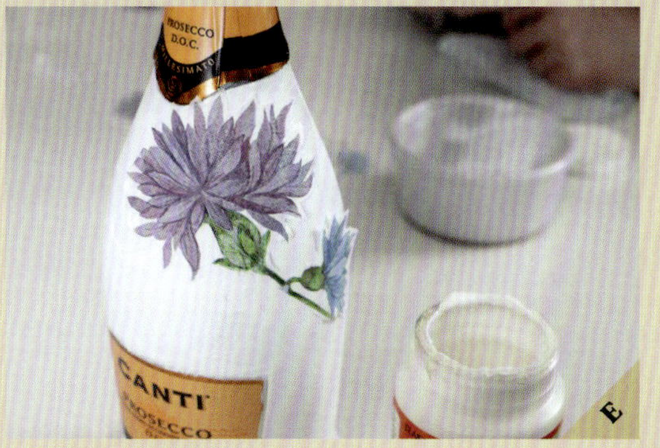

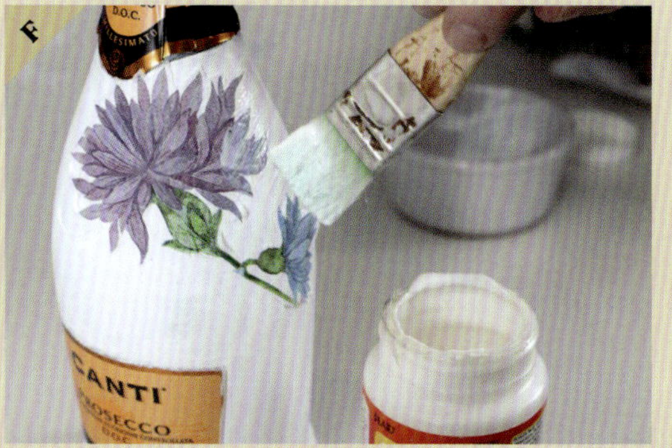

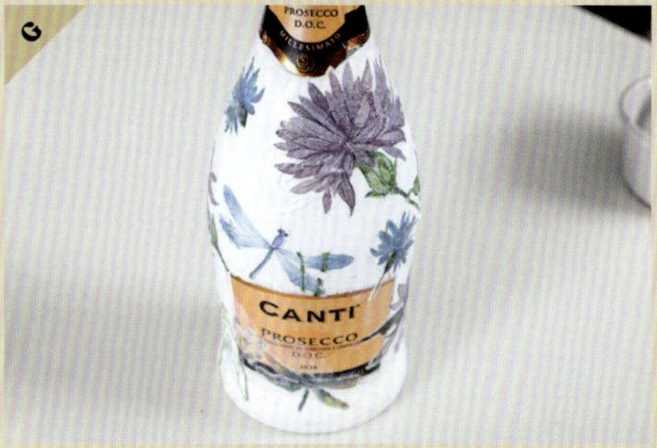

6 Apply another thin layer of Mod Podge over the top of the napkin to seal it in place. **(F)**

7 Repeat steps 5–6 until you are happy with the overall design and coverage. It's fine to leave some of the painted background showing through if you prefer a lighter look. **(G)**

8 Set the bottle aside to dry completely. Once dry, tie a ribbon around the neck if you'd like to add a little something extra!

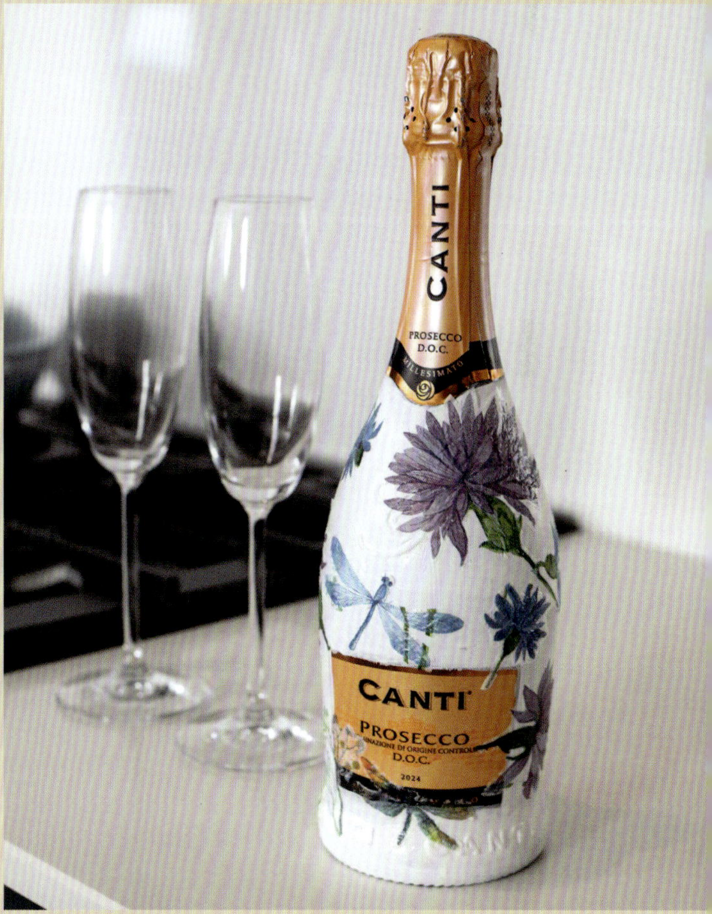

Easy

Favour Box

Present your wedding favours in a super-stylish way with these beautiful paper favour boxes. Using just one sheet of patterned paper, you can create an elegant box that's perfect for filling with sweet treats, confetti or small keepsakes for your guests. They're easy to customize to match your wedding colour scheme, and the ribbon tie gives a lovely finishing touch. Best of all, they're quick to make in batches, so you can create something truly personal for your big day without the stress.

TOP TIP You can change the size of the favour boxes by adjusting the size of the circular template.

You will need:

- 12″ × 12″ patterned paper
- Pencil
- Dinner plate or similar-sized circular template
- Scissors
- Ruler
- Glue tape pen
- Hole punch
- Ribbon
- Treats

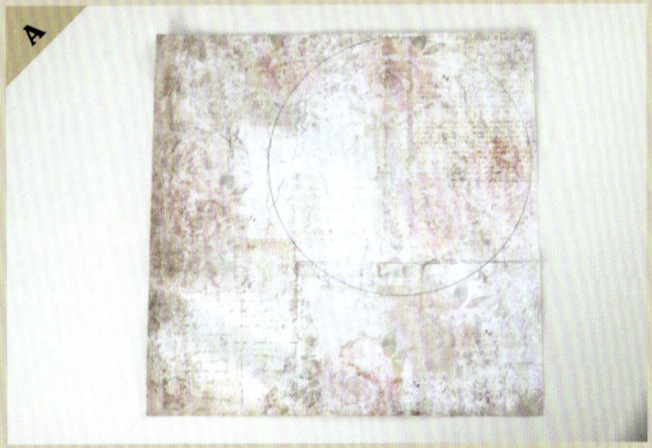

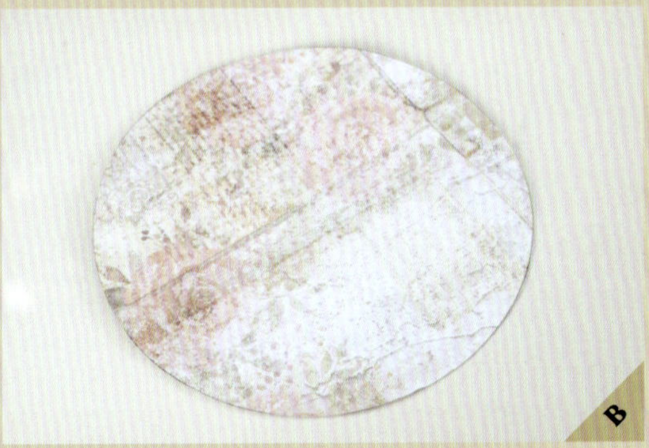

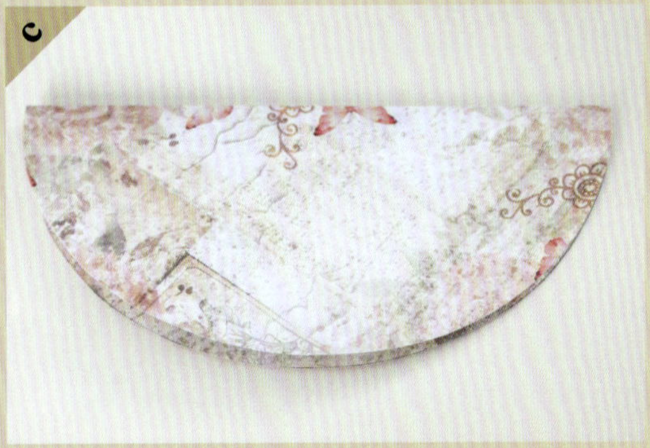

1 Take a piece of 12″ × 12″ patterned paper.

2 Using a dinner plate or other circular object as a template, draw a large circle on to the paper. The larger the circle, the bigger your box will be. **(A)**

3 Carefully cut out the circle. **(B)**

4 Fold the circle in half. **(C)**

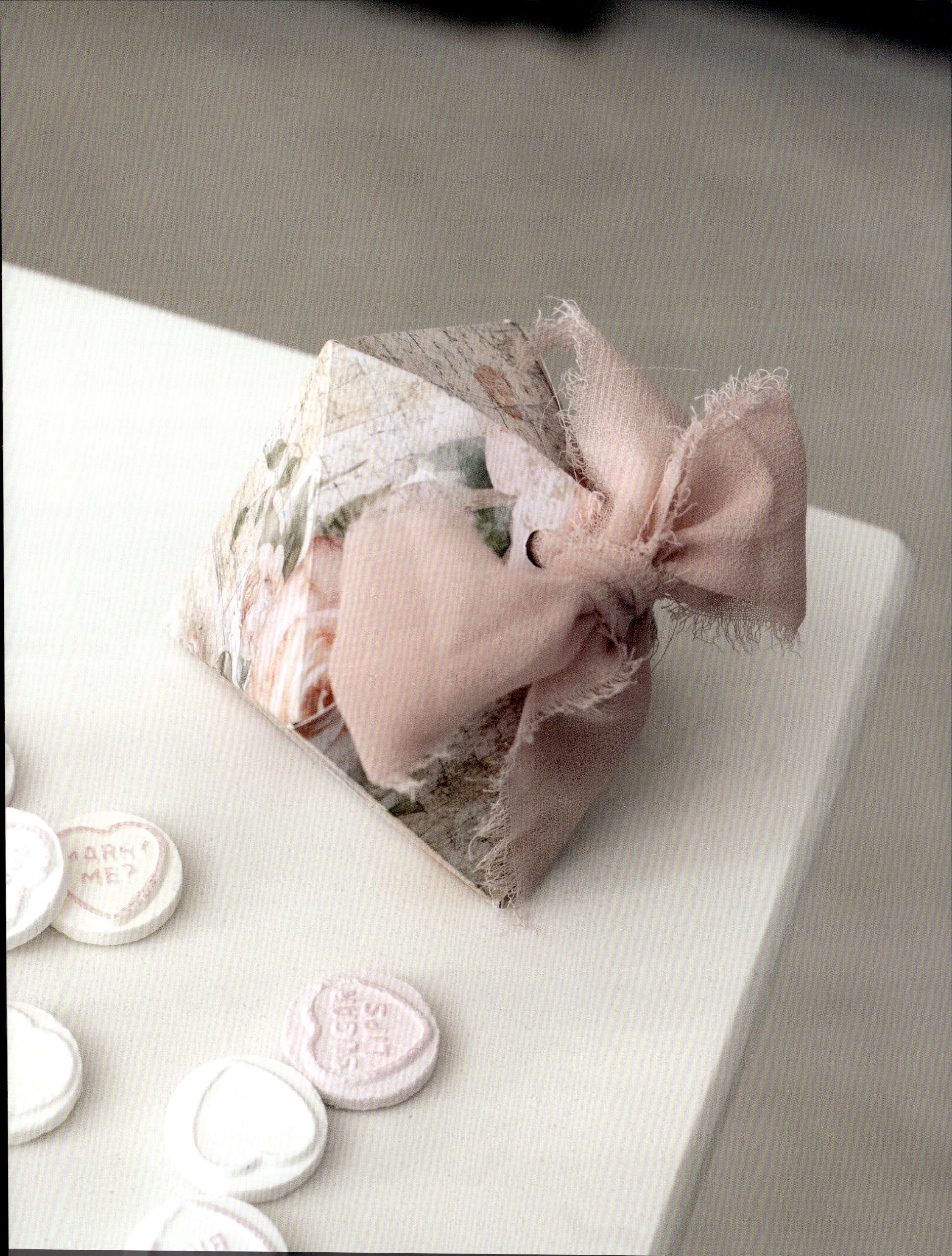
MARRY ME?
SUGAR LIPS

5 Fold it in half again. **(D)**

6 Fold the piece once more. **(E)**

7 Measure the halfway point on each edge of the folded paper. Using the plate again, draw a curved edge on both sides. **(F)**

8 Cut away the curved sections on either side. **(G)**

9 Open the shape out and cut away two of the pointed sections, as shown. **(H)**

10 Bring the two remaining sections together and adhere them in place using a tape pen to form a cone shape. **(I)**

11 Use a hole punch to make a hole in each pointed flap. **(J)**

12 Thread a length of ribbon through each hole. **(K)**

13 Fill the cone with treats, then tie the ribbon ends into a bow to close the cone. **(L)**

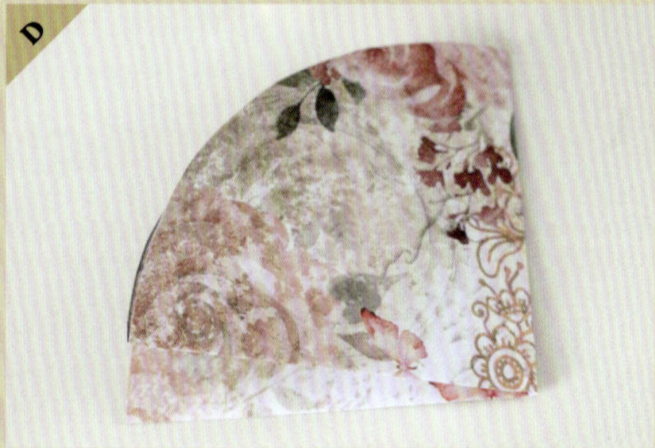

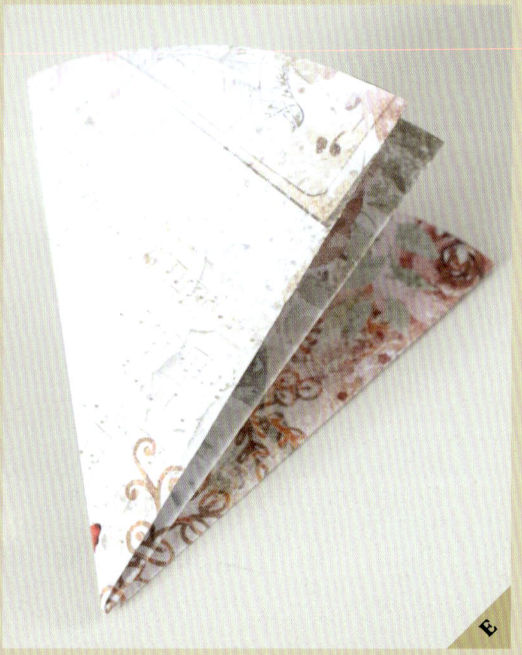

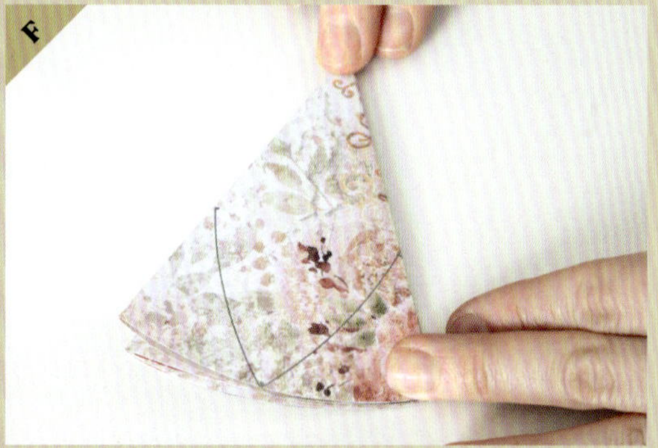

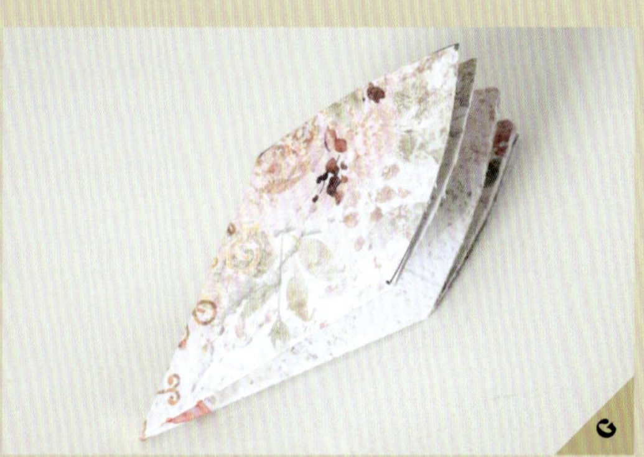

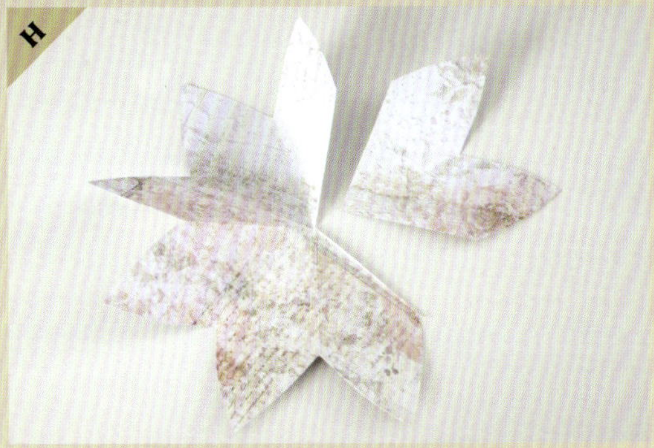
H
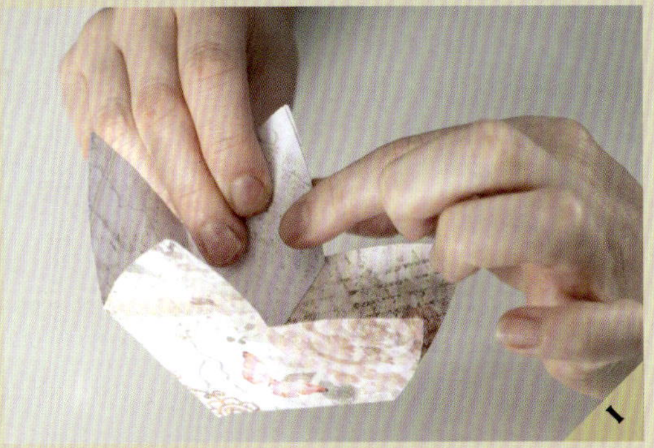
I
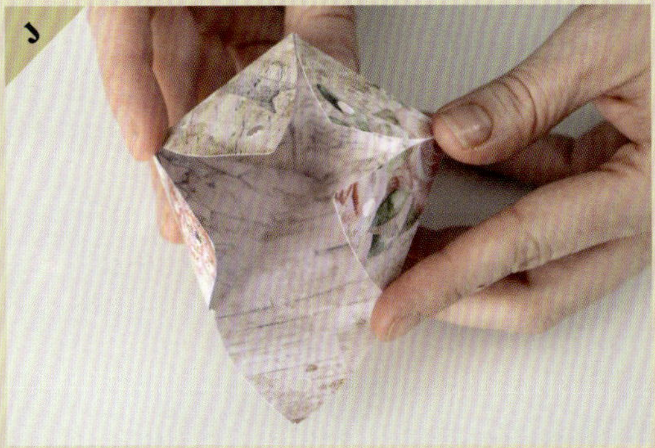
J
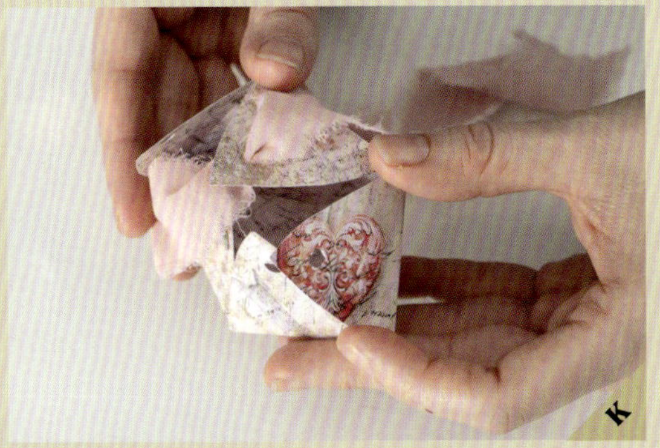
K
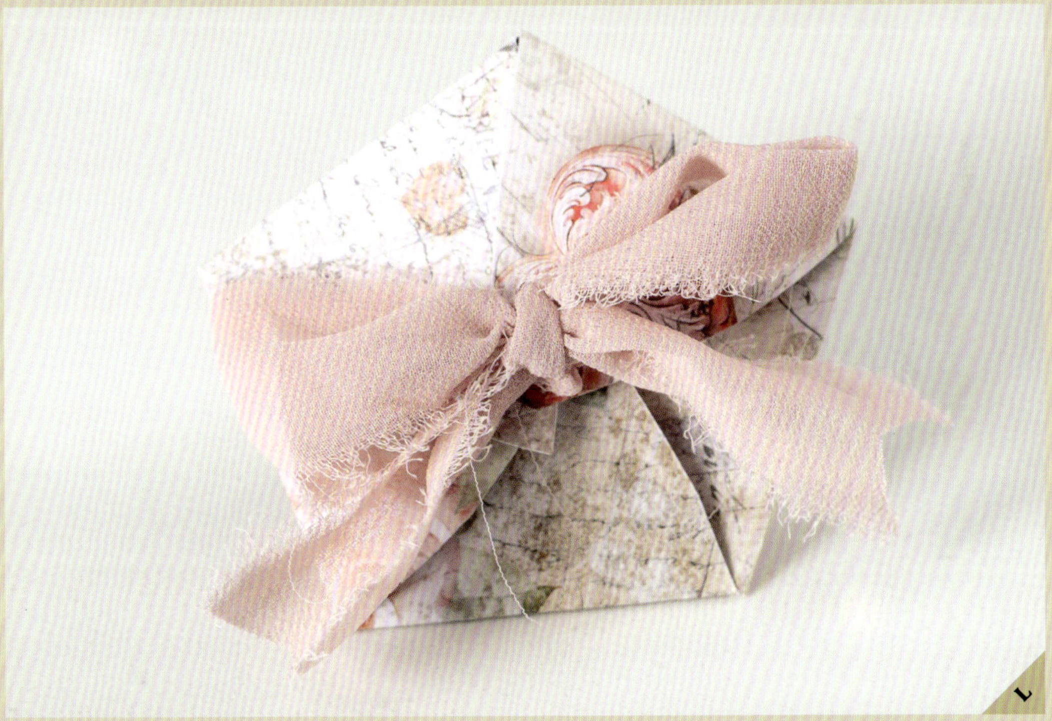
L

Intermediate

Heart Place Setting

Looking for a simple yet really special way to dress your wedding table? This beautiful heart place setting is the perfect handmade finishing touch. Best of all, it's created from just one piece of paper. No fancy tools, no fuss – just a few clever folds that come together to create something truly lovely. Quick to make, affordable and ideal for batch crafting, these paper hearts sit neatly at each place setting, holding your guests' names and making everyone feel that little bit extra special.

You will need:

- 5″ × 5″ patterned paper (double-sided works best)
- Brown paper or card
- Scissors
- Black fine liner

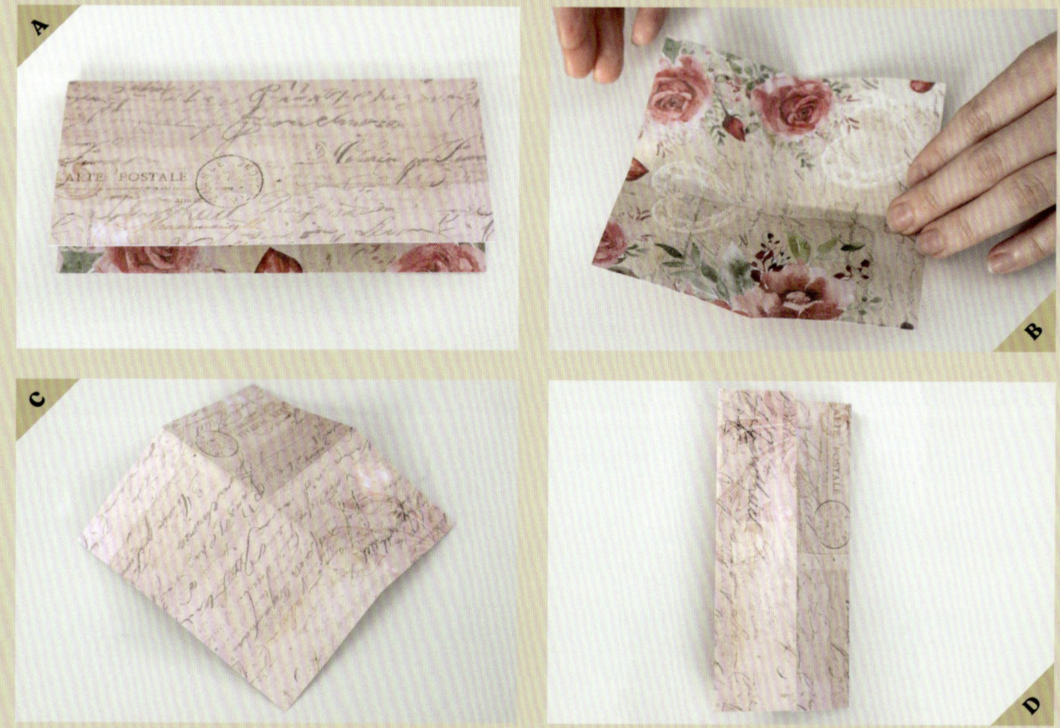

1 Fold the 5″ × 5″ piece of paper in half, then unfold. **(A and B)**

2 Fold the paper in half again in the opposite direction, then unfold it so you have four equal square sections. **(C)**

3 Fold two opposite edges in towards the centre crease to form a vertical rectangle. **(D)**

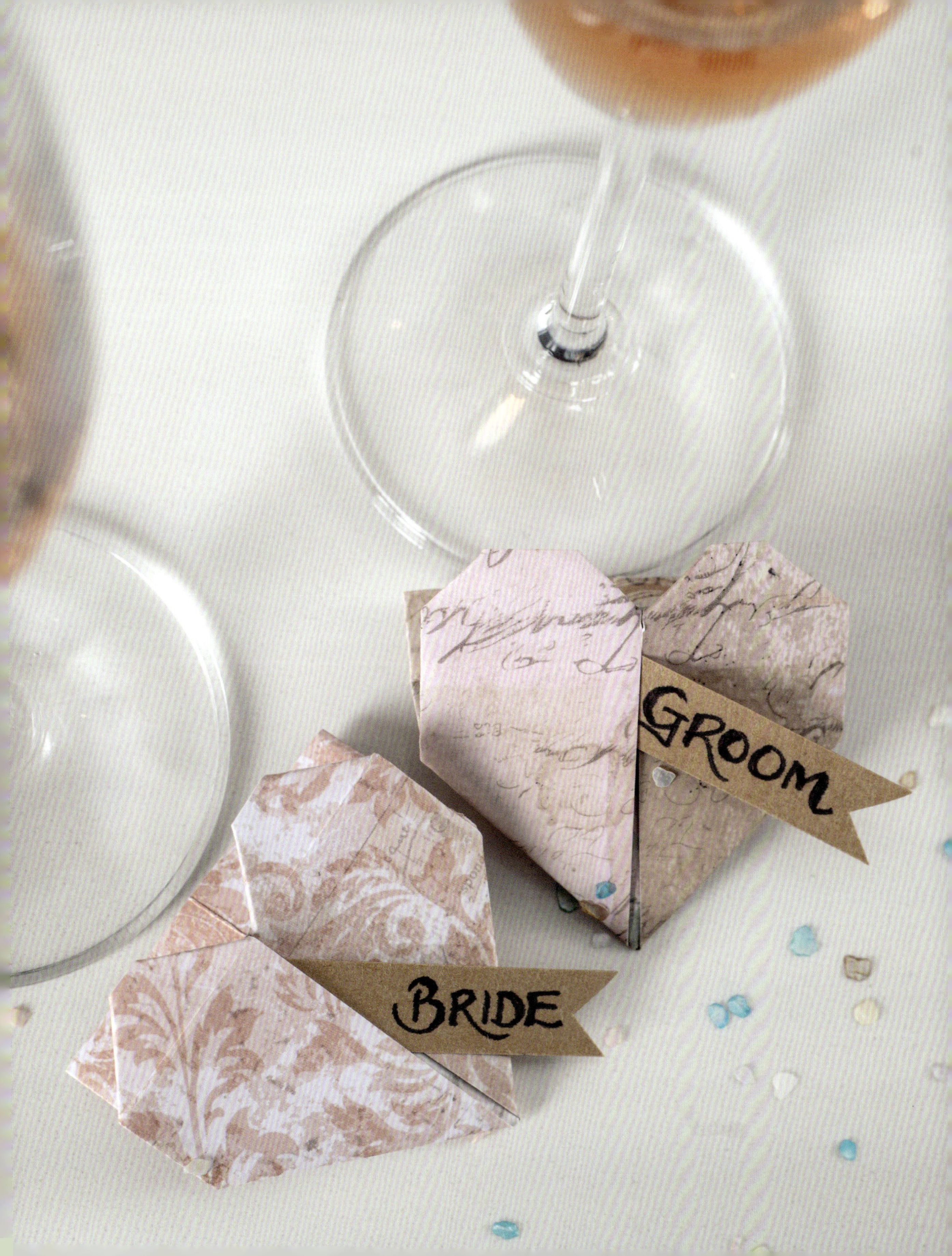
GROOM
BRIDE

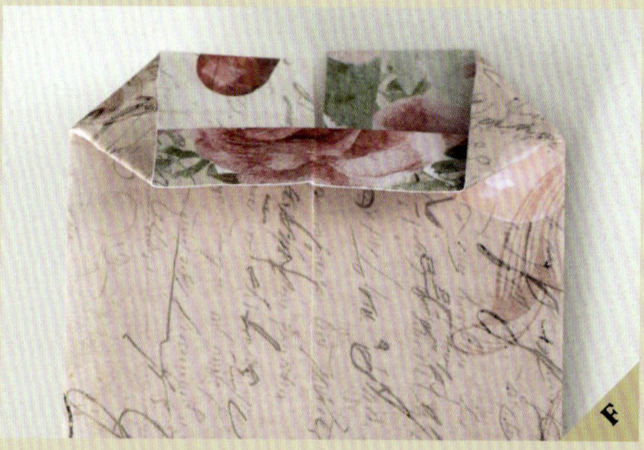

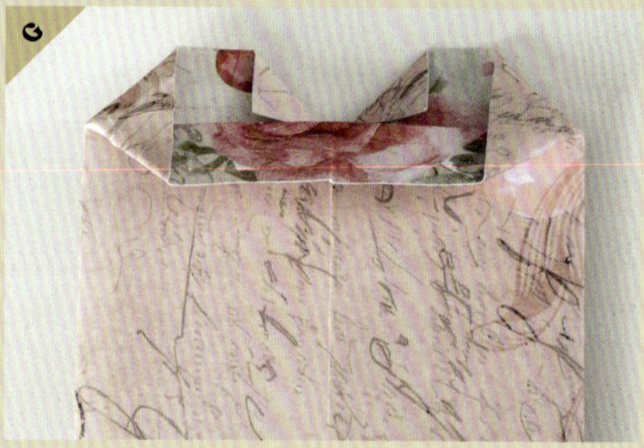

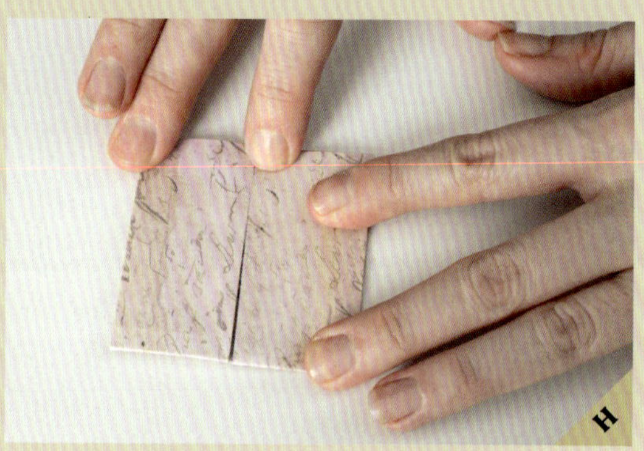

4 Fold the top end of the rectangle down by ½". **(E)**

5 Open this fold, flip the rectangle over, then gently push in the sides with your fingers to create triangular shapes on each side. **(F)**

6 Fold the two middle sections in to form the top curves of the heart. **(G)**

7 Fold the bottom half of the shape up and over the top of the heart. **(H)**

8 Next, fold both bottom corners up to create the point of the heart. **(I)**

9 Fold the top rectangle down to form a stand so the heart sits upright. **(J and K)**

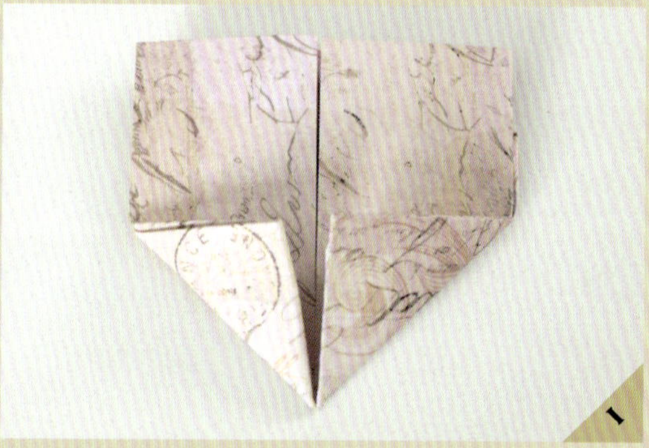

10 Cut a narrow strip of paper or card and trim the ends into a ribbon shape.

11 Write the guest's name on the strip using a black fine liner, then tuck it neatly into the front of the heart to finish. **(L)**

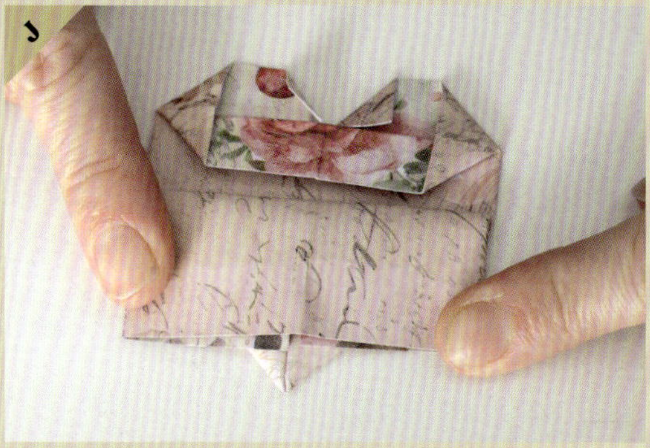

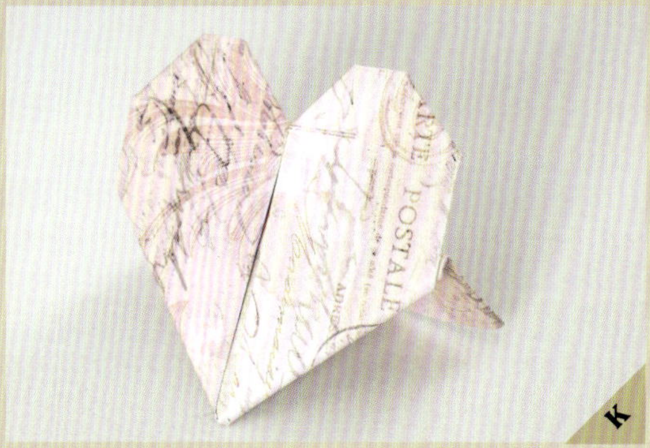

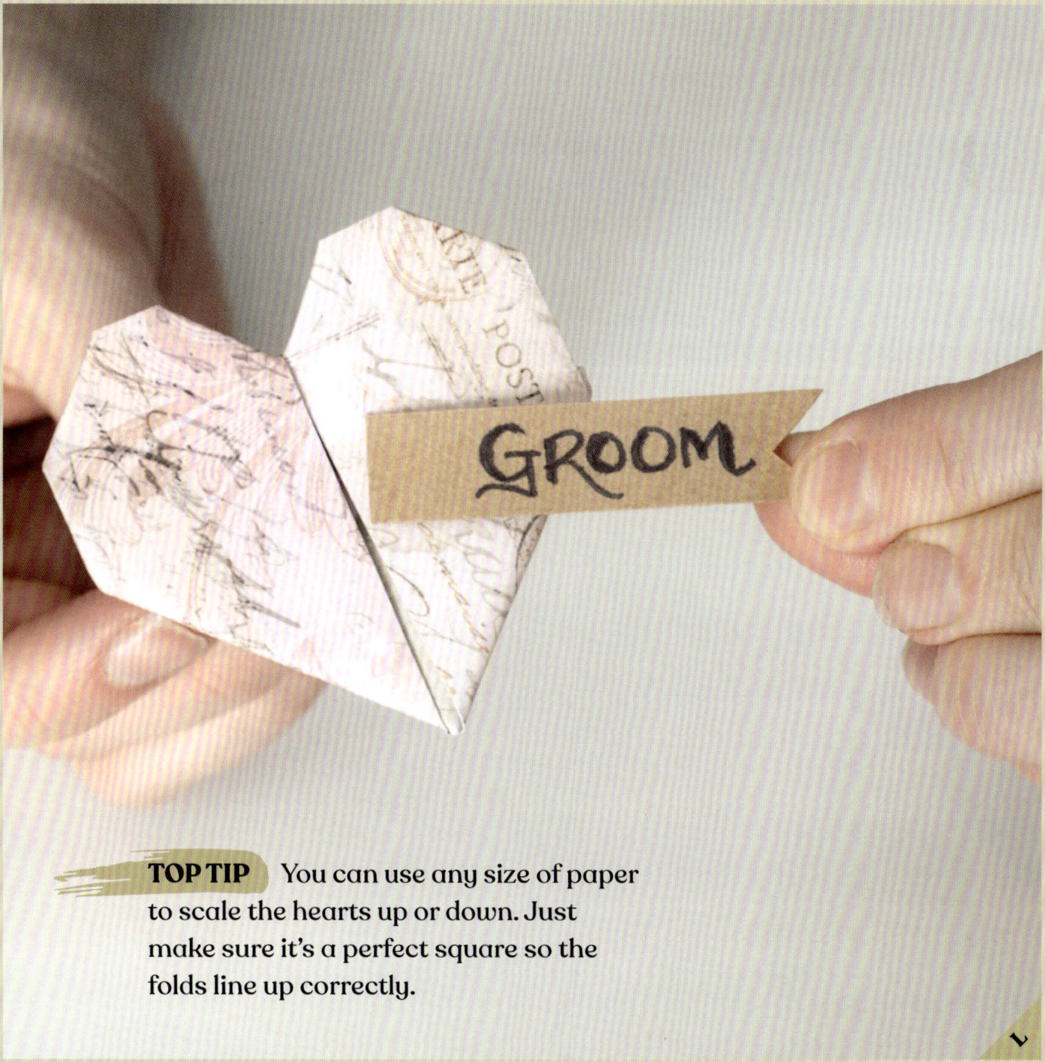

TOP TIP You can use any size of paper to scale the hearts up or down. Just make sure it's a perfect square so the folds line up correctly.

Easy

Romantic Roses

You don't need expensive materials to create something truly beautiful, and these paper towel roses prove it! They're soft, romantic and perfect for weddings, whether you're decorating tables, creating a backdrop, or adding a handmade touch to your big day. The watercolours give each flower a gorgeous finish, and because you're blending the colours yourself, every single bloom turns out slightly different.

TOP TIP **You can use whatever watercolours you like in this project to complement your colour scheme.**

You will need:

- Glass craft mat or greaseproof paper
- Kitchen paper towel
- Spray bottle with water
- Watercolour palette
- Water
- Small/medium paintbrush
- Scissors
- String
- Glue gun
- Bamboo skewers

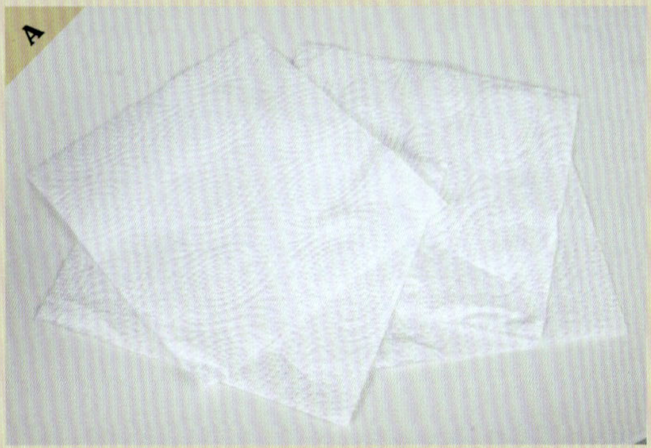
A

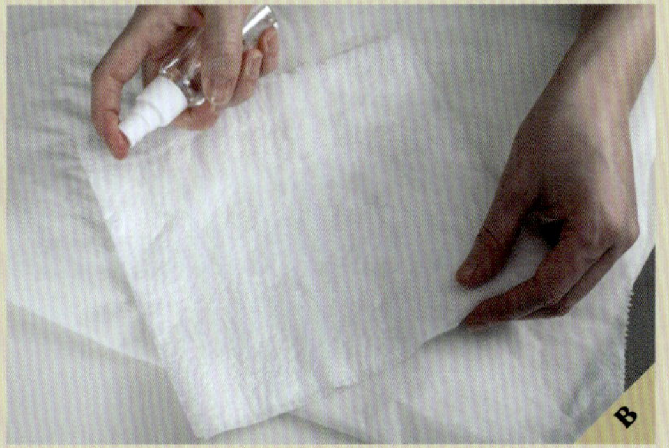
B

1 Prepare your workspace by laying out a glass craft mat or a sheet of greaseproof paper.

2 To create one flower, take four sheets of kitchen paper towel and stack them neatly on top of each other. **(A)**

3 Mist the sheets with the spray bottle of water until they are evenly damp and able to absorb the watercolour paint. **(B)**

4 Using a paintbrush, pick up some yellow watercolour paint and run a line down the centre of the stacked paper towels. Gently drag the brush from side to side to allow the colour to bleed outwards. **(C)**

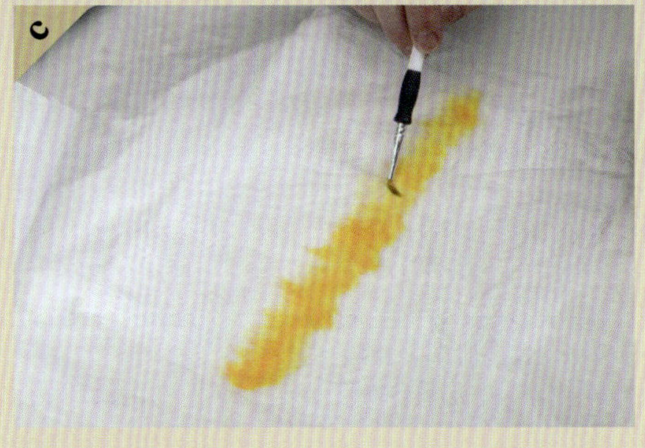

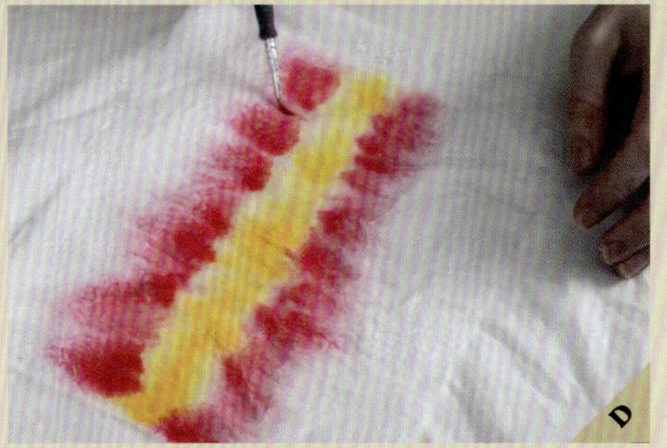

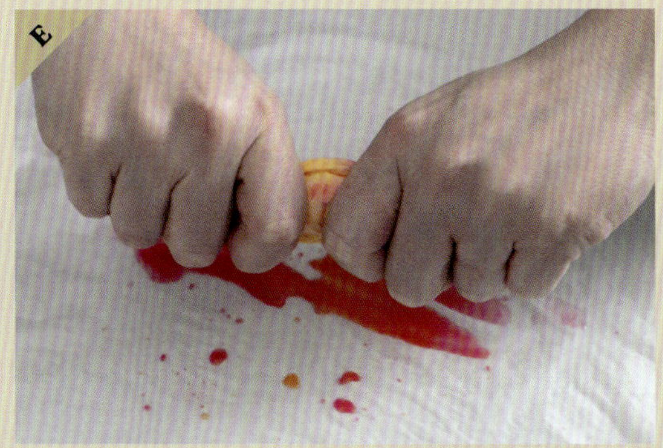

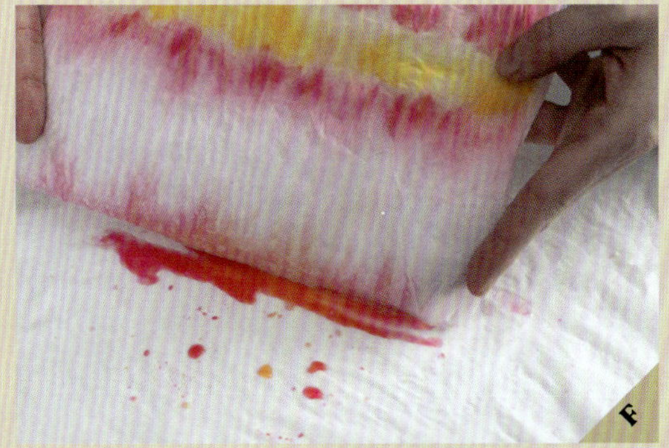

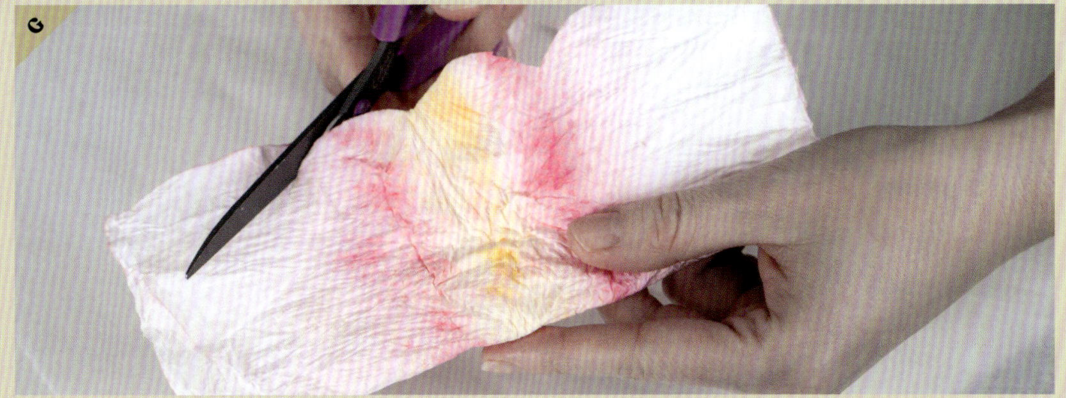

5 Repeat the previous step using pink watercolour paint on either side of the yellow. **(D)**

6 Scrunch the four sheets together between both hands, squeezing out any excess water so it drips on to your work surface below. **(E)**

7 Once the paper towels have been wrung out, carefully unfold them and dip the outer edges into the pooled watercolour paint on your work surface. **(F)**

8 Fold the sheets in half and set them aside to dry completely. Once dry, trim a scalloped edge along the long open side to create a petal effect. **(G)**

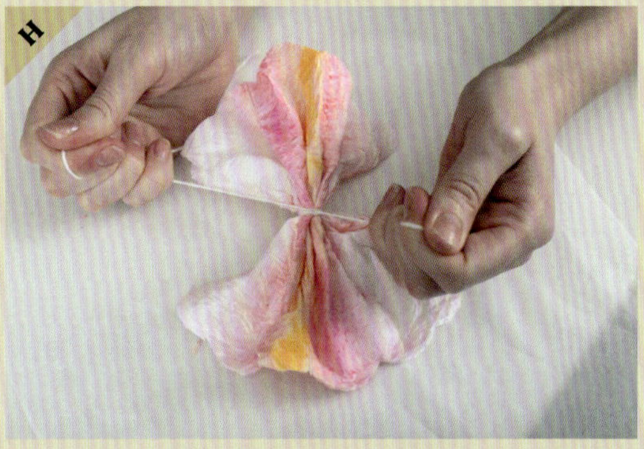

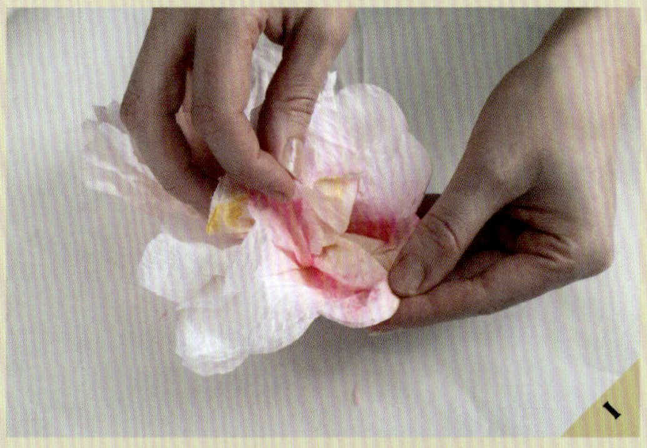

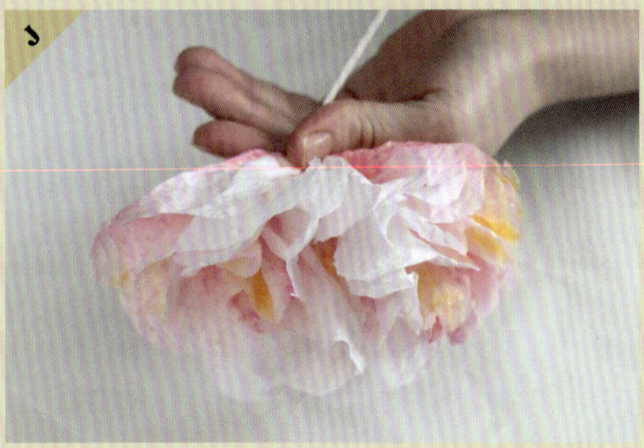

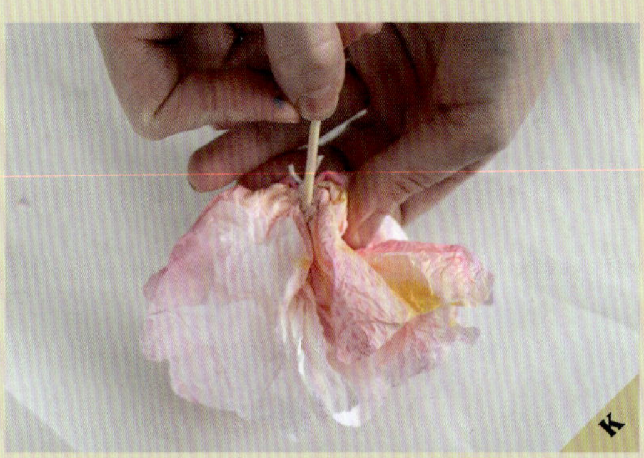

9 Unfold the sheets then scrunch them lengthways and secure tightly in the centre with a length of string. **(H)**

10 Gently separate the layers of paper towel, pulling them apart to form petals until a flower shape emerges. **(I)**

11 Cut away any excess string, then use hot glue to attach a bamboo skewer to the centre of the flower. The easiest way to do this is to sandwich the skewer between the two central layers, as shown. **(J and K)**

12 Repeat steps 2–11 to create the desired number of flowers for your wedding display! **(L)**

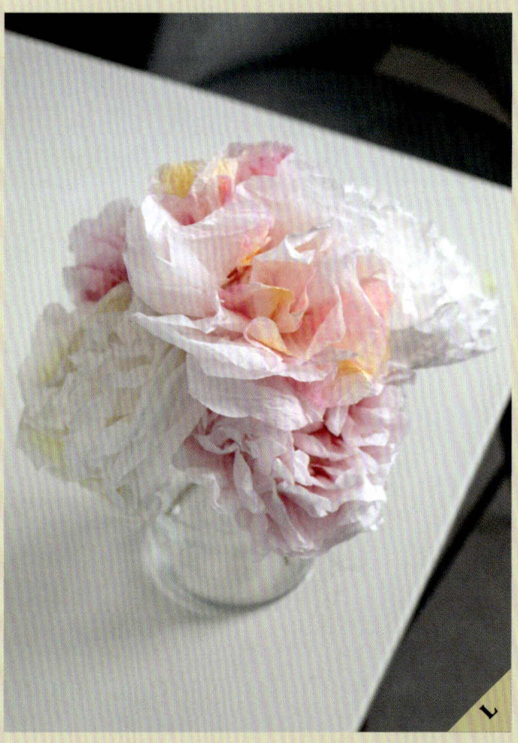

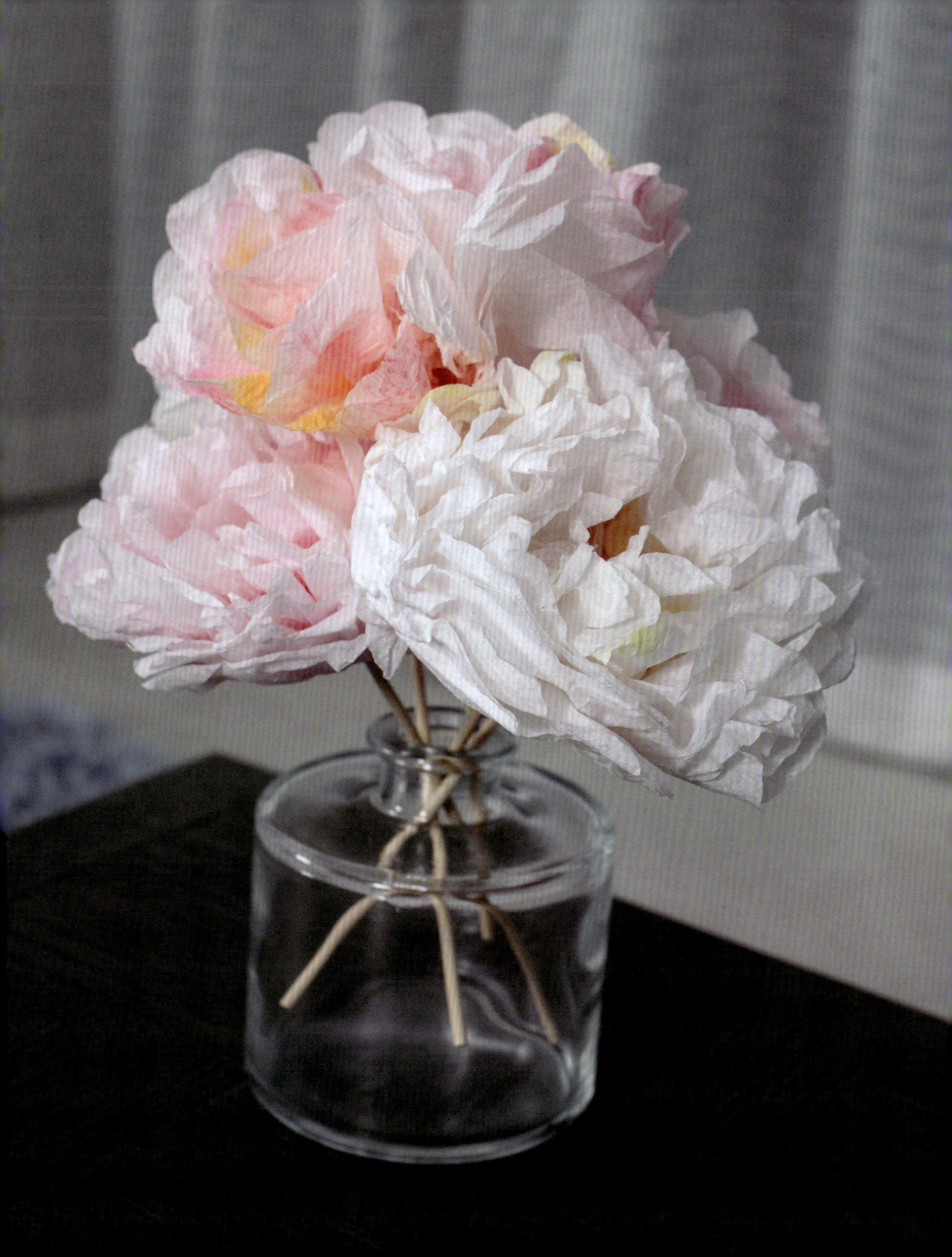

Easy

Wildflower Paper

There's something really special about giving a gift that keeps on giving, and that's exactly what this handmade wildflower seed paper does. Not only is it a beautiful, tactile craft to make yourself, it also doubles as a lovely, eco-friendly touch for weddings or parties – perfect for tags, place settings or little favours your guests can treasure. There's something magical about knowing that the paper you've made can bloom into a patch of colourful wildflowers. It's a gift that grows, literally!

You will need:

- Copier paper
- Mixing bowl
- Water
- Blender
- Tea towel
- Baking parchment (optional)
- Rolling pin (optional)
- Wildflower seeds
- Scissors
- Gold or silver gel pen
- Gold or silver thread

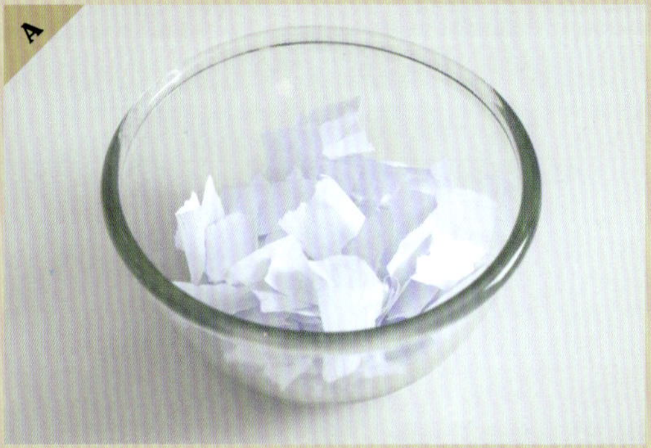

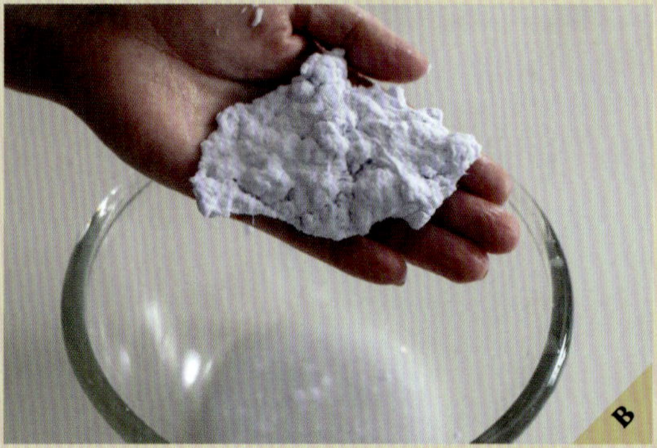

1 Tear 6–8 sheets of copier paper into small pieces and place them in a mixing bowl. **(A)**

2 Cover the paper with water and leave it to soak overnight.

3 Transfer the paper-and-water mixture to a blender and blitz until it becomes a smooth pulp. If the mixture sticks to the sides or blades, add a little more water.

4 Once you're happy with the consistency, carefully remove the pulp from the blender and use your hands to gently squeeze out any excess water over the bowl or kitchen sink. It's easiest to do this in small batches. **(B)**

5 Flatten the pulp on to a tea towel to absorb any remaining water. If you need extra help, place a sheet of baking parchment over the pulp and gently roll it out with a rolling pin.

TOP TIP **Smaller blenders used for protein shakes and smoothies work best for this project.**

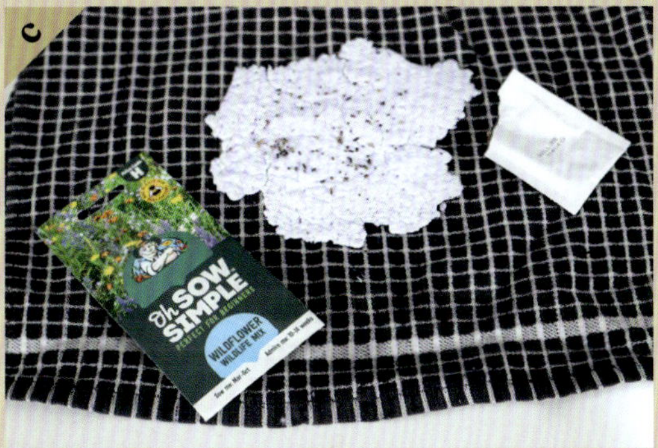

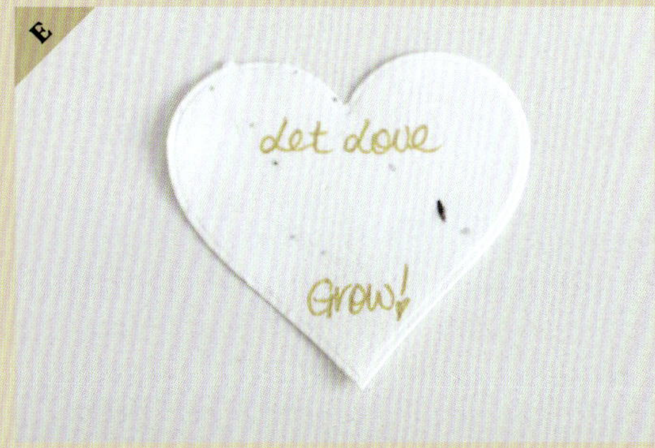

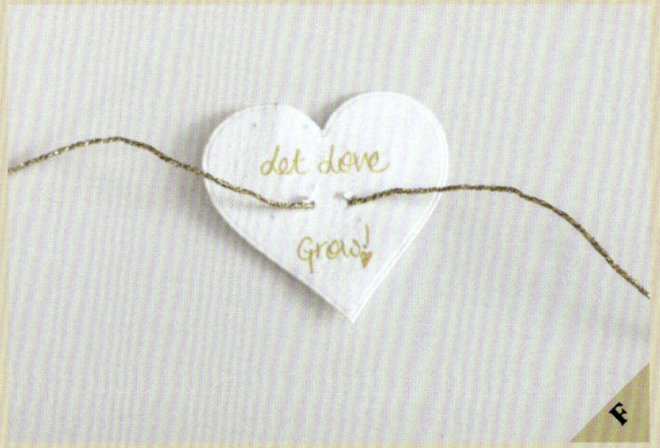

6 Sprinkle your wildflower seeds evenly over the pulp and press them in gently. **(C)**

7 Leave the seed paper to dry overnight. **(D)**

8 Once fully dry, cut into shapes as desired, write your message in gold or silver gel pen and thread through with matching thread – perfect for wedding tags, party favours or thoughtful gifts. **(E and F)**

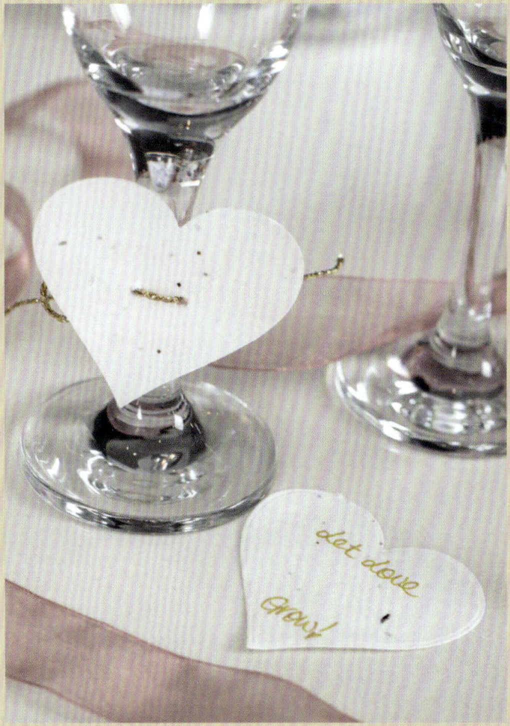

Intermediate

Get Well Soon Card

Sometimes cards aren't sent to celebrate happy moments but to let someone know you're thinking of them when they need a little lift. This get well soon card does exactly that. With playful torn layers, textured details and cute paper 'plasters', it's a thoughtful and light-hearted way to show you care. Handmade and heartfelt, this design balances warmth with a touch of humour, making it a comforting card that's guaranteed to raise a smile when it matters most.

You will need:

- 6″ × 4″ card base
- Patterned paper
- Scissors or paper trimmer
- White card
- Ruler
- Finer liner or pen
- Alphabet stamps and ink pad (optional)
- Glue tape pen
- Kraft card
- Brown pen
- Foam pads

1 Cover the front of a 6″ × 4″ card base with patterned paper, trimming to fit if needed. **(A)**

2 Cut a piece of white card measuring 6″ × 3½″. **(B)**

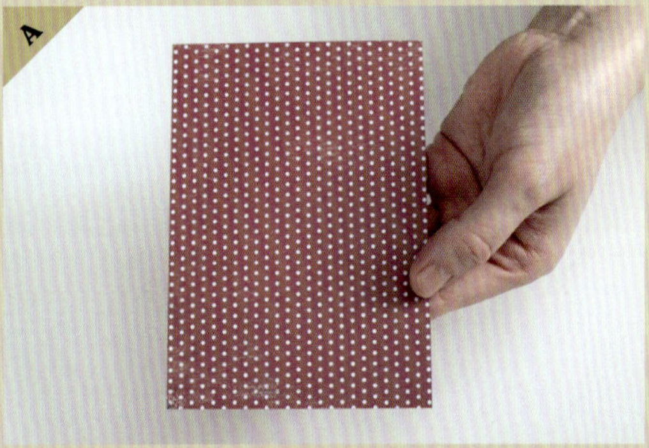

3 Tear along the bottom third of the white card to create two separate pieces, then tear a further ½″ strip from the larger piece. **(C)**

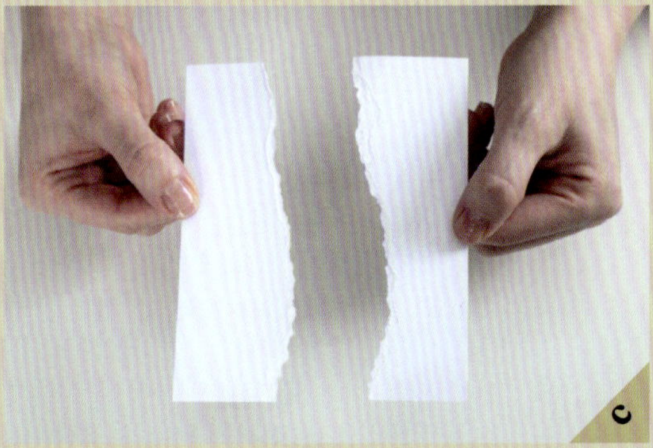

TOP TIP Add personality to your 'plasters' by doodling small details with a pen. This gives a playful, handmade feel and helps the design really pop.

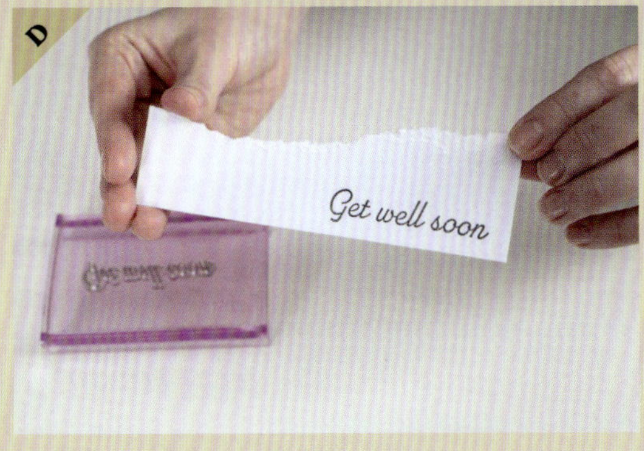

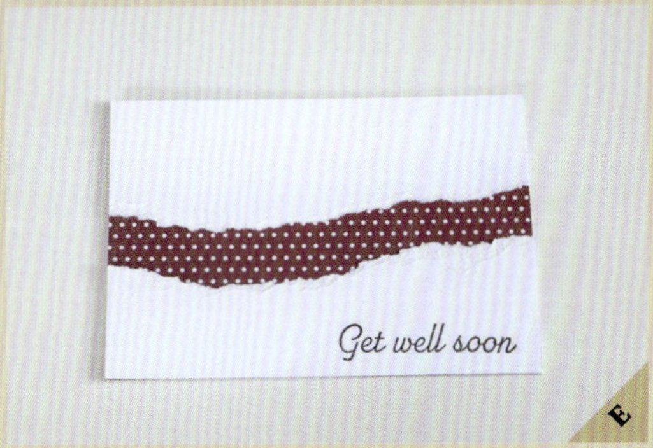

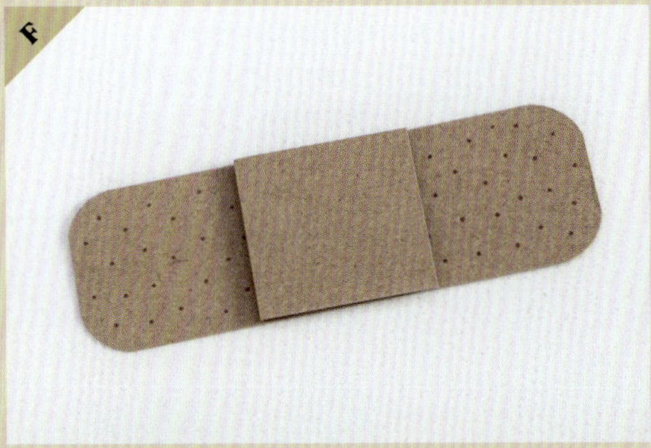

4 Handwrite or stamp a 'get well soon' sentiment on to one of the torn pieces of paper that will sit at the bottom of the card. **(D)**

5 Using a tape pen, adhere the two torn pieces on to the card front so that the patterned paper remains visible between the torn layers. **(E)**

6 Cut a piece of Kraft card measuring 3″ × 1″ and round off the corners. Use a brown pen to add small dots across the surface so that it resembles a plaster.

7 Cut a second piece of Kraft card measuring 1″ × 1″, attach foam pads to the back, then adhere it to the centre of the larger Kraft strip to create a layered 'plaster'. **(F)**

8 Finish by adhering the plaster to the card front at a slight angle.

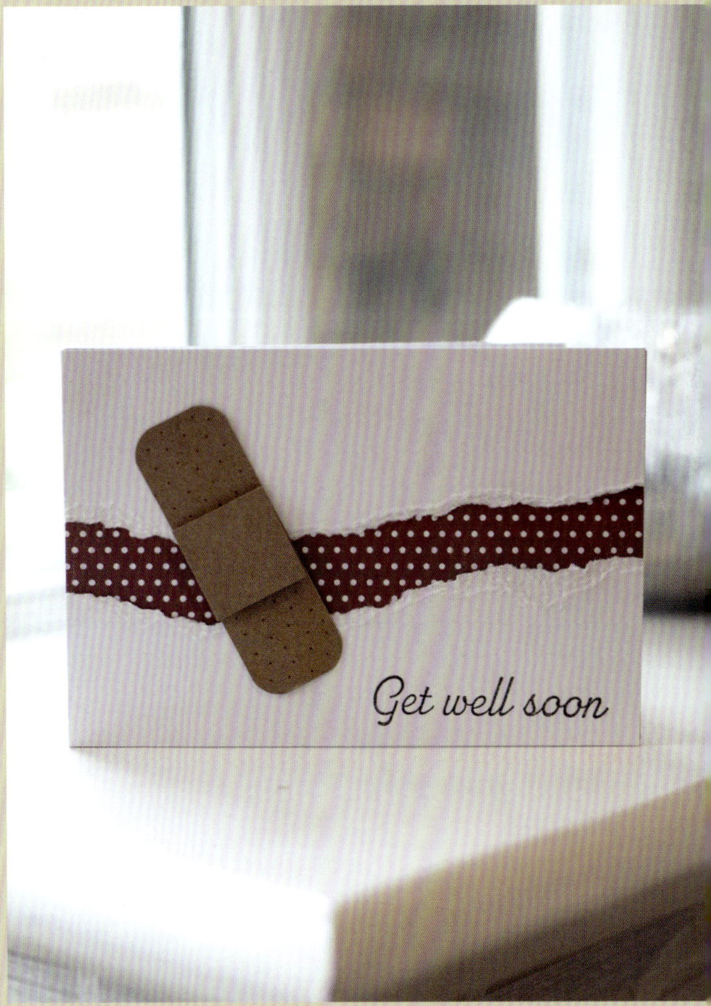

Intermediate

Thinking of You Card

These heart envelope cards are such a thoughtful way to let someone know you're thinking of them, especially when words alone don't quite feel enough. I love how the hearts bursting out of the envelopes add a warm, expressive touch. Once you've made this card, the technique is easy to adapt for other occasions, and you'll be itching to return to it again and again!

You will need:

- 3 6⁄8" × 7 6⁄8" white paper (for card front)
- 3⅞" × 7⅞" patterned paper, plus extra for hearts
- 4¼" × 8¼" card base
- Glue tape pen
- Heart-shaped die
- Scissors
- Coloured paper
- Bone folder or ruler
- Glue gun
- Embossed label maker or pen

1 Adhere the white card front to the patterned paper panel, aligning the edges neatly. **(A)**

2 Attach this layered panel to the card base.

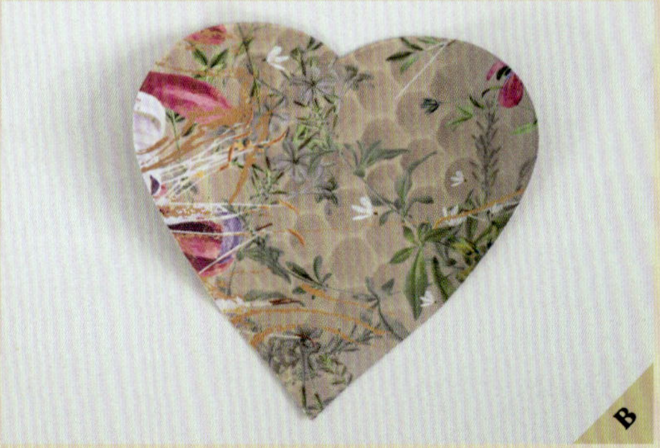

3 Using a heart-shaped die or template, cut three heart shapes from patterned paper. Each heart should measure approximately 4" × 3½". **(B)**

4 Take one heart and turn it upside down so the point is facing away from you. Fold both curved sides inwards towards the centre to form the sides of the envelope. **(C)**

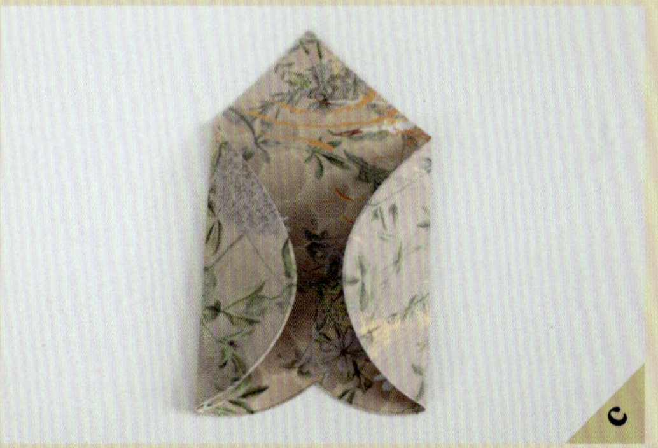

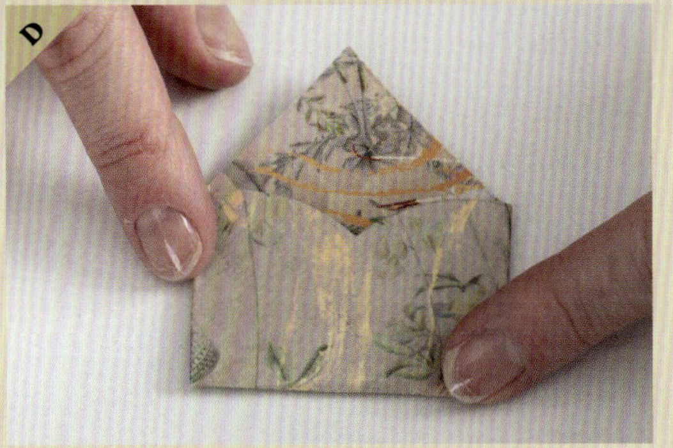

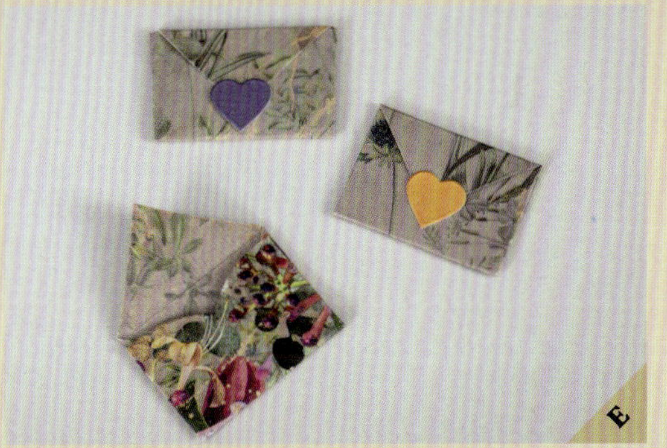

5 Fold the curved edges of the heart upwards to create an envelope shape, then glue this flap into place. **(D)**

6 Repeat steps 4–5 to create two more heart envelopes, leaving one envelope unglued at the top so it appears open.

7 Create two small hearts from coloured paper, one for each of the closed envelopes, and glue them in place. **(E)**

8 Cut an additional seven or eight small hearts to create the effect of hearts bursting out of the open envelope.

9 Arrange the three heart envelopes on the front of the card, then secure them in place using a tape pen or hot glue.

10 Add a 'thinking of you' sentiment to the card front using an embossed label maker or pen.

11 Finish by gluing the small hearts in place so they appear to spill out of the open envelope, creating a lovely dimensional effect.

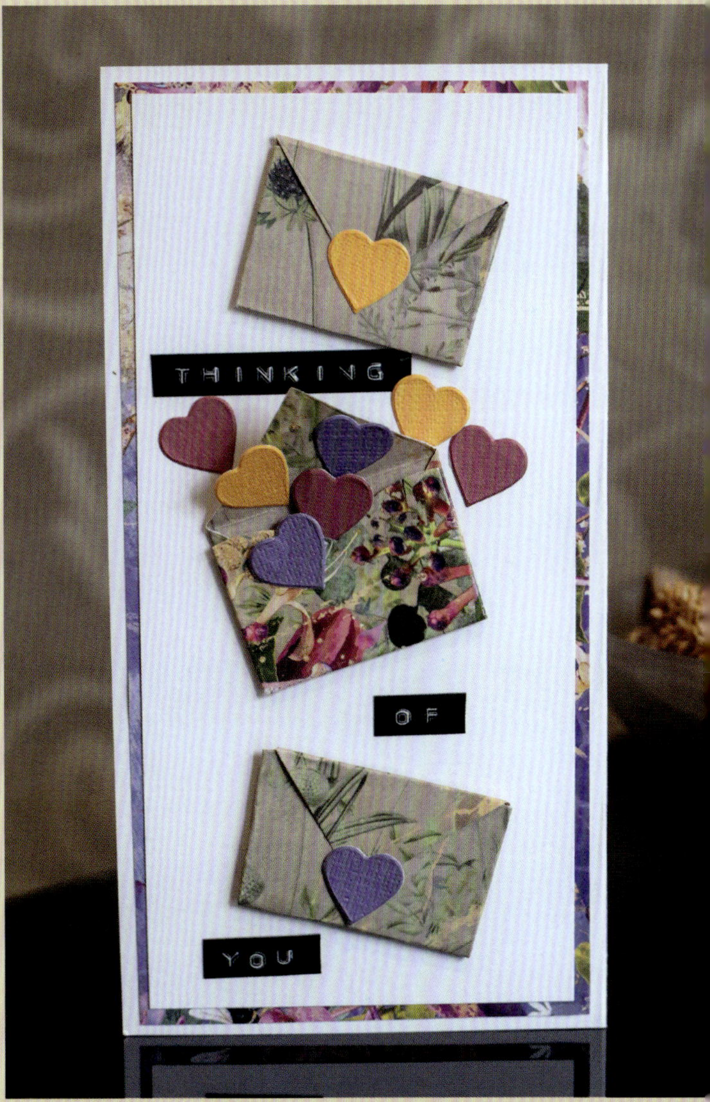

Advanced

Happy Retirement Card

Celebrate a wonderful milestone with this 3D retirement card that's full of charm and personality. Featuring cute little road signs and a winding map, this 3D map is the perfect way to highlight all the exciting opportunities that lie ahead in someone's next chapter of life.

You will need:

- Kraft card
- Scoring tool
- Ruler or scoring board
- Scissors
- Map paper
- Glue tape pen
- Bone folder
- Glue gun
- Ice lolly sticks or wooden craft sticks
- Brown pen or pencil (optional)

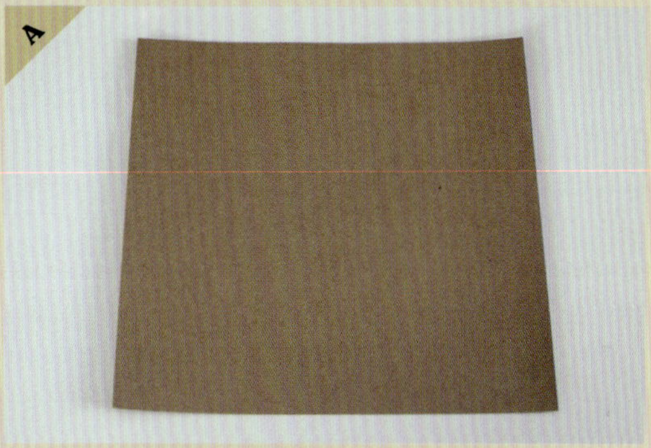

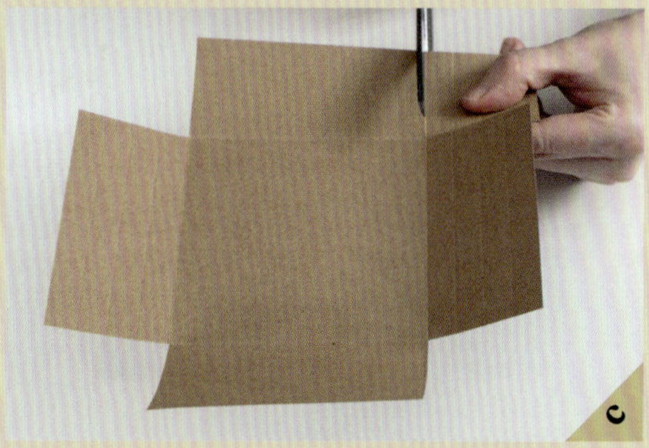

1 Cut a piece of Kraft card measuring 8″ × 8″. **(A)**

2 Score all four sides at ½″, 1″, 1½″ and 2″. **(B)**

3 Cut away all four corners. **(C)**

4 On one side, cut diagonally from the top corner to the ½″ score line, then cut straight down to 1″ score line. From there, cut diagonally again to remove a trapezium-shaped section. Repeat this cutting process on the opposite side of the same edge.

TOP TIP Use a brown pen or pencil to mark the edges of the ice lolly sticks to add an aged and natural effect.

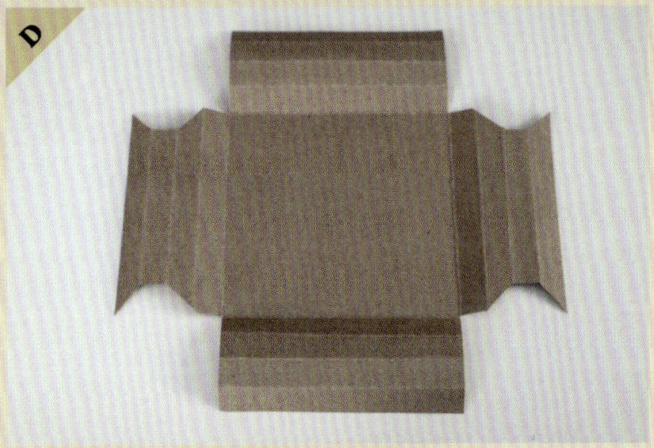

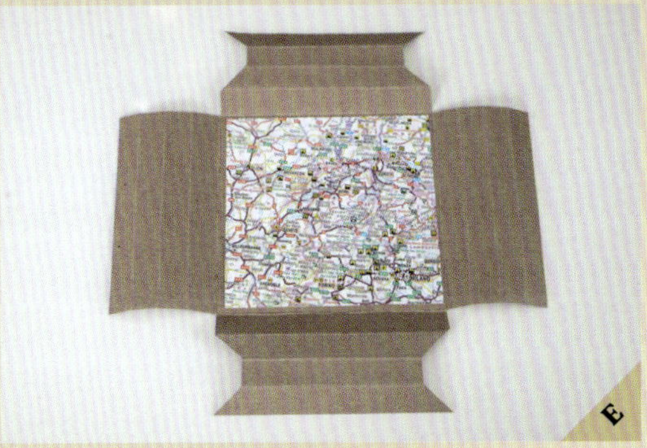

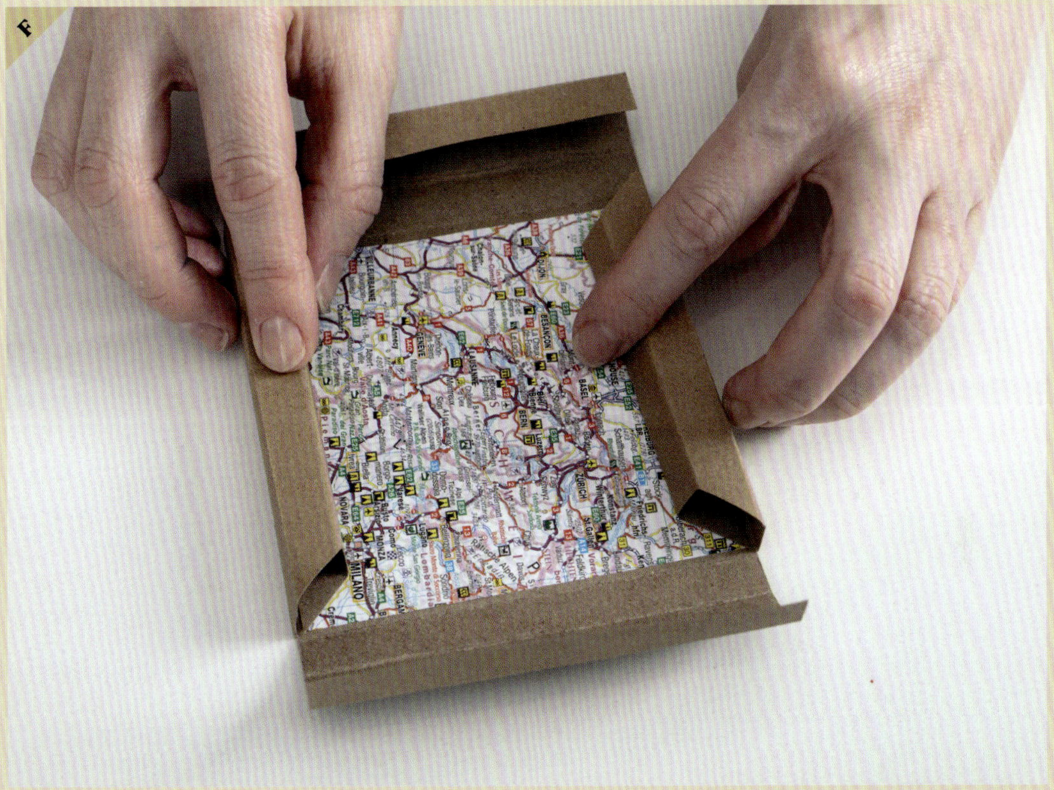

5 Depending on which sides you have cut away, repeat the same cutting process on the opposite side of the card. **(D)**

6 Trim a piece of map paper to just over 3″ × 3″ and glue it to the centre of the scored card using the tape pen. **(E)**

7 Crease and burnish all of the score lines. Take one of the sides with the cut-away section, roll it inwards to form the frame edge, and glue it into place. Repeat with the other side. **(F)**

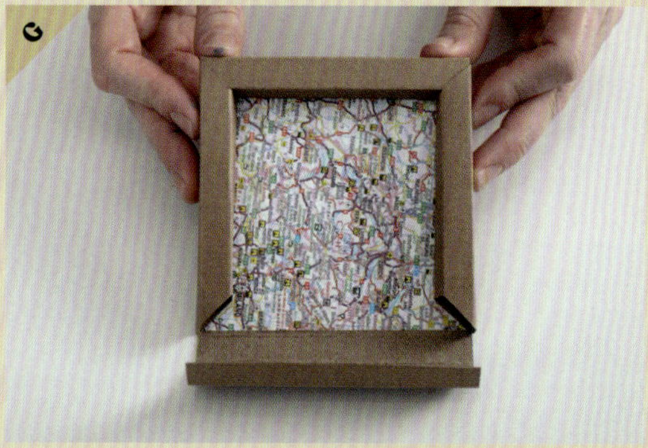

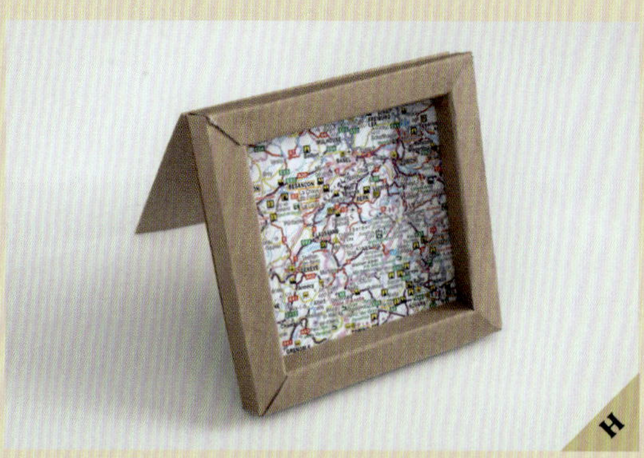

8 Fold in the remaining sides, tucking the corners neatly underneath the sides that are already secured, to complete the dimensional frame. **(G)**

9 Glue the finished frame on to a 4" × 4" card front. **(H)**

10 Cut one ice lolly stick in half and write your chosen sentiment across the two pieces. Use a brown pen or pencil to create an aged effect if desired. Glue the two halves to a second lolly stick, as shown, then adhere to the edge of the frame to resemble a road sign.

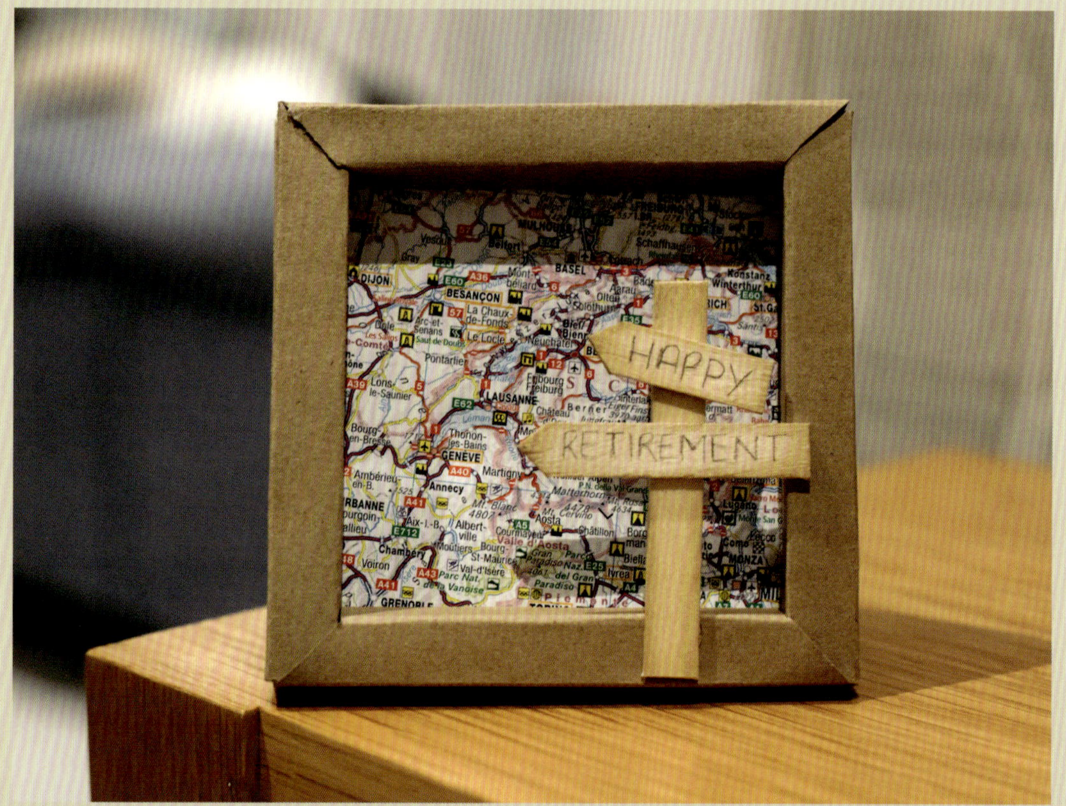

Intermediate

Adventure Awaits Card

This vibrant paper-plane card is a cheerful way to send best wishes as someone embarks on the next exciting chapter of their life in their retirement. The folded heart-shaped plane adds a playful 3D element, while the dashed trail symbolizes all the adventures and journeys ahead!

You will need:

- 5″ × 7″ card base
- Light blue card
- Red card
- Ruler
- Pencil
- Paper trimmer or scissors
- Black fine liner
- Glue tape pen
- Glue gun

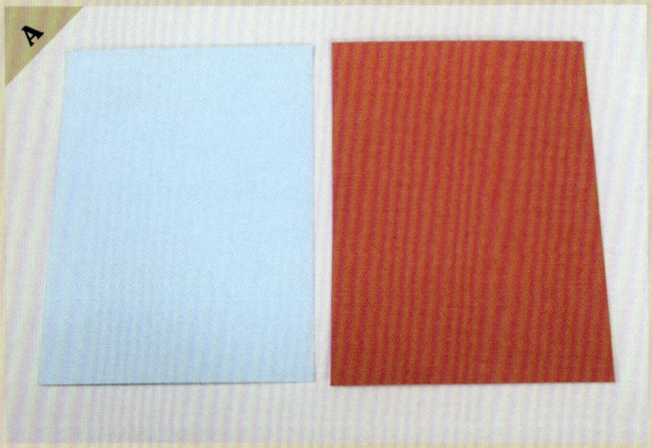

TOP TIP Take your time when folding the wings and shaping the heart. Neat, accurate folds make a big difference to how the plane comes together.

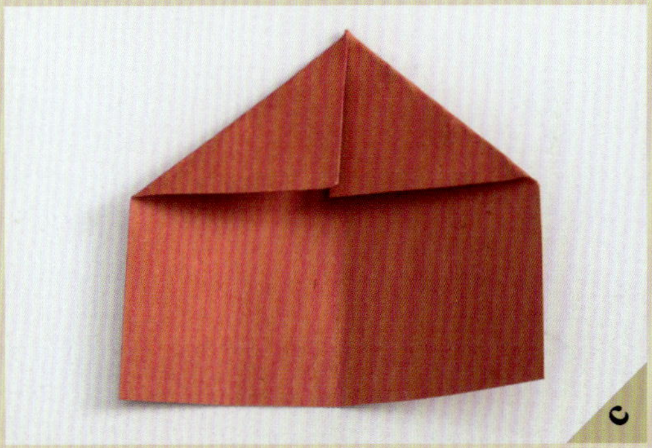

1 Cut a piece of light blue card measuring 4⅝″ × 6⅝″ and a piece of red card measuring 4¾″ × 6¾″. **(A)**

2 Cut a square of red card measuring 3″ × 3″, then fold it in half. **(B)**

3 Open it out, then take the top two corners and fold them inwards so they meet at the centre line. **(C)**

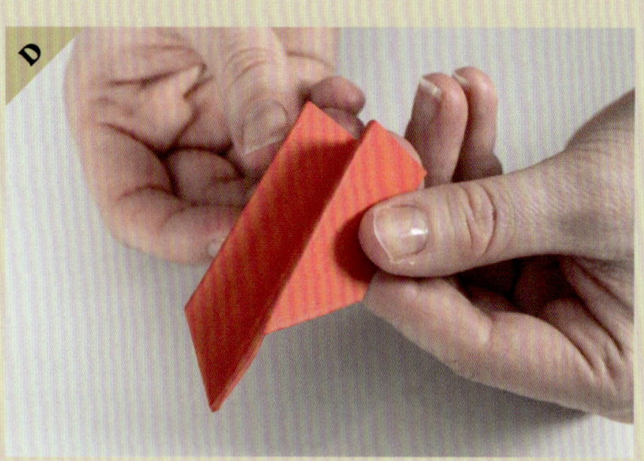

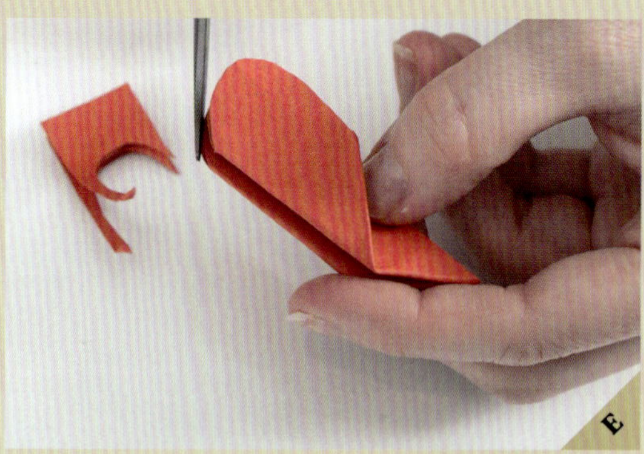

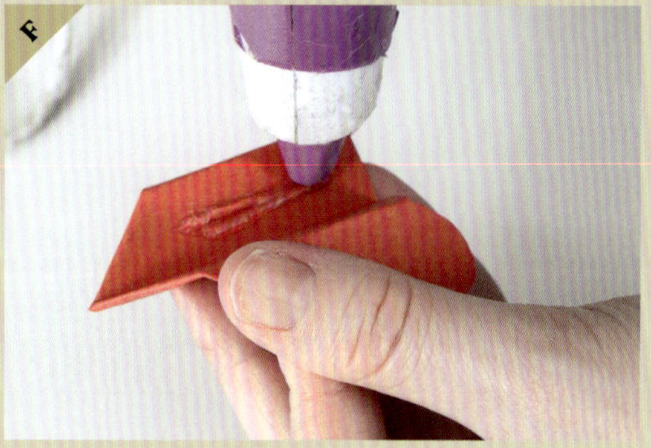

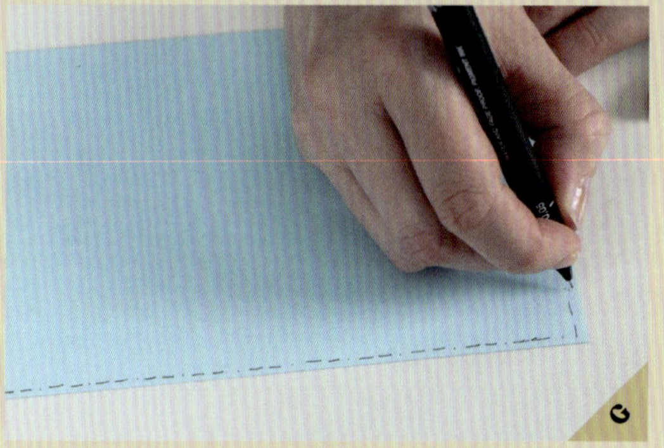

4 Fold the shape in half again. Fold one side down, leaving approximately ¼" visible, then repeat on the opposite side. **(D)**

5 Fold the wings down. Carefully cut a curved line around the folded edges so that when the wings are opened out, they form a heart shape. **(E)**

6 Trim the bottom edge straight along the ¼" section to neaten the shape and glue the folds together into a plane shape. **(F)**

7 Using a black fine liner, draw dashed lines around the edges of the light blue card panel. **(G)**

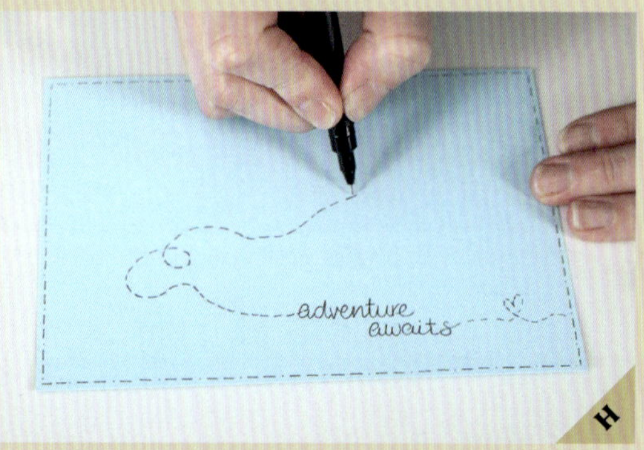

8 Write the sentiment 'adventure awaits' in the bottom-right corner and add a dashed trail for the plane. **(H)**

9 Adhere the light blue panel on to the red card panel from step 1 using a tape pen. **(I)**

10 Glue the paper plane on to the blue panel, positioning it at the end of the dashed trail.

11 Attach the layered panels to the 5″ × 7″ card base to finish!

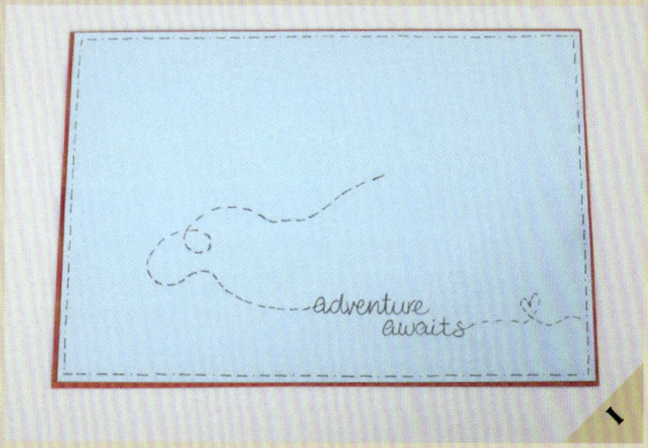

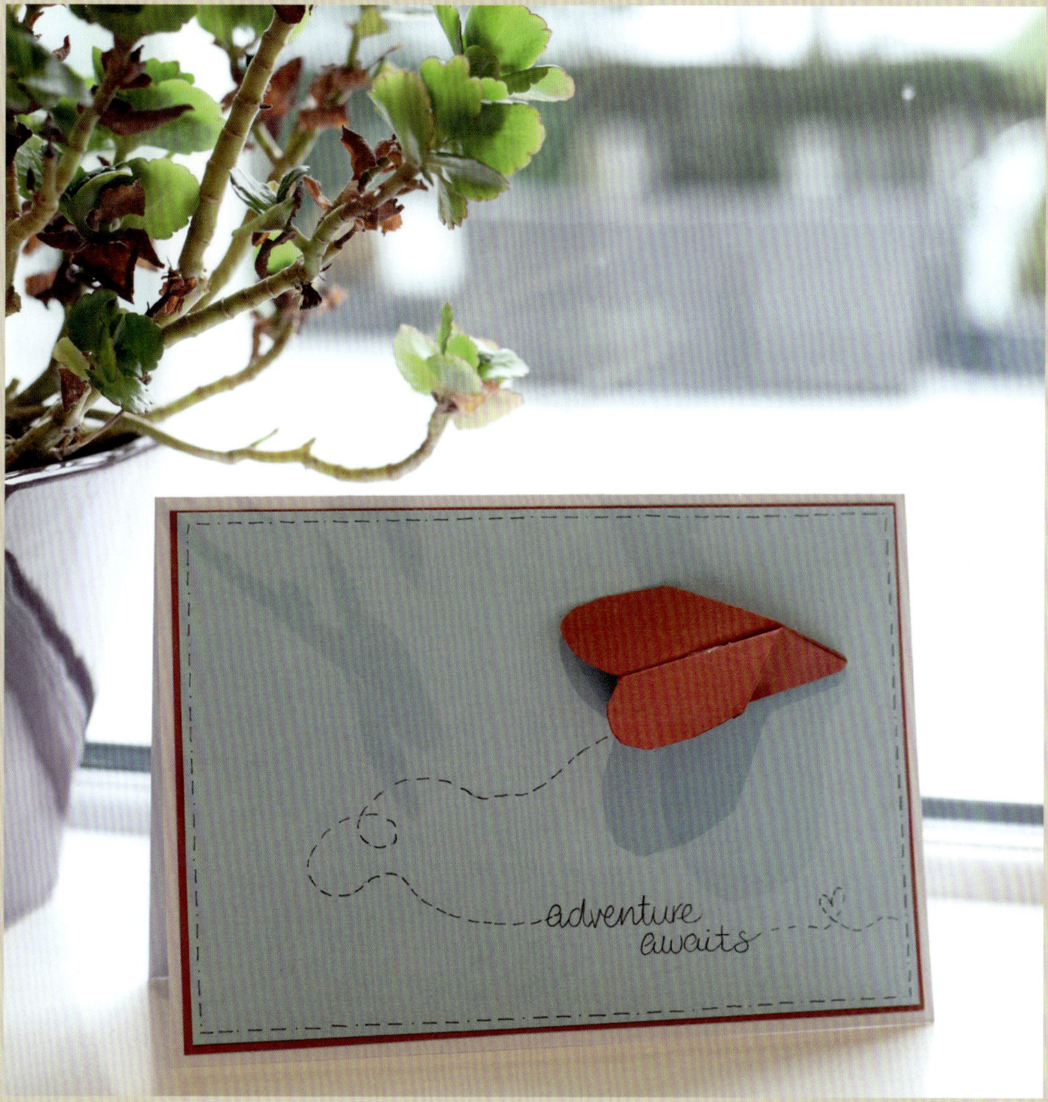

Intermediate

Apple Gift

This is one of those makes that looks so impressive but is actually really clever and achievable once you break it down. By layering simple shapes, you can create a striking 3D apple that makes a thoughtful handmade thank-you gift for a brilliant teacher. Personal, meaningful and long-lasting, it's a gorgeous keepsake that shows real care and appreciation.

TOP TIP **Open the glued structure carefully to avoid tearing.**

You will need:

- Paper
- Red card
- Pencil
- Ruler
- Scissors
- Scoring tool
- Glue gun
- Small twig from the garden
- Tag or card (optional)
- Black fine liner (optional)

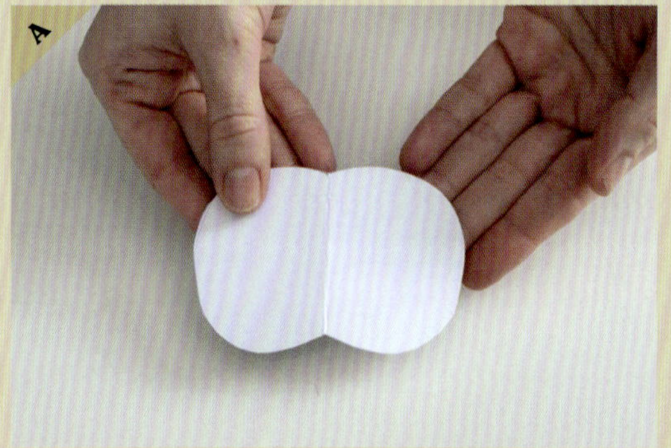

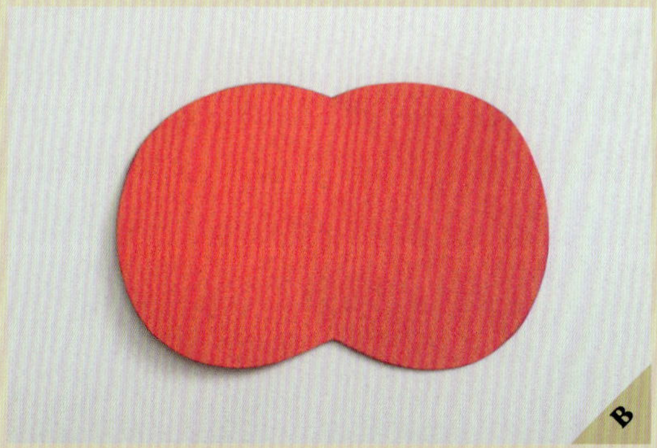

1 Draw an apple template on to a folded piece of paper measuring approximately 1¾" × 2⅝" and cut out. **(A)**

2 Use the template to draw the apple shape multiple times on to red card. Carefully cut out 24 identical apple shapes in total. **(B)**

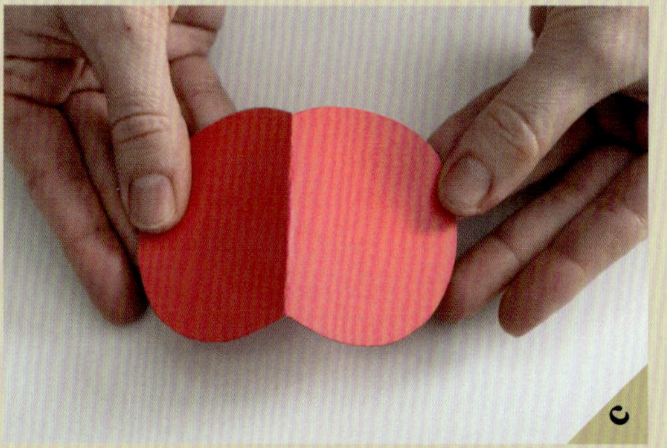

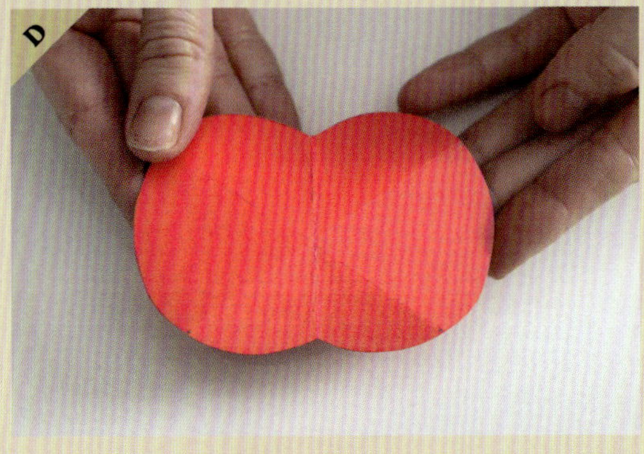

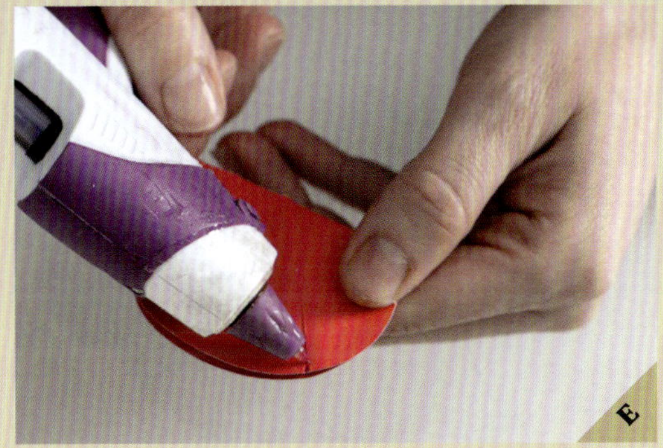

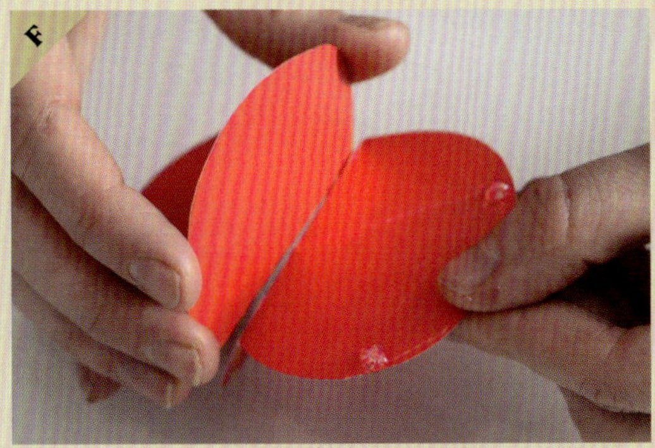

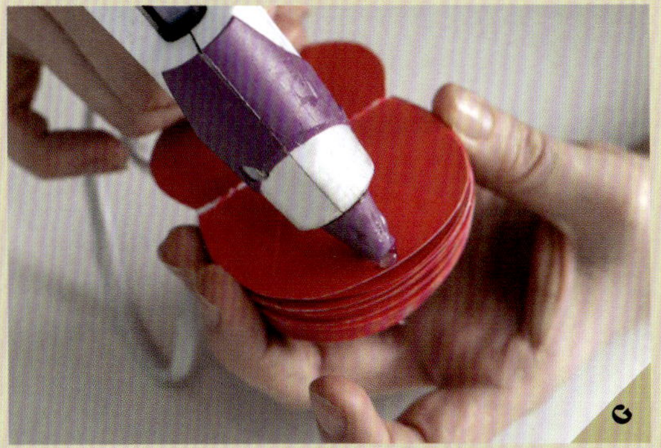

3 Fold each apple shape in half. **(C)**

4 On one folded apple, mark ¼" up from the bottom on each side and ½" down from the top on each side.

5 Using a ruler and scoring tool, join the marks diagonally to score an X shape across the folded apple. **(D)**

6 Take one folded apple and apply adhesive at the ends of the top and bottom score lines, as shown. **(E)**

7 Place a second folded apple on top, aligning the edges carefully, and press to secure. **(F)**

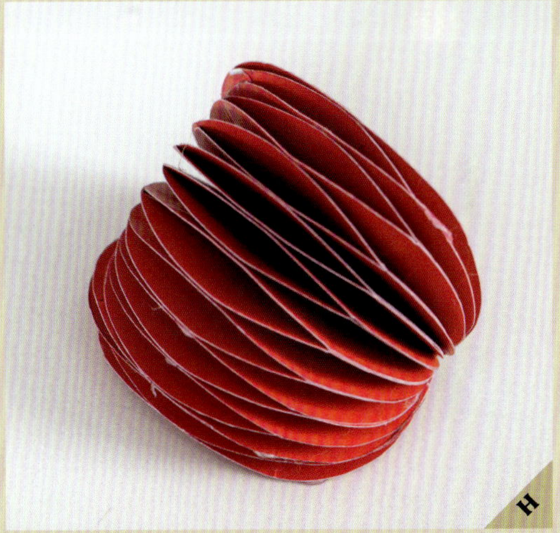

8 Apply adhesive to the edge points again, and add another folded apple on top.

9 Repeat this process until all apple layers have been stuck and secured. **(G and H)**

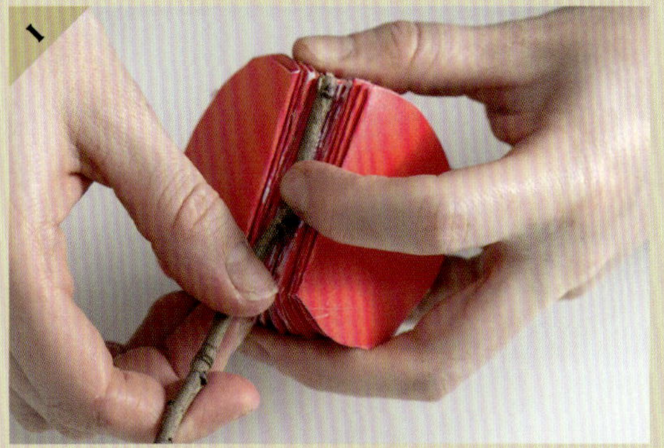

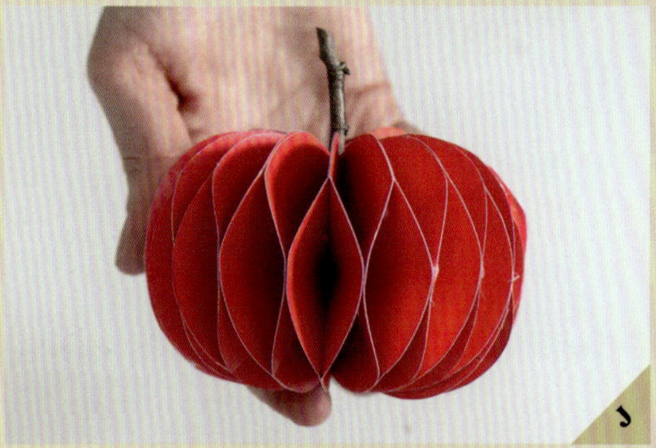

10 Once all layers are secure, glue a small twig in the centre of the apple to form the stalk. **(I)**

11 Add a small dot of glue along the outer edge of the middle section as you work, continuing until you reach the point where the top and bottom layers are glued together, forming a complete 3D apple. **(J)**

12 Finish by adding a personalized name tag, if desired.

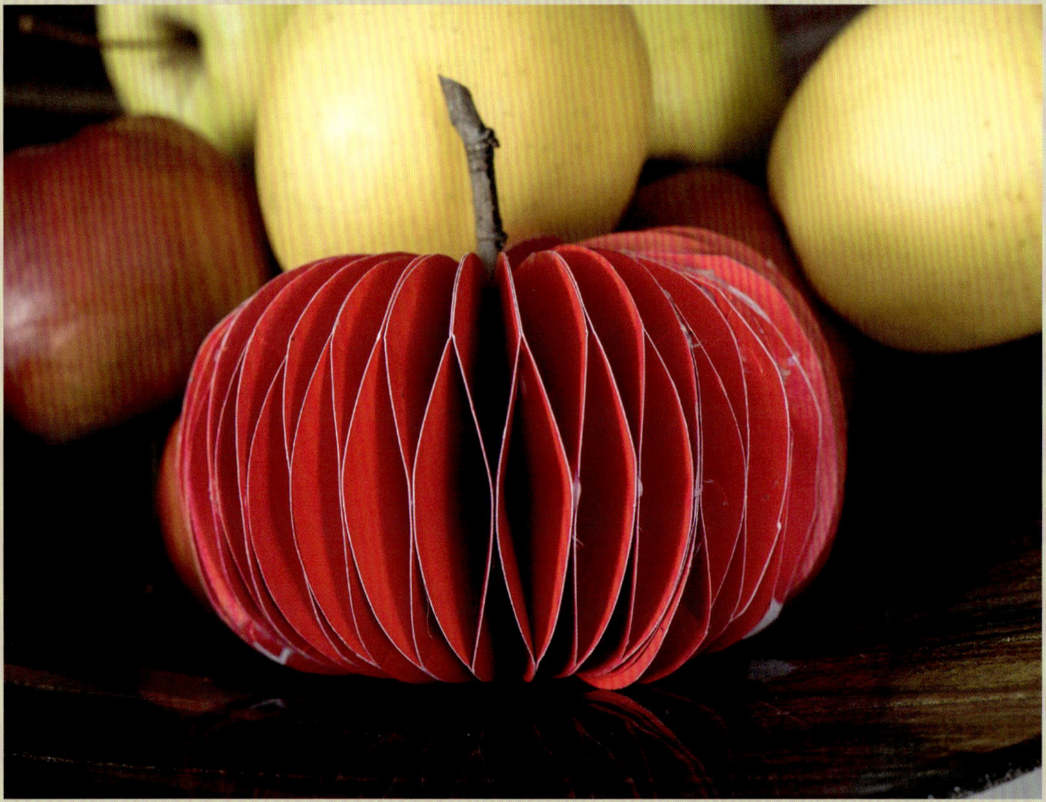

Intermediate

Pencil Card

This pencil card is a fun way to say a big thank-you to a special teacher! It's bright, cheerful and full of personality, making it perfect for the end of term, a class thank-you, or even a first-day-back treat. By simply shaping your card base and layering a few colourful pieces of card, you can create something that looks really impressive.

You will need:

- Yellow, pink, silver, cream and black card
- Ruler
- Pencil
- Paper trimmer
- Scissors
- Glue tape pen or other adhesive
- Pen
- Decorative string

TOP TIP Before sticking anything down permanently, test all the pencil layers first. This makes it much easier to line up the tip, lead and eraser neatly, and ensures your finished card looks professional.

1 Create a slimline 8″ × 4″ card base from yellow card. **(A)**

2 Mark the centre point at the top of the card at 2″. Then measure 2¼″ down both sides and draw two lines joining these points to the 2″ mark. **(B)**

3 Cut away both sides of the card to form the tip of the pencil. **(C)**

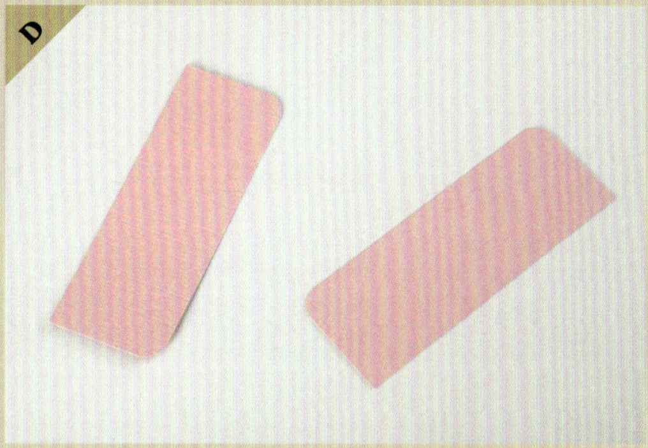

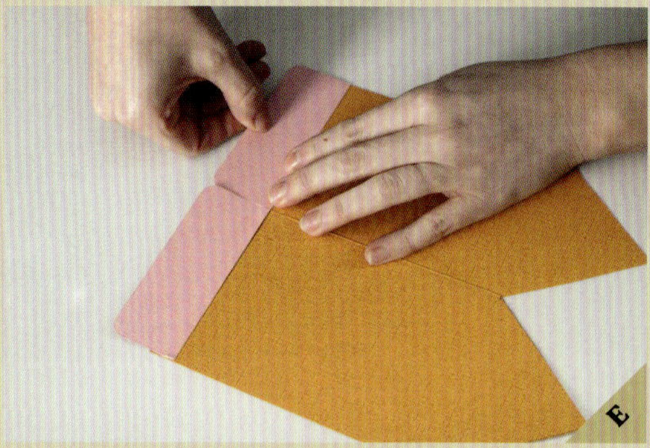

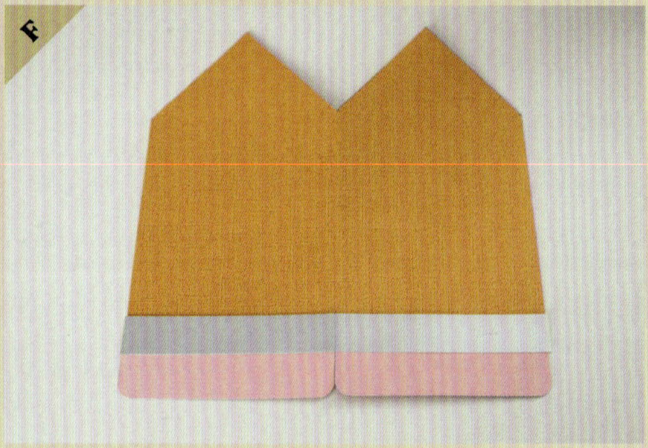

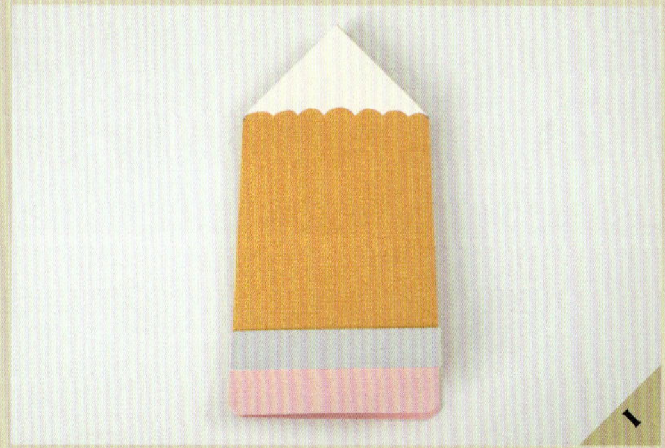

4 Cut two strips of pink card measuring 4″ × 1½″. Use scissors to round the two corners on each piece as shown. **(D)**

5 Adhere them to the bottom of each side of the card base to create the eraser. **(E)**

6 Add a strip of silver card measuring 8″ × ¾″, gluing it across the pink card pieces. **(F)**

7 Cut two triangular pieces of cream card using the tip of the card base as a template. **(G)**

8 Cut a scalloped edge along the bottom of each piece. **(H)**

9 Adhere these in place at the top of the pencil. **(I)**

10 Cut two small triangles from black card and glue them to the tip of the pencil to create the lead. **(J)**

11 Create a sentiment tag and glue it to the card front with a decorative string bow to finish. **(K)**

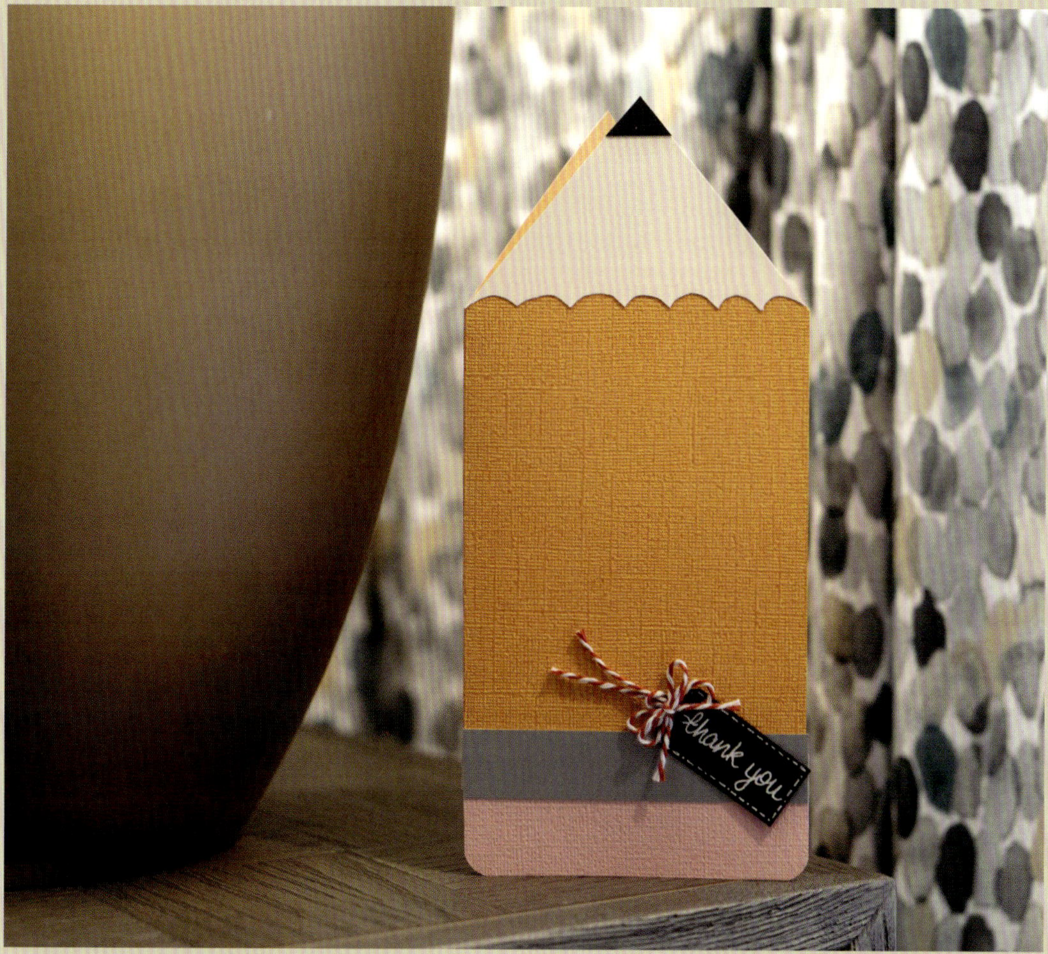

Advanced

Stationery Gift

If you're looking for a really thoughtful way to say thank you to an amazing teacher, this handmade stationery gift with a notepad and pen holder is just perfect. It's practical, personal, and something they can use every single day in the classroom or at home. With its clever folds and pockets, this project is a joy to make and looks beautifully professional once finished. A heartfelt, handmade gift that truly shows your appreciation and celebrates all the hard work they do!

TOP TIP **Personalize the gift with the teacher's name and favourite colours!**

You will need:

- Kraft card
- Ruler
- Scissors or craft knife
- Scoring tool
- Scoring board
- Glue tape pen
- Patterned paper
- Red liner double-sided tape
- Notepad
- Pen or pencil

1 Cut a piece of Kraft card measuring 5½" × 8½". **(A)**

2 Score at 2¼" and 2¾" from the bottom, then at ⅜" and ⅞" along both long sides. **(B)**

3 Cut away the two side sections down to the 2¾" score line. Next, cut away the ⅜" section, leaving two small tabs above the wider bottom section. **(C)**

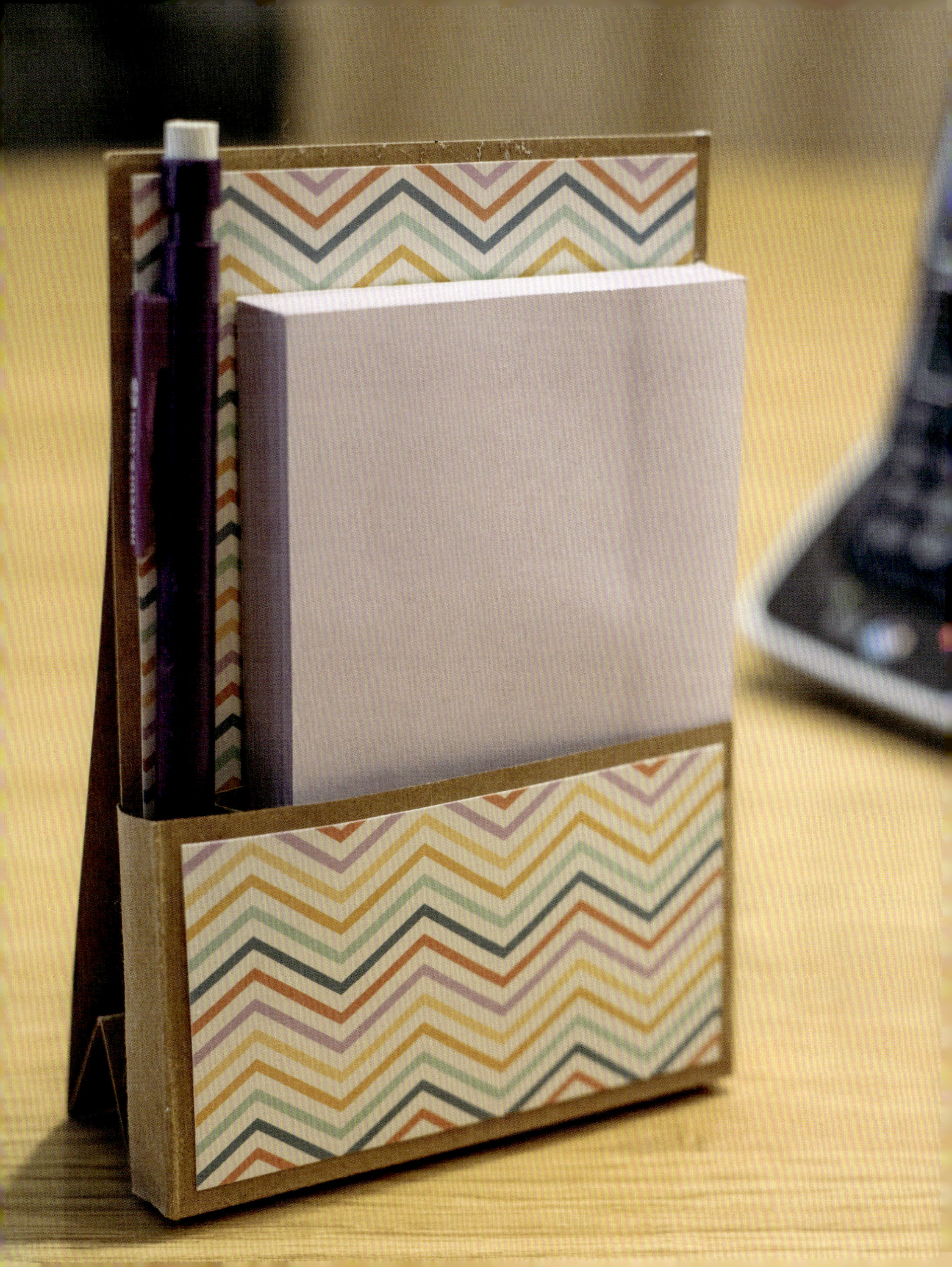

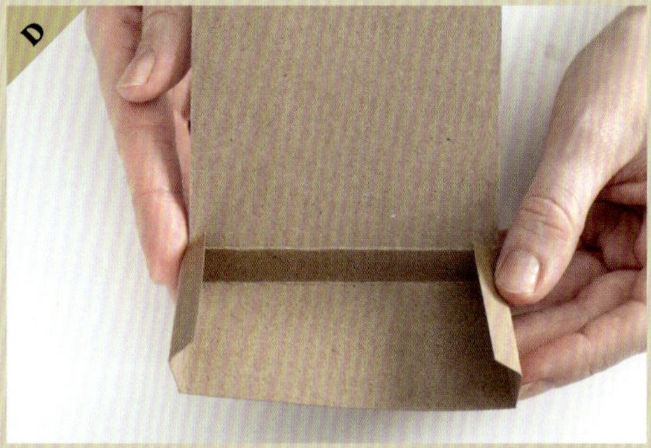

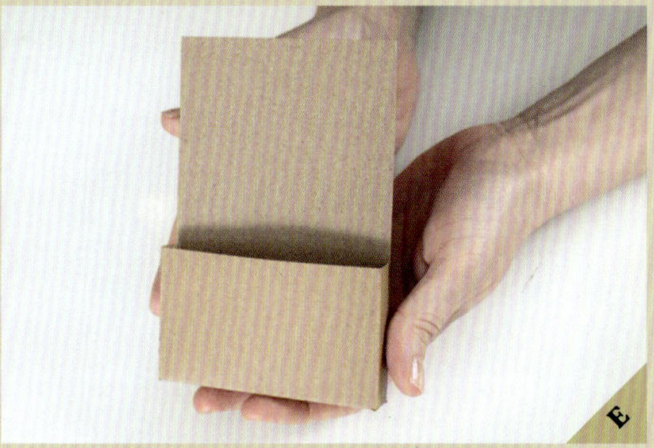

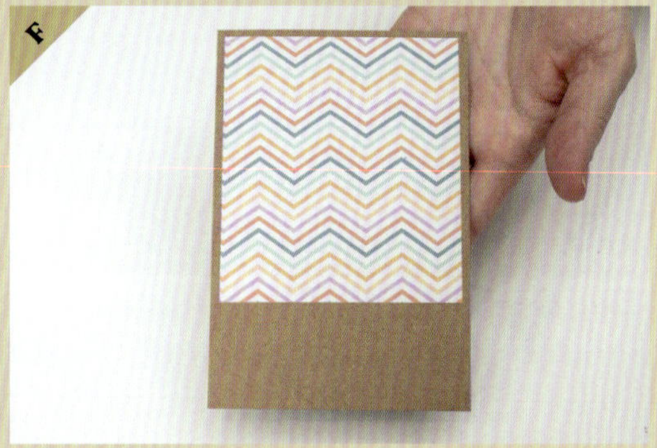

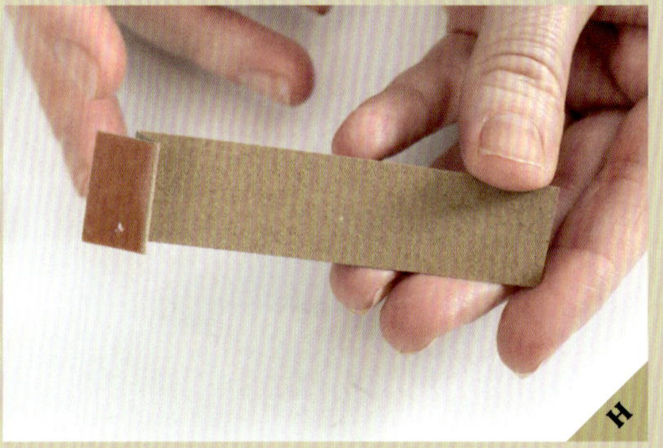

4 Take the 5½″ × 8½″ base piece and fold up the bottom section along the score line. **(D)**

5 Apply adhesive and glue it into place to form a pocket. **(E)**

6 Cut a piece of Kraft craft card 3¾″ × 5¾ then glue a piece of patterned paper measuring 3½″× 4″ to it. **(F)**

7 Adhere it to the back panel of the holder. **(G)**

8 Cut a separate piece of Kraft card measuring ⅞″ × 4¼″ and score it at ½″ and 1″. Fold along the score lines and add strip of red liner tape to the smallest tab. **(H)**

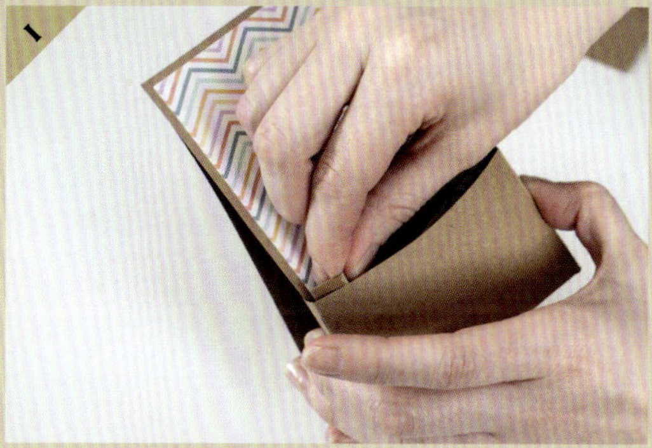

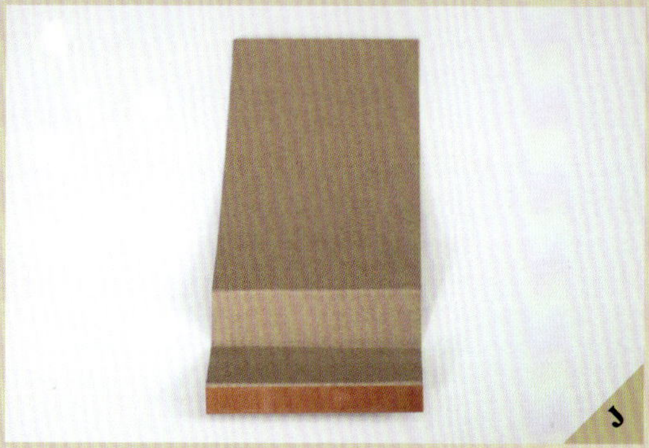

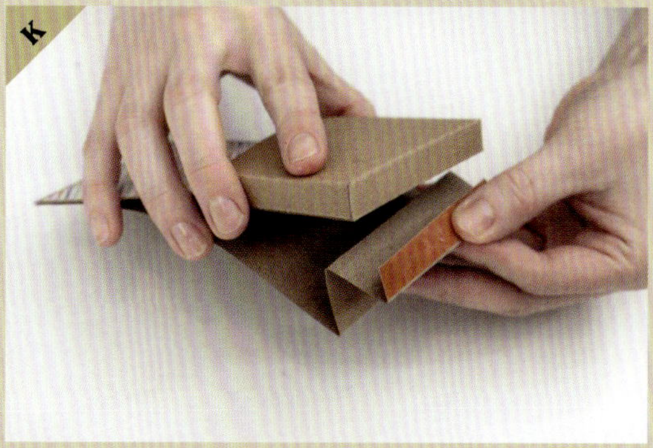

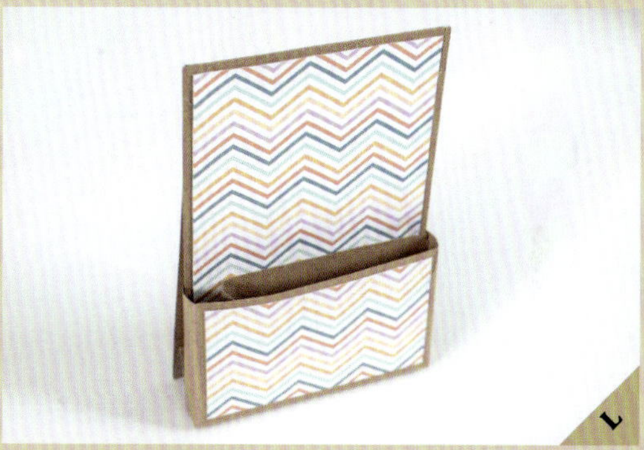

9 Remove the tape backing and affix the tab inside the pocket to create two separate compartments for a notepad and a pen. **(I)**

10 Cut another piece of Kraft card measuring 3¾" × 8¼" and score it at 2½", 1½" and ½".

11 Fold the 3¾" × 8¼" piece along the score lines to create alternating mountain and valley folds. Add red liner tape to the bottom tab. **(J)**

12 Remove the liner tape backing and affix the tab to the bottom of the pocket. **(K)**

13 Apply adhesive along the top of the pocket panel to form the closing flap.

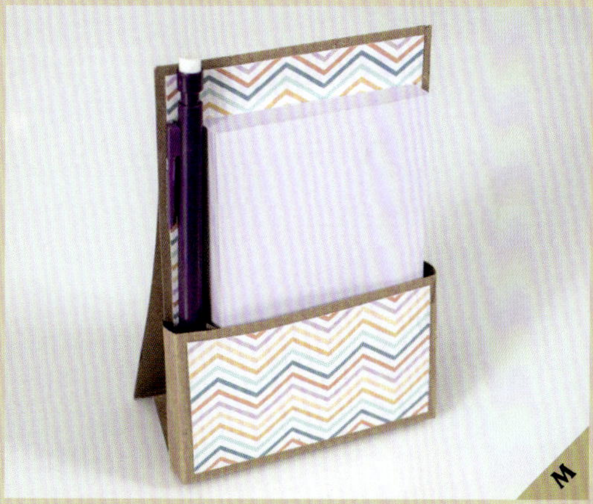

14 Cut patterned paper measuring 3½" × 2" and adhere it to the front of the pocket. **(L)**

15 Finish by adding a notepad and a pen or pencil to the stationery holder. **(M)**

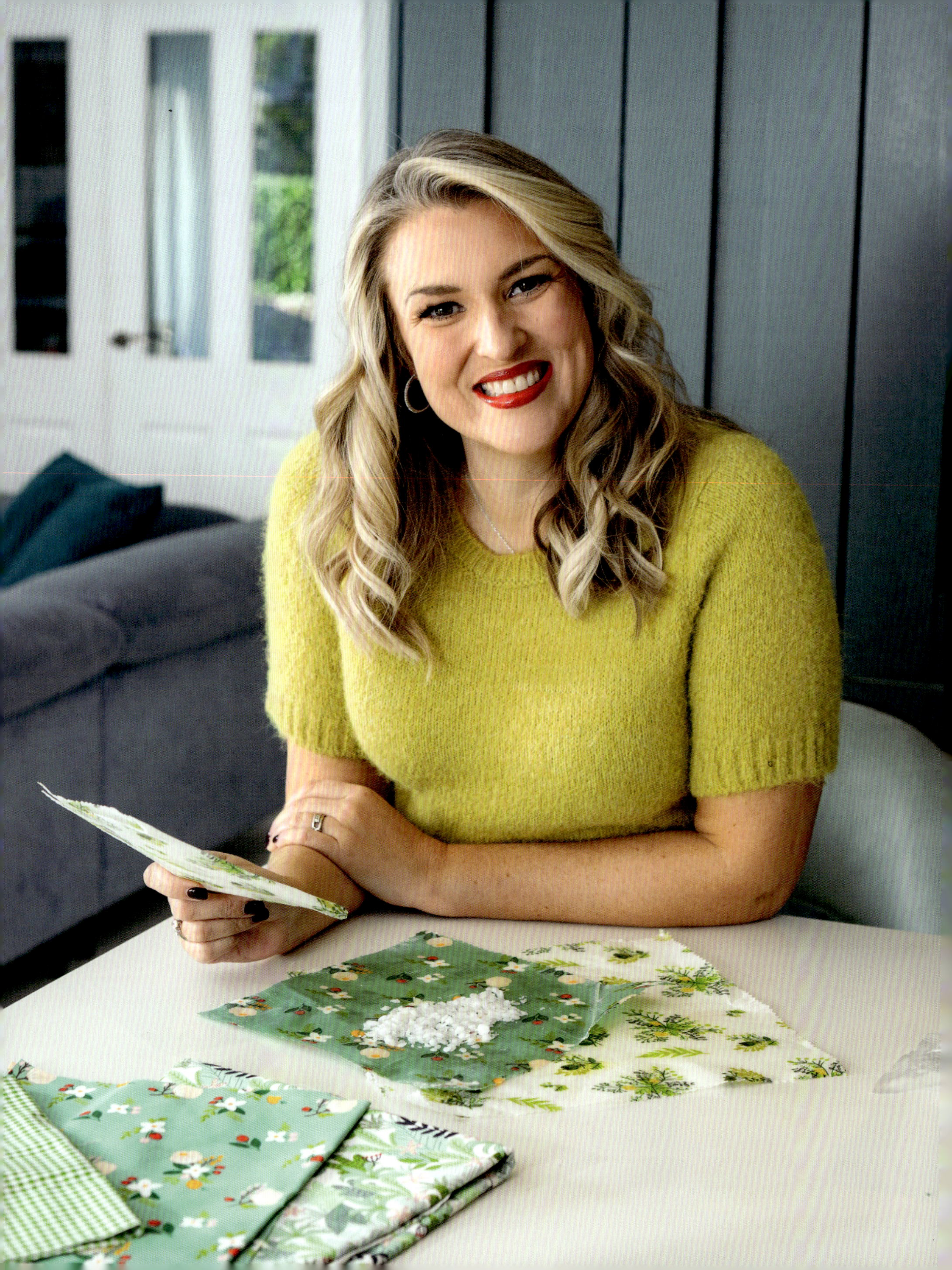

Something New

New Job

New Home

New Baby

Intermediate

New Job Card

There's no better way to celebrate a big achievement than with a handmade card, and the notepad detail in this design gives you the freedom to make your message truly personal. It's a thoughtful and creative way to tell someone you're proud of them, and a card that feels just as special to give as it does to receive!

TOP TIP **Use different coloured papers or vary the notepad messages to personalize this card for that special someone.**

You will need:

- 5″ × 7″ card base
- Patterned paper
- Black card
- Kraft card
- Scissors or paper trimmer
- Ruler
- Glue tape pen
- Copy paper or notepad pages
- Blue and red pens (if creating your own notepad pages)
- Foldback clip or paper clip
- Black pen

1 Cut a piece of patterned paper measuring 5″ × 5″ and adhere it to the top of the 5″ × 7″ card base, aligning it neatly along the top edge. **(A)**

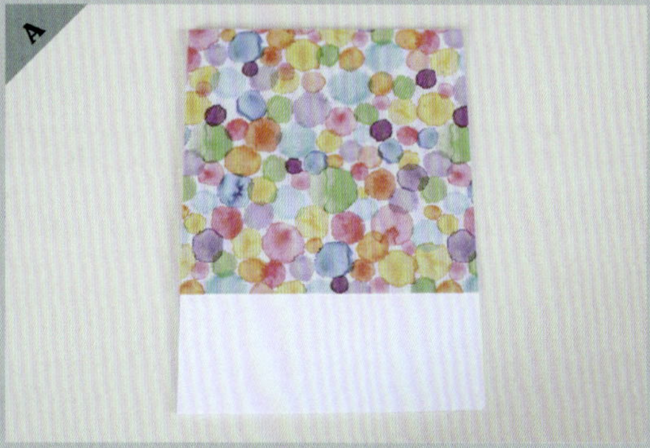

2 Cut a ¼″ strip of black card and glue it along the bottom edge of the patterned paper panel. **(B)**

3 Cut a piece of Kraft card measuring 3″ × 4½″ and use scissors to round off all four corners. **(C)**

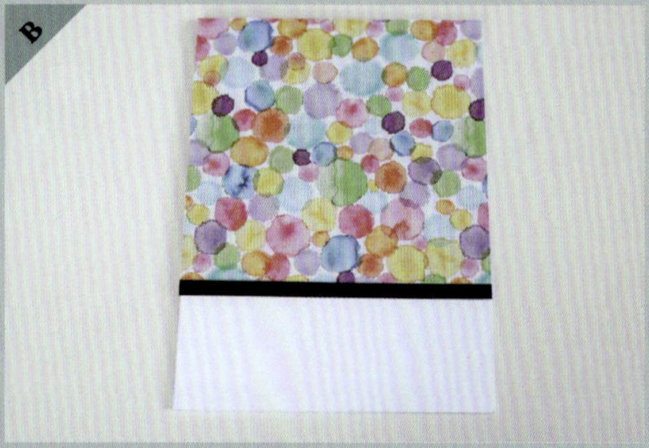

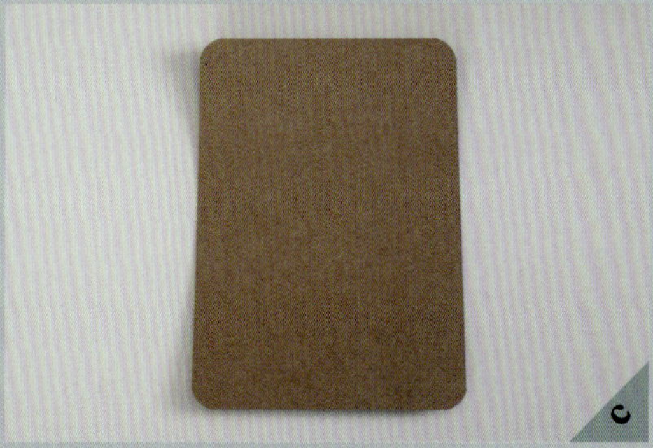

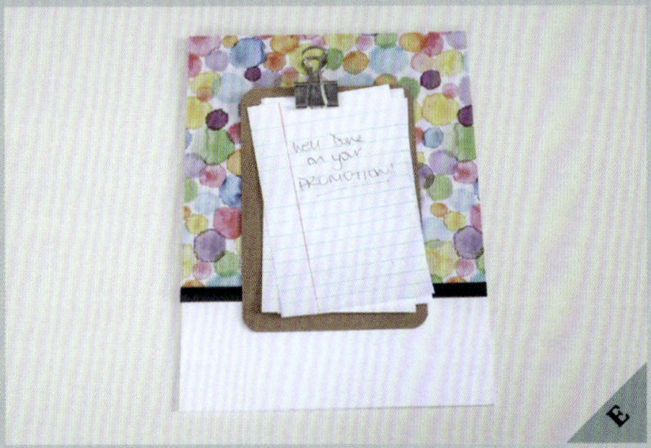

4 Cut a sheet of copy paper (or notepad paper) to 2½" × 4". If creating your own pages, draw horizontal blue lines starting ½" down from the top edge, spaced at ¼" intervals, then add a vertical red line ½" in from the left-hand edge. **(D)**

5 Repeat the previous step to create several sheets of lined paper. Stack them on to the Kraft card and secure them at the top using a small foldback clip or paper clip.

6 Write a personalized message on to the paper using a black pen, then adhere the notepad panel to the front of the card. **(E)**

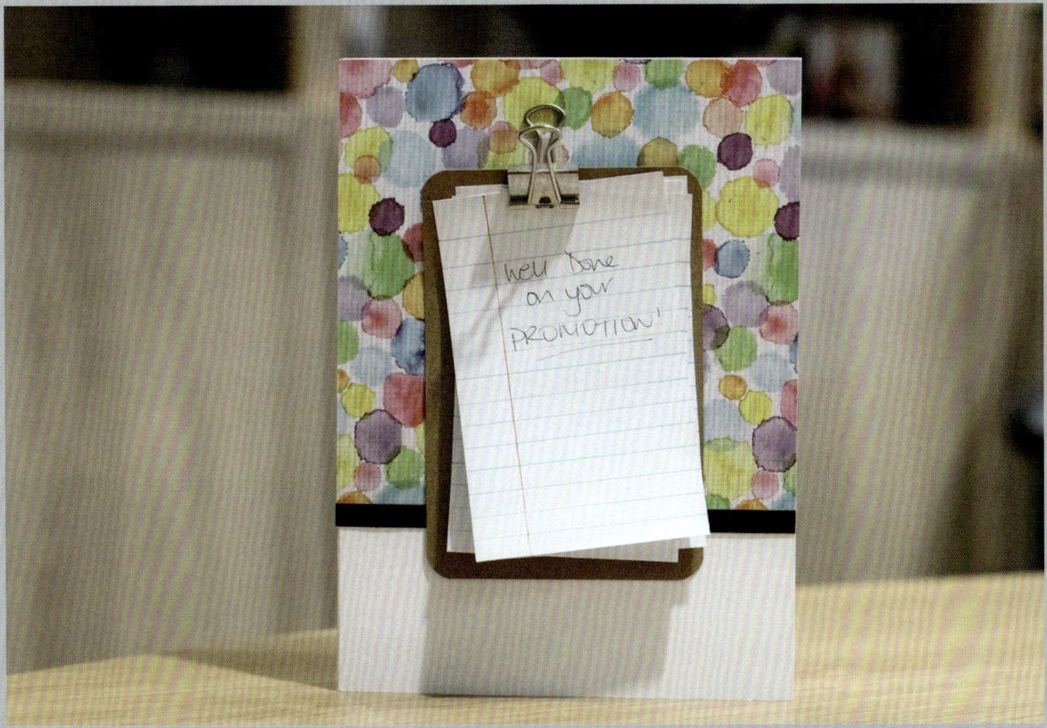

Easy

Beeswax Wraps

These beeswax wraps are a beautiful way to wrap bread, snacks or small treats for someone settling into a new home, while also offering an eco-friendly alternative to cling film or foil. So you're giving a gift that's kind to the planet too! Simple to make, reusable and easy to personalize with fabric choices, they add a thoughtful handmade touch to a housewarming present that's both stylish and sustainable.

You will need:

- Cotton fabric
- Yellow beeswax pellets
- Scissors (pinking shears optional, for a nice serrated finish)
- Iron
- Greaseproof paper

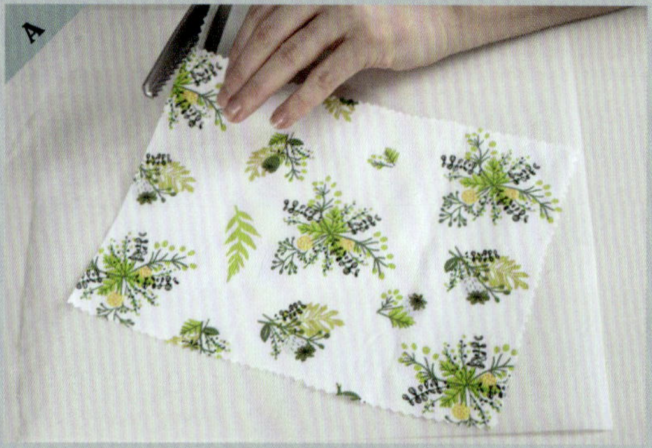
A

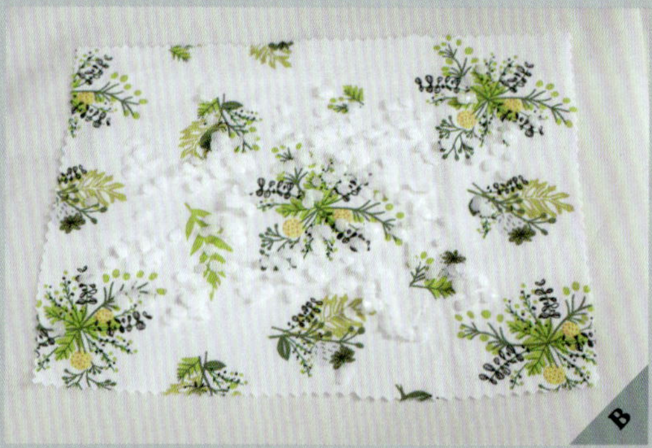
B

1 Lay your cotton fabric flat on a heatproof surface and cut it to your desired size. **(A)**

2 Scatter beeswax pellets evenly across the fabric, leaving a small margin around the edges to prevent wax from running over. **(B)**

3 Set your iron to medium-high heat, with the steam function turned off.

4 Cover the fabric with a sheet of greaseproof paper to protect both the fabric and the iron. **(C)**

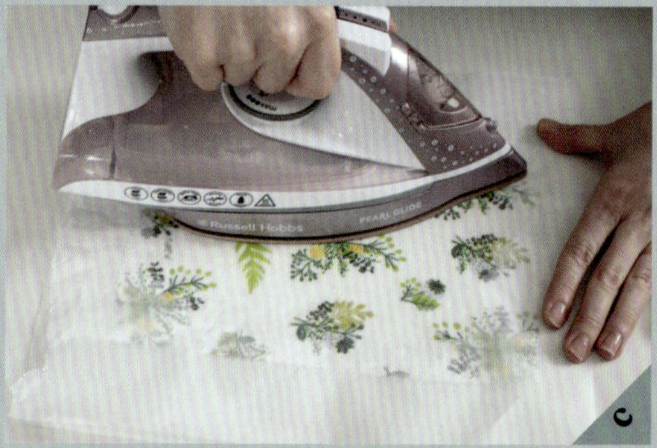

C

5 Gently move the iron over the paper, allowing the beeswax pellets to melt and spread evenly across the fabric. Lift and reposition the iron as needed to avoid overheating any one area.

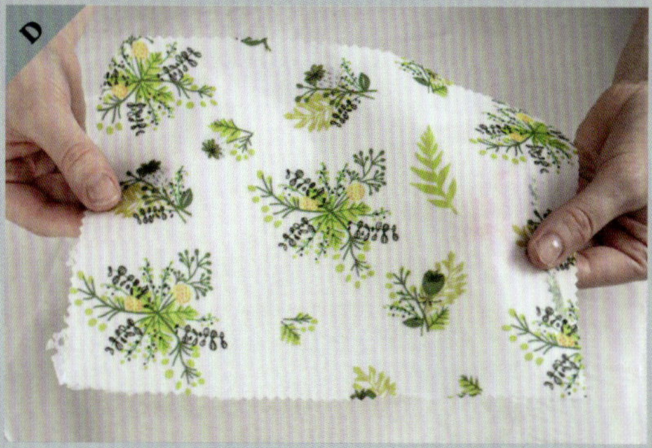

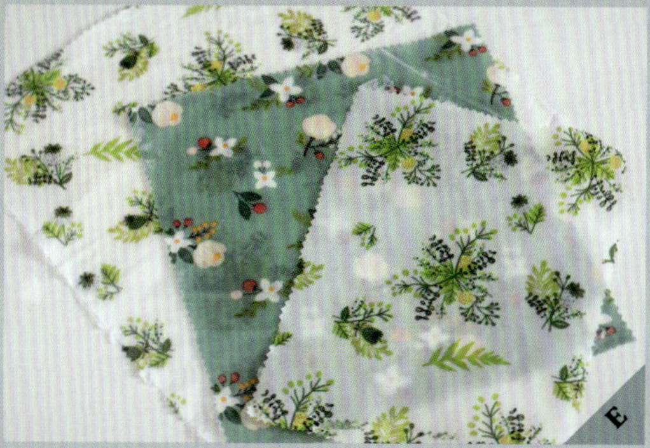

6 Once the fabric is fully coated with melted wax, carefully lift it and set it aside to cool completely. **(D)**

7 Once cool and set, your beeswax wraps are ready to use! **(E)**

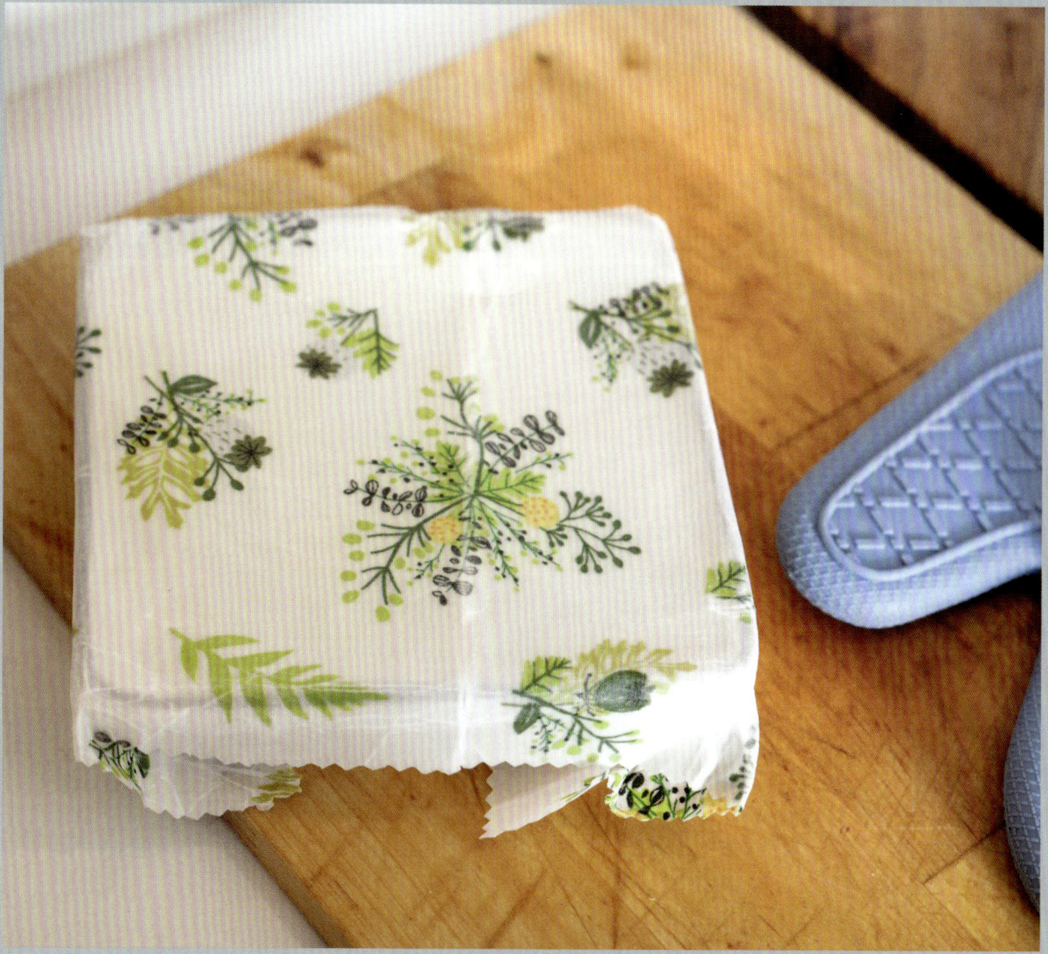

Easy

Handmade Soap

These floral soaps look beautiful and smell amazing, making them a thoughtful gift for someone moving into a new home (or a lovely treat for yourself!). With the option to customize colours, scents and dried flowers, each soap can be tailored to suit different styles and personal preferences. Do check the allergen advice on the soap base and include that when gifting the soaps.

You will need:

- 500g melt-and-pour soap base (makes approximately six small round soaps)
- Sharp knife
- Heatproof bowl
- Dried flowers
- Tweezers (optional)
- Heatproof jug
- Soap mould (silicone works best), with six equal sections
- Spoon or spatula
- Soap dye
- Essential oils

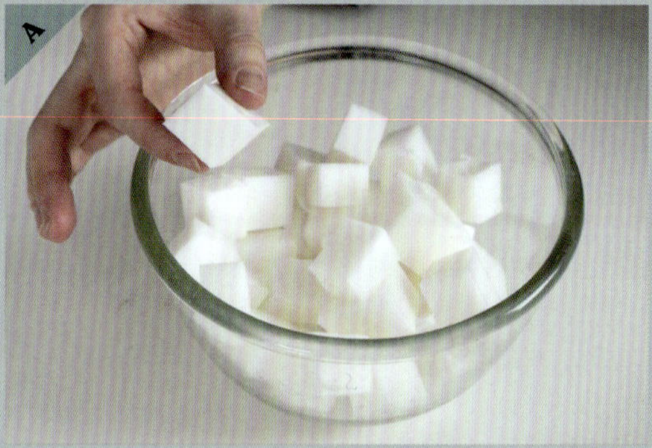

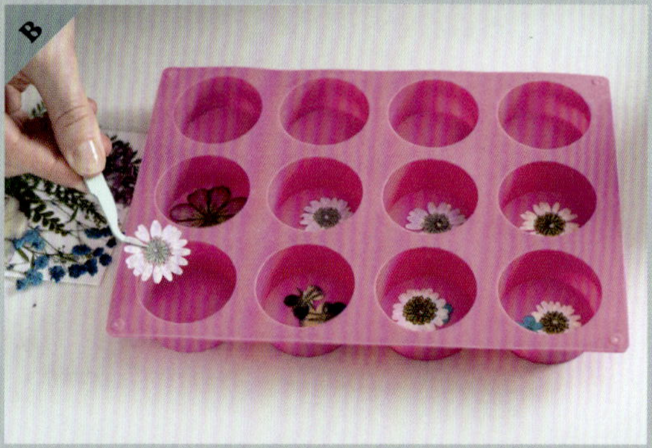

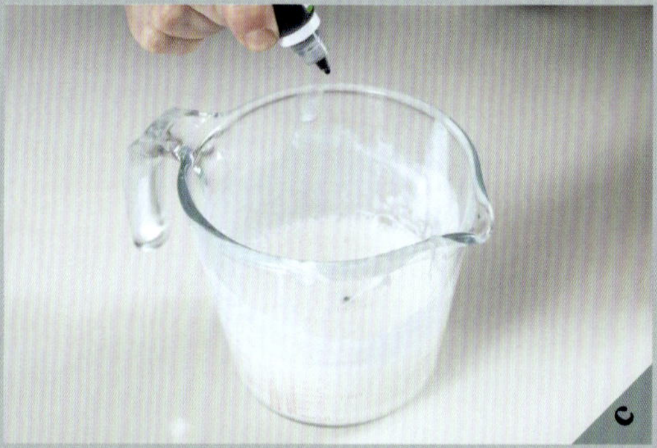

1 Chop your soap base into small chunks. Place the chunks in a heatproof bowl. **(A)**

2 Place dried flowers face down in the base of each section of the soap mould. Using tweezers can help prevent the flowers from breaking. **(B)**

3 Melt the soap base in the microwave for 20 seconds at a time, stirring between each burst, until the soap is fully melted and smooth.

4 Transfer the melted soap to a heatproof jug, add a few drops of soap dye and stir well, adjusting the colour gradually. Be careful – a little goes a long way! **(C)**

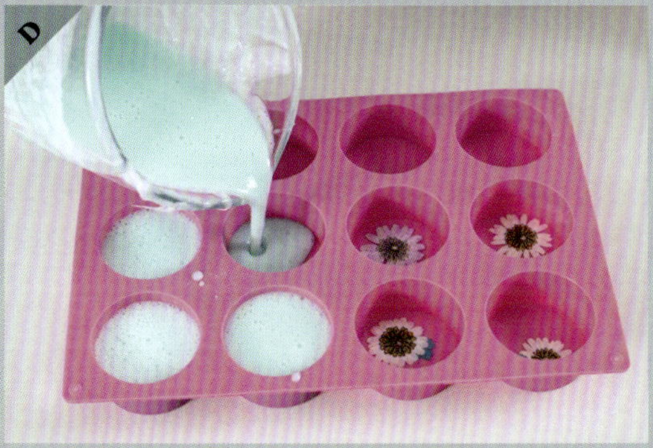

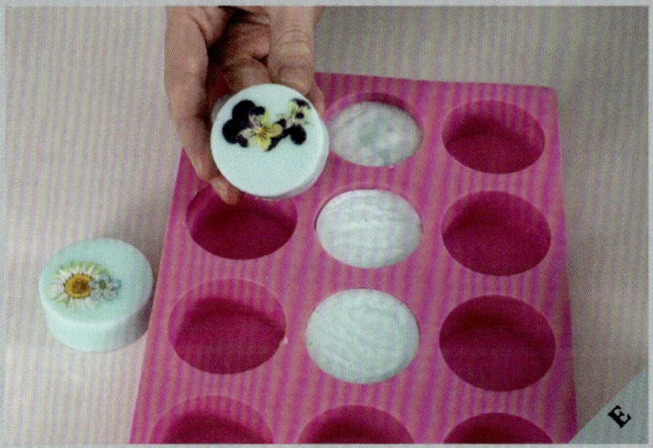

5 Add a few drops of your chosen essential oils and stir thoroughly to combine.

6 Carefully pour the mixture into the moulds, covering the dried flowers. **(D)**

7 Leave the soaps to set in a cool place, or in the fridge, for several hours until completely firm.

8 Once set, gently remove the soaps from the mould and admire your handmade creations! **(E)**

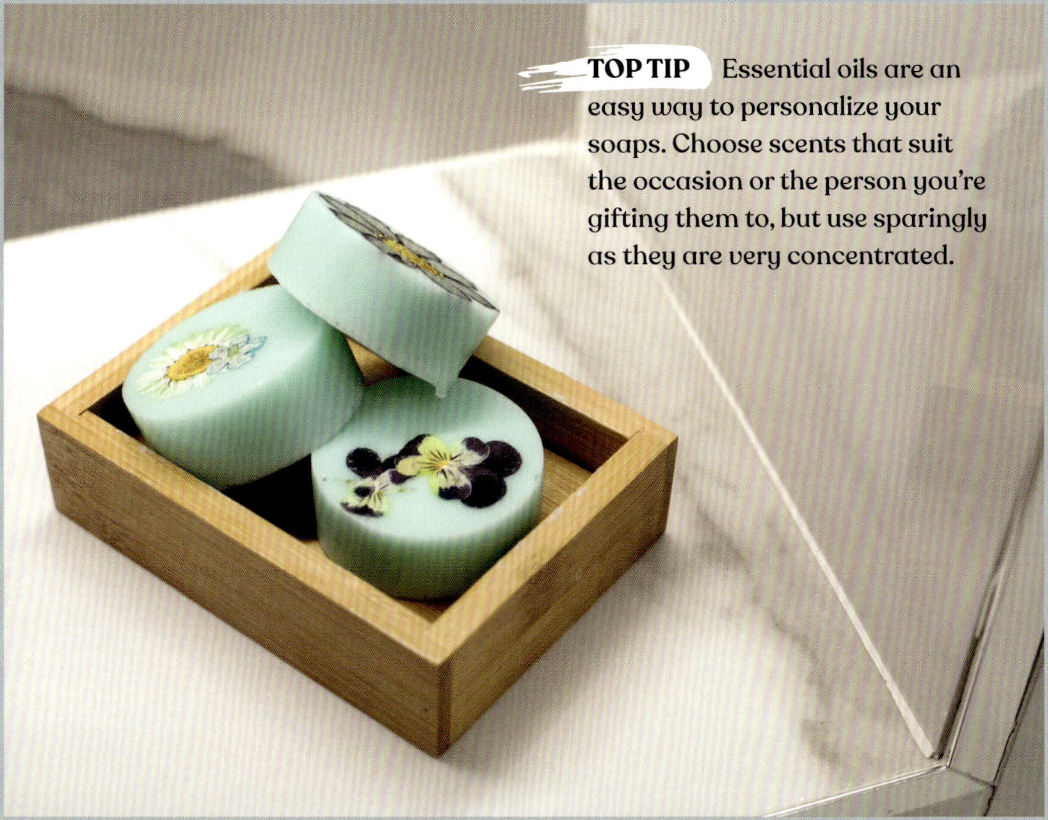

TOP TIP Essential oils are an easy way to personalize your soaps. Choose scents that suit the occasion or the person you're gifting them to, but use sparingly as they are very concentrated.

Intermediate

Keyhole Card

If you're looking for a way to celebrate someone moving into a new home, then look no further than this gorgeous keyhole card. The clever aperture design gives a peek at the sparkling sequins inside, adding a playful, interactive element. It looks impressively detailed but is very satisfying to make, and with a few careful steps you can create a card that's full of charm.

TOP TIP The handmade tag on the card front gives you the option to personalize this for your recipient.

You will need:

- Kraft card
- Pencil
- Ruler
- Scissors
- Pokey tool
- Acetate
- Red liner double-sided tape
- Foam tape
- Glue tape pen
- Patterned paper
- Sequins
- Black fine liner
- Cream card
- String

1 Create a 5″ × 7″ card base from Kraft card and set it aside. **(A)**

A

2 To create the keyhole shape, take a piece of scrap paper and draw a triangle measuring 2⅜″ on two sides, with a 1⅞″ base. Add a circle to the top of the triangle. Drawing a light pencil cross first can help position the circle accurately. **(B)**

3 Cut the keyhole shape out to use as a template and draw around it on to a piece of Kraft card measuring 4¾″ × 6¾″ to form the card front. Using a pokey tool and scissors, cut out the shape to create an aperture. **(C)**

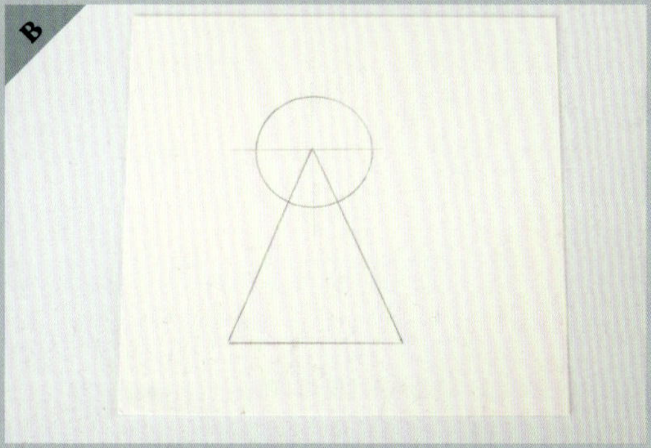

B

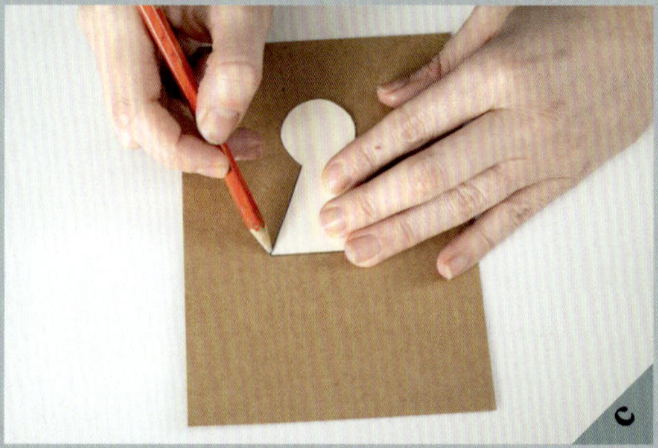

C

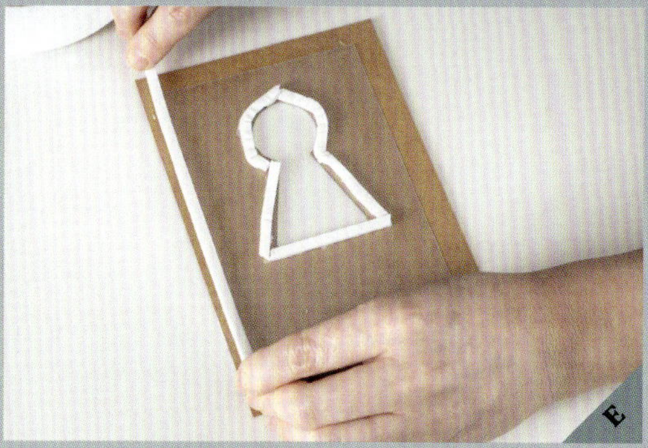

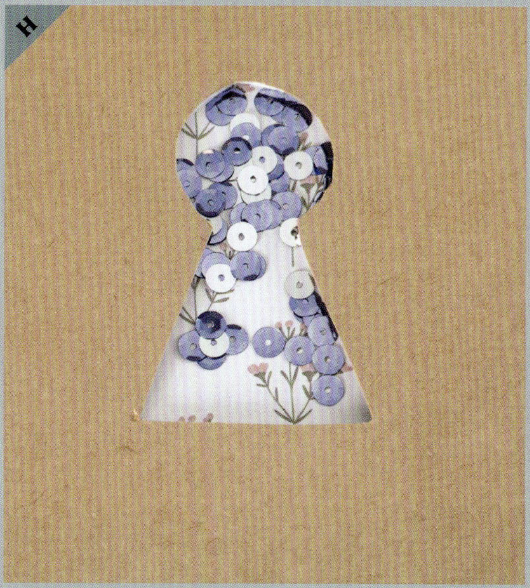

4 Cut a piece of acetate large enough to cover the aperture and secure it to the back of the card front using red liner tape around the edges. **(D)**

5 Apply foam tape around the outer edges of the back of the card front and around the keyhole aperture. This will keep the sequins securely contained and add dimension to the design. **(E)**

6 Take the 5″ × 7″ card base and use a tape pen to adhere a piece of patterned paper large enough to show through the aperture window. **(F)**

7 Place the sequins on to the centre of the patterned paper. **(G)**

8 Remove the backing from the foam tape and carefully position the card front on to the card base, sealing the shaker elements inside. **(H)**

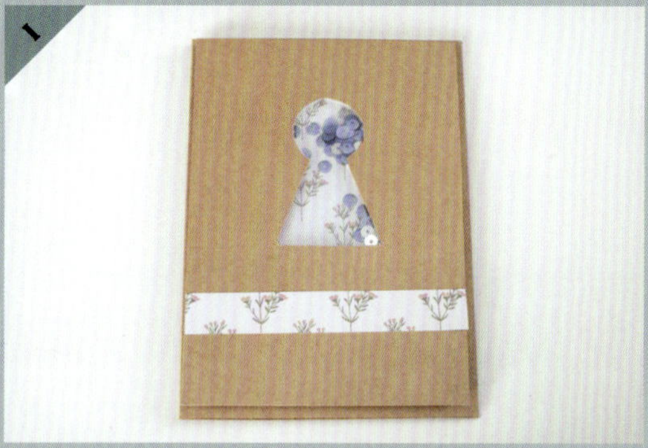

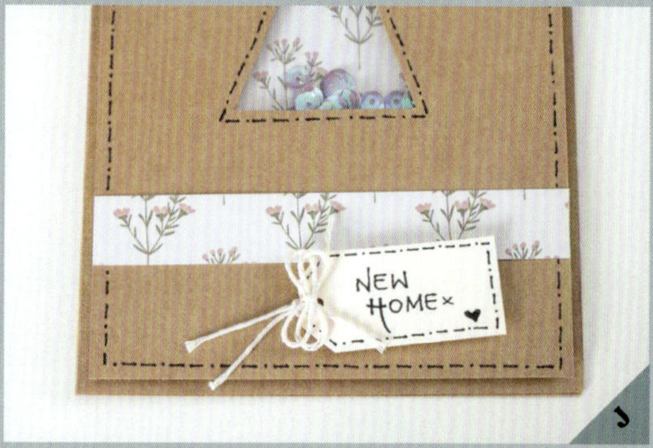

9 Use a tape pen to attach a ¾" wide strip of patterned paper across the card front. **(I)**

10 Using a black fine liner, add stitching detailing around the keyhole shape and the outer edges of the card. Finish by adding a tag with a handwritten message or sentiment, securing it with foam tape for extra dimension. **(J)**

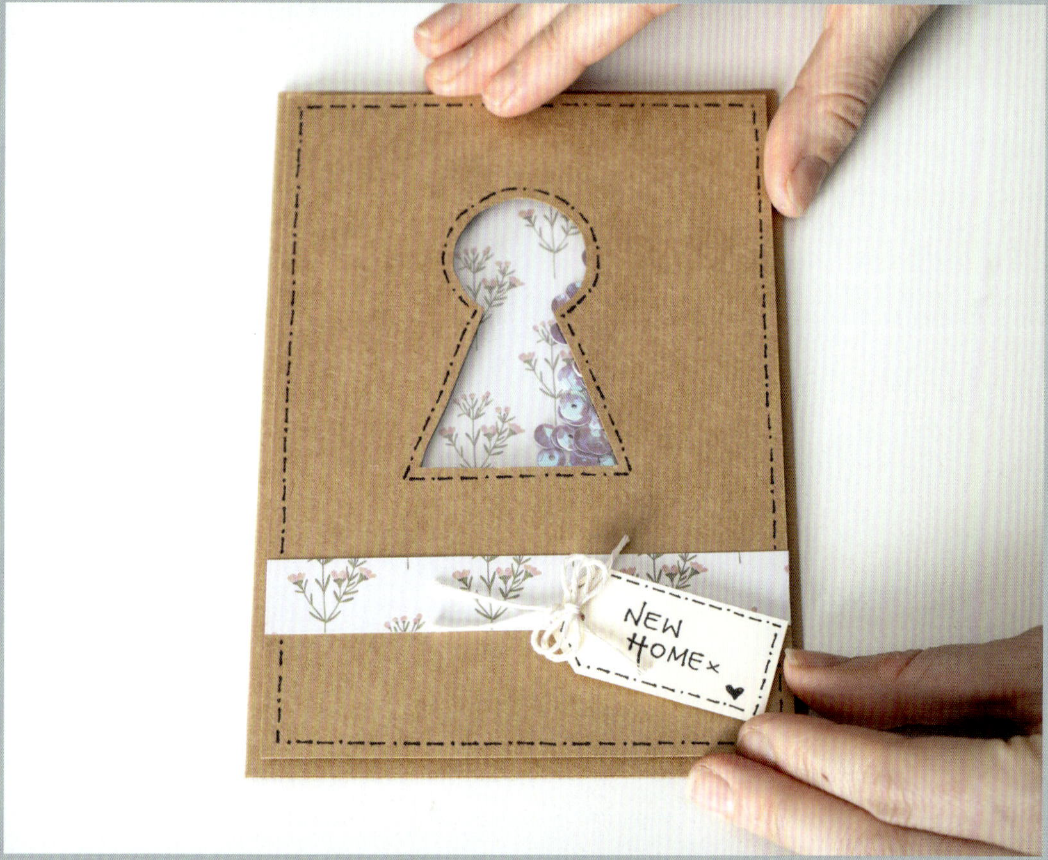

Easy

New Home Card

Moving into a new home is such a special milestone, and this watercolour balloon card is a lovely way to say congratulations. It's a really relaxing project that's perfect for taking your time on and enjoying the creative process. The result is a beautiful handmade card that feels thoughtful, personal, and is ideal for welcoming someone into their new space.

TOP TIP **Don't overload your brush with paint. Building up the watercolour in light layers will give the balloons a soft, floaty look and add real depth to the design.**

You will need:

- 5⅞" × 5⅞" card base
- Metallic-finish, black and watercolour card
- Ruler
- Pencil
- Scissors
- Watercolour palette
- Water
- Paint palette or glass craft mat
- Fine paintbrush
- Small circular object such as a bottle lid (for balloon template)
- Black fine liner
- Glue tape pen

1 Create a 5⅞" × 5⅞" card base.

2 Cut a piece of metallic card measuring 5 6/8" × 5 6/8", a piece of black card measuring 5⅝" × 5⅝", and a piece of watercolour card measuring 5½" × 5½". **(A)**

3 Place the watercolour card in front of you. Using a paintbrush, water and a watercolour palette, mix one of the paint colours on a glass mat or palette, adding extra water to dilute the colour. **(B)**

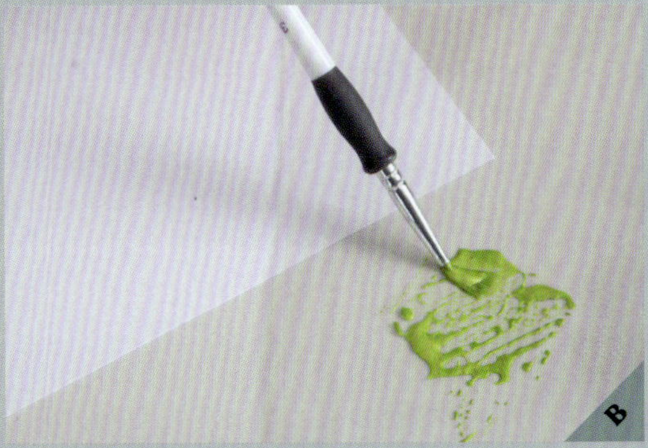

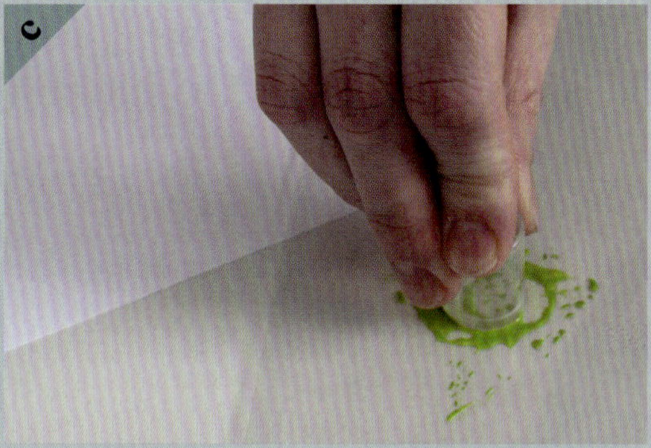

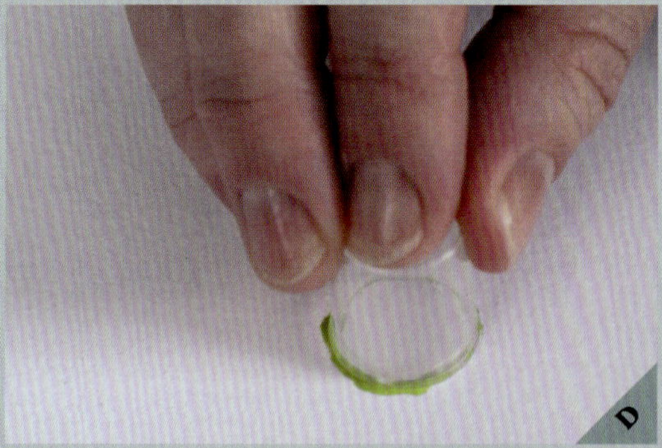

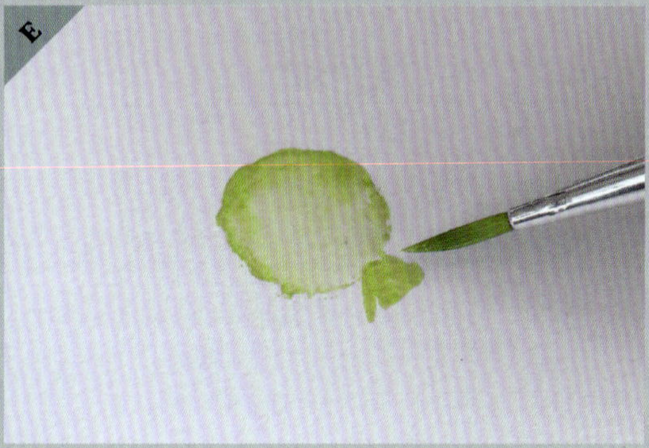

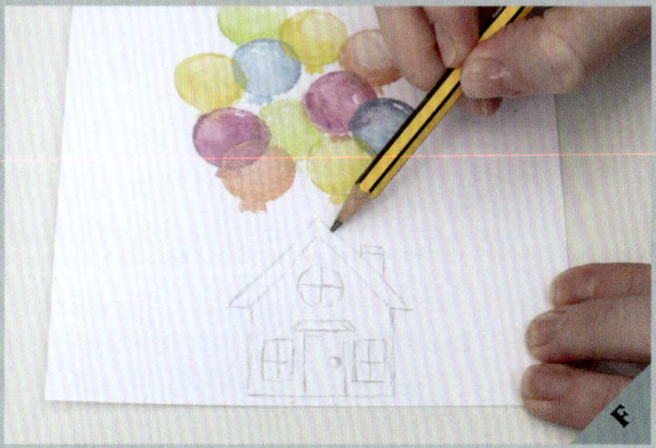

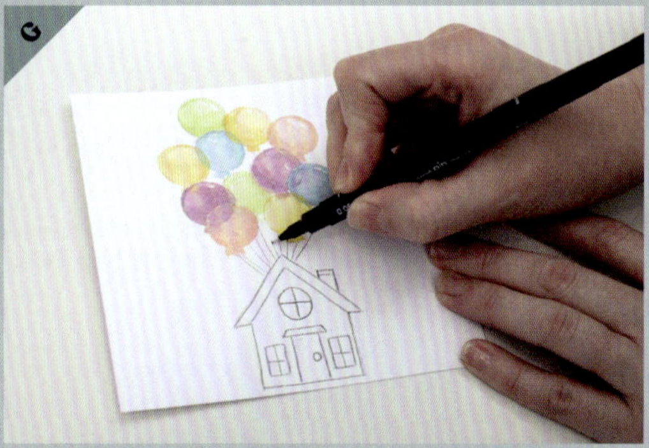

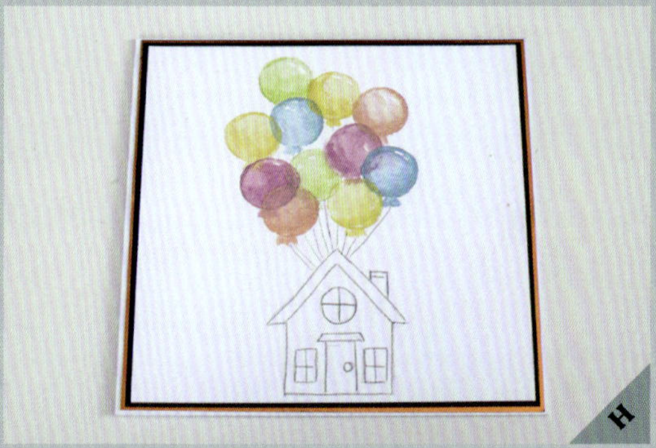

4 Take a small circular object to use as a balloon template and gently press its rim into the paint mixture. **(C)**

5 Press the paint-covered rim on to the watercolour card to form the outline of a balloon. **(D)**

6 Using a damp brush, pull colour away from the edge of the circle to fill in the balloon, leaving lighter areas for a soft, dimensional effect. **(E)**

7 Repeat steps 3–6 to create a cluster of different coloured balloons towards the top of the card, leaving space at the bottom for a house illustration.

8 Once the balloons are complete, lightly sketch a house beneath them in pencil. **(F)**

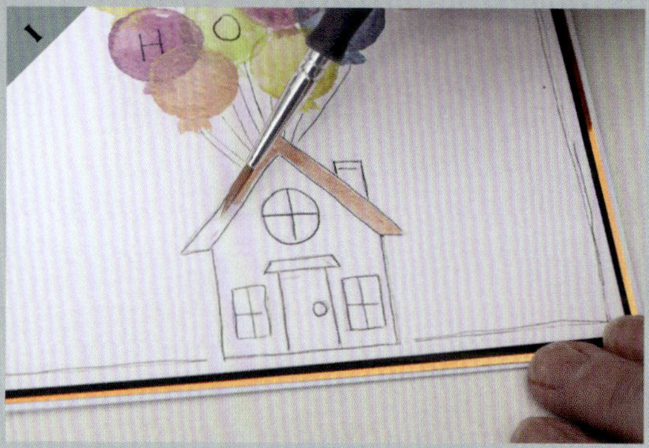

9 When you're happy with the shape, trace over the drawing with a black fine liner and draw strings connecting the balloons to the house. **(G)**

10 Adhere the metallic, black and painted watercolour layers to the front of the card base in order, finishing with the balloon panel on top. **(H)**

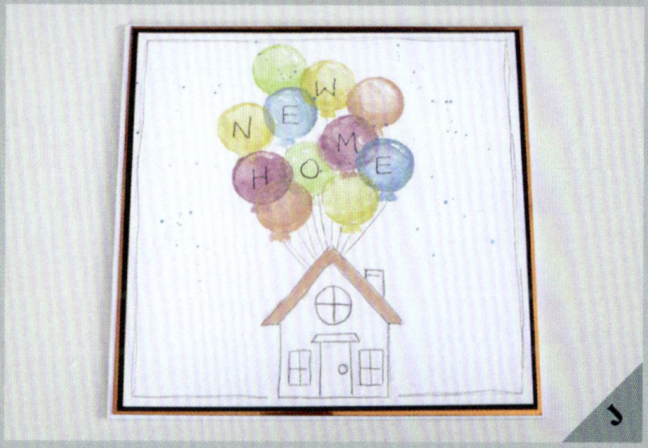

11 Write 'New Home' across some of the balloons using a black fine liner.

12 Sketch a border if desired, then use watercolour paint to fill in the house roof. **(I)**

13 Add light paint spatters to finish. **(J)**

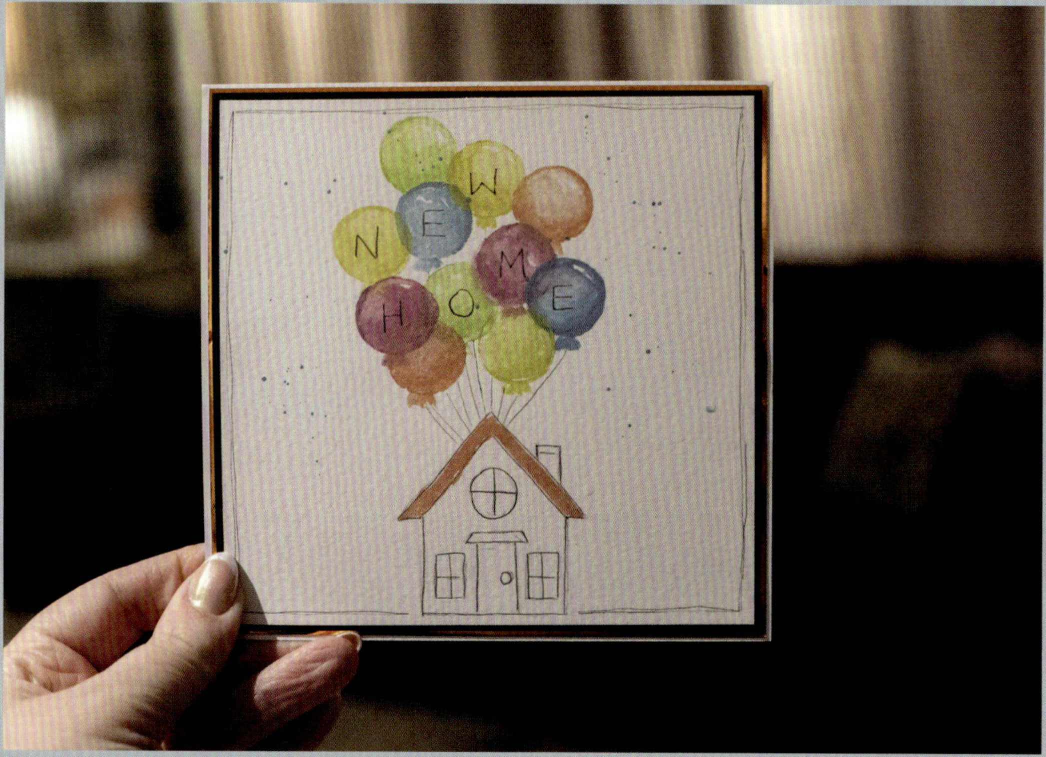

Intermediate

Baby Shower Invitation

Make your baby shower invitations extra special with this adorable nappy-shaped card. It's a clever and creative way to get guests excited for the celebration, transforming a simple folded card into a charming keepsake. Using careful scoring and folding along with patterned paper and personalized tags, each invitation feels thoughtful while remaining perfectly achievable with accurate measuring and a steady hand.

TOP TIP Take your time with scoring and folding. Precise measurements and crisp folds will help the invitation hold its shape neatly.

You will need:

- White card
- Patterned paper
- Kraft card
- 2½″ circle template, punch or die
- Scissors or paper trimmer
- Scoring board
- Glue tape pen
- Hole punch
- Ribbon
- Safety pin

A

1 Cut a piece of card measuring 8¼″ × 8¼″.

2 Cut the card in half diagonally to create two triangles. Use one triangle for the invitation. **(A)**

3 Place the triangle in front of you with the right angle positioned on the right-hand side.

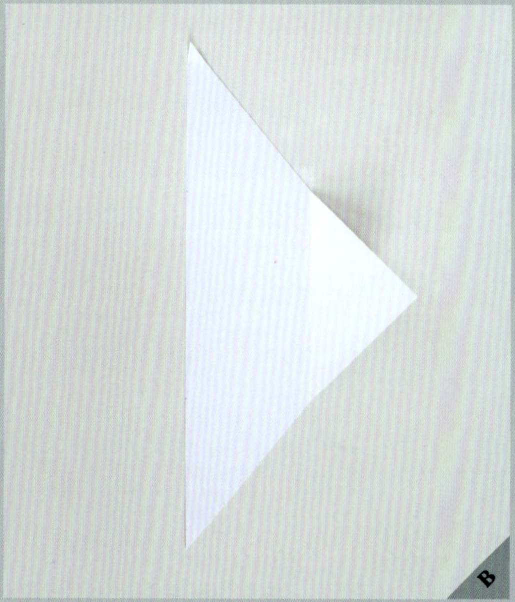

B

4 Measure 4½″ from the straight vertical edge, make a vertical score line, then fold along this line. **(B)**

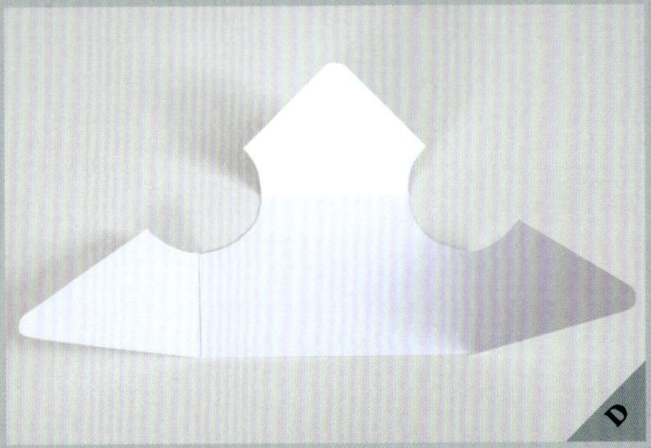

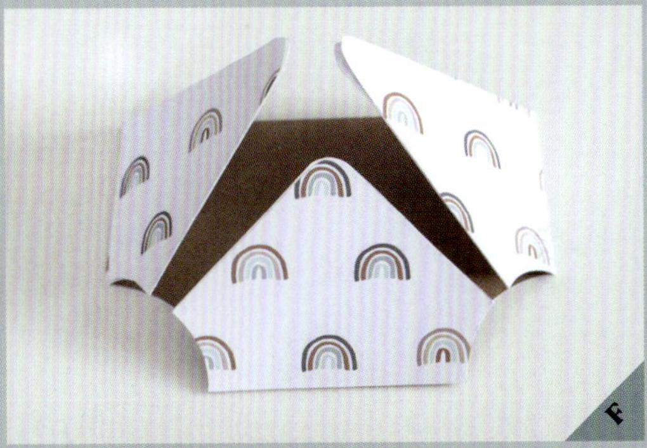

5 From the bottom point, measure 3″ up the vertical edge and make a horizontal score line. Then, from the top point, measure 3″ down the vertical edge and make another horizontal score line. **(C)**

6 Using a template, circle punch or die, cut a half-circle approximately 2½″ in diameter into the crossed score lines to form the leg openings. **(D)**

7 Cut a piece of Kraft card to fit neatly into the centre section of the nappy and adhere it in place. This can now be used to write your invitation details. **(E)**

8 Draw around the front sections of the nappy onto patterned paper, cut

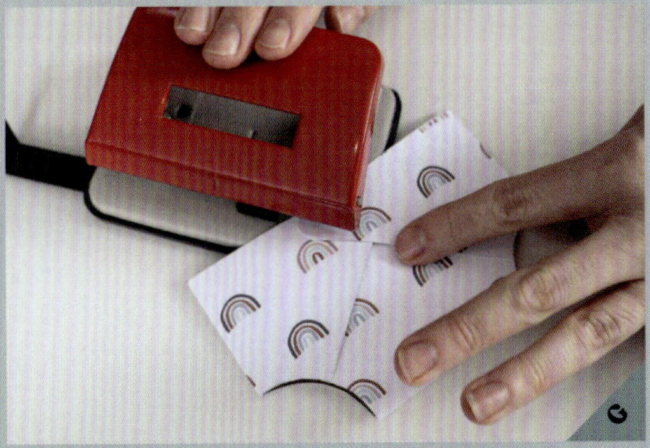

them out and adhere them to the card using a tape pen. **(F)**

9 Fold the left and right panels over the bottom section to form the nappy shape.

10 Punch a hole through both the left- and right-side panels. **(G)**

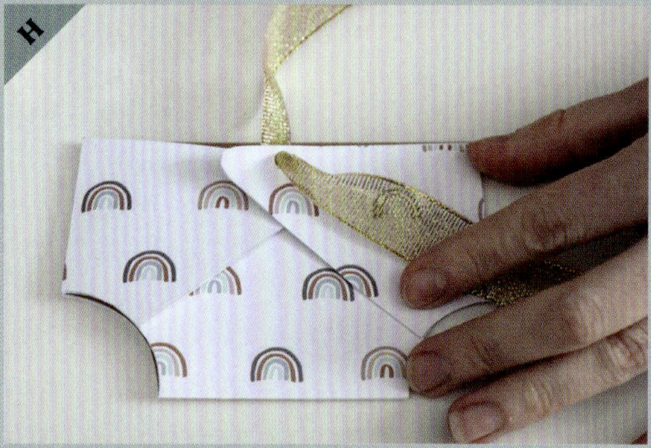

11 Thread ribbon through the holes and tie into a bow to secure the nappy closed. **(H)**

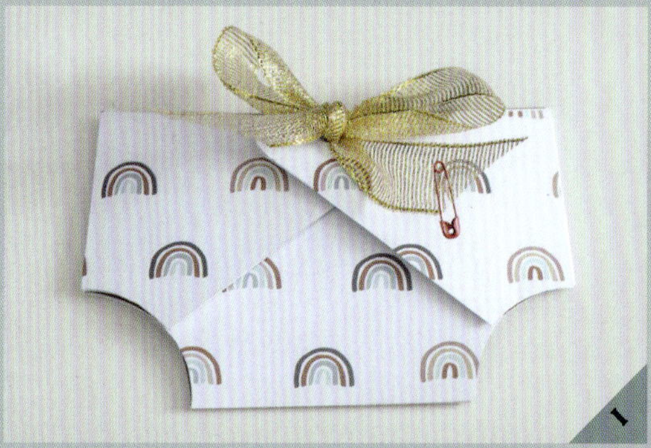

12 Finish by adding a safety pin and using it to attach a personalized name tag. **(I)**

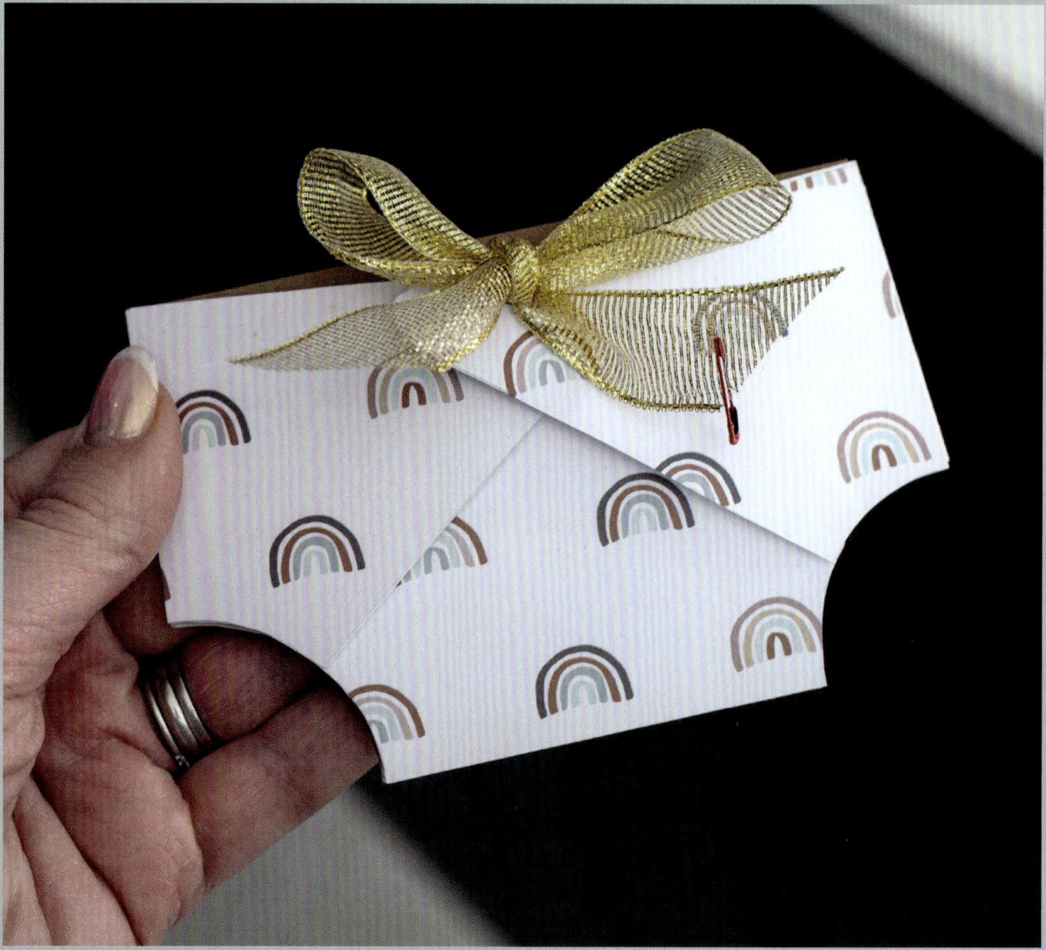

Easy

Baby Bunting

This baby bunting is a lovely handmade addition to a baby shower or welcome-home celebration. Using soft felt, colourful buttons and a few simple techniques, you can create beautiful decorative bunting that feels both playful and personal.

Whether you spell out the baby's name, a sweet message or a simple 'baby shower' banner, this project is easy to customize and makes a keepsake that can be enjoyed long after the celebrations are over.

TOP TIP **Lay all of your pennants, buttons and flowers along the string before gluing anything in place. This helps you check spacing and ensures your wording is centred and balanced before committing.**

You will need:

- Scrap card
- Ruler
- Pencil
- Scissors
- Felt
- Buttons
- Glue gun
- Calico fabric
- Small paintbrush
- White acrylic paint
- Glitter
- String or cord

1 Create a pennant template by trimming a piece of card to 5" × 7". **(A)**

2 Draw a vertical line down the centre of the card at 2½".

3 Measure 2⅜" up from the bottom edge and draw a horizontal line across the card.

4 From where the two lines meet, draw a diagonal line out to each bottom corner of the card. **(B)**

5 Cut away the central triangle to reveal your pennant template shape. **(C)**

6 Use the template to cut out as many pennants as needed from felt. **(D)**

7 Arrange buttons on each felt pennant to spell out your chosen letters. Once you're happy with the layout, secure each button in place using hot glue. **(E)**

8 To make the flowers, cut one strip of fabric measuring approximately 3" × 18" for each flower needed. **(F)**

9 Fold the fabric strip in half lengthways and run a thin line of hot glue along the open edge to secure it. **(G)**

10 Once the glue is set, cut small snips at ¼" intervals, stopping approximately ¼"

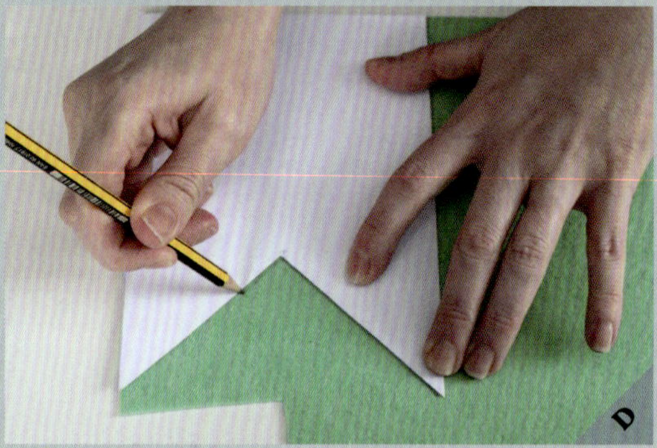

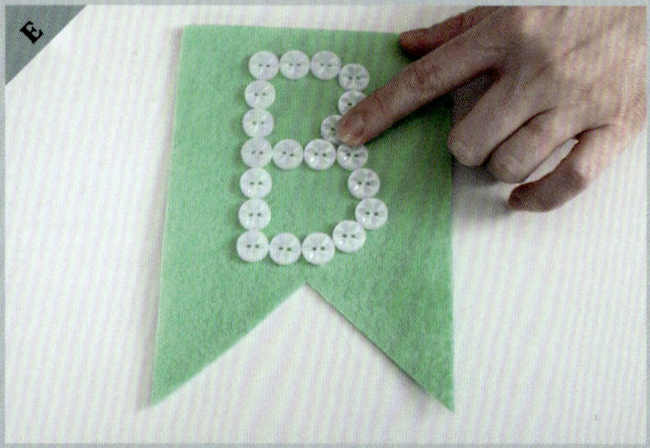

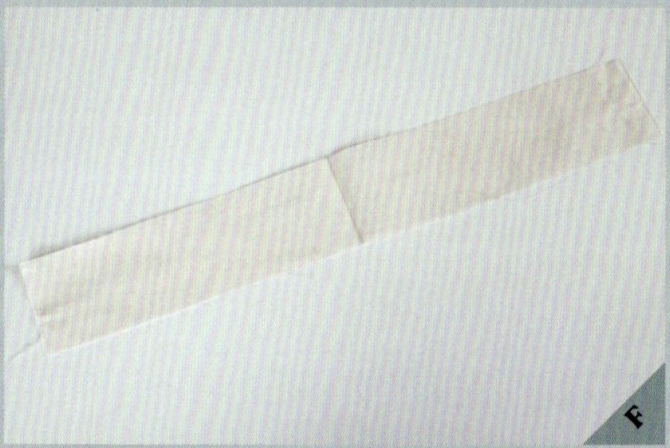

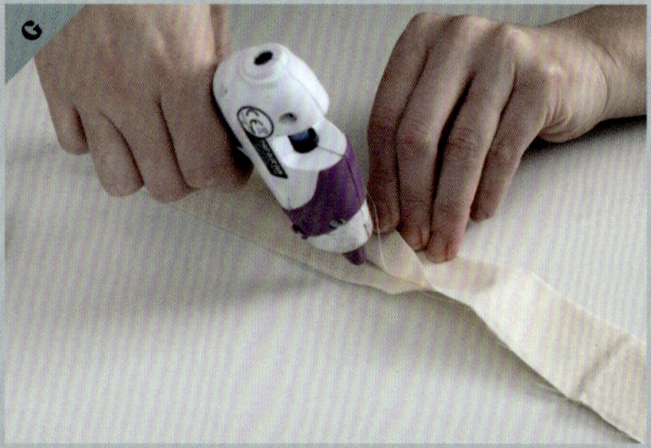

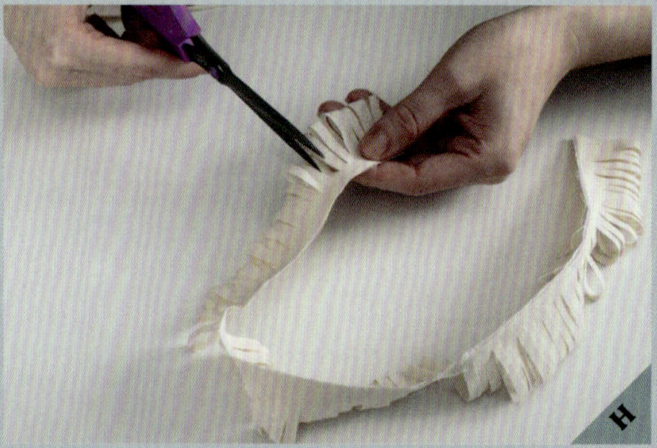

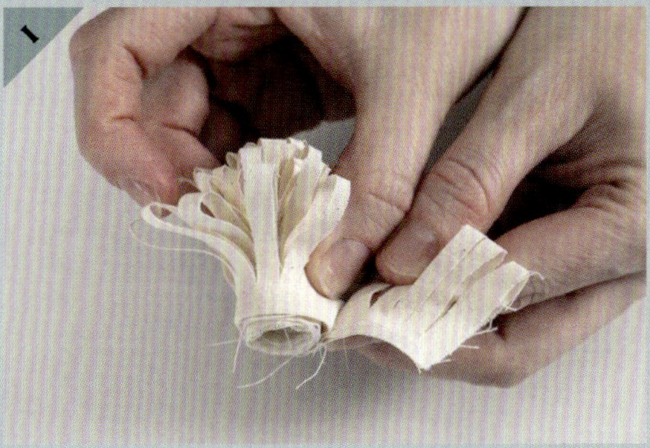

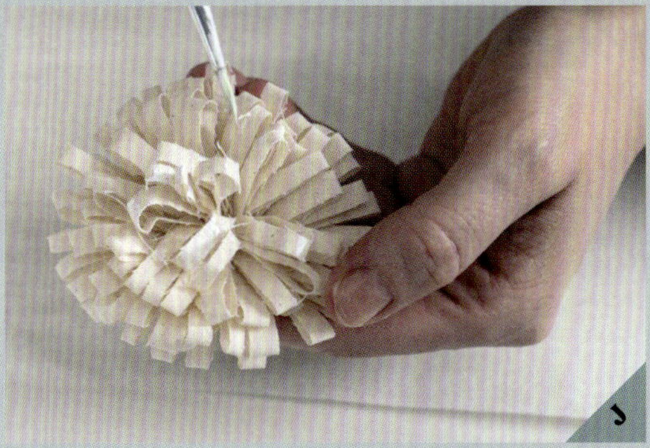

from the glued edge, to create a fringed effect. **(H)**

11 Add a small amount of hot glue to one end of the strip and roll it tightly to form a flower, continuing to glue along the edge as you roll. **(I)**

12 Repeat steps 9–11 for as many flowers as needed. Dab each flower with a small amount of white acrylic paint and add glitter or paint to the centre for extra detail. **(J)**

13 Finally, adhere the felt pennants and flowers evenly along a length of string or cord to create your finished bunting!

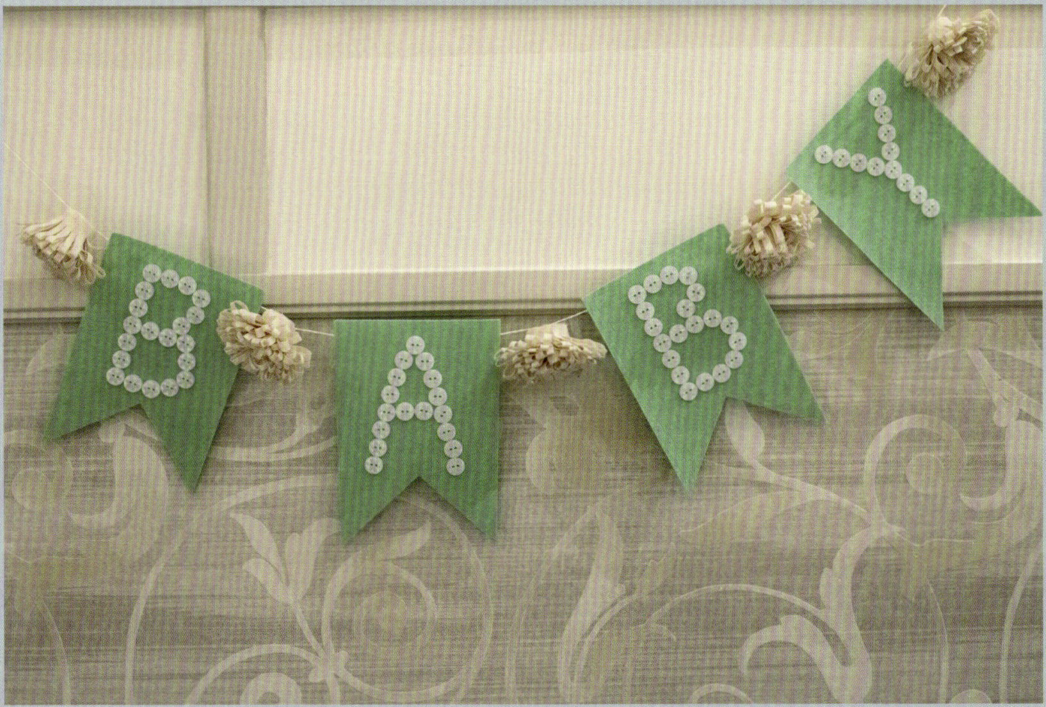

Intermediate

It's a Boy Card

This baby-rattle shaker card is a real showstopper! It's bright, fun and full of movement, making it perfect for celebrating a new arrival or a baby shower. The clever shaker element adds that extra 'wow' factor, while the rattle shape keeps the design playful and adorable. There are a few tricky steps to this project, but take your time and enjoy the process because you'll be rewarded with a card that looks professionally made and is guaranteed to be treasured.

TOP TIP Take care when sealing in the shaker element – any gaps could mean your sequins slip out of the sides!

You will need:

- 5" × 7" card base
- 2½" circle template, punch or die
- White card
- Ruler
- Scissors or craft knife
- Paper trimmer (optional)
- Red liner double-sided tape
- Acetate
- Foam tape
- Kraft card
- Patterned papers
- Glue tape pen
- Sequins
- Ribbon
- Gold pen
- Embossed label maker or pen
- Foam pads

A

1 On a piece of card measuring 4¾" × 6¾", cut out a 2½" circle in the top left-hand corner to create an aperture. **(A)**

2 Flip the card over and use red liner tape to attach a piece of acetate over the back of the circle aperture. **(B and C)**

B

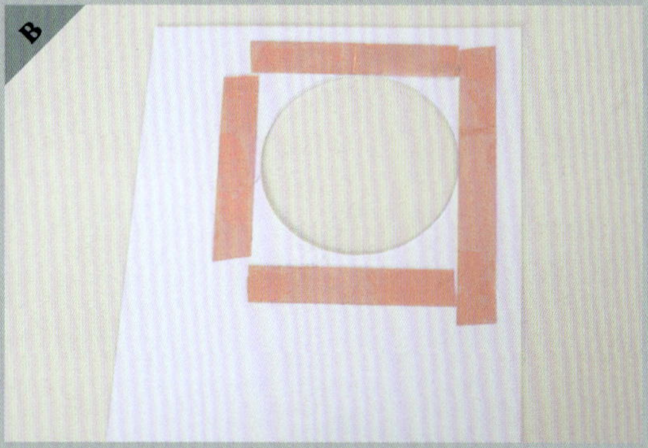

C

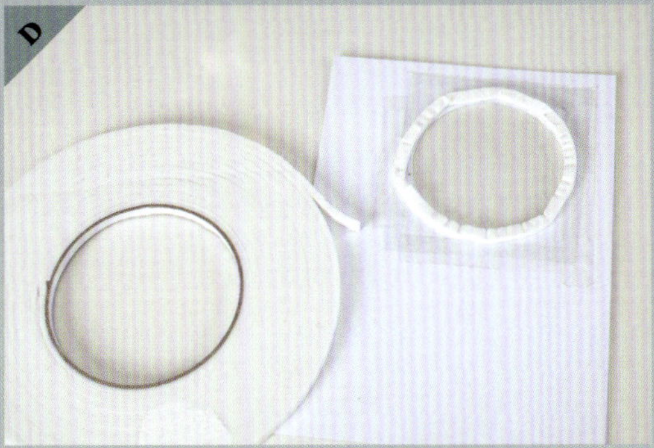

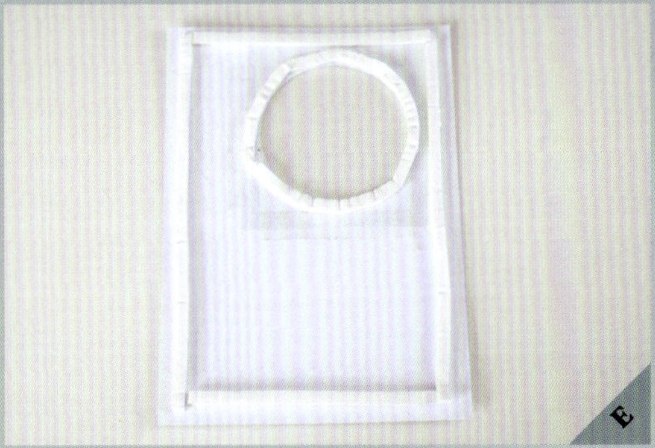

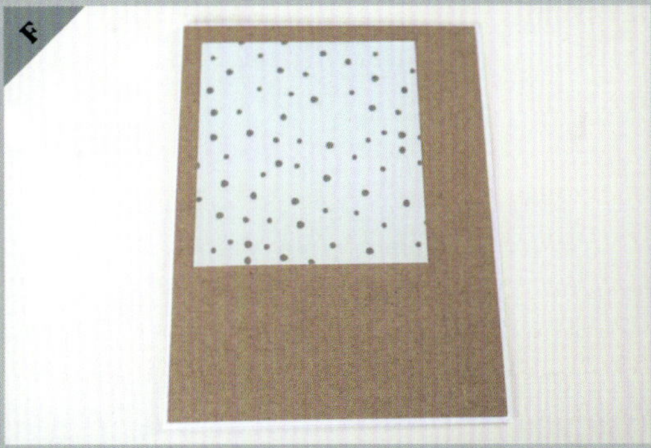

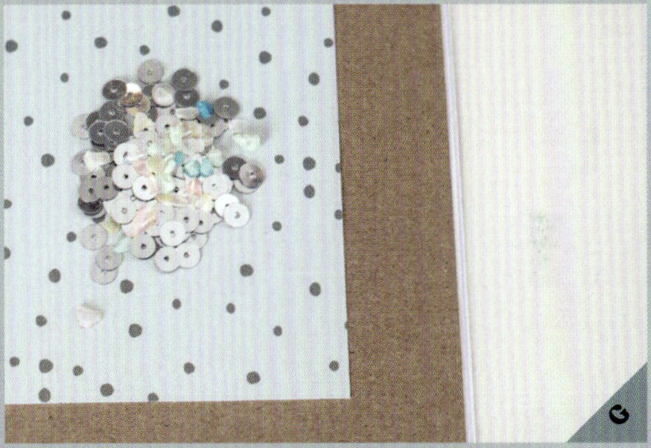

3 Apply foam tape around the circle opening, ensuring there are no gaps at the joins so shaker elements cannot escape. **(D)**

4 Apply additional foam tape around the remaining edges of the panel so it will sit raised when attached to the card base. **(E)**

5 Cut a mat measuring 4⅞" × 6⅞" from Kraft card and adhere a piece of patterned paper large enough to be visible through the circle aperture. **(F)**

6 Place your sequins on to the patterned paper, positioning them so they sit neatly within the circle area. **(G)**

7 Return to the aperture panel, remove the backing from the foam tape and carefully adhere it over the patterned paper, sealing the shaker elements inside. Adhere the panel to the front of the card base. **(H)**

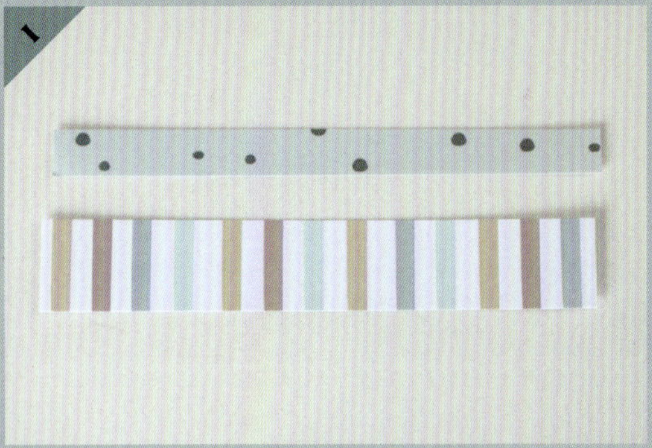

I

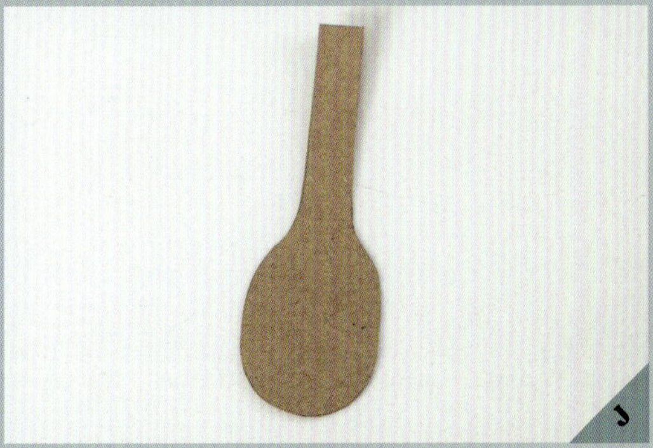

J

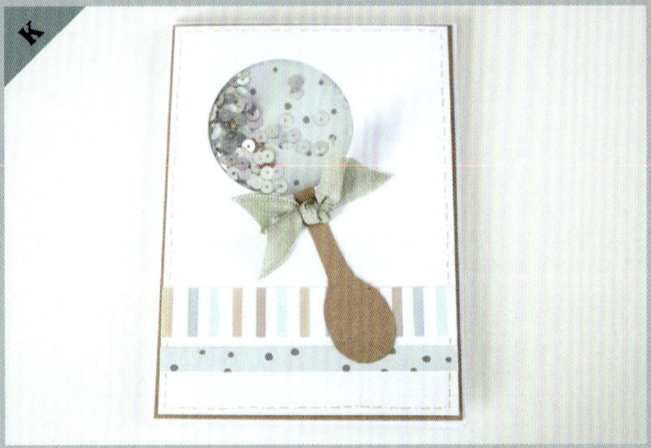

K

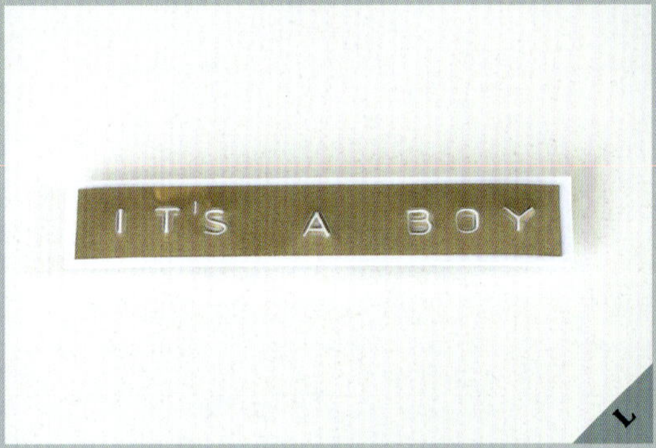

L

8 Cut two strips of patterned paper to glue across the bottom third of the card front. **(I)**

9 Draw a handle shape on to some Kraft card, cut it out and glue it in place below the circle aperture to form the baby rattle. **(J)**

10 Create a bow from ribbon and adhere it to the handle. Using a gold pen, draw dashed lines around the edge of the card front. **(K)**

11 Using an embossed label maker or pen, add your chosen sentiment to a strip of white card. Attach it to the card front using foam pads to complete the design. **(L and M)**

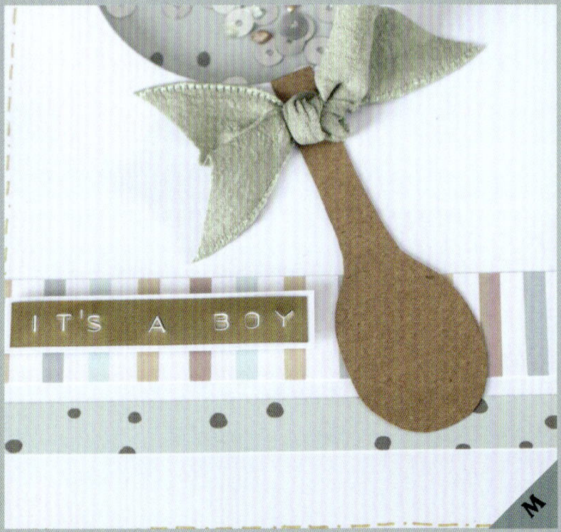

M

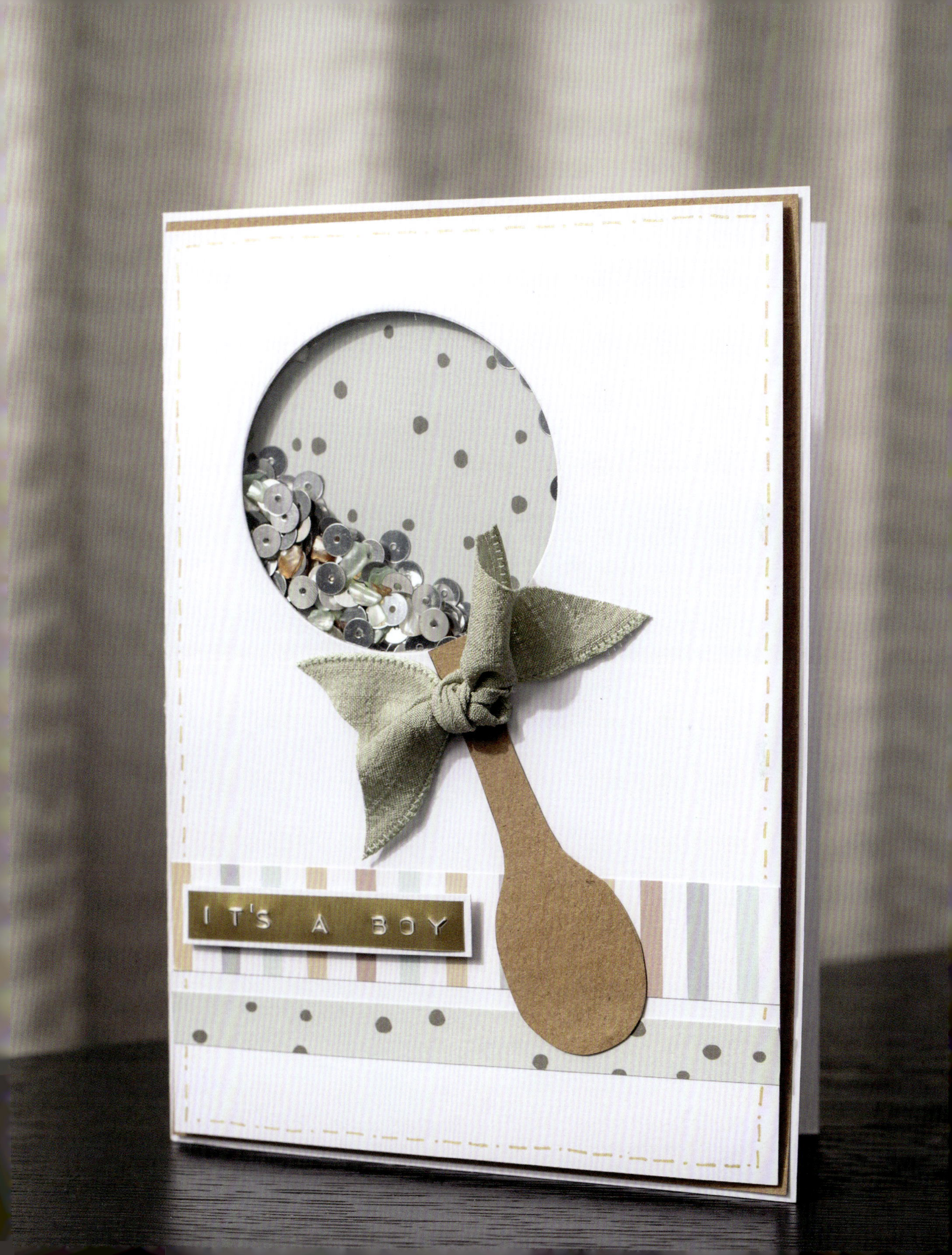
IT'S A BOY

Intermediate

It's a Girl Card

My favourite types of cards are those with a bit of movement or dimension, and this 'It's a Girl' design is a perfect example. Featuring super-cute details such as bunting and a tiny baby vest, it's a really sweet and personal way to welcome a new baby or celebrate parents-to-be.

You will need:

- White card
- Ruler
- Pencil
- Scissors or paper trimmer
- String
- Glue gun
- Patterned paper
- Pink card
- Glue tape pen
- Pen or fine liner
- Gems
- Foam pads

1 Create a 5″× 7″ card base from white card. **(A)**

2 Set the card base in landscape orientation. Using a ruler and pencil, draw a rectangle 1″ in from each short edge and 2″ up from the bottom edge. **(B)**

3 Carefully cut out the rectangle. Cut a length of string and glue it across the opening to create a washing line. **(C)**

A

B

C
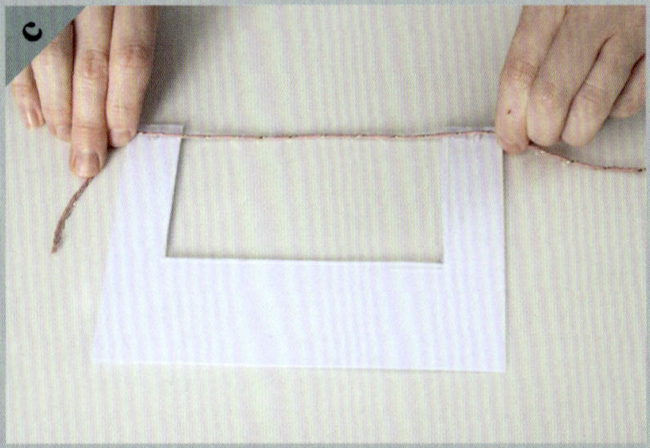

TOP TIP Using a folded template is a great way to create symmetrical images, helping your designs look neat and balanced.

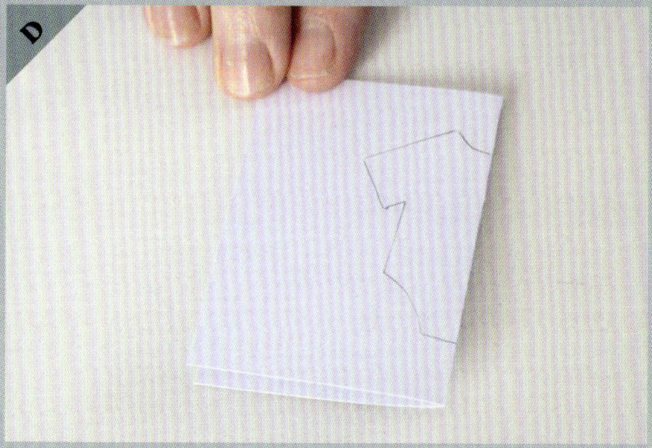

D

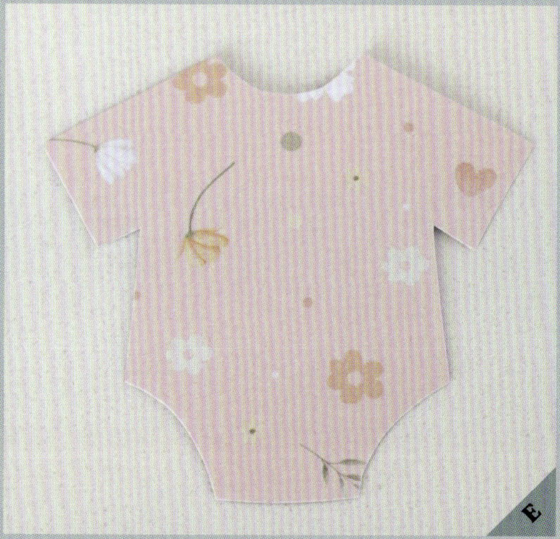

E

4 Fold a piece of scrap card or paper in half, draw half of a baby vest shape along the folded edge, then cut it out to create a symmetrical template. **(D)**

5 Use the template to cut a baby vest shape from patterned paper. **(E)**

6 Glue the vest on to the washing line so it appears to be hanging. **(F)**

7 Cut bunting shapes from 1″× 1″ pieces of pink card and patterned paper. Attach them to the washing line using small dabs of hot glue. **(G)**

8 Tie small bows from the same string and add them to the card using glue. **(H)**

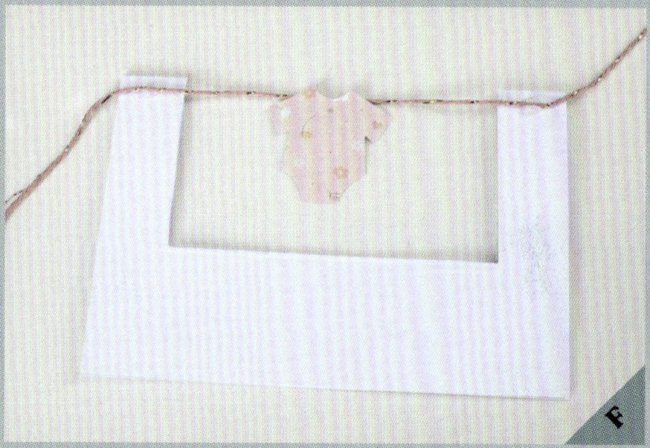

F

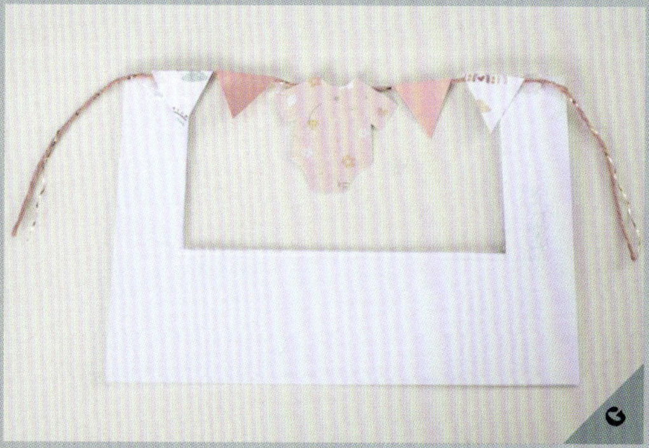

G

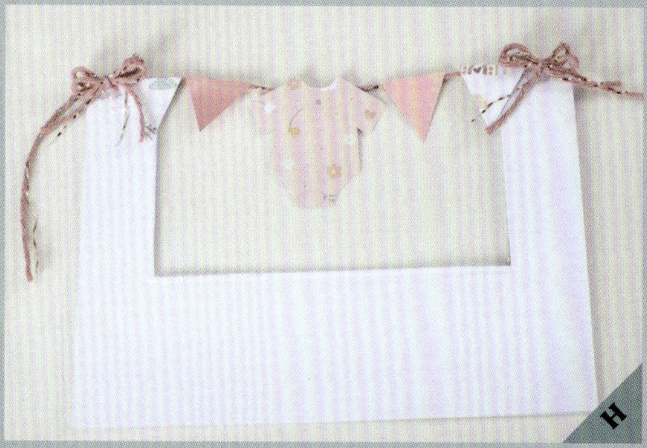

H

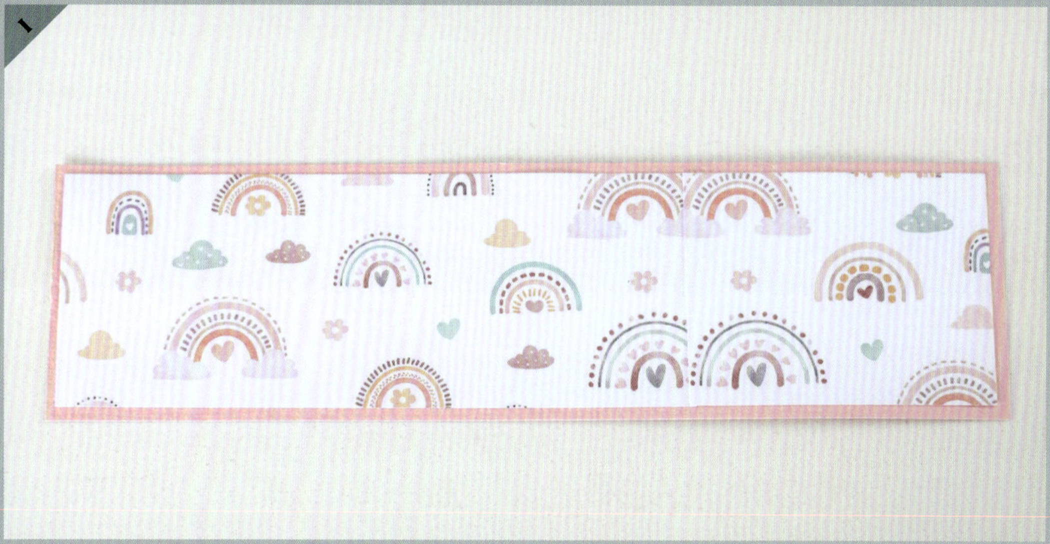

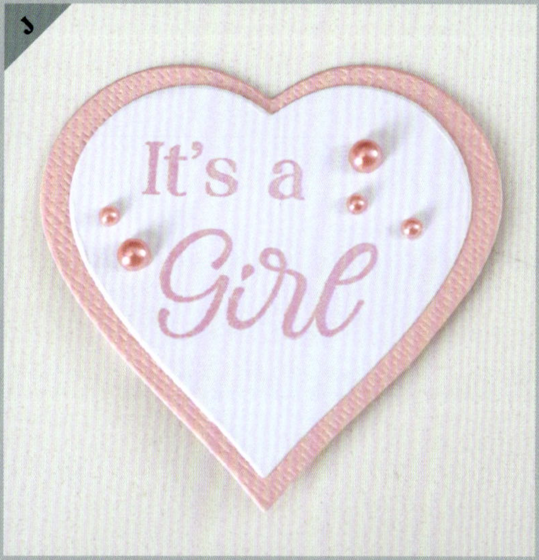

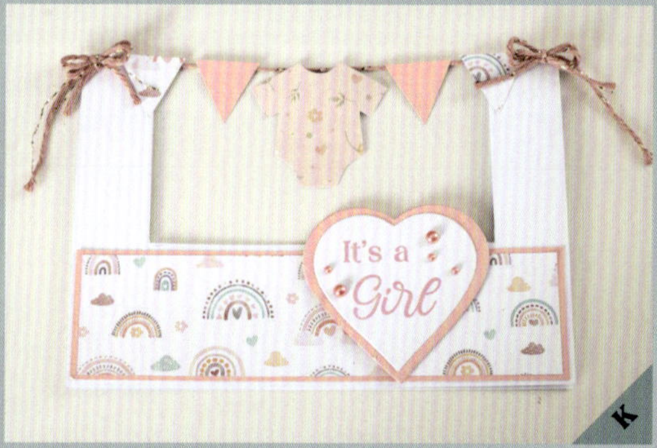

9 Cut a panel from pink card measuring 6⅞" × 1⅞" along with a piece of patterned paper measuring 6¾" × 1¾". Adhere to the front of the card using a tape pen. **(I)**

10 Mat and layer a heart shape with a sentiment and add gems for decoration. **(J)**

11 Attach the heart panel to the card front using foam pads to finish. **(K)**

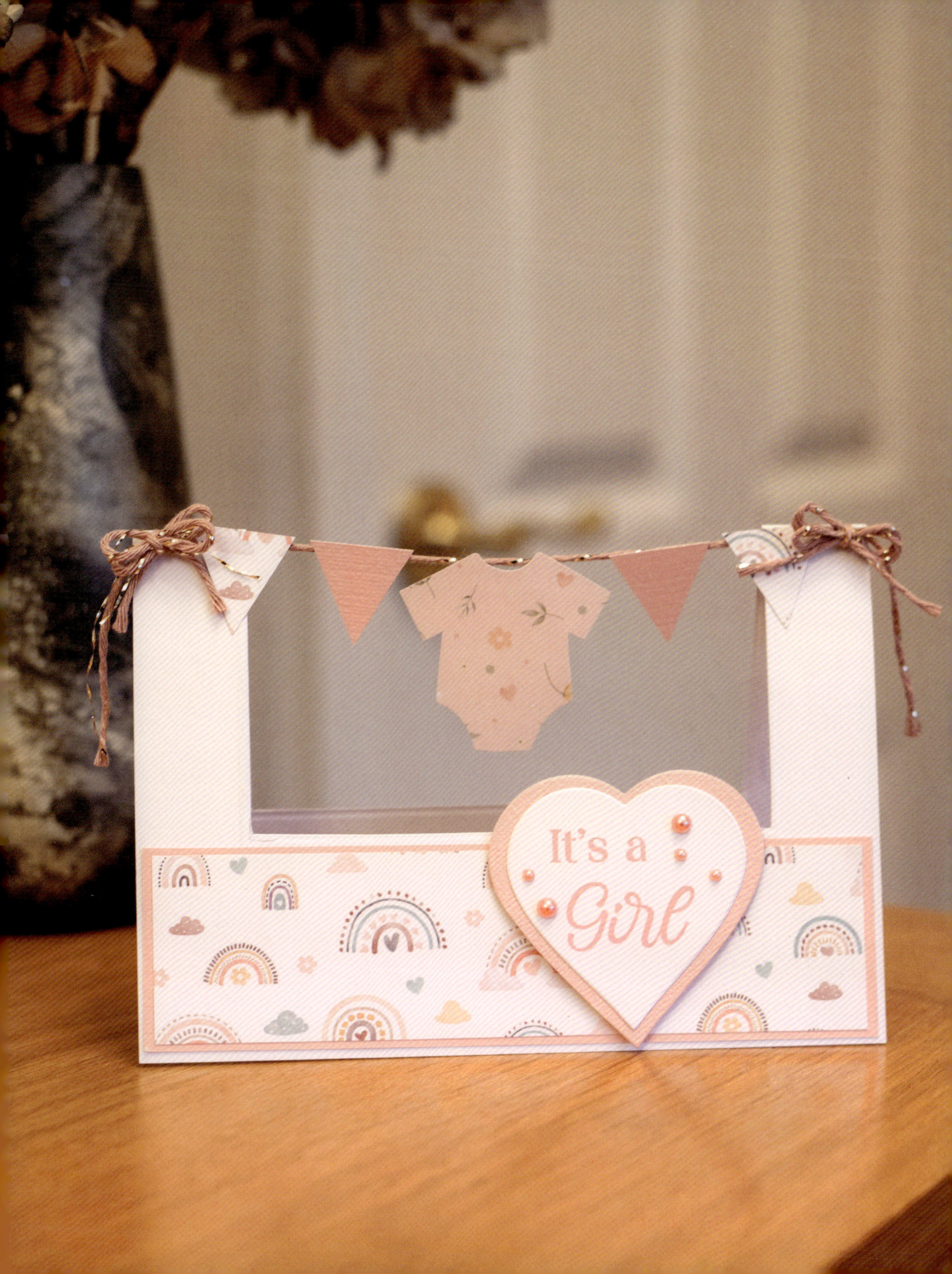
It's a
Girl

Advanced

Macramé Dummy Holder

This handmade macramé dummy holder is both beautiful and practical. It's a lovely project that parents can use every day. With its soft texture, neutral tones and handcrafted feel, it makes a thoughtful gift for a new baby or baby shower. The dummy holder should only be used under adult supervision, and please regularly check the clip to ensure no parts break away.

You will need:

- Macramé cord
- Ruler or tape measure
- Dummy clip
- Blu Tack
- Scissors
- Comb or fine-tooth brush (for finishing)

1 Attach a length of macramé cord measuring 84" to the dummy clip using a Lark's Head knot. To do this, fold the cord in half, place the folded section underneath the ring, then take the loose ends, thread them through the loop and pull tight. **(A)**

TOP TIP **Use Blu Tack behind the dummy clip to keep it securely in place on your work surface while you knot.**

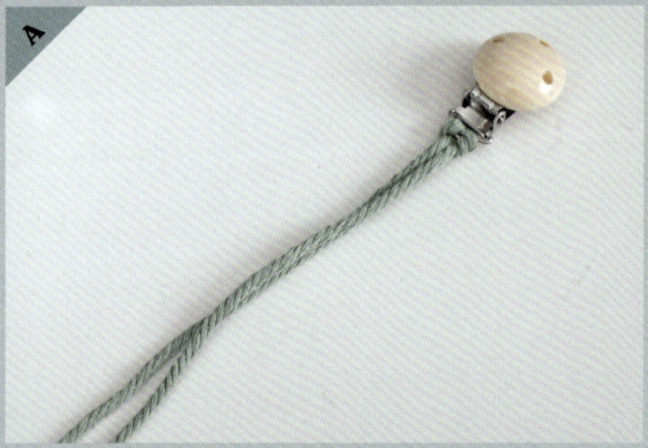

2 Tie a second length of macramé cord, also measuring 84", around the strands from step 1. **(B)**

3 Take the left-hand cord and place it over the two centre cords and underneath the right-hand cord. Then take the right-hand cord and loop it through to the left-hand side, as shown. **(C)**

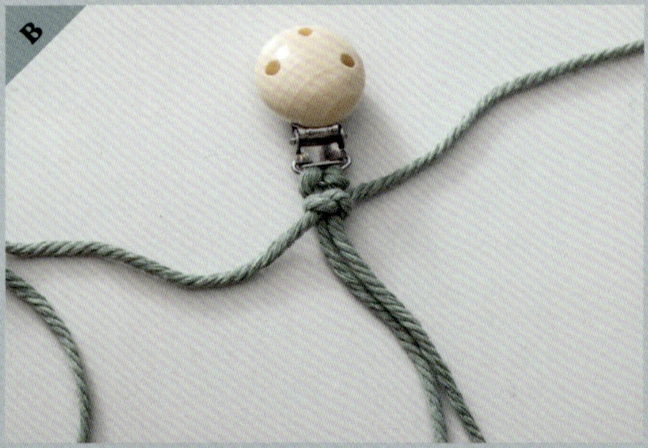

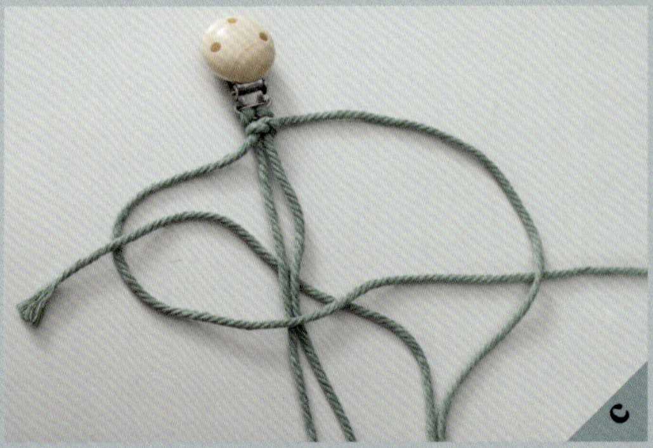

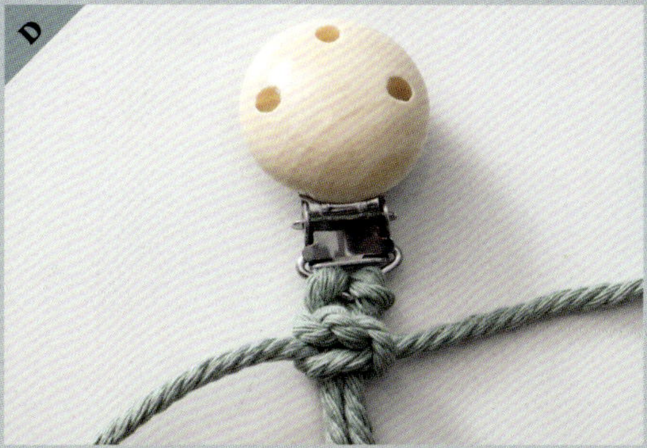

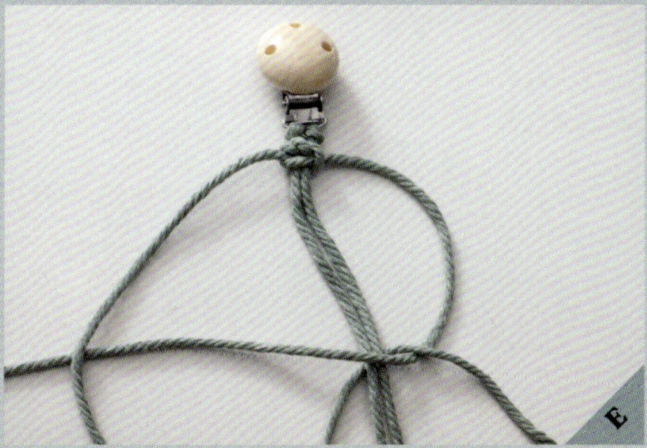

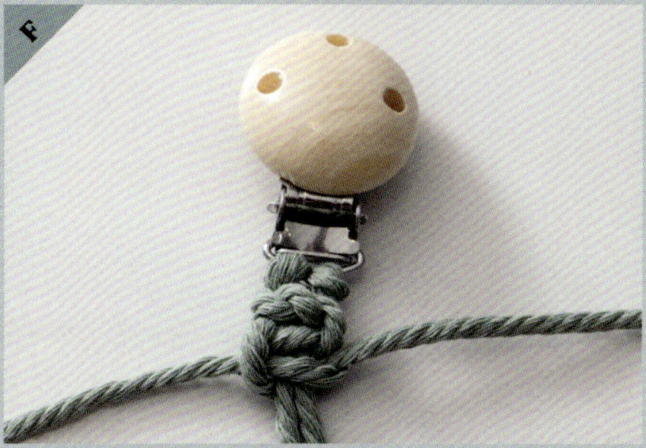

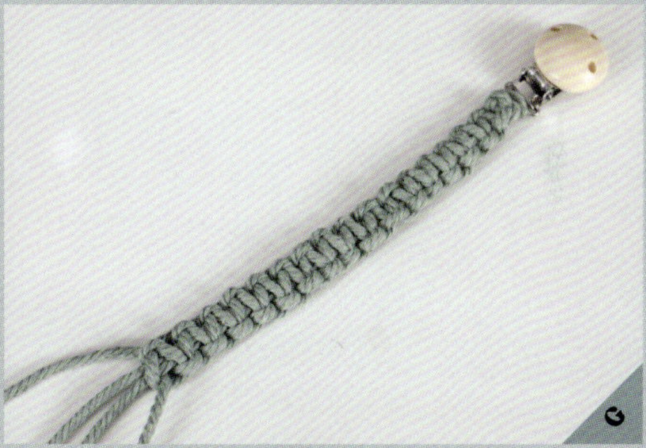

4 Pull the cords tight to create the first knot. **(D)**

5 Repeat step 3, but leading with the right-hand cord first, to form the second knot. **(E)**

6 Pull tight to complete the full knot sequence. **(F)**

7 Continue working your way down the cords, repeating these steps until the knotted section is a maximum of 7⅞" long to meet safety standards. **(G)**

8 Fold one of the cord ends back on itself to form a loop for the dummy holder. Take an additional length of cord measuring 8", fold it in half to create a loop, and place it behind the folded cords. For safety reasons, the loop should never be larger than 4". **(H)**

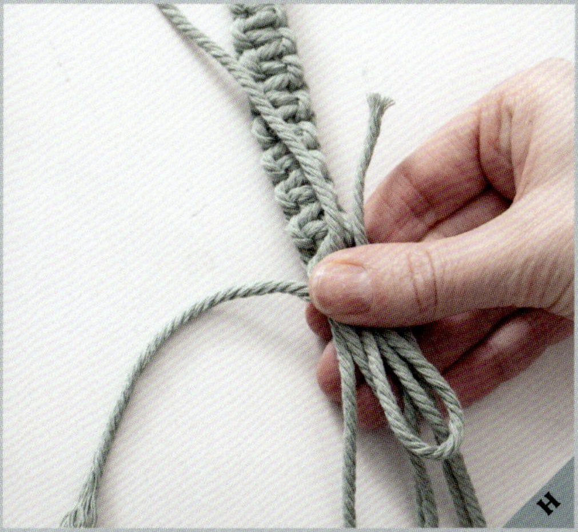

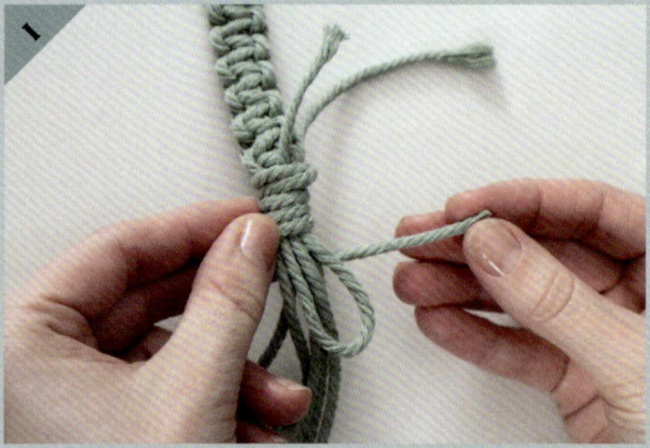

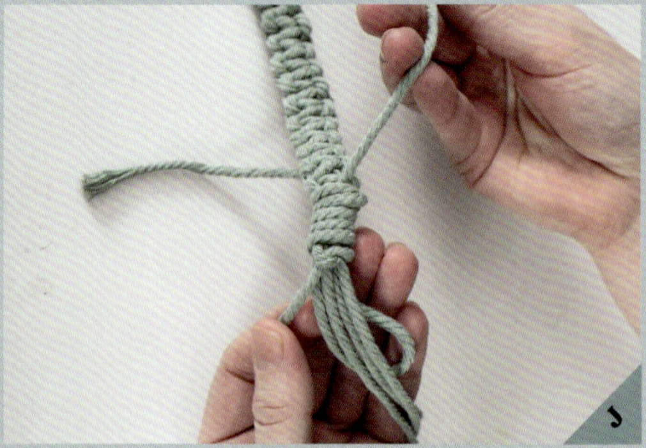

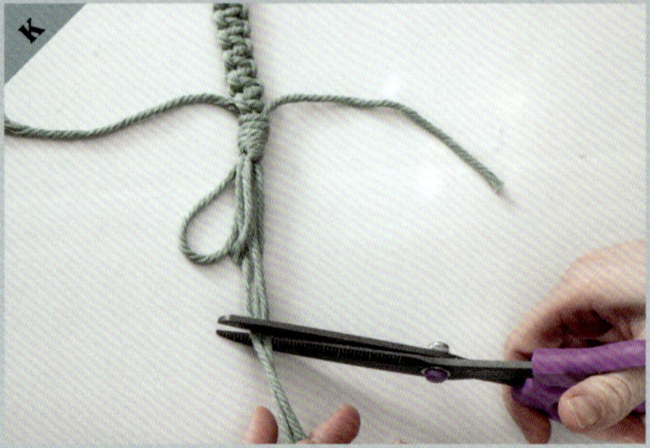

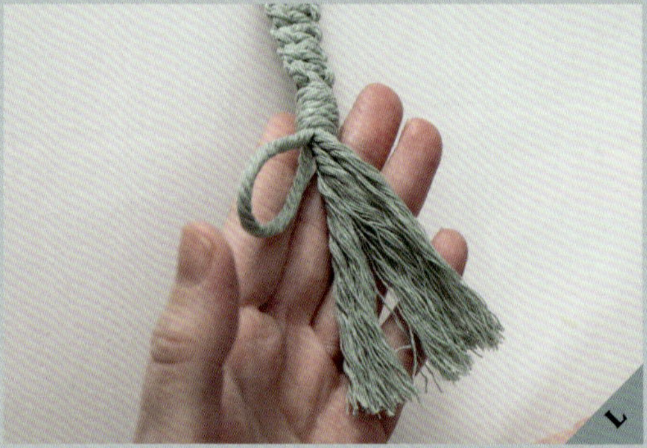

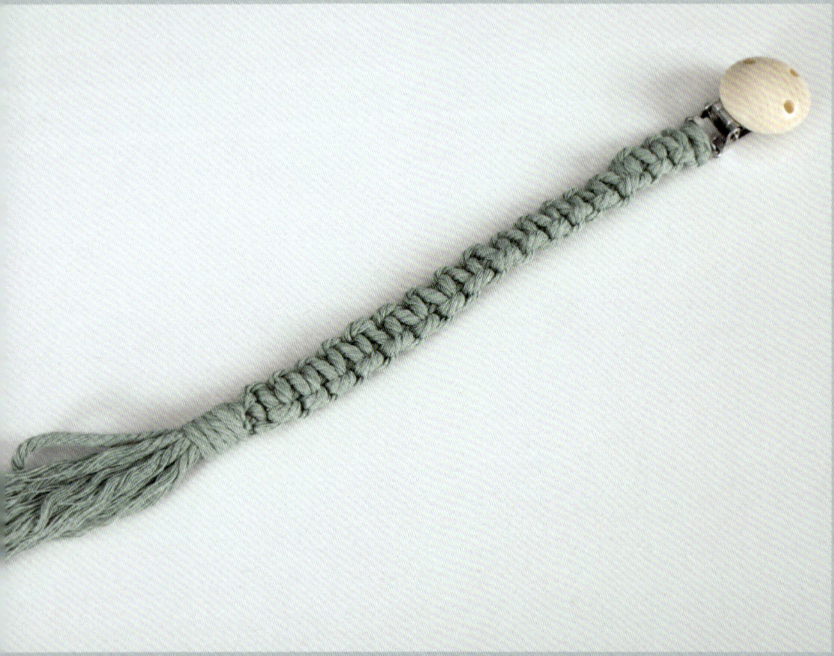

9 Wrap the loose ends of this cord around the folded section approximately five times. Thread the ends through the loop to secure. **(I)**

10 Pull the two loose ends to tighten. The knot will slide under the wrapped section to create a neat finish. **(J)**

11 Trim away any excess cord from the bottom of the holder and the two loose cords above the wrapped section. **(K)**

12 Finish by combing out the remaining cord to create a soft, fringed effect. **(L)**

Easy

Mammy Bag

Whether it's for a parent-to-be or a special mother in your life, this handmade bag is a thoughtful way to give a gift that feels truly personal and considered. Personalize it with their name, a sweet message or a simple heart, then fill it with treats or essentials for a gift that's both practical and meaningful. Not only is it simple to assemble but it's also a lovely keepsake that can be used long after the goodies inside have been enjoyed!

TOP TIP **If you're using a glue gun, work in small sections and lay the wool down quickly, as hot glue sets fast.**

You will need:

- Calico zip bag
- Paper
- Pen or pencil
- Scissors
- Sponge or foam mat
- Pokey tool
- Glue gun or fabric glue
- Wool

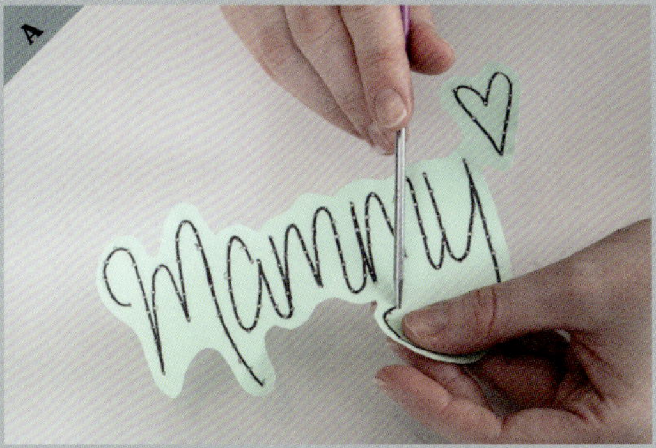

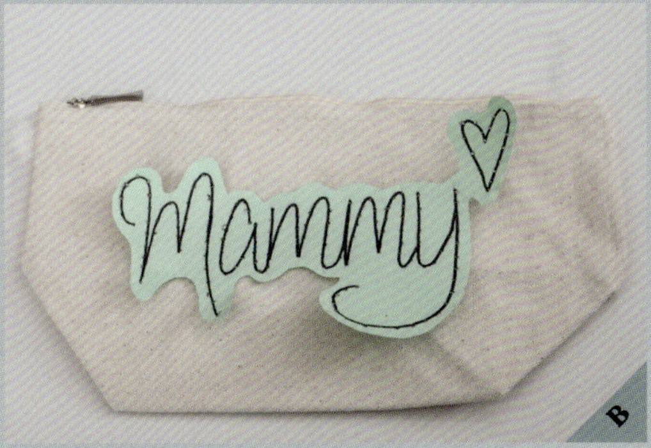

1 Print a template or freehand your chosen word (and optional heart) on to paper. Carefully cut it out, leaving a generous border around the design.

2 Place the paper template on a soft surface, such as a sponge or foam mat, and use a pokey tool or similar sharp implement to create evenly spaced holes along the entire design. **(A)**

3 Position the perforated template on to the front of the calico bag. **(B)**

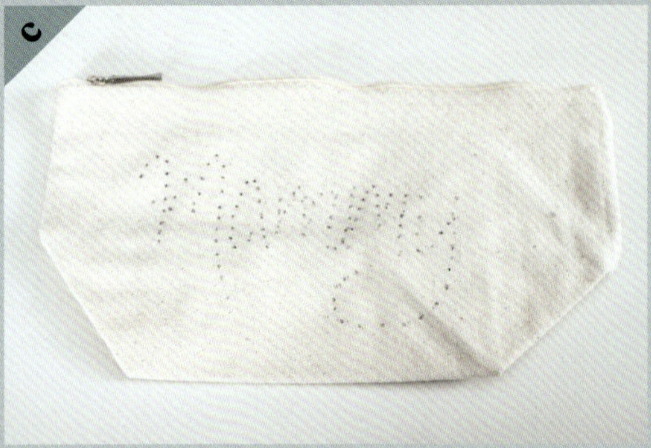

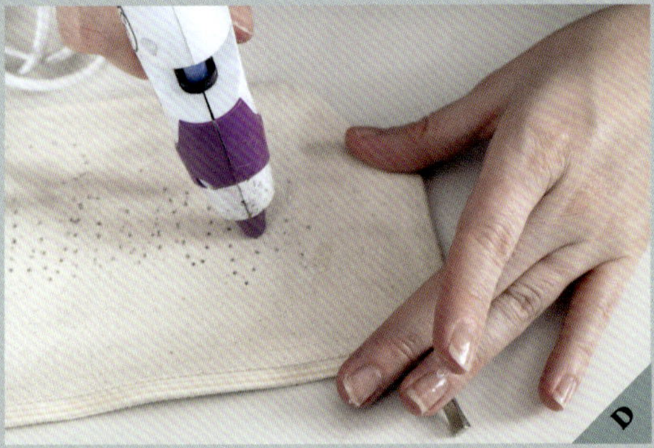

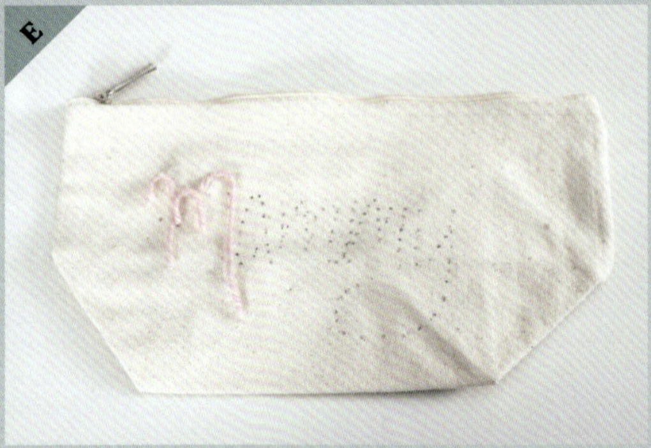

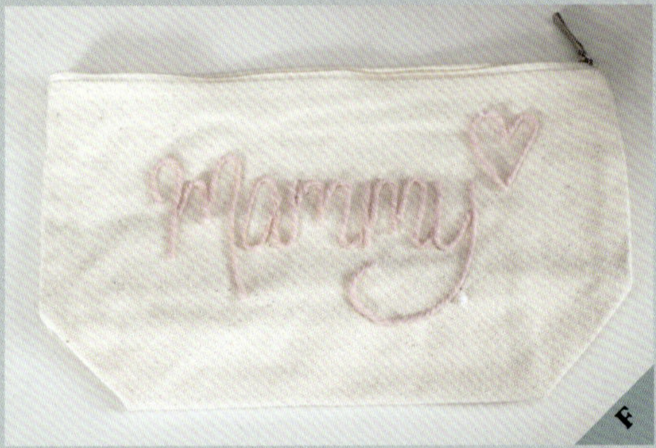

4 Using a pen or pencil, mark through each hole on to the fabric beneath to transfer the design. **(C)**

5 Remove the paper template. Using a glue gun or fabric glue, carefully trace over the marked lines to recreate the design on the bag. **(D)**

6 Working in short sections, lay a length of wool directly on to the glue, pressing gently to secure it. For tighter curves, cut the wool and start a new section for a cleaner finish. **(E)**

7 Continue until all letters and any decorative shapes are fully covered with wool. **(F)**

8 Allow the glue to dry completely before handling, then fill the bag with treats or goodies for that special mammy in your life!

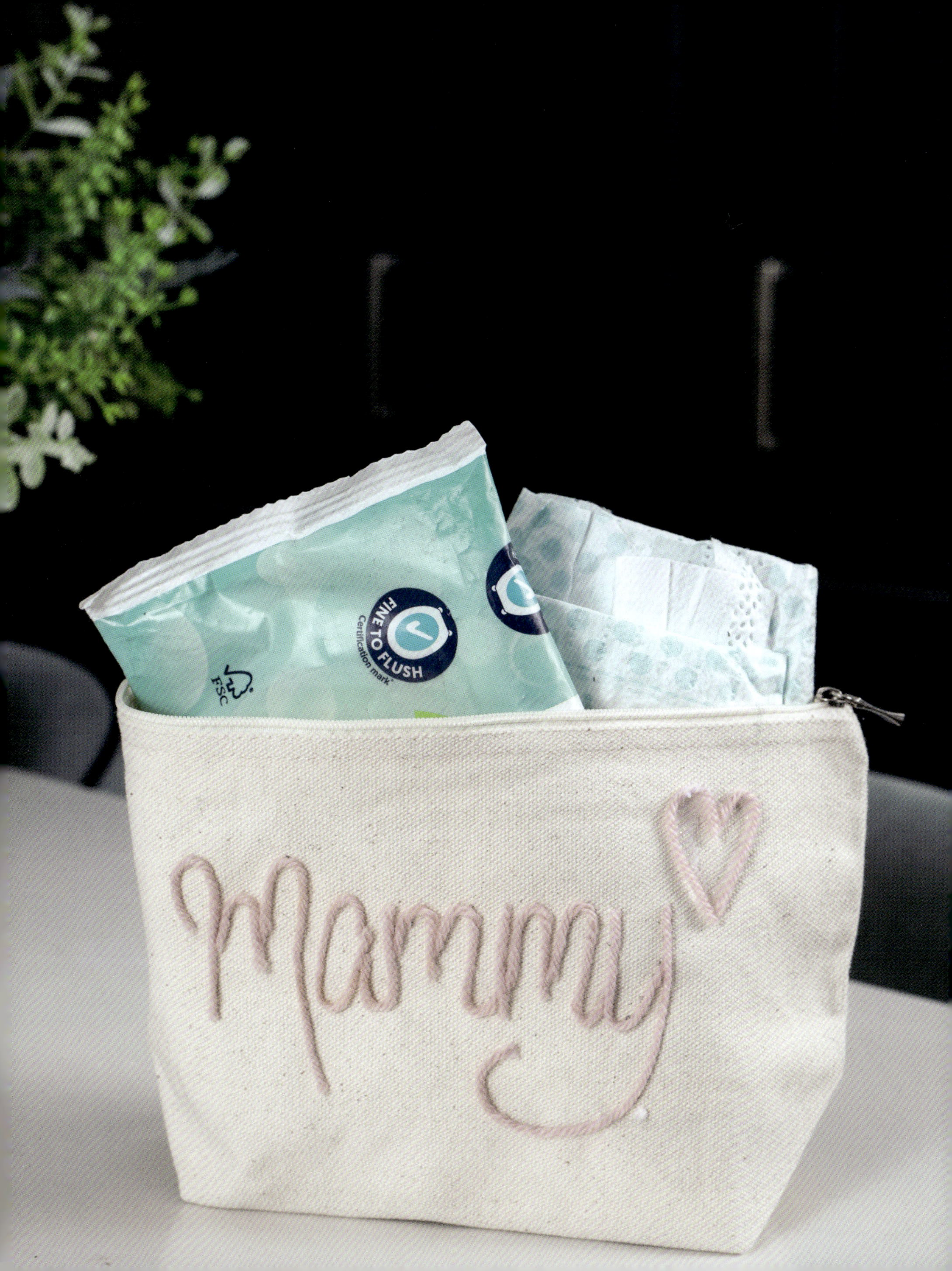
FINE TO FLUSH
Certification mark
FSC
Mammy

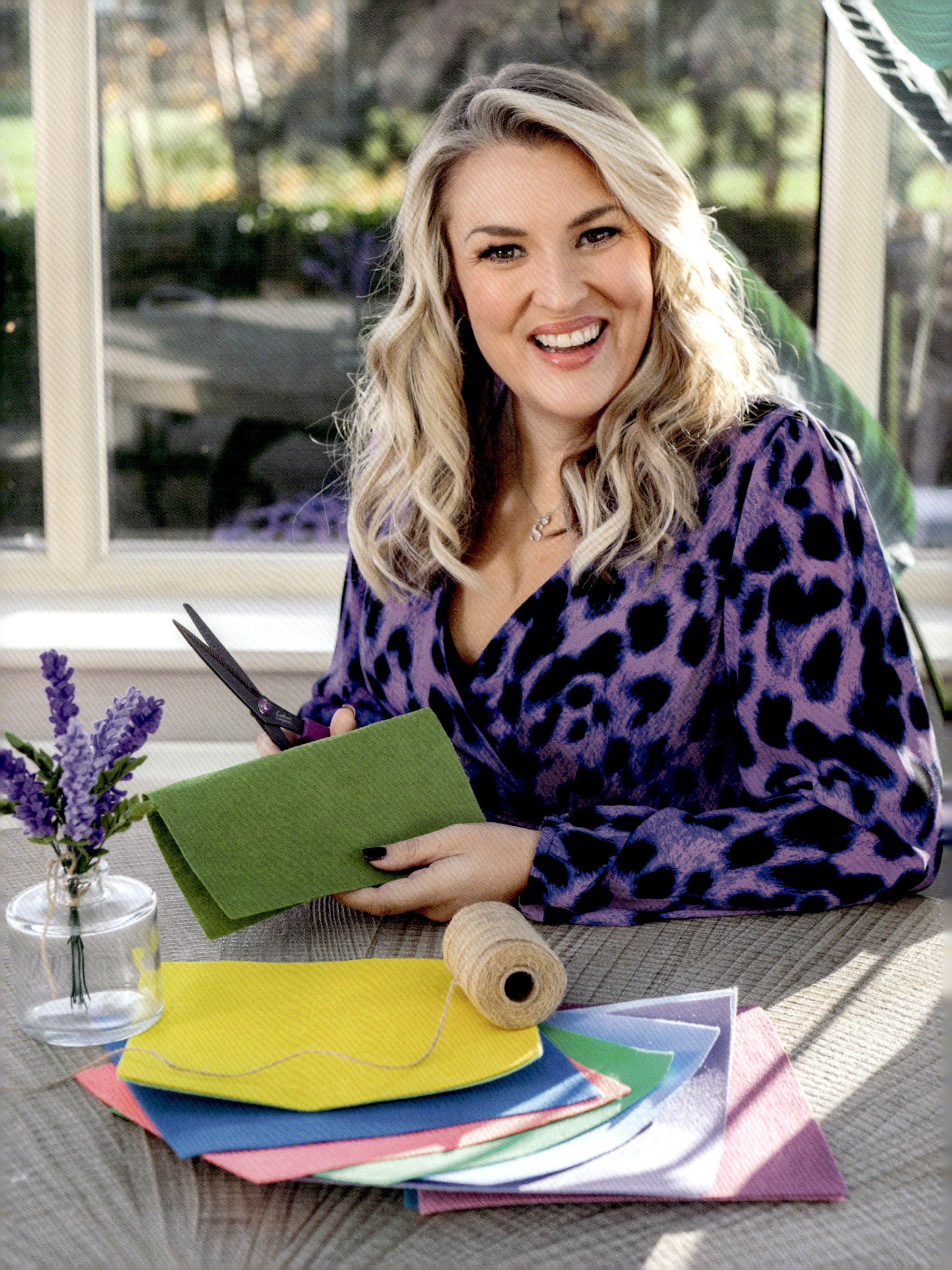

I Love You

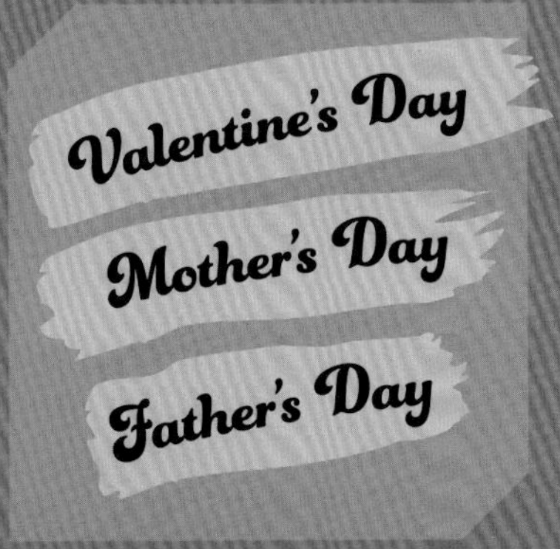

Intermediate

Heart Bunting

I've been known to find any excuse to decorate my house (because why not), and what better occasion than Valentine's Day? This heart bunting is a lovely way to add charm to your space while also putting those nostalgic fan-making techniques many of us learned at school to good use. With simple mountain and valley folds, you'll create eye-catching heart shapes that look beautiful when strung together.

You will need:

- Pink and red paper or thin card
- Scissors
- Glue gun
- Yarn

TOP TIP **Make the circles bigger to create larger hearts! Mixing different sizes will give the bunting a great look and feel.**

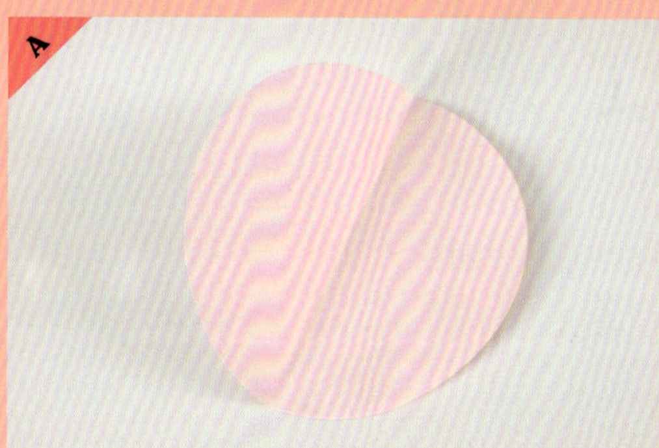

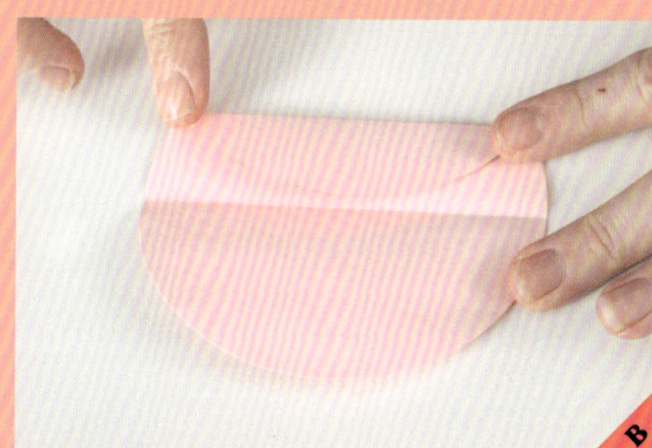

1 Cut out a circle measuring 3" from paper or thin card.

2 Fold the circle in half then open it back out to reveal a centre crease. **(A)**

3 Fold the bottom edge up to meet the centre crease. **(B)**

4 Turn the circle round and repeat on the other side. **(C)**

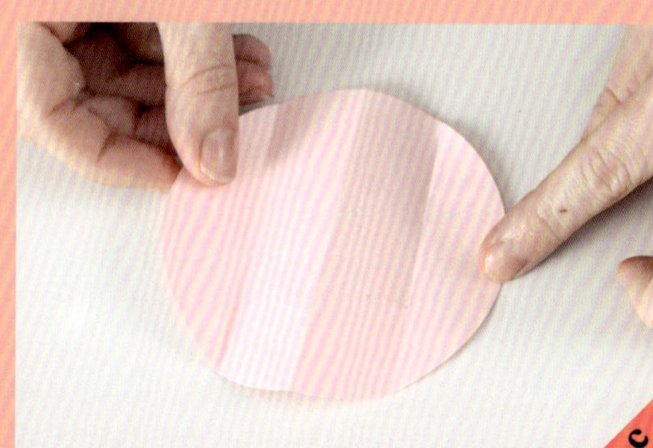

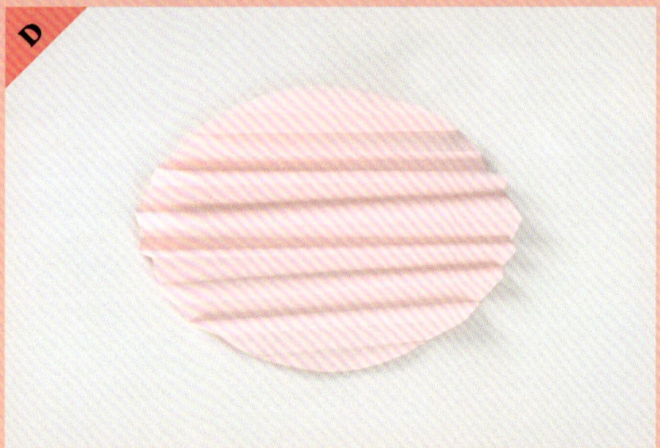

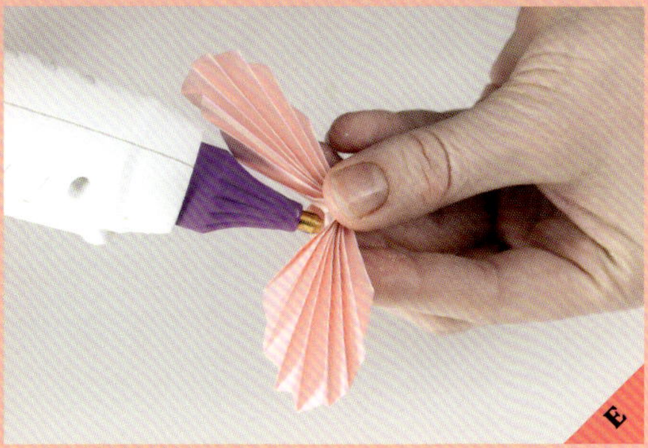

5 Flatten the circle. Fold the bottom edge to the first crease, unfold, then fold to the top crease. Turn the sheet round and repeat: fold to the first crease, unfold, then fold to the second crease from the top.

6 With the folds running horizontally and the creases facing upwards, fold along the pre-made creases to create alternating mountain and valley folds. Continue until the entire circle has been folded into a concertina shape. **(D)**

7 Trim the bottom edge to create a straight line, then repeat on the opposite side so that both edges are neat and even.

8 Fold the concertina-shaped oval in half. Once the heart shape is visible, apply glue to one of the end sections and press firmly to secure. **(E)**

9 Repeat the steps above to create as many hearts as you'd like for your bunting.

10 Finally, use a glue gun to attach the hearts evenly along a length of yarn to create your finished heart bunting.

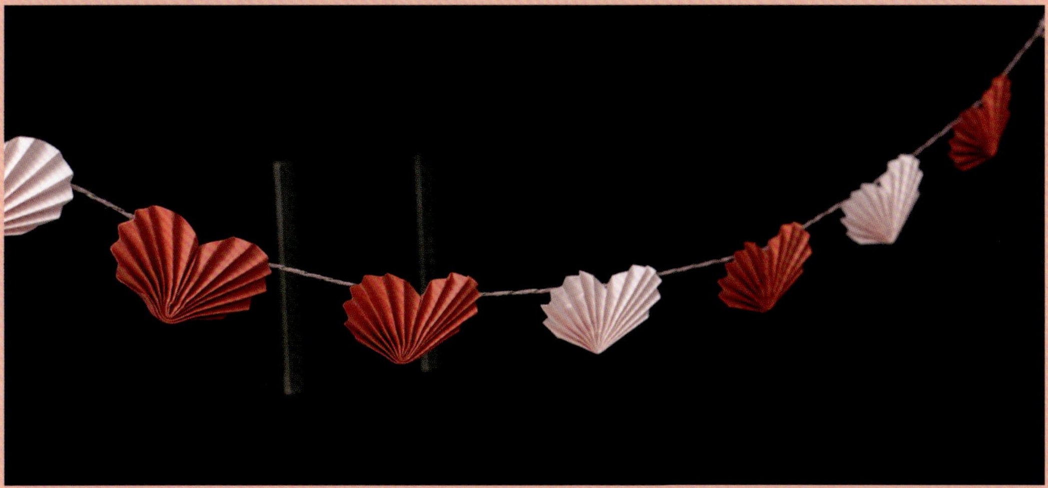

Easy

Photo Iron-On Tea Towel

I love projects that are both practical and personal, and this photo iron-on tea towel is a perfect example. It's a simple way to turn a favourite memory into something useful that friends and family will actually see and enjoy every day. Whether you choose a family photo, a beloved pet portrait or a fun snapshot, this project is super simple to make but feels thoughtful and special, making it ideal for gifting. Plus, it's a brilliant way to add a handmade touch to your kitchen!

You will need:

- Computer and printer
- Iron-on transfer paper
- Scissors
- Microfibre tea towel
- Heatproof surface, such as an ironing board
- Iron
- Greaseproof paper

TOP TIP **Take your time when using the iron. Rushing the process can affect the quality of the transfer, so steady pressure and patience will give the best results.**

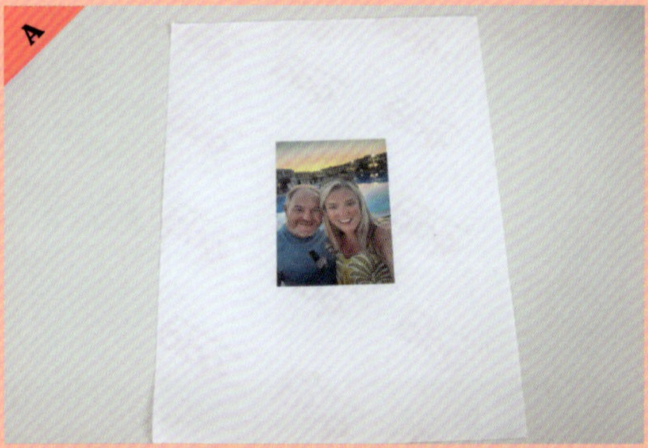

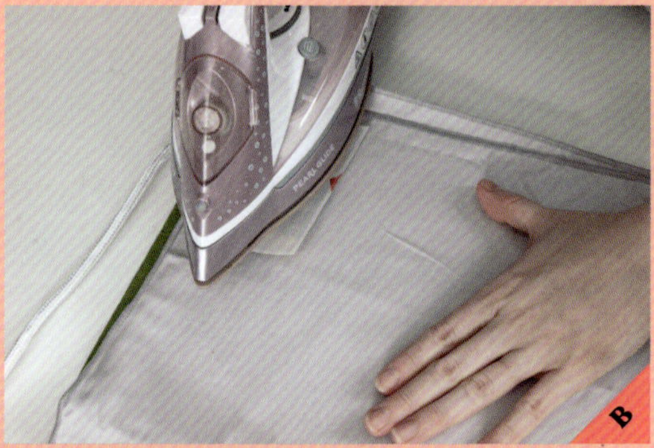

1 Select a photo on your computer, phone or tablet, and print it on to iron-on transfer paper, following the manufacturer's instructions. **(A)**

2 Cut out the printed image into a square or your desired shape. On a heatproof surface, position the image face down on the tea towel where you want the design to appear.

3 Heat your iron to the highest setting, ensuring the steam function is turned off. Carefully press the iron over the image, applying firm, even pressure. **(B)**

4 After approximately one minute, place a sheet of greaseproof paper between the iron and the transfer. Continue applying heat. This creates a non-stick barrier and protects both the towel and the iron.

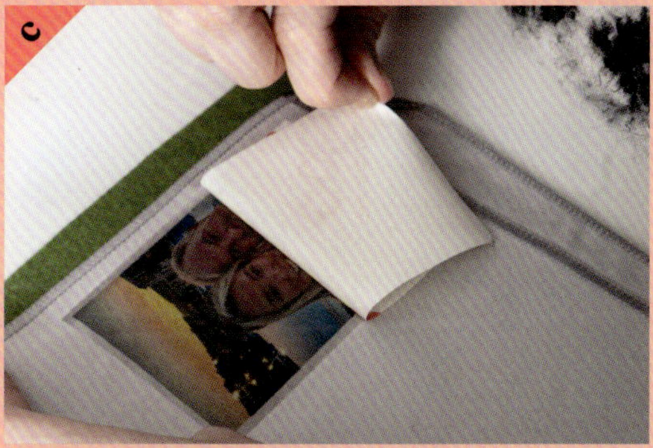

5 Carefully lift one corner of the transfer paper to check whether the image has adhered. If the transfer is complete, peel away the paper. If not, lower the paper back down and press again with the iron for a few more seconds. **(C)**

6 Allow the tea towel to cool completely before handling, then admire your finished personalized creation!

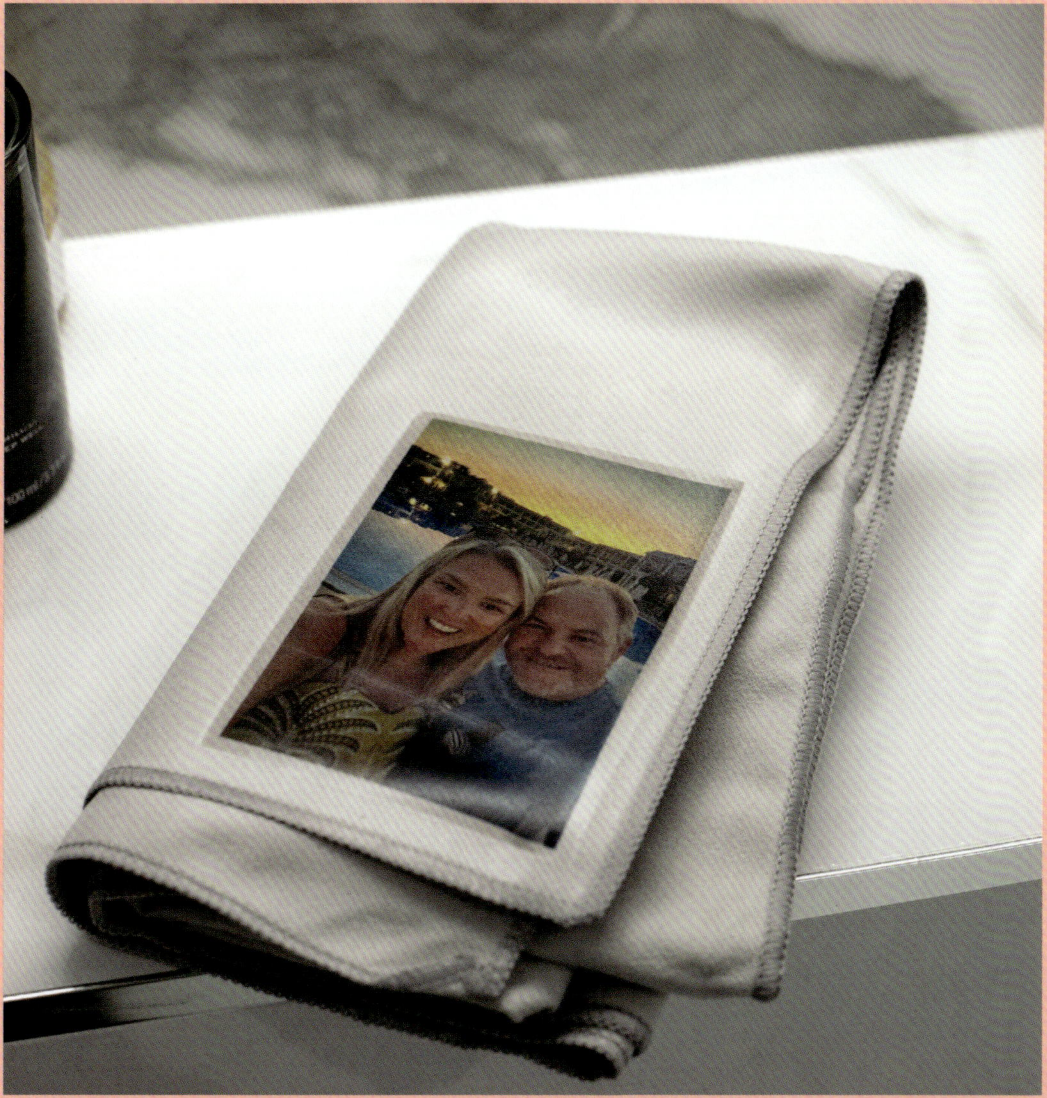

Advanced

Picture Reveal Card

This beautiful Valentine's project looks like a gatefold card at first glance, but open it up and there's a hidden photo revealed inside. I love projects like this because they're personal and have a real 'wow' factor, yet when you break them down step by step, they're completely achievable. It's thoughtful, creative, and such a lovely way to celebrate someone you care about because, honestly, handmade always means more!

TOP TIP Print out a selection of images and see which fits best behind the aperture.

You will need:

- White card
- Ruler
- Pencil
- Scissors or paper trimmer
- Scoring tool
- Patterned papers
- Glue tape pen
- Circle die or circular template
- Photograph or image

1 Create a gatefold card from an 8″ × 5½″ piece of white card. In landscape orientation, score vertically at 2″ and 6″.

2 Glue patterned paper to the front and inside of the card. You'll need four pieces measuring 5¼″ x 1¾″ for the outer and inner side panels, and one piece measuring 5¼″ x 3¾″ for the larger centre panel. **(A)**

3 Cut two pieces of white card measuring 3″ × 3″.

4 On the first square, draw a vertical pencil line halfway across at 1½″. Measure 1⅛″ from the bottom edge and mark this point on the centre line. From there, draw a diagonal line to each bottom corner of the card. Cut out the central triangle to create a pennant shape. **(B)**

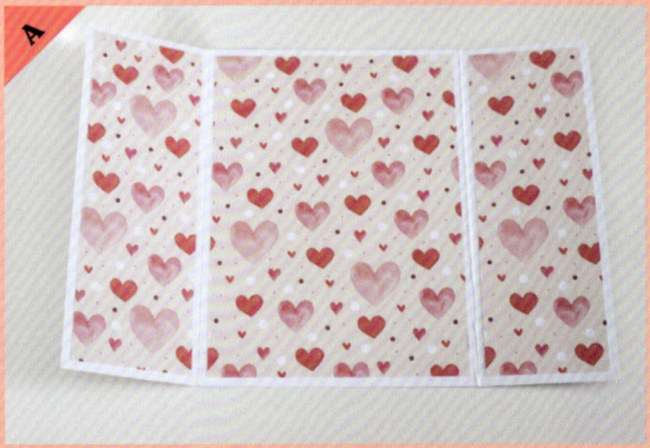

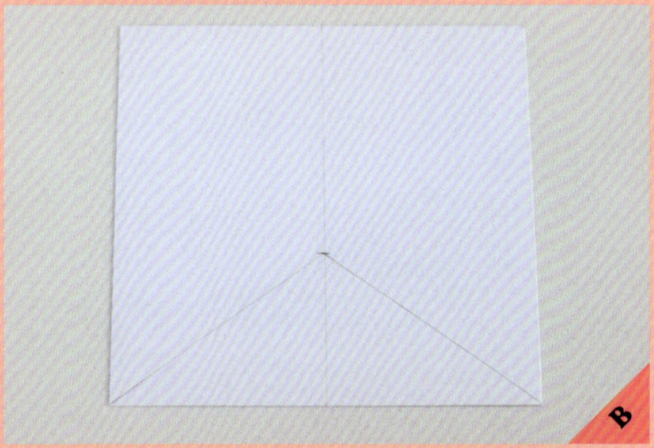

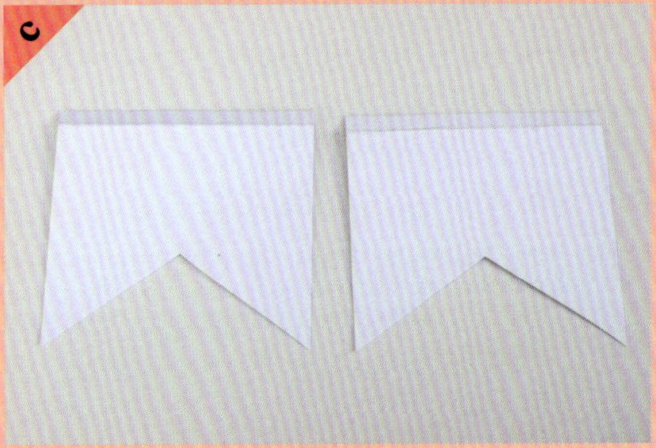

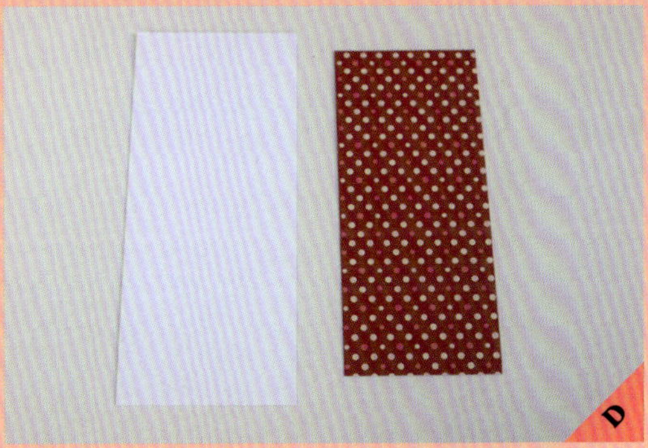

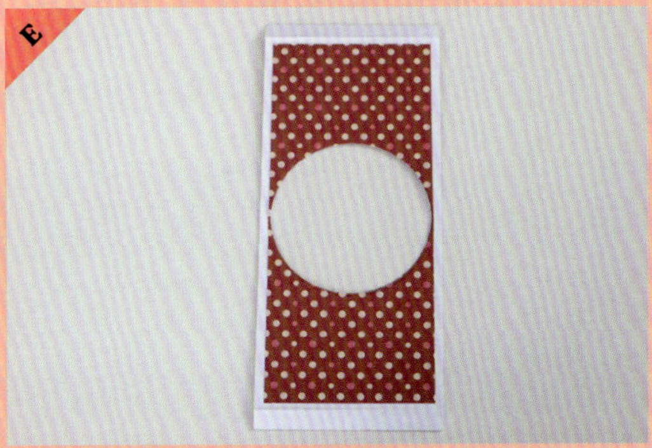

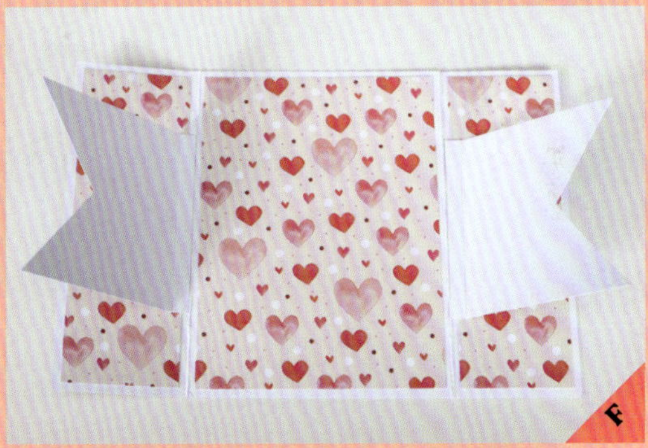

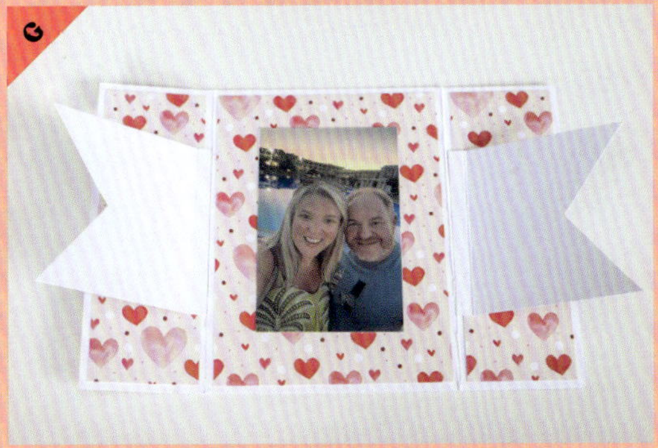

5 At the top edge of the pennant, score a ¼″ line to create a tab.

6 Repeat steps 4–5 on the second square of card to create two pennant panels with tabs. **(C)**

7 Cut a piece of card measuring 6″ × 2½″ and a piece of patterned paper measuring 5″ × 2″. **(D)**

8 Score at ¼″ along the top and bottom of the short edges. Mark the centre point of the panel with a pencil cross, then cut a 2¼″ diameter circle to create an aperture in the middle, using the cross as a guide. **(E)**

9 Add adhesive to the ¼″ tabs on the pennant pieces and glue one to the left of the gatefold centre score line and the other to the right. **(F)**

10 Position your image on the centre panel, aligning it so it sits neatly in the aperture. **(G)**

11 Fold the pennant panels over so they overlap when the card closes.

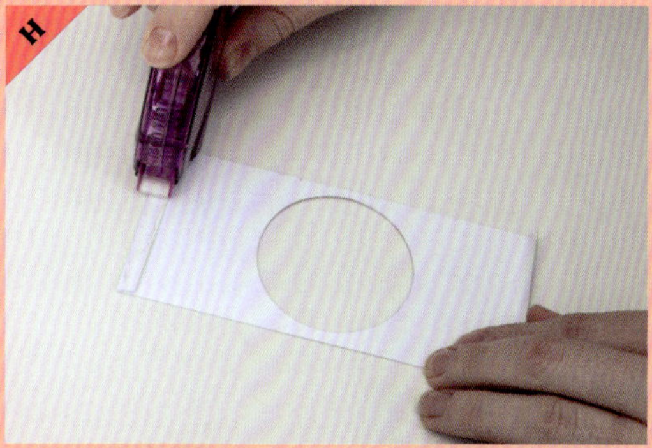

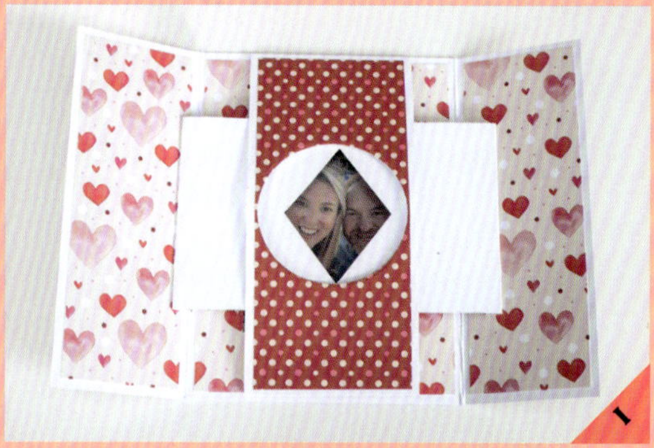

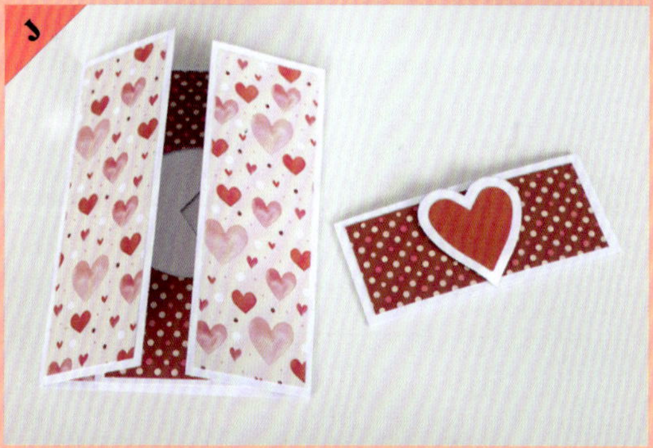

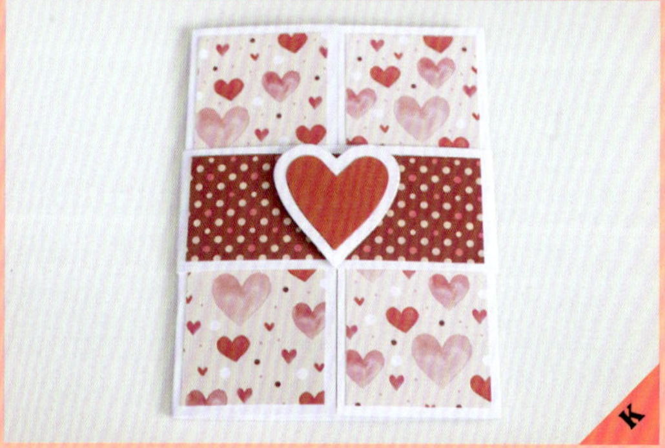

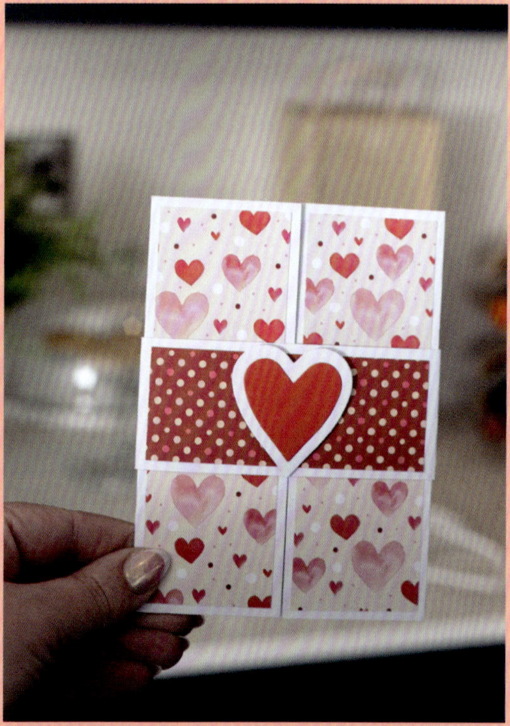

12 Add adhesive to the ¼" scored tabs on the aperture panel. **(H)**

13 Secure the mechanism by gluing the aperture panel into place on the card base. **(I)**

14 To create a belly band, cut a piece of card measuring 1¾" x 9". Wrap it around the closed card so it slides on and off easily, then glue the ends together. Add patterned paper panels measuring 1½" × 3¾" to the front and back of the band. **(J)**

15 Finish by adding a heart embellishment to decorate. **(K)**

Intermediate

Heart Treat Box

If you're looking to make something truly heartfelt this Valentine's Day, this sweet little treat box is a lovely project to try. Simple yet stylish, it's ideal for filling with chocolates, love notes or a small surprise for someone special.

Starting with sturdy Kraft card for the base, you'll add a pop of red for that classic Valentine's feel, then finish with a ribbon pull that makes opening the box just as delightful as what's inside. With plenty of satisfying scoring and folding, you'll get that fabulous 'I made this!' moment once it all comes together.

TOP TIP One of the best bits about this box is how easy it is to customize every detail. Change the colours, cardstock or ribbon to suit the recipient or occasion.

You will need:

- Kraft card
- Red card
- Pencil
- Ruler
- Scissors or paper trimmer
- Scoring board
- Scoring tool
- Hole punch or pokey tool
- Quick-dry craft clue (e.g. Collall Tacky Glue)
- Ribbon
- Scrap card

1. Trim a piece of Kraft card to 8¾" × 3¼". **(A)**
2. Cut a separate piece of red card measuring 6" × 6". **(B)**
3. Setting the Kraft card in landscape orientation, use a scoring board and tool to score at 2⅛", 4¼", 6⅜" and 8½" along the long edge. **(C)**

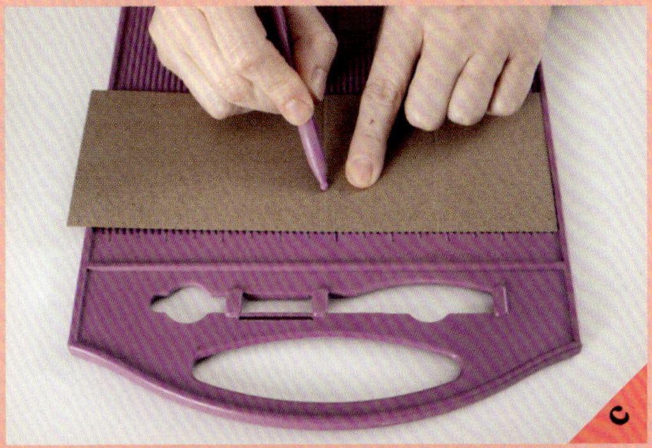

4 Rotate the Kraft card into portrait orientation and score at 1⅛″ from the right-hand edge. **(D)**

5 With the smaller panels positioned at the bottom, cut along the first three vertical score lines up to the horizontal score line. **(E)**

6 At the fourth score line, cut away the small lower panel entirely, leaving a 2⅛″ × ¼″ side tab intact with a diagonal cut as shown. **(F)**

7 On the 6″ × 6″ red card, score at 2″ and 4″, then rotate the card and repeat to create a grid with a 2″ centre square. **(G)**

8 Score again at 1¾″ and 4⅛″, stopping at the first score line. Rotate the card so

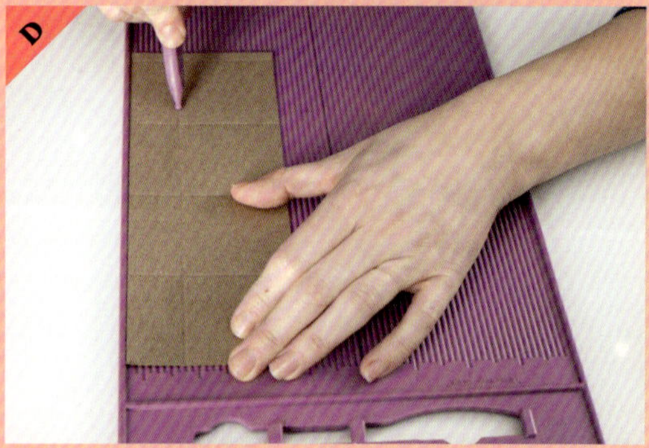

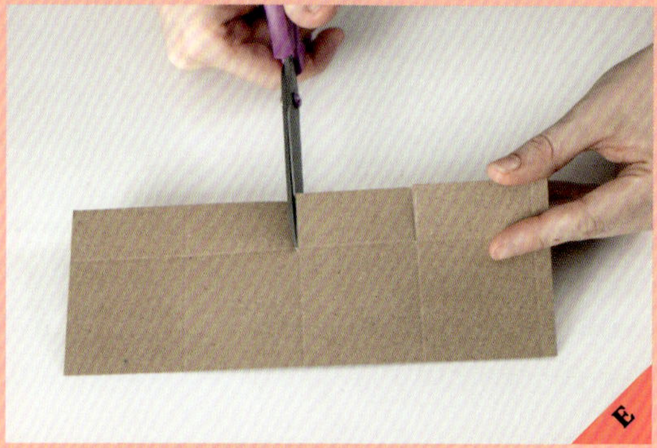

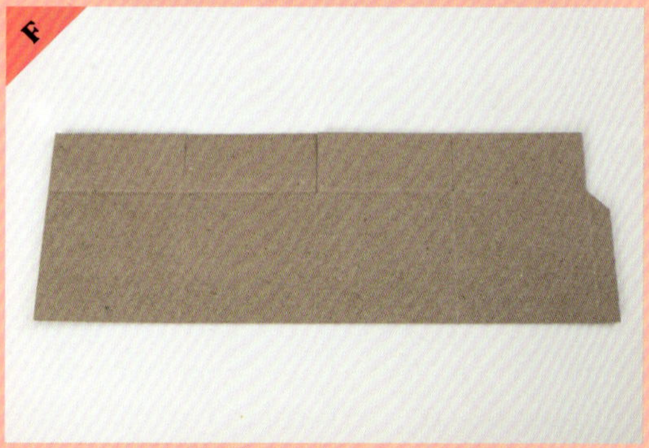

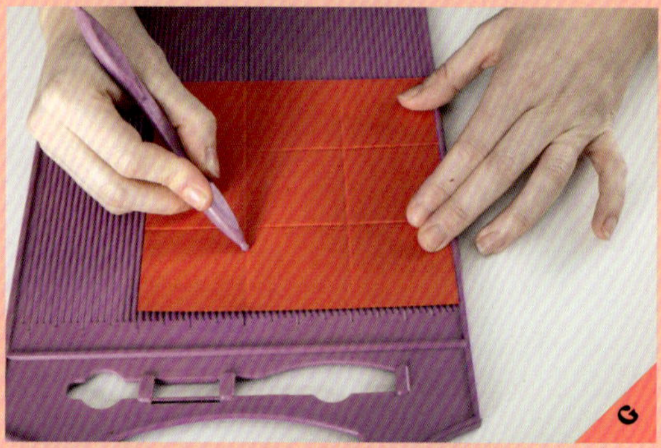

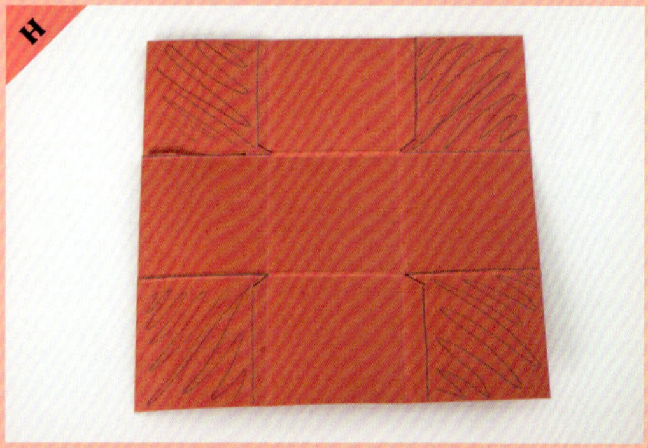

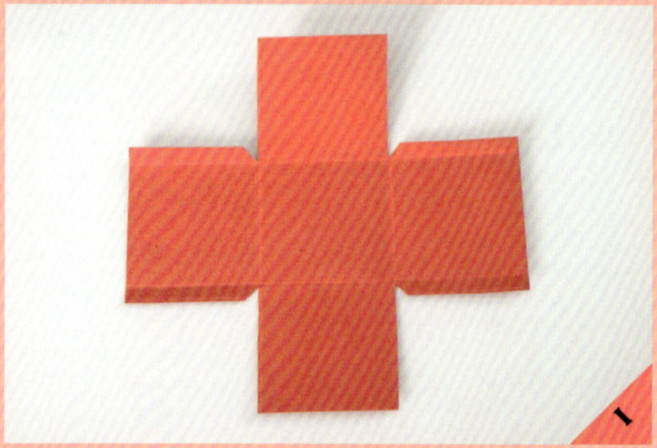

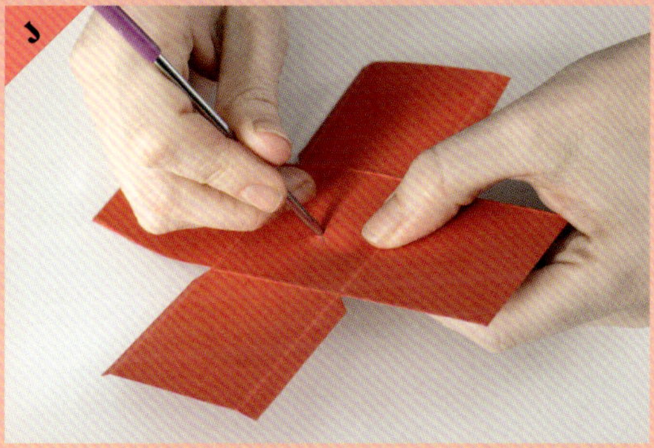

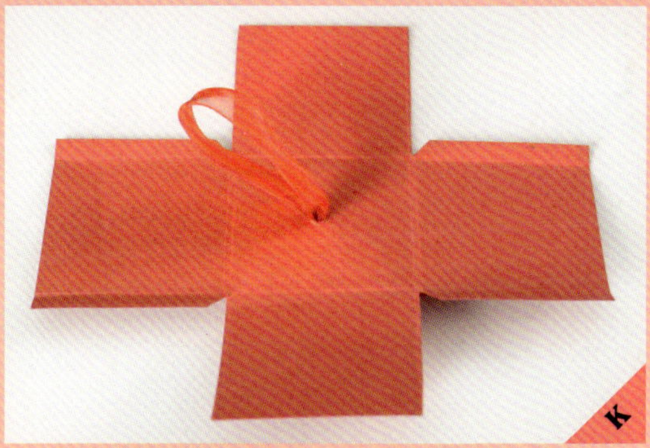

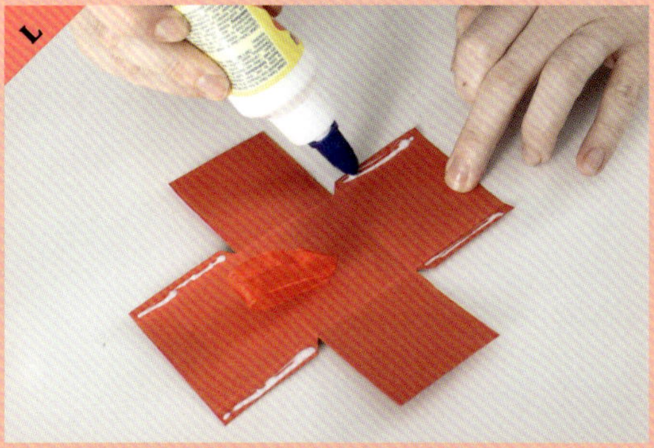

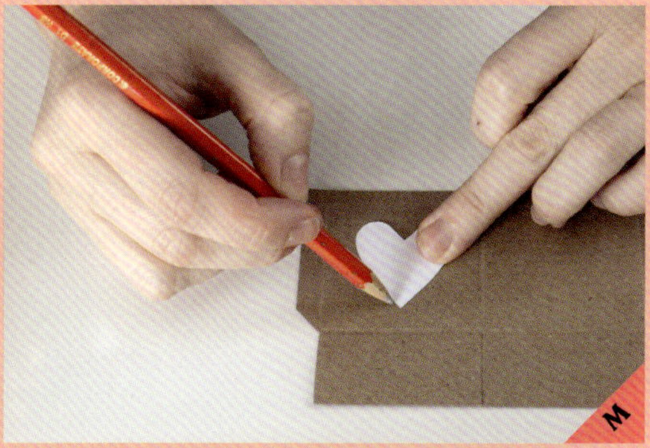

these two score lines sit at the bottom, then repeat the same scoring along this edge. **(H)**

9 Cut away the four corner sections, taking care to leave the ¼″ tabs in place. Cut each tab on a diagonal as shown. **(I)**

10 Mark the centre of the middle square and, using a hole punch or pokey tool, create a hole. **(J)**

11 Cut a length of ribbon, fold it in half, and tie a knot at the loose ends. Thread the ribbon through the hole from underneath so the loop sits on top. Trim any excess ribbon beneath the knot. **(K)**

12 Apply adhesive to the four tabs and assemble the red piece to form the box lid. **(L)**

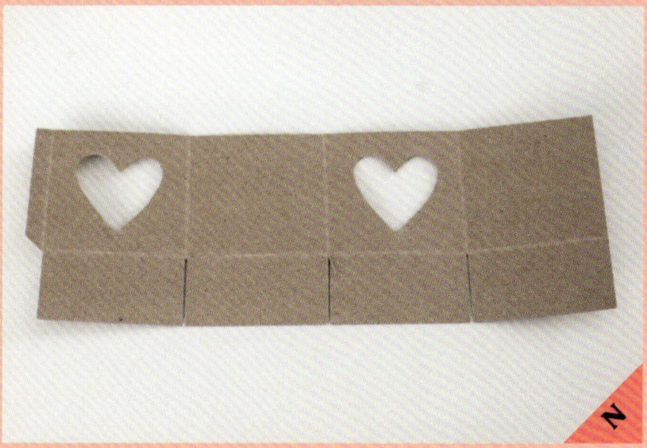

13 Draw and cut out a heart shape from some scrap card to create a template. **(M)**

14 Use a pencil to draw around the template on the first and third panels of the Kraft card as shown and cut out. **(N)**

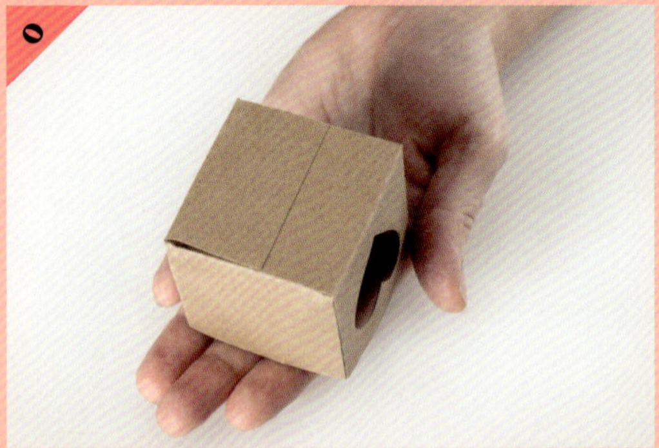

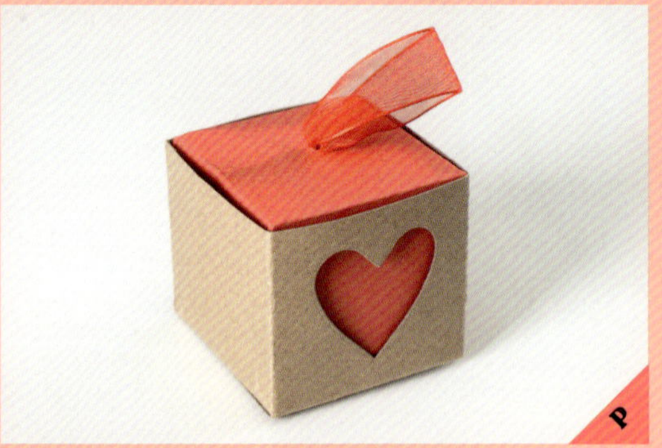

15 Add glue to the ¼″ side tab on the Kraft piece and adhere it to the inside of the first square to form the box base.

16 Fold in the rest of the bottom panels and glue them into place to complete the base. **(O)**

17 Slide the assembled red lid into the Kraft base to finish the treat box. **(P)**

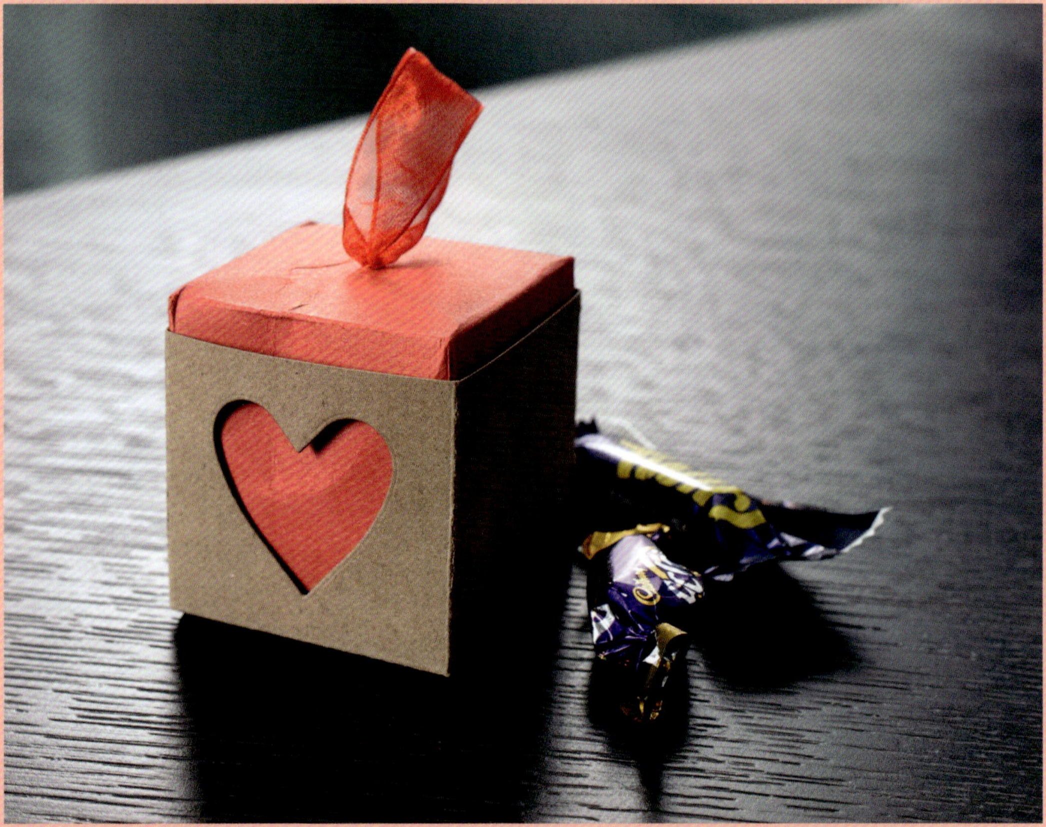

Advanced

Waterfall Card

If you're looking for a showstopper of a card then this waterfall design is such a fun one to make! With every pull of the tab, a new image flips over, whether that's favourite photos, sweet messages or special memories. It's interactive, thoughtful and perfect for any occasion. There are a few steps involved but super satisfying once you see the mechanism come together!

TOP TIP **Before securing the mechanism inside the card base, test the movement a few times to make sure each panel flips smoothly.**

You will need:

- 6" x 4" card base
- White and coloured card
- Patterned paper
- Scissors or paper trimmer
- Ruler
- Glue tape pen or glue gun
- Scoring board
- Scoring tool
- Images or photos measuring approximately 1⅞" × 1⅞" (or 2" × 2" and trimmed to fit)

1 Mat and layer the front and back of a 6" × 4" card base with coloured card and patterned paper. **(A)**

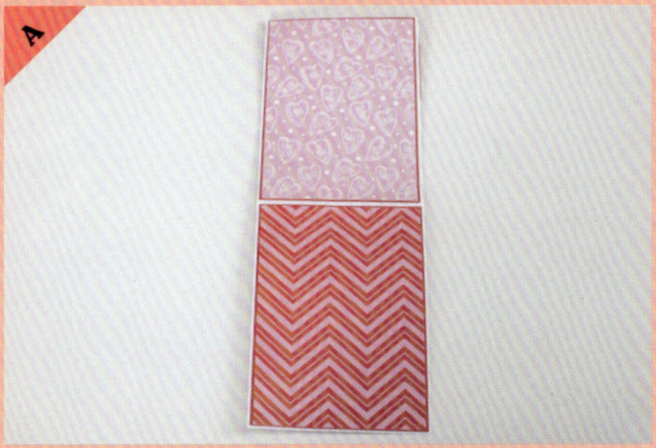

2 Cut a piece of white card measuring 2" × 9". **(B)**

3 Measure and score this strip at 2", 2¾", 3½" and 4¼". **(C)**

4 Cut four pieces of card measuring 2" × 2".

5 With the scored strip positioned in front of you, use a tape pen or glue gun to adhere the first square to the top section of the strip, aligning it carefully. **(D)**

6 Continue adhering the remaining squares, fixing one to each scored section in order. **(E)**

7 Adhere your chosen images on to the four square panels. **(F)**

8 Open the strip fully. Cut a piece of card measuring ¾" × 3⅞" and glue it in place at the bottom of the strip to act as the pull mechanism. **(G)**

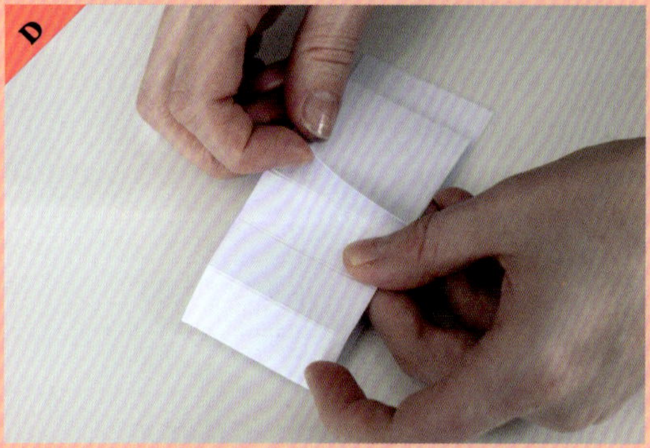

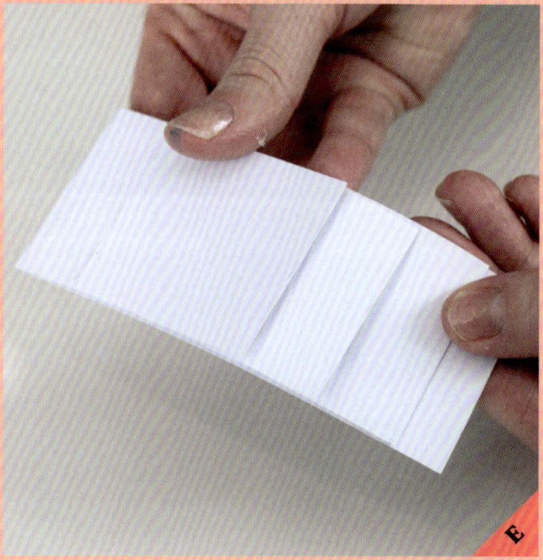

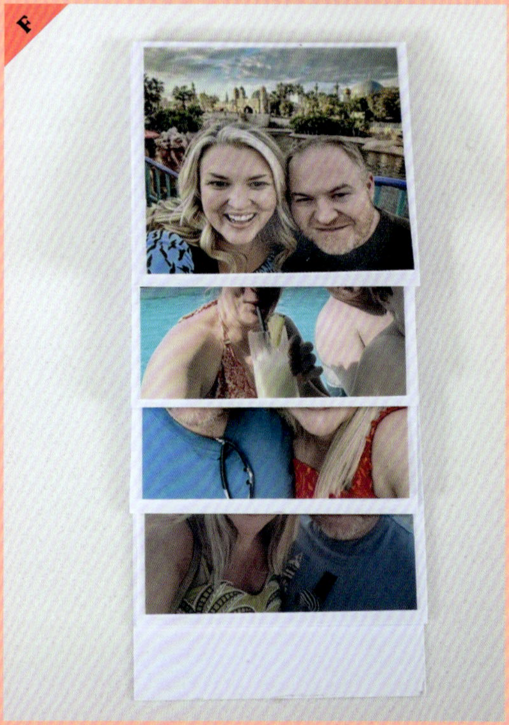

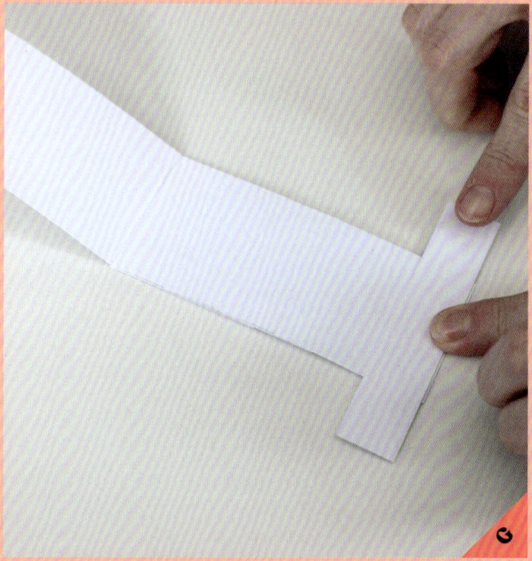

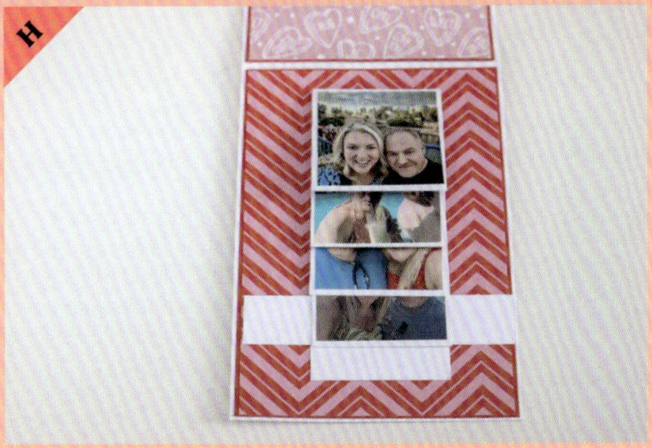

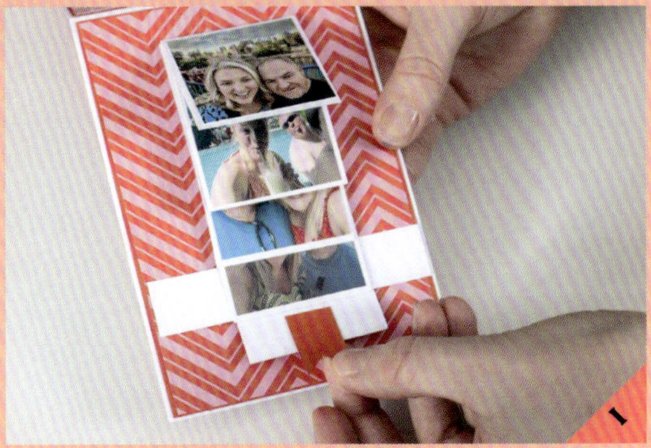

9 Fold the top end of the 9″ strip under, so a small section extends beneath the fourth image.

10 Apply adhesive to the overhanging ends of the ¾″ strip and glue them to the inside of the card base to secure the mechanism. **(H)**

11 Create a pull tab from coloured card and adhere it to the exposed section below the final image.

12 Gently pull the tab to check the mechanism moves smoothly! **(I)**

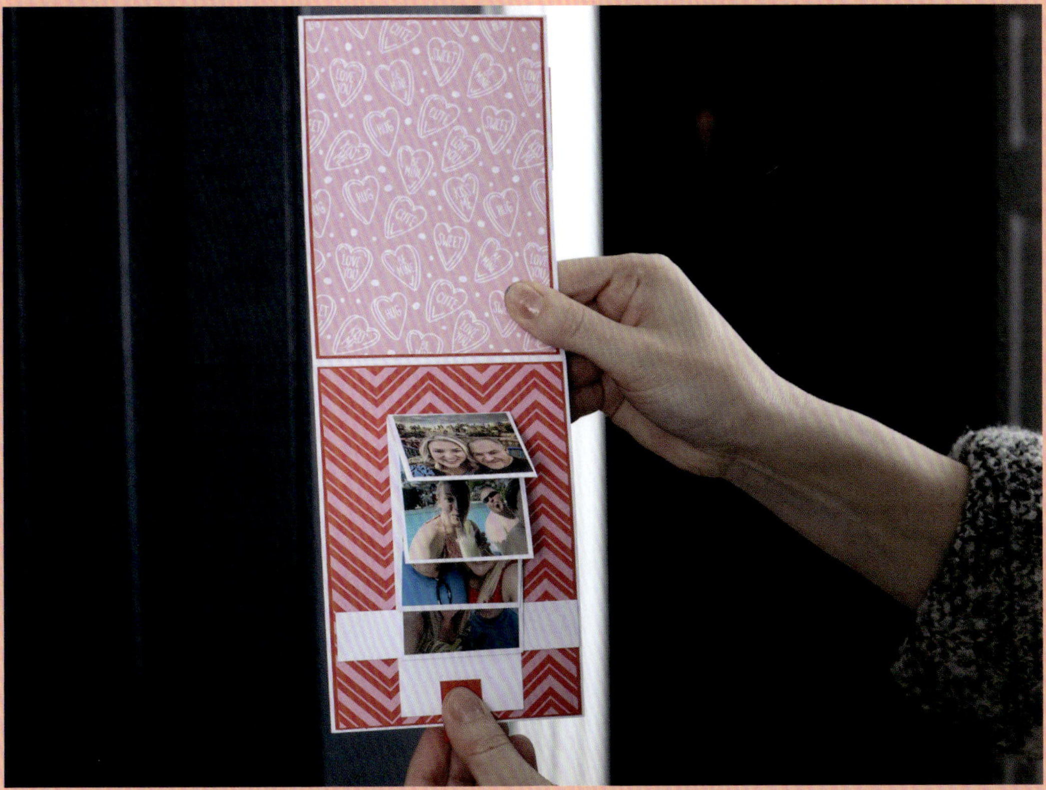

Advanced

Bursting Flowers Card

If you're looking for a card that really wows, then look no further than this Bursting Flowers Card. It's intricate, colourful and full of impact, making it a showstopping design for Mother's Day, birthdays and other special occasions. This project is ideal for crafters who enjoy detail, precision and a satisfying creative challenge!

TOP TIP **When creating the flowers, use different coloured papers. This makes it much easier to see which petals need to be glued at each stage.**

You will need:

- Coloured paper
- Pencil
- Ruler
- Scissors
- Glue tape pen
- Alcohol markers or felt-tip pens
- White card
- Coloured card
- Patterned paper

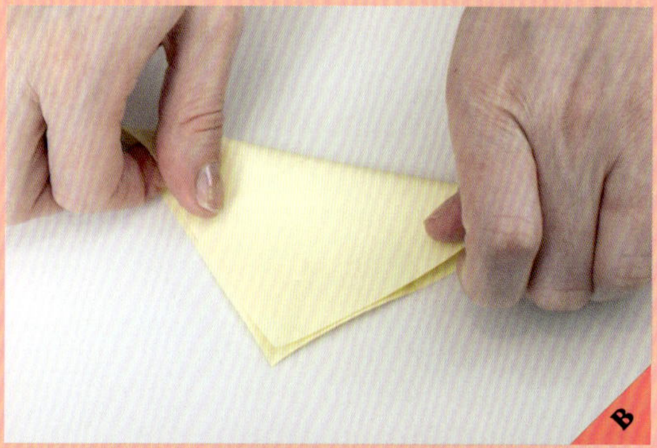

1 Cut seven pieces of coloured paper, each measuring 4" × 4". **(A)**

2 Fold each square in half diagonally. **(B)**

3 Repeat this fold two further times, keeping the folds aligned. **(C)**

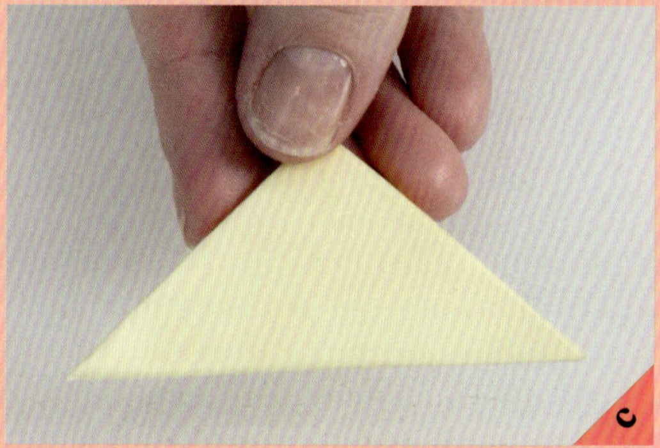

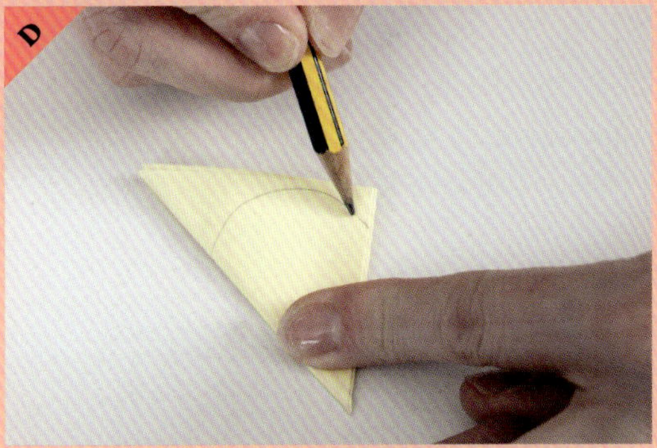

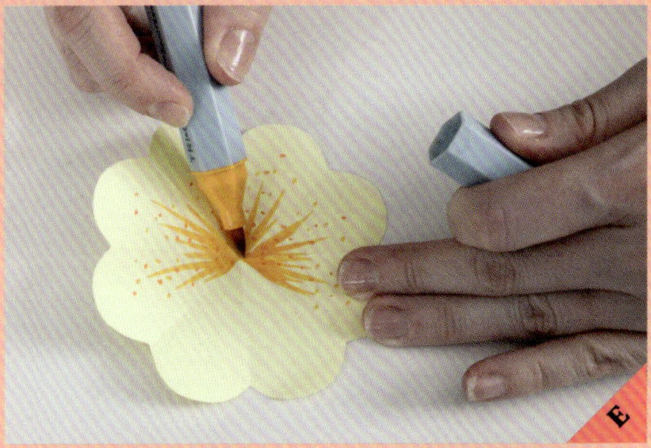

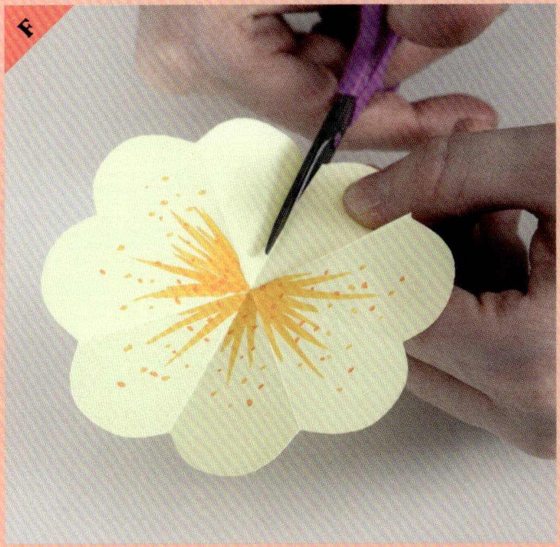

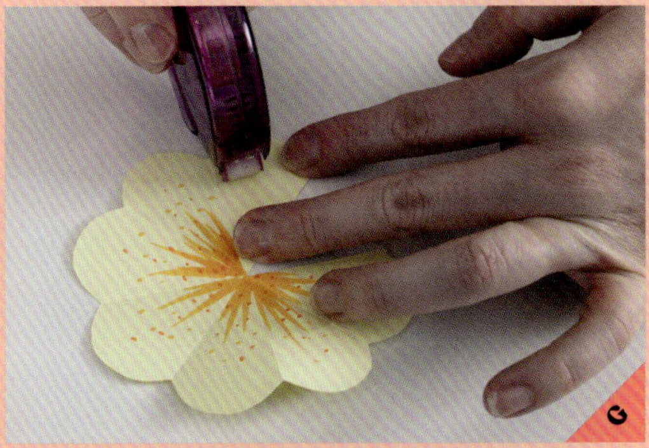

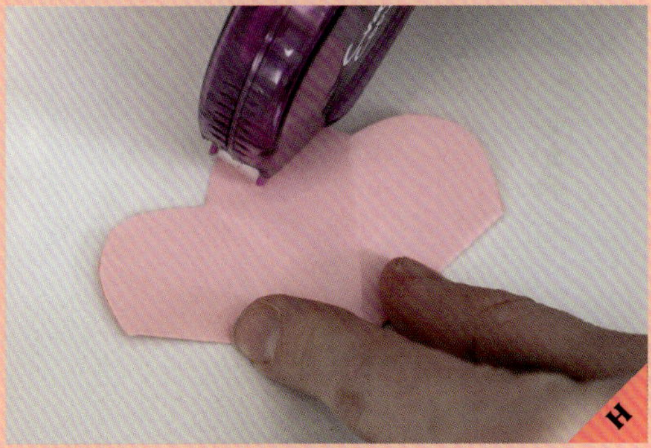

4 With the folded piece positioned so the open edges are on the left and at the top, draw a curved line across them using a pencil. Cut carefully along the drawn line, then open the paper out flat. **(D)**

5 You should now have an eight-petal flower. Add detail to six of the petals, using alcohol markers or felt-tip pens, leaving two petals plain. **(E)**

6 Cut away one of the plain petals. **(F)**

7 Repeat steps 2–6 for the remaining six pieces of paper. Apply glue to the remaining plain petal on each flower and join it to the opposite petal to form a shallow cone shape. Repeat this for all seven flowers. **(G)**

8 Fold all seven flowers in half. Take one folded flower and apply glue to the top edge only of the centre and outer petals. Avoid gluing too far down, as this will restrict the movement of the petals. **(H)**

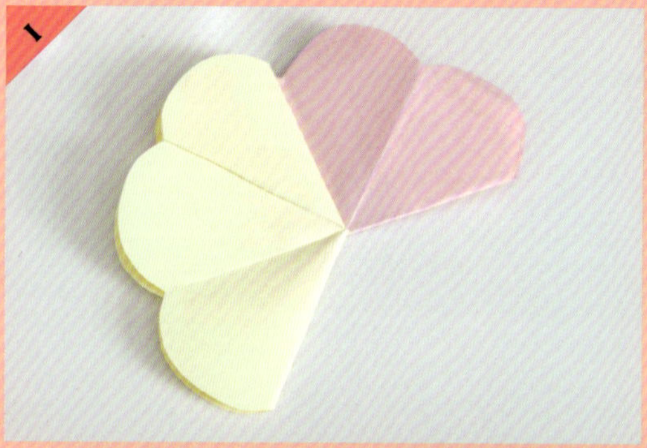

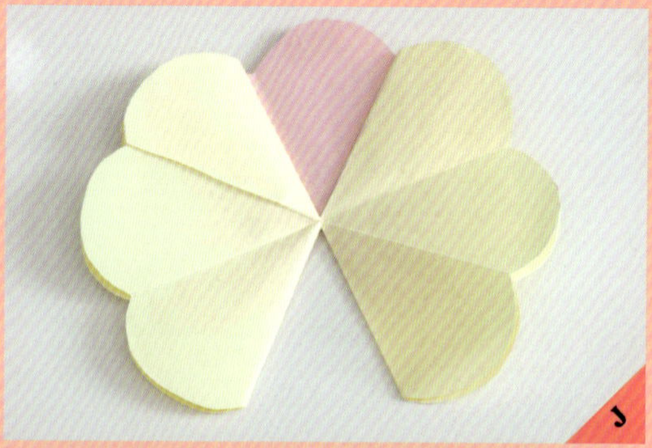

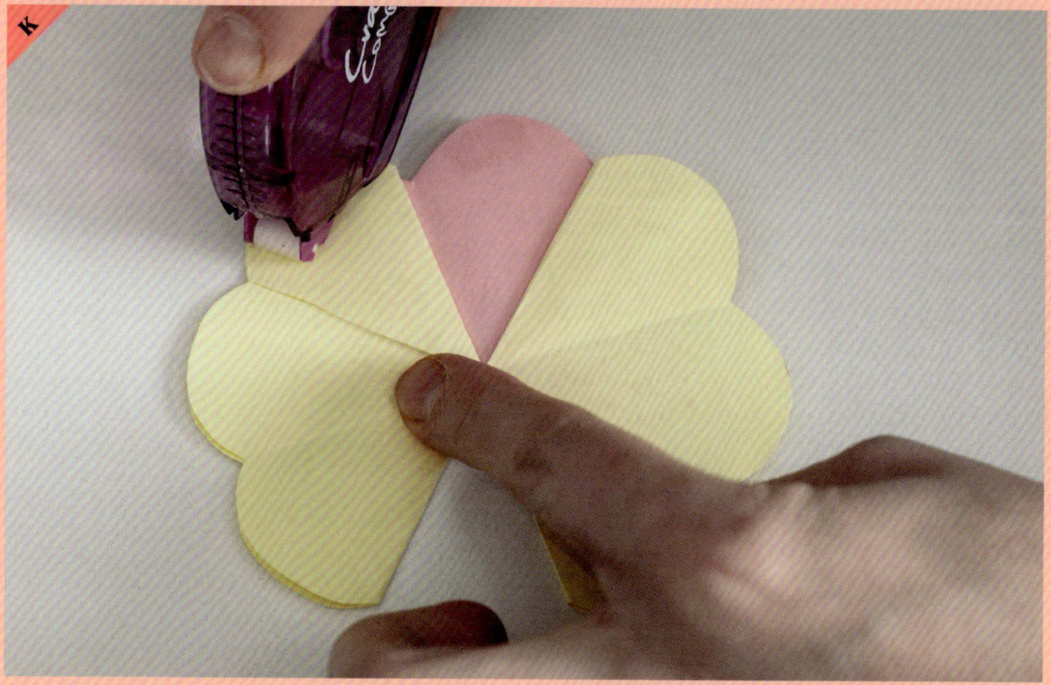

9 Attach one folded flower to each glued section so the flowers begin to form a cluster. **(I)**

10 Repeat on the opposite side. **(J)**

11 Apply a small amount of adhesive to the top edges of the newly attached sections. **(K)**

12 Adhere another folded flower on top. **(L)**

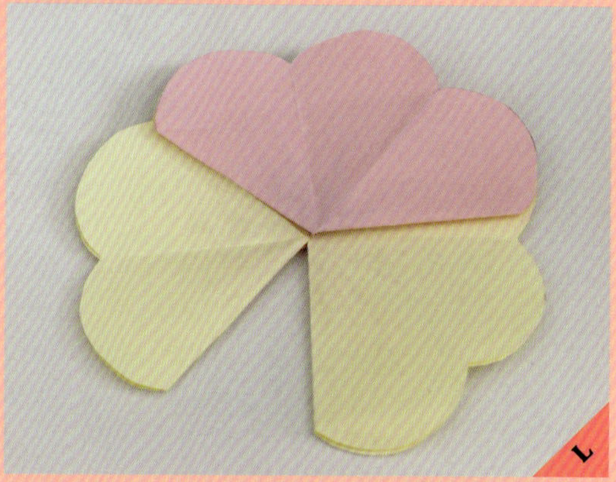

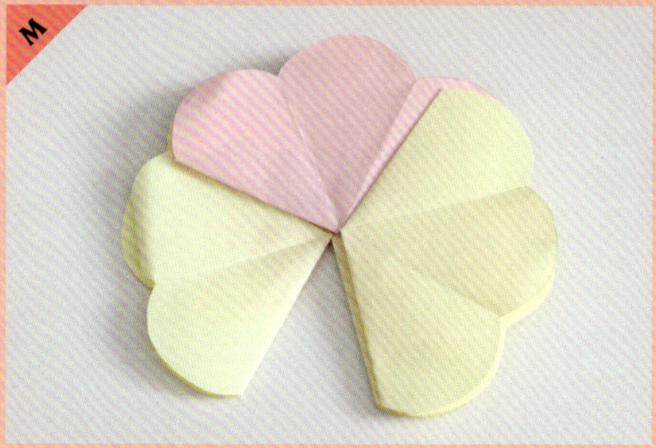

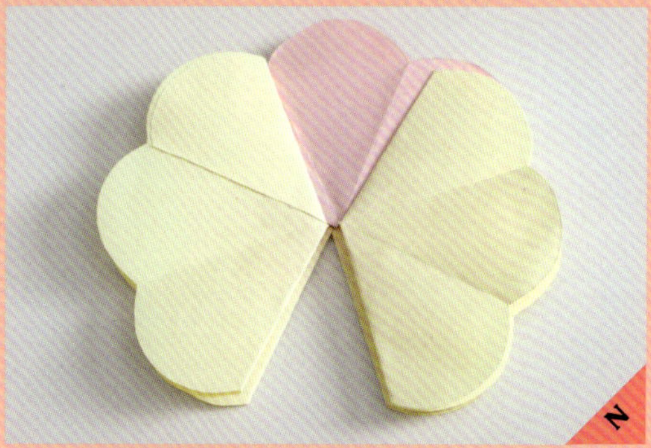

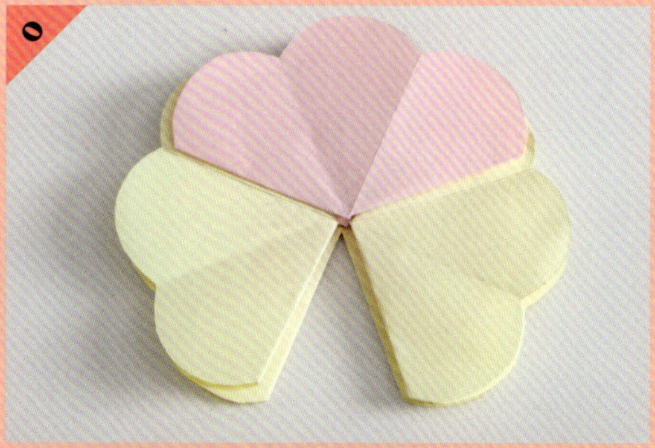

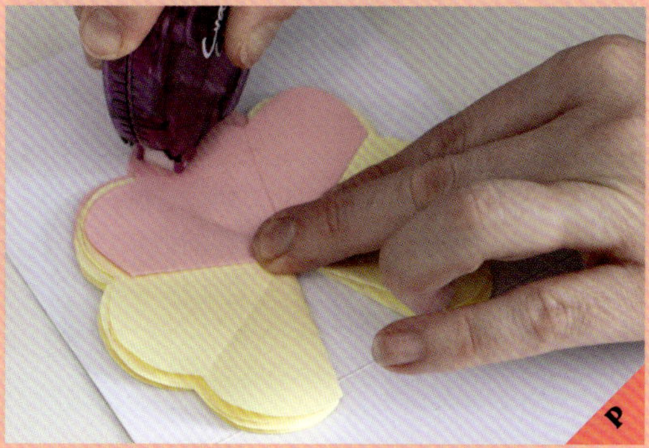

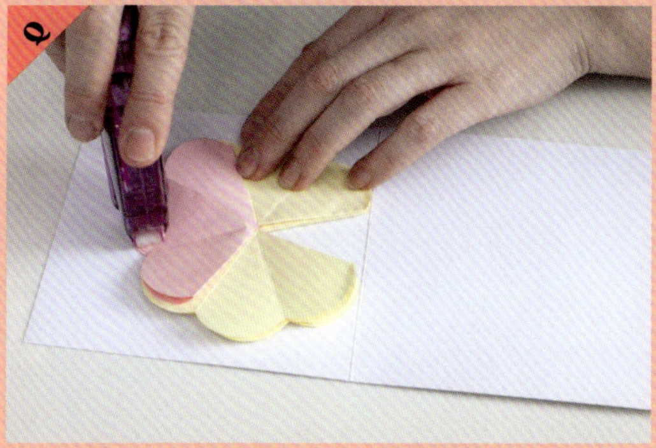

13 Attach two more folded flowers, one on each side. **(M and N)**

14 Adhere the final folded flower on top to complete the floral structure. **(O)**

15 Create a card base large enough for the flower to sit comfortably inside.

16 Apply adhesive to the top centre petal and adhere it to the inside of the card, aligning it with the centre fold, as shown. **(P)**

17 Press the flower into place, then apply glue to the same petal on the opposite side. Close the card to secure the flowers evenly. **(Q)**

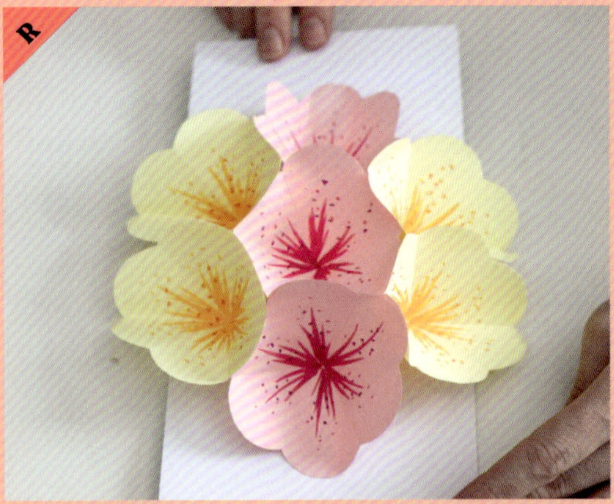

18 When the card is opened, the flowers should bloom and open fully. **(R)**

19 To finish, mat and layer the card front with coordinating card and patterned paper.

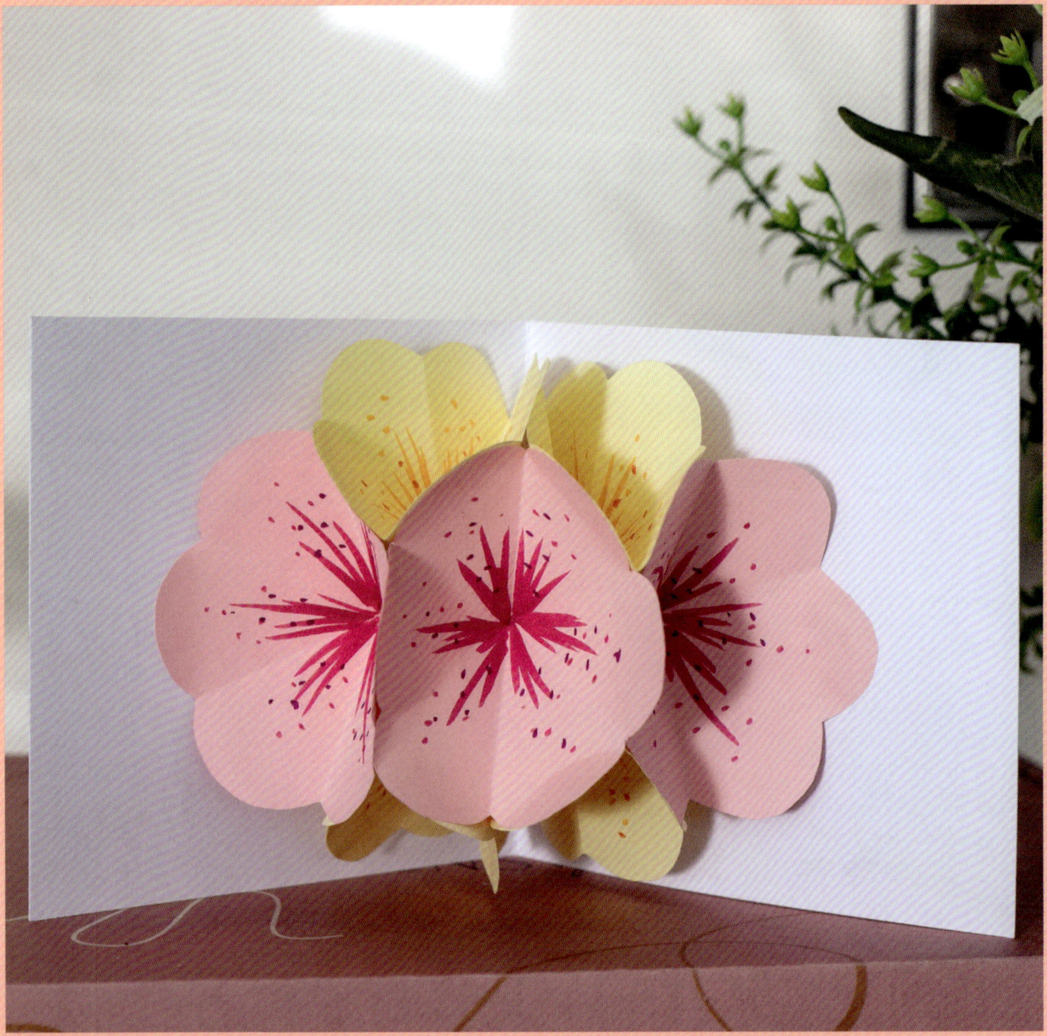

Intermediate

Embroidered Card

Mother's Day is the perfect opportunity to create something truly heartfelt, and this embroidered floral wreath card is exactly that. Combining soft watercolours, simple stitching and a standout heart centrepiece, it's a thoughtful way to say 'thank you' and 'I love you' in a way that really steals the show.

If painting isn't your strongest skill, don't worry. This design celebrates loose, relaxed brushstrokes over precision. With a few basic supplies and a little time, you can create a card that looks incredibly impressive while remaining achievable, even for beginners. So pop the kettle on, clear a little crafting space and make something Mum will treasure long after Mother's Day has passed.

TOP TIP If you're feeling unsure about painting the florals, practise a few simple shapes on scrap paper first.

You will need:

- White card
- Ruler
- Scissors
- Pencil
- Circular template (optional)
- Pokey tool or needle
- Eraser
- Watercolour palette
- Water
- Small paintbrush
- Embroidery thread
- Sewing needle
- Pink card and contrasting card (for the lettering)
- White gel pen
- Quick-dry craft glue (e.g. Collall Tacky Glue)

1 Create a 6″ × 6″ card base. **(A)**

2 Lightly draw a circle in pencil on the front of the card, using a circular template if you prefer. The circle in this project measures approximately 2¾″ in diameter. **(B)**

3 Using a ruler as a guide, evenly mark small dots around the circle approximately ½″ apart. These will act as your stitching guide.

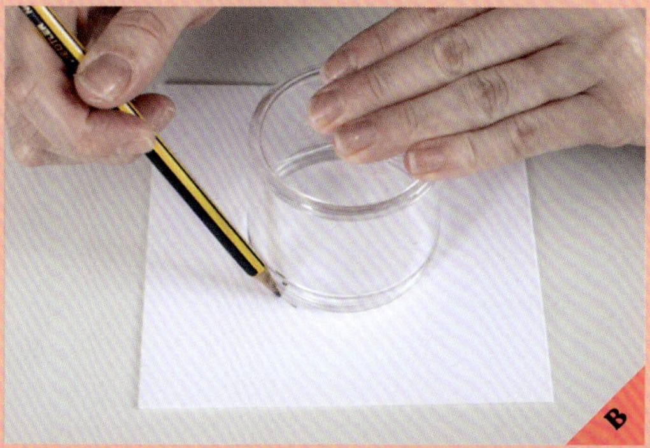

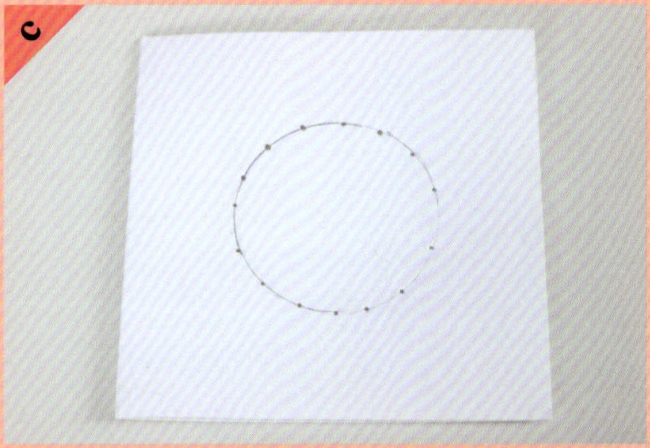

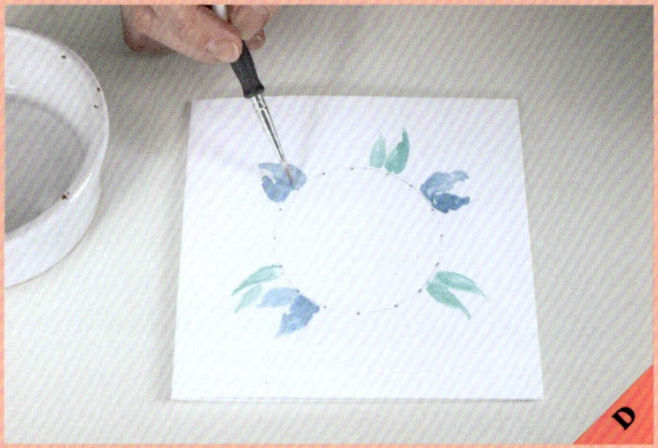

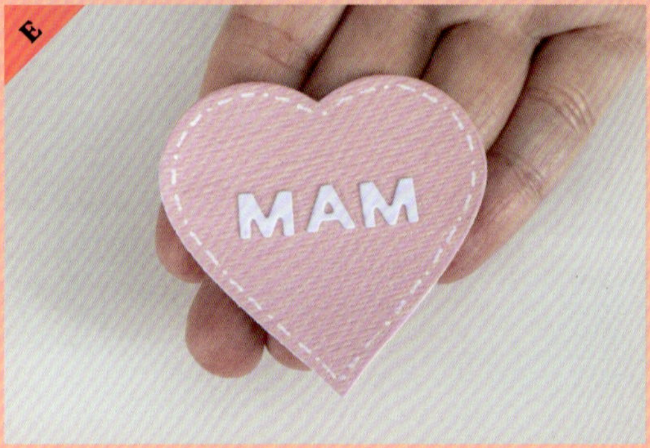

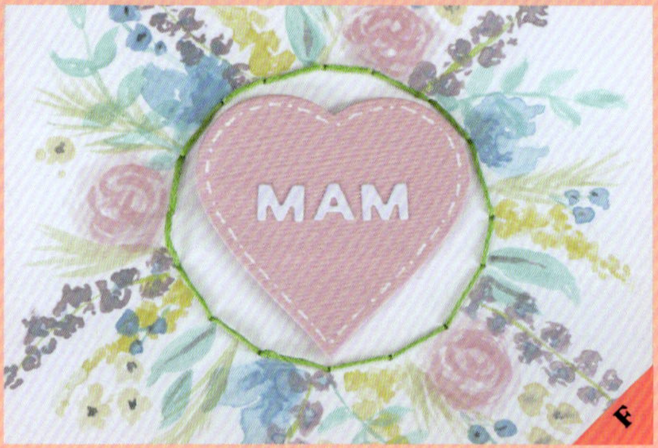

4 Using a pokey tool or needle, carefully pierce a hole through each marked dot. Gently erase any remaining pencil marks. **(C)**

5 Using watercolour paints, begin adding flowers and foliage around the circle. Start with simple shapes such as ovals, brushstrokes and dots in lighter shades, then layer darker tones on top to add detail and depth. **(D)**

6 Continue painting a variety of flowers and foliage, extending some leaves and stems towards the edges of the card to give the wreath a natural, full appearance.

7 Thread a needle with embroidery thread and stitch around the circle, working through the holes you created to form the stitched base of the wreath.

8 From pink card, cut out a heart shape for the centre of the design. Use a template if you prefer.

9 Using a white gel pen, draw small, evenly spaced marks around the edge of the heart to create a stitched effect.

10 Draw and cut out the letters for your sentiment from contrasting card, then glue them neatly on to the centre of the heart. **(E)**

11 Adhere the finished heart to the centre of your wreath on the card front to complete the design. **(F)**

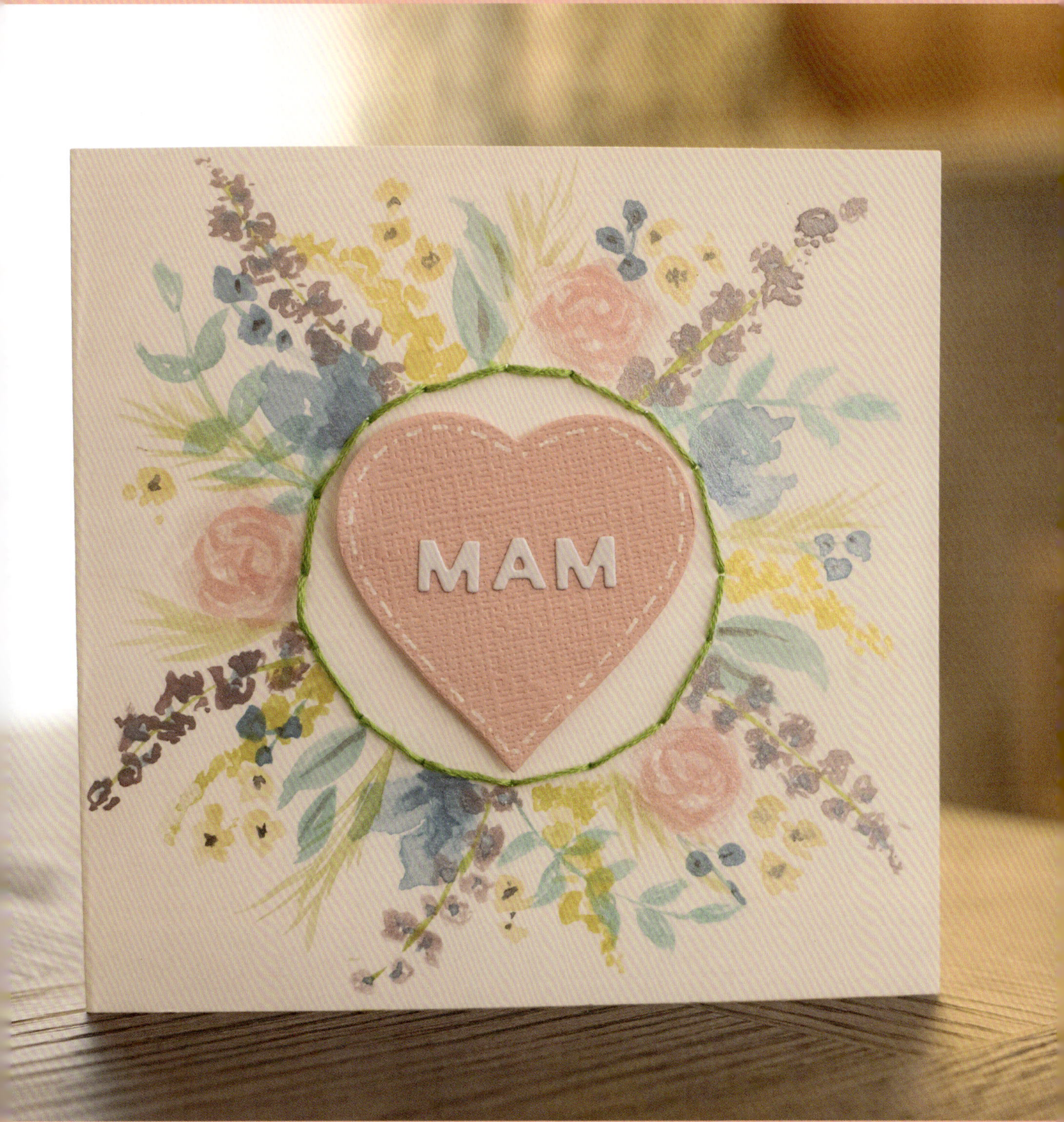
MAM

Intermediate

Lavender Bouquet

Fresh flowers are beautiful, but they don't last, which is why this felt lavender bouquet makes such a thoughtful Mother's Day gift. These delicate felt blooms capture the look of real lavender while lasting far beyond the season. Whether displayed on its own or arranged in a pretty vase, this everlasting bouquet is a lovely way to show Mam – or a special lady in your life – just how much she's appreciated.

You will need:

- Purple and green felt
- Scissors
- Ruler
- Glue gun
- Green craft wire
- Twine

TOP TIP **Add a drop or two of lavender essential oil to the felt stems as you assemble them to create a bouquet that delights with scent as well as appearance.**

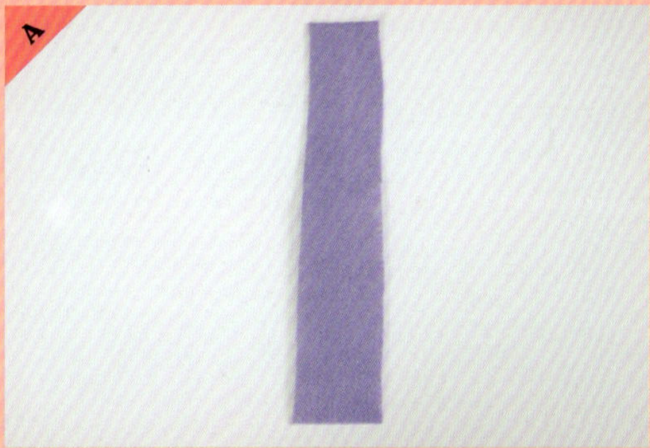

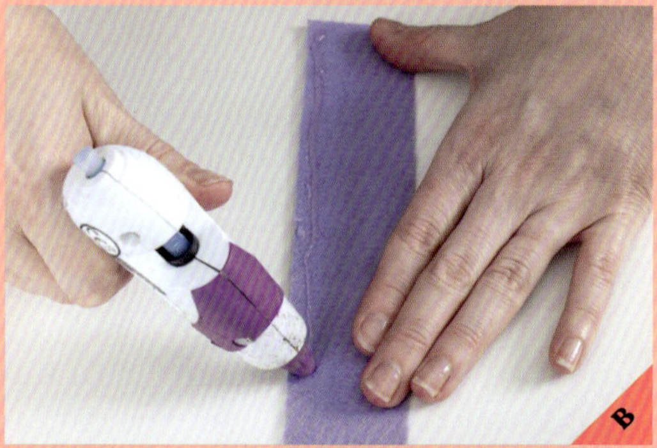

1 Cut a strip of purple felt measuring approximately 1" × 9". **(A)**

2 Run a thin line of hot glue along one long edge of the felt strip. **(B)**

3 Fold the felt strip in half lengthways and press along the glued edge to seal it securely. **(C)**

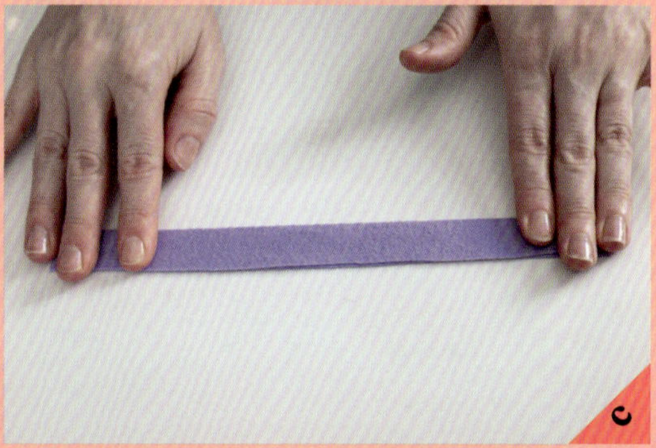

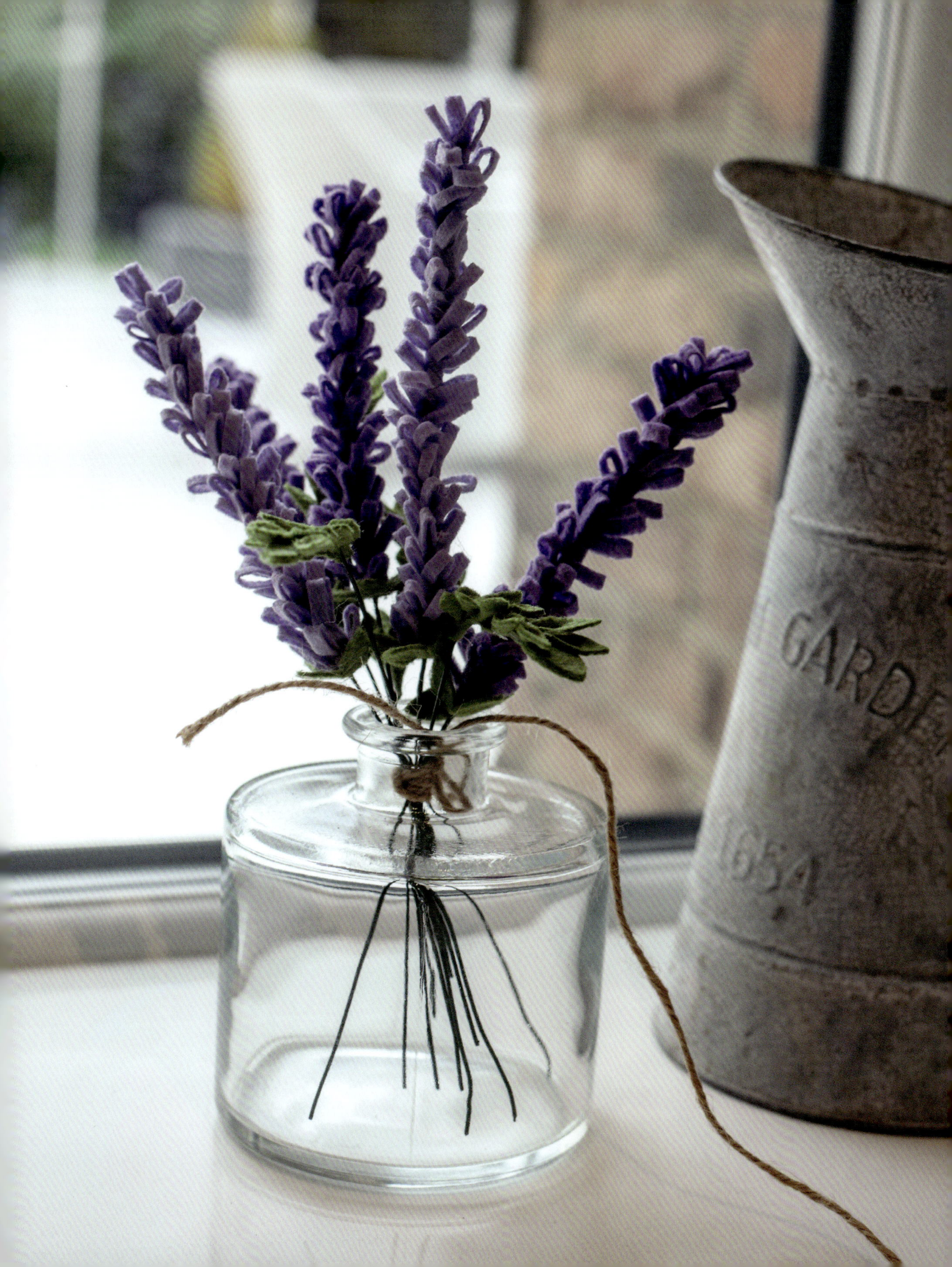
GARDE

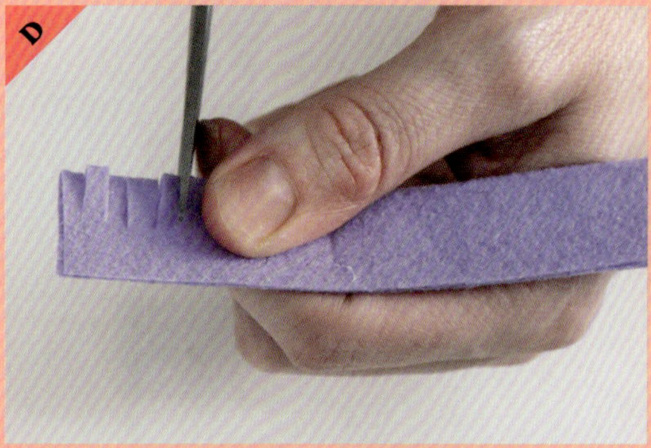

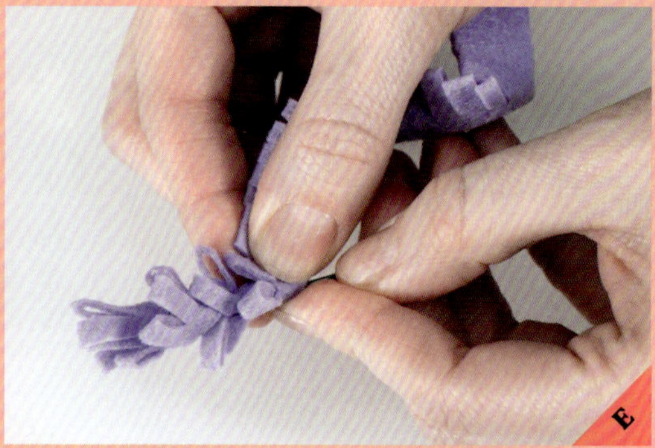

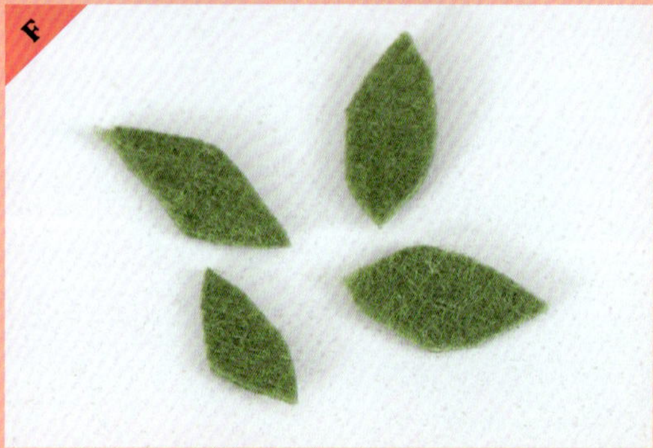

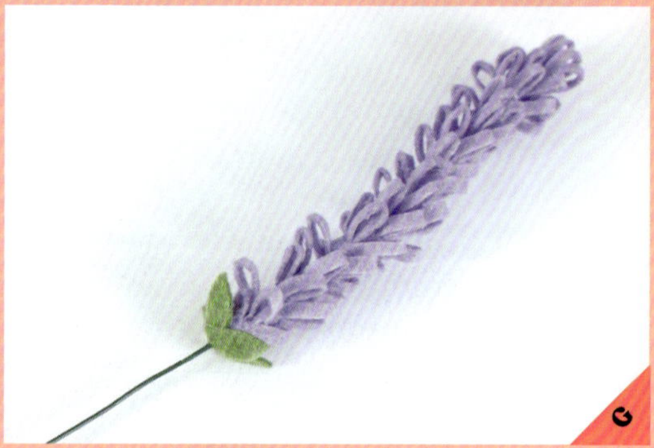

4 Once the glue has fully set, use scissors to snip evenly along the folded edge to create a fringe, taking care not to cut through the sealed edge. **(D)**

5 Add a small amount of hot glue to one end of the felt strip and attach it to the end of a piece of green craft wire measuring approximately 8".

6 Wind the fringed felt tightly down the length of the wire, adding small dabs of glue as you go to secure it in place and prevent gaps. **(E)**

7 Cut small leaf shapes from green felt and glue them to the base of the lavender stem. **(F)**

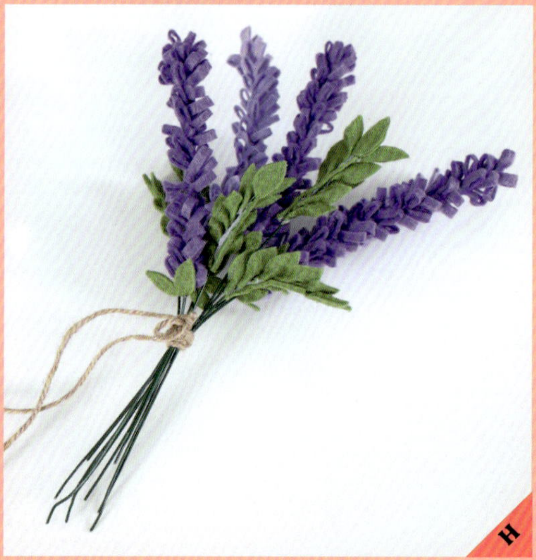

8 Repeat steps 1–7 to create as many lavender stems as you like, then gather them together and tie with twine to form a finished bouquet ready to gift. **(G and H)**

Easy

Lotion Bars

These homemade lotion bars are practical, pampering and ideal for gifting. Whether you're making a birthday present, a small treat for a friend, or a luxurious pick-me-up for yourself, they're a simple way to create something that feels indulgent and considered. Made with cocoa butter, coconut oil and beeswax, these bars melt gently on contact with the skin, leaving hands and bodies soft and nourished. Straightforward to make and completely handmade, they're a lovely introduction to DIY skincare. Please be aware that people can be allergic to some of the ingredients, so always ask about allergies before giving or using these bars.

TOP TIP If you prefer the bars fragrance-free and natural, simply skip the essential-oil step.

You will need:

- ½ cup beeswax pellets
- ½ cup cocoa butter
- ½ cup coconut oil
- Heatproof bowl
- Saucepan (for a bain-marie)
- Spoon or spatula
- Heatproof jug
- Essential oils (optional)
- Mould (silicone works best), with six equal sections
- Box or glass container, for gifting

To create six small lotion rounds:

1 Measure out all the ingredients and place them into a heatproof bowl.

2 Set the bowl over a saucepan of gently simmering water to create a bain-marie, making sure the base of the bowl does not touch the water. **(A)**

3 Stir the mixture continuously until the beeswax, cocoa butter and coconut oil have completely melted into a smooth, golden liquid. **(B)**

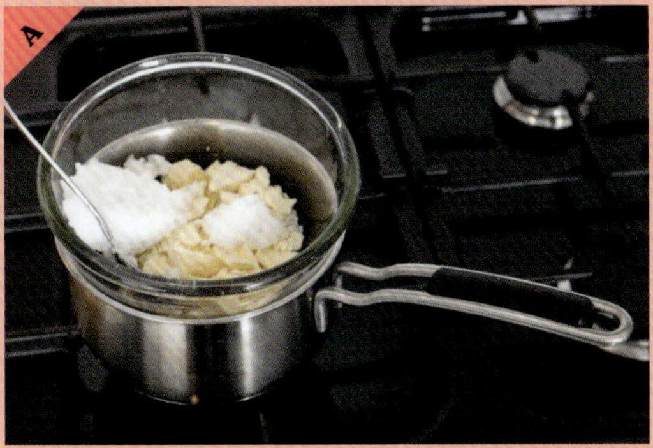
A

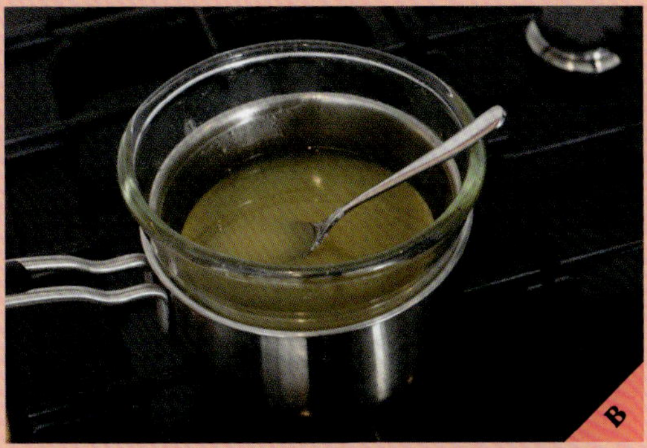
B

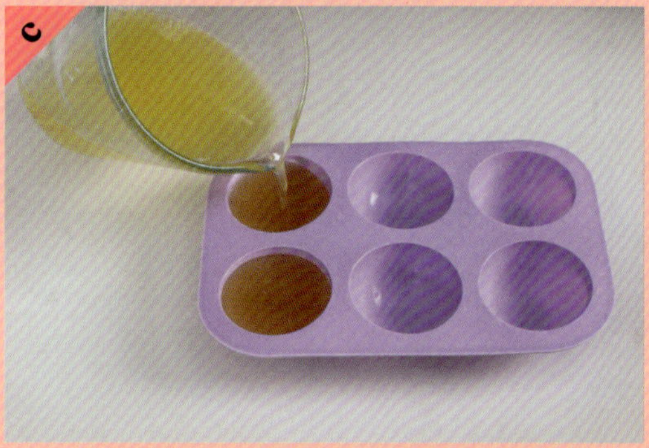

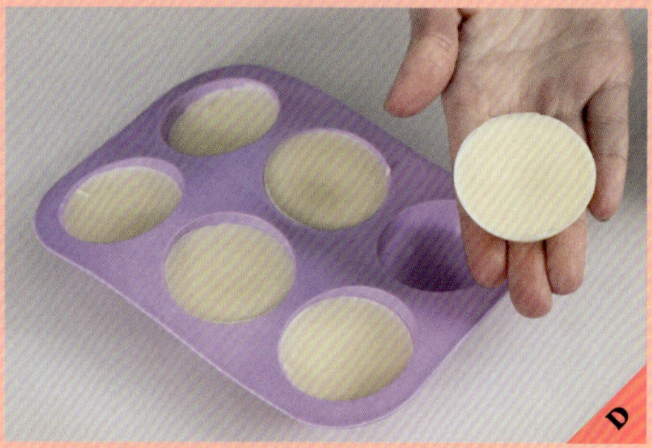

4 Carefully pour the melted mixture into a heatproof jug to make pouring easier.

5 If using essential oils to personalize the scent, add a few drops now and stir well, then pour the mixture evenly into the moulds. **(C)**

6 Leave the lotion bars to harden in a cool place or in the fridge for several hours, until fully set. **(D)**

7 Once set, gently remove the bars from the moulds and package them in a pretty box or glass container, ready for gifting or treating yourself!

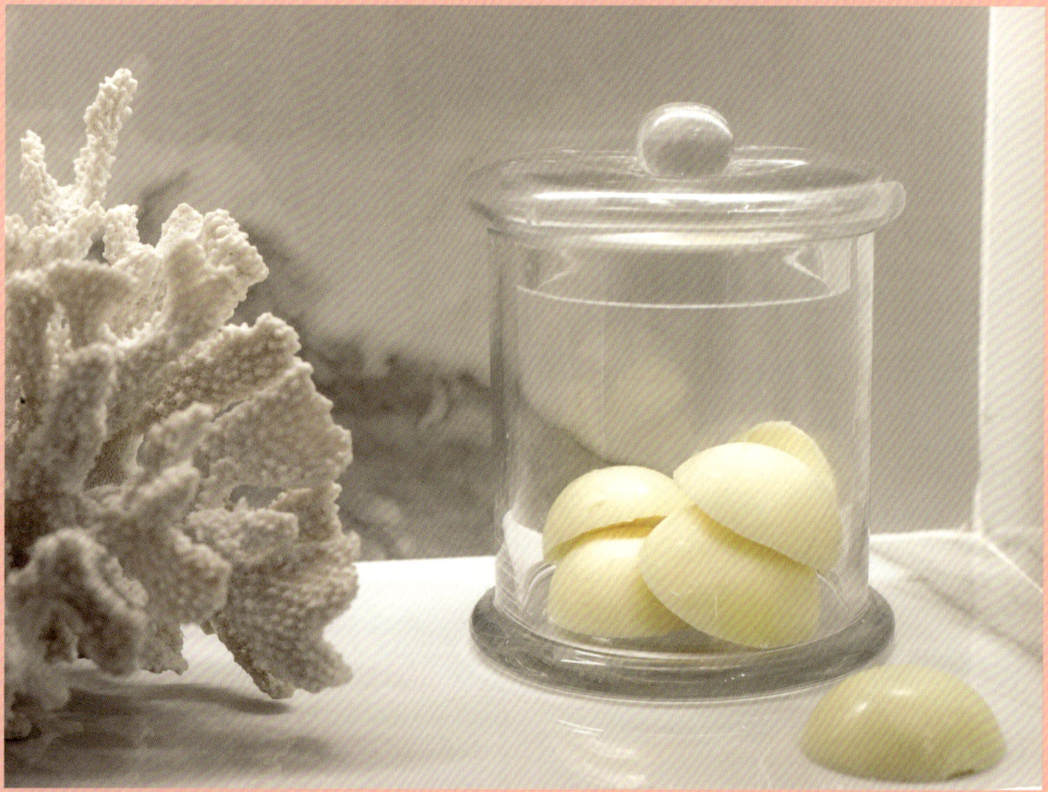

Advanced

Show Your Love Card

Mother's Day is such a lovely opportunity to make something truly meaningful, and this make is guaranteed to make her feel extra special. There are a lot of steps to this card, but the intricate handmade roses, along with the bursting hearts when the card opens out, create such a gorgeous surprise. I always think a handmade card says so much more than something shop-bought. It shows time, care and love!

You will need:

- Kraft card
- Pink and patterned paper
- Pencil
- Scissors (small and medium-sized)
- Ruler
- Glue tape pen
- Cocktail stick
- Glue gun

1 Fold a piece of card measuring 10″ × 10″ in half. Turn it and fold it again to create four equal squares. **(A)**

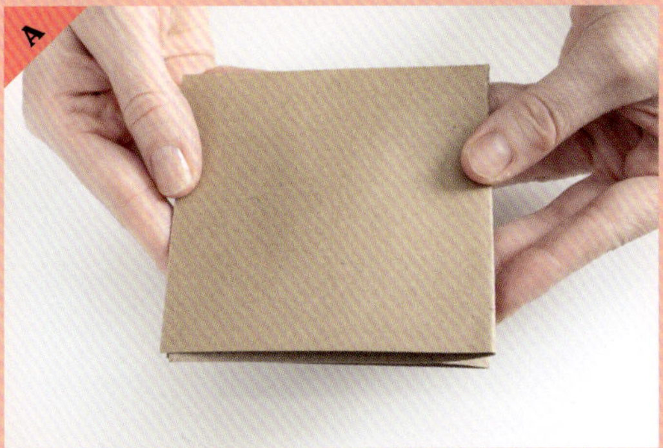
A

2 Open the piece back out and fold it in half diagonally. **(B)**

3 With the card positioned like a diamond in front of you, fold it upwards so the two diagonal folds come together and are sandwiched between the outer layers. You should now have a folded square measuring 5″ × 5″. **(C)**

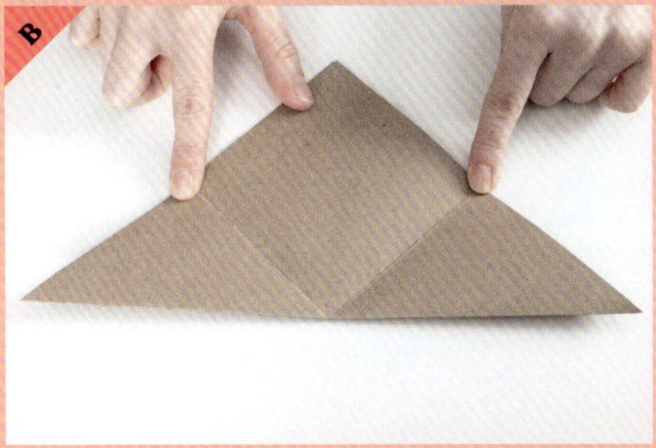
B

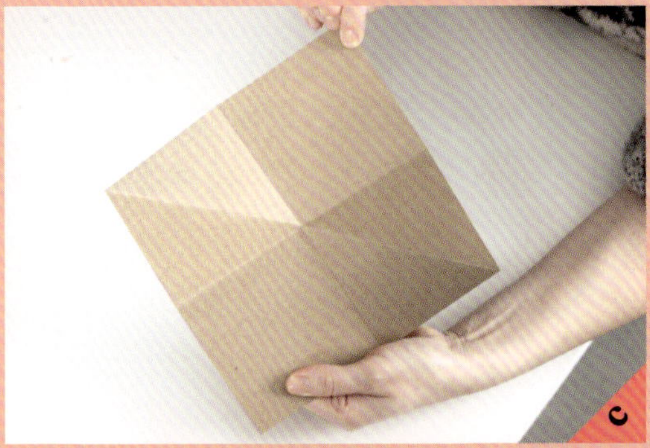
C

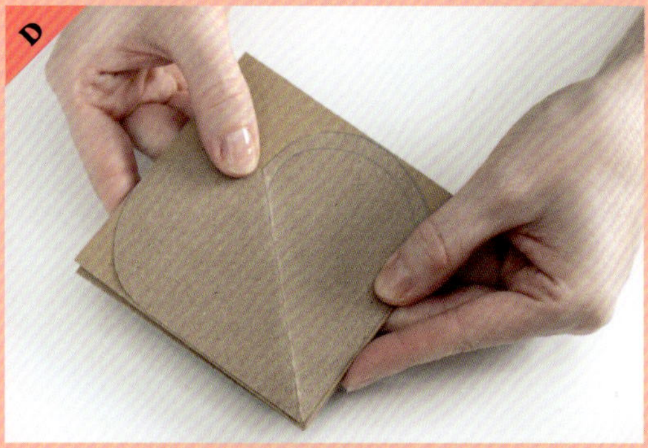

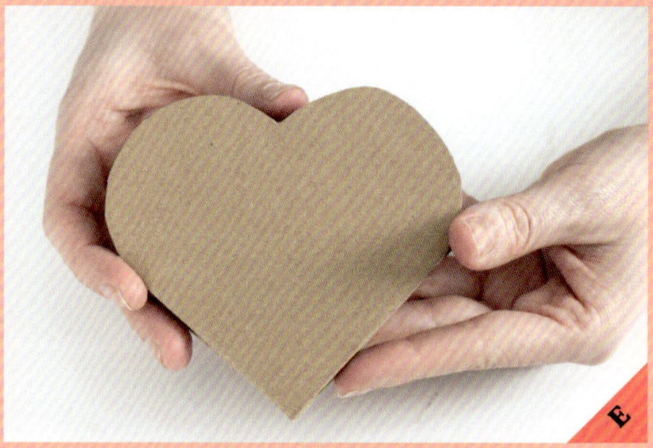

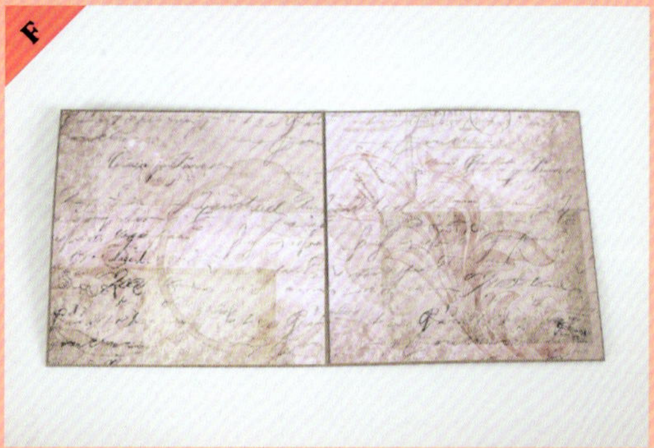

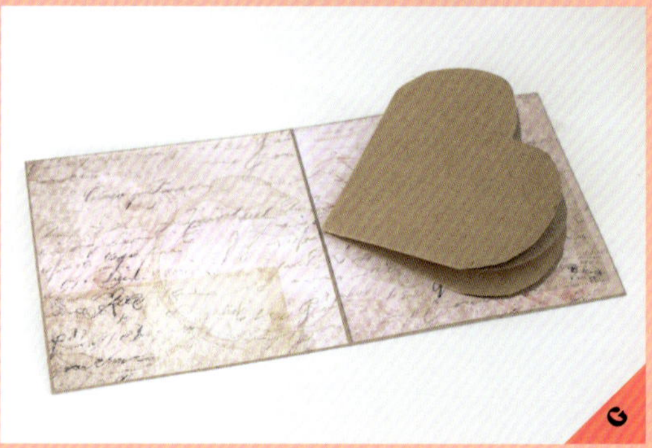

4 Set the card to one side and create a heart template by folding a 5" × 5" piece of scrap paper in half, then drawing half a heart shape along the folded edge and cutting it out. Use a pencil to mark a ¼" border on the heart.

5 With all the folded edges positioned at the bottom, draw the top half of a heart along the open edge of the card, using the template. **(D)**

6 Carefully cut along the drawn line, then open the card out to reveal the full heart shape. **(E)**

7 Create a 5" × 5" card base and mat the inside with patterned paper. **(F)**

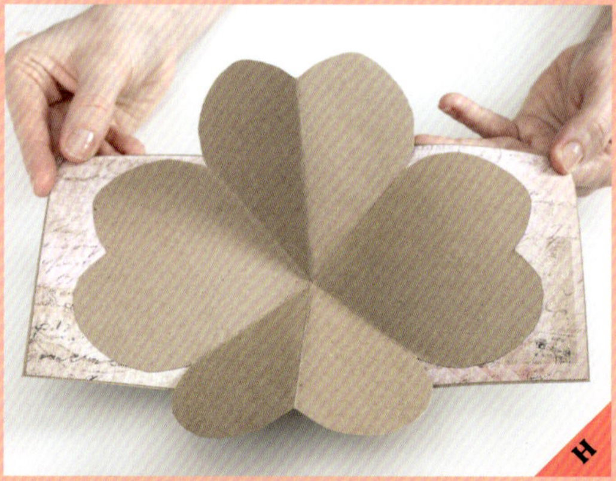

8 Take the heart shape and use some adhesive to attach it to the right-hand inside panel. **(G)**

9 Repeat this step on the left-hand side so that when you open the card, the hearts unfold. **(H)**

10 Take the heart template and cut away the ¼" border marked in step 4.

11 Use this template to cut out four hearts from pink paper then adhere them to the four heart panels inside the card. Split the top and bottom pink hearts into four separate pieces to prevent the paper from tearing when opening, and to ensure the card opens and closes neatly. **(I and J)**

12 Mat and layer a piece of 4½" × 4½" Kraft card onto some patterned paper measuring 4¾" × 4¾" then draw around the heart template. **(K)**

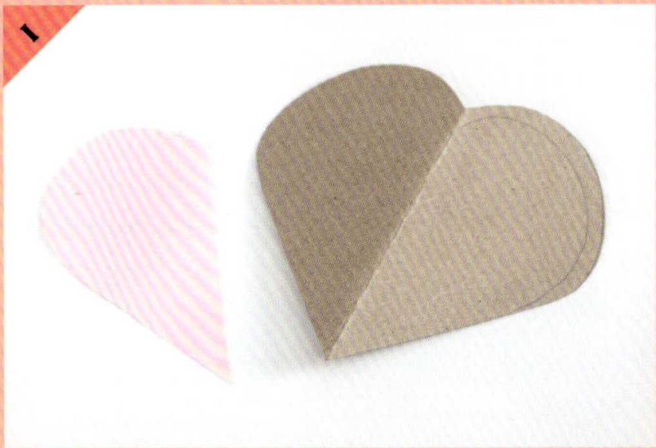

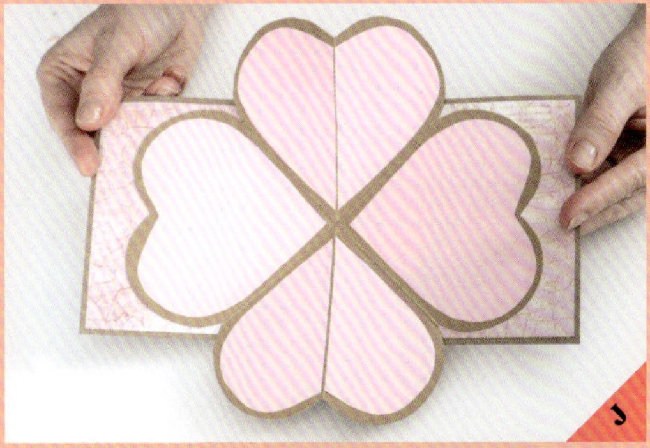

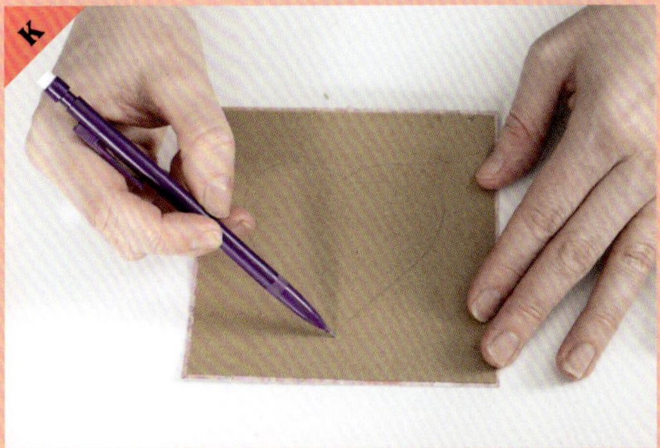

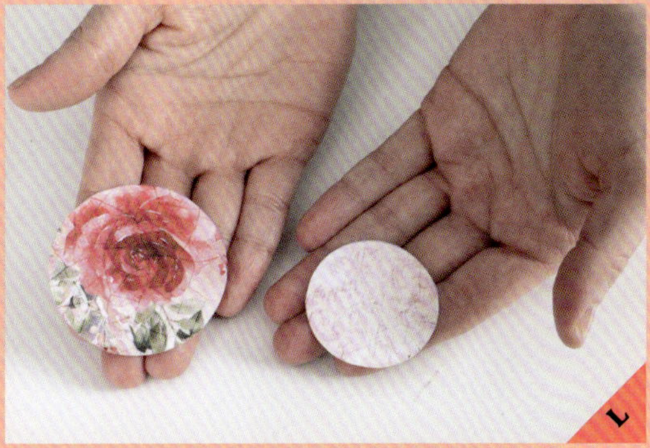

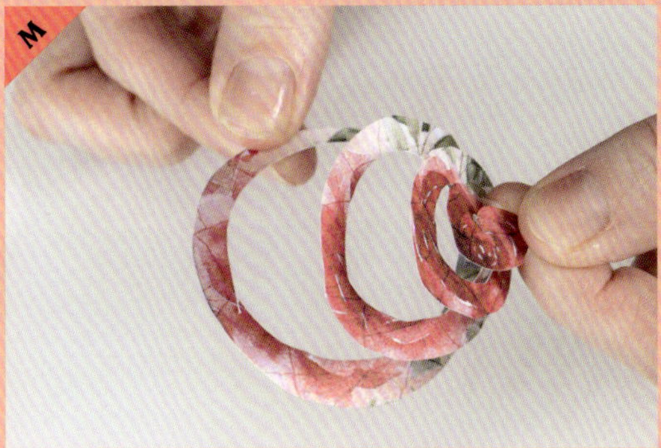

13 Use two circular templates to cut out two different-sized circles from patterned paper – a small circle of 1¼" diameter and a larger one of 1¾" diameter. **(L)**

14 Use a small pair of scissors to cut into one of the circles and work your way towards the centre until you have a spiral. **(M)**

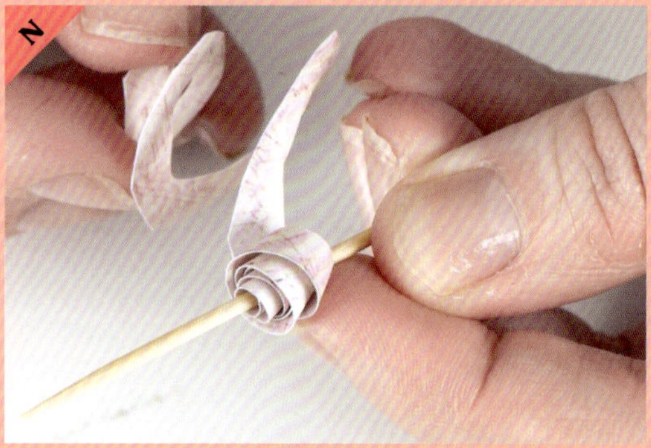

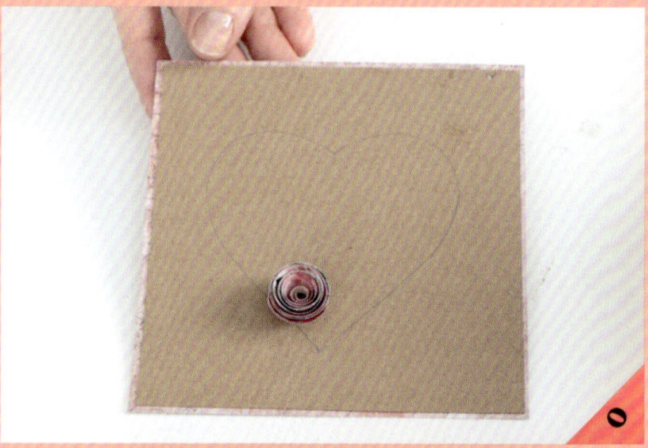

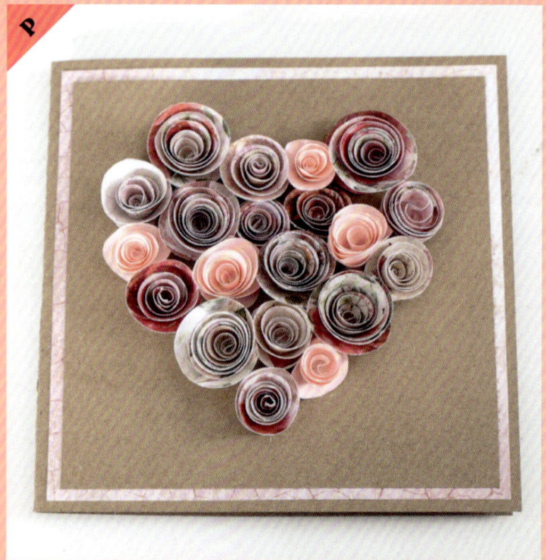

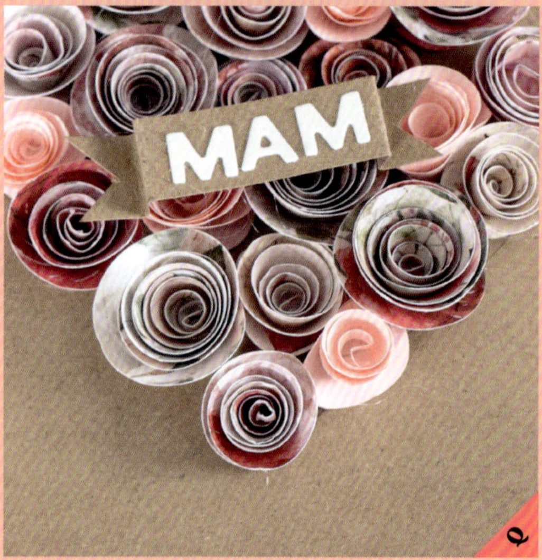

15 Take a cocktail stick and wind the paper tightly around it to create a rose shape. **(N)**

16 Slide the rose off the end of the stick and add some hot glue to its base to keep its shape.

17 Using hot glue, adhere the rose to the Kraft card panel inside the heart shape. **(O)**

18 Repeat steps 13–17 until you have completely filled the heart shape with roses then fix this panel to the card front. **(P)**

19 Cut a small ribbon shape from Kraft card. Add cut-out white card letters to spell your chosen sentiment, then glue the ribbon to the front of the card to finish. **(Q)**

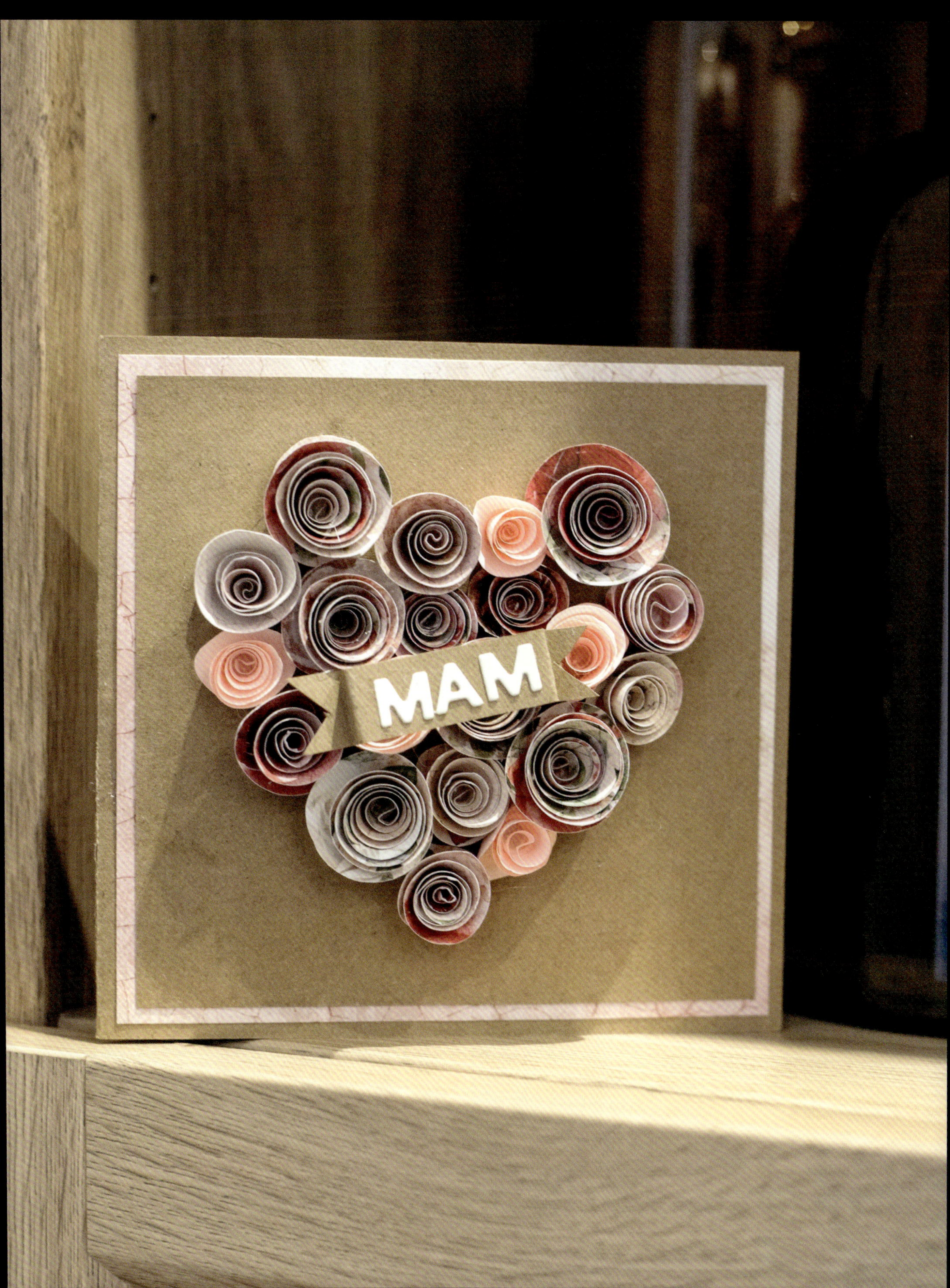
MAM

Intermediate

Chocolate Truffle Bouquet

If you enjoy projects that look really impressive but are actually wonderfully simple to make, you're going to adore this one! These cheerful paper flowers add a bright pop of colour to your home and make a gorgeous handmade gift – perfect for Mother's Day, birthdays, or just because.

What makes this project especially appealing is how clever it is. Using just a few paper strips and some recycled packing paper, you can create a long-lasting bouquet that's inexpensive and ideal for batch crafting. It's a great way to use up scraps while turning everyday materials into something decorative and special. So grab your glue gun, get everything prepped and let's get blooming – because handmade always means more!

You will need:

- ½" × 6" strips yellow crepe paper
- 2½" × 14" strips white crepe paper
- 2½" × 7" strips green crepe paper
- Scissors
- Foil-wrapped chocolate truffles
- Wooden skewers
- Glue gun
- Recycled packing paper
- Glass vase or jar
- Ribbon

1 Fold a yellow paper strip into quarters.

2 Using scissors, snip thin vertical cuts along one long edge, leaving approximately ½" uncut at the bottom to create a fringe. **(A)**

3 Take a white paper strip, fold it into quarters and cut petal shapes along one long edge, stopping approximately ¼" from the bottom so the strip remains intact. **(B)**

A

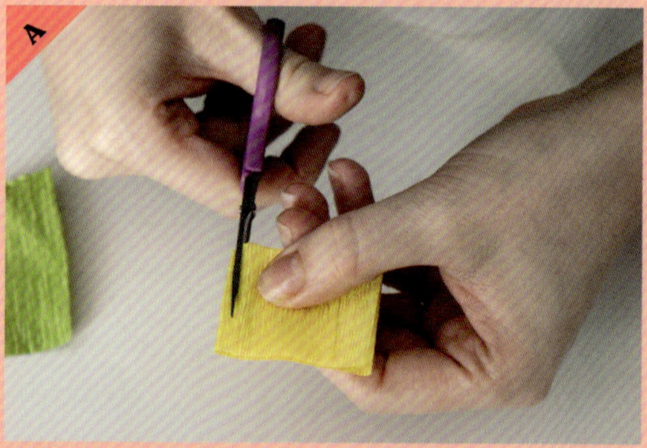

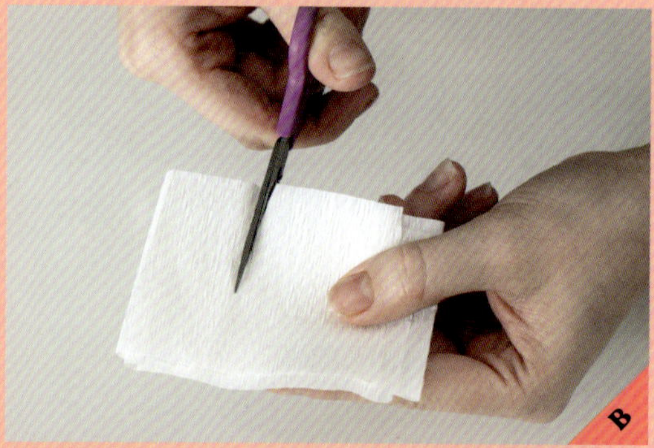

B

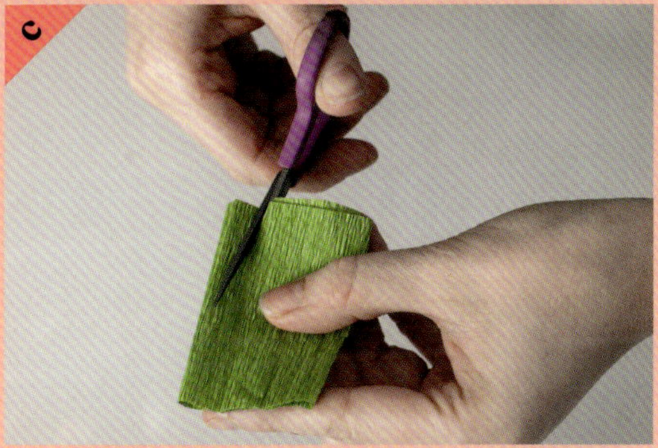

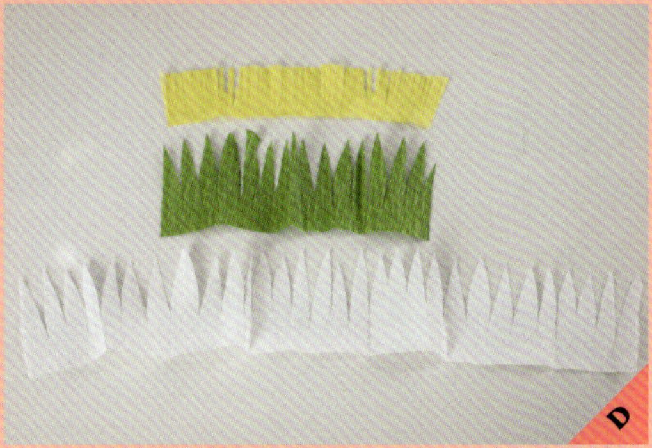

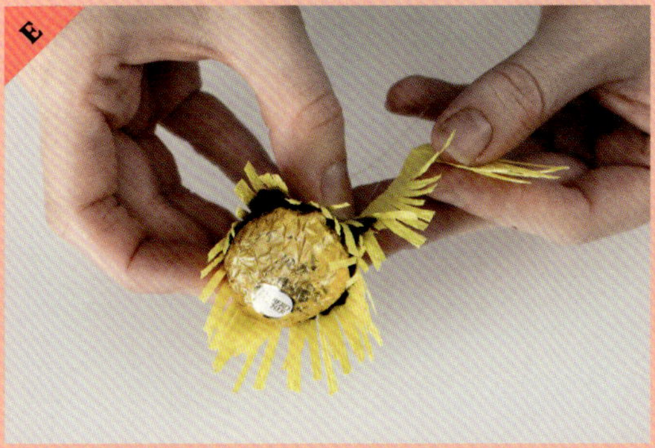

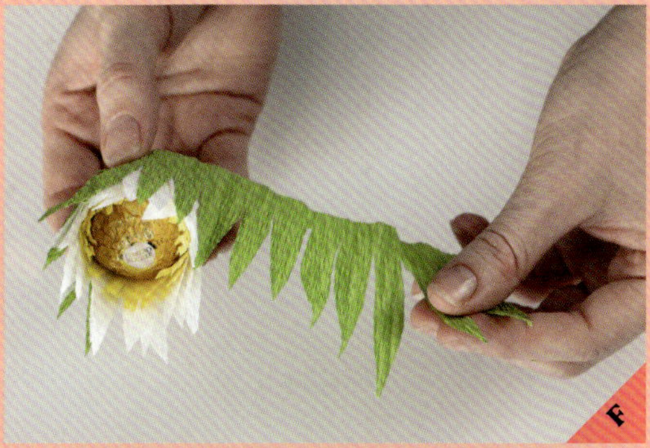

4 Repeat the same folding-and-cutting process with a green paper strip to create leaf shapes. **(C and D)**

5 Apply a small amount of hot glue to the edge of a truffle paper and secure the yellow fringed strip in place. Wrap the remaining crepe paper around the truffle, adding small dabs of glue as needed to keep it secure. **(E)**

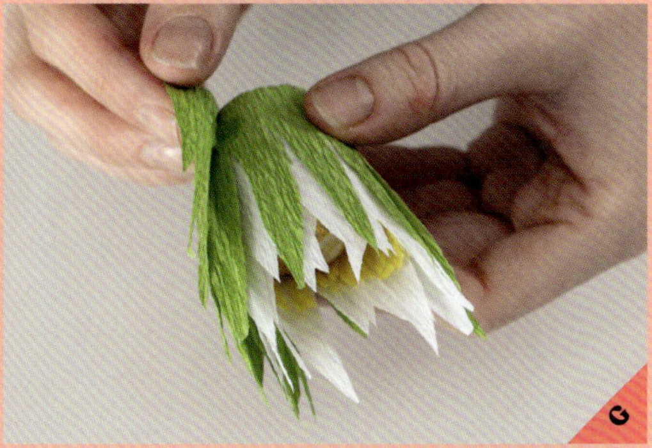

6 Repeat the wrapping process with the white and green strips. As you work, gently stretch the paper to give the petals and leaves a more natural shape. **(F and G)**

7 Insert a wooden skewer into the base of the flower, securing it with hot glue if needed. **(H)**

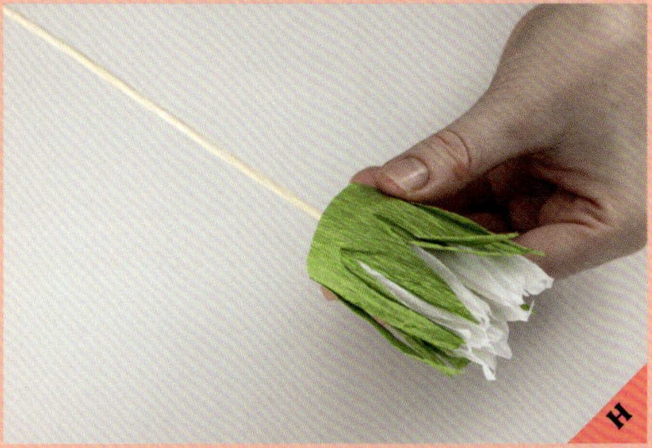

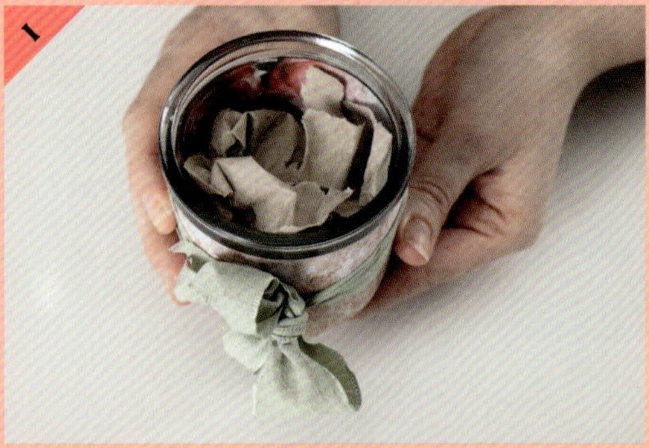

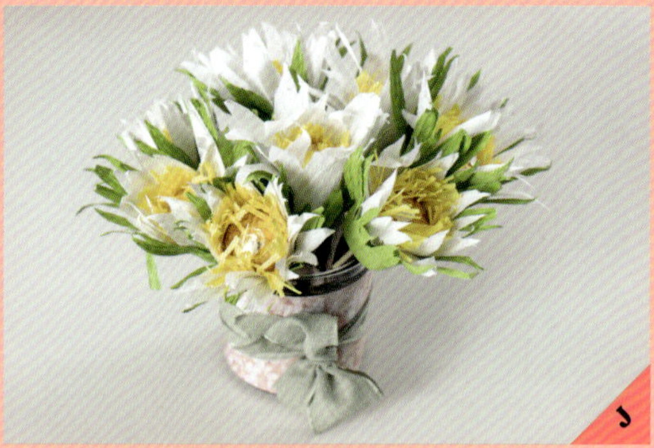

8 Repeat steps 1–7 to create enough flowers to fill your vase or jar.

9 Arrange the flowers in the vase and use recycled packing paper to hold them securely in place. If your container is shallow, trim the skewers to size using scissors. Finish with ribbon if desired. **(I and J)**

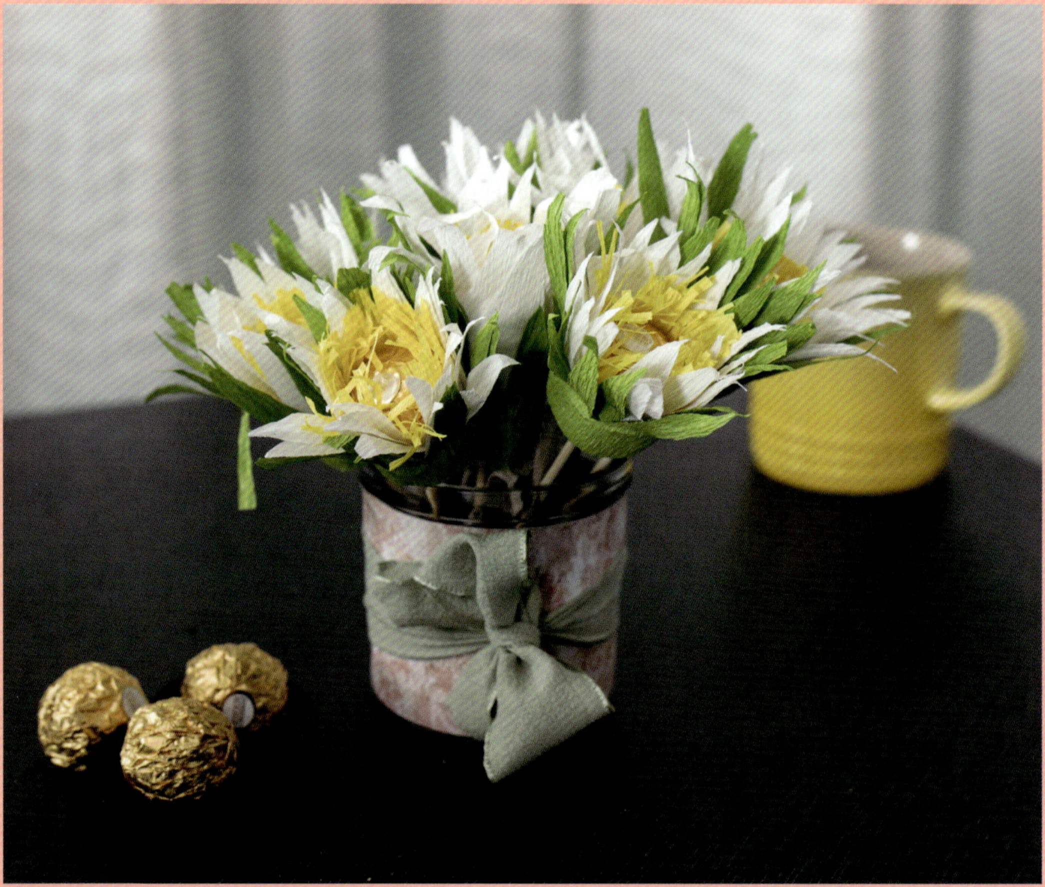

Intermediate

Photo Plaque

This personalized DAD plaque transforms a simple piece of wood into a stylish display for photos and memories. Designed as a heartfelt gift for Father's Day, it's a thoughtful way to celebrate dads and show just how much care and effort has gone into making something by hand.

TOP TIP **Take your time when creating the starter holes with the pokey tool. Even spacing will give the nails a stronger hold and make winding the string much easier and more controlled.**

You will need:

- 6" × 12" piece of wood
- Paper or copy paper
- Pencil
- Pokey tool
- Chopping board
- Sheet of felt (or similar material)
- Picture-hanging nails
- Hammer
- String
- Wood glue or super glue
- Mini craft pegs
- Photos or Polaroids
- Additional string (for hanging)

1 Decide which word or letters you want to feature on the plaque. For this project, the letters spell DAD, with each letter measuring 4" × 3".

2 On a sheet of paper, draw the letters by hand or print a template from your computer. Cut out the letters and trace around them directly on to the wood. **(A)**

3 Using a pokey tool, create starter holes around the outline of each letter, spacing them approximately ¾" apart. **(B)**

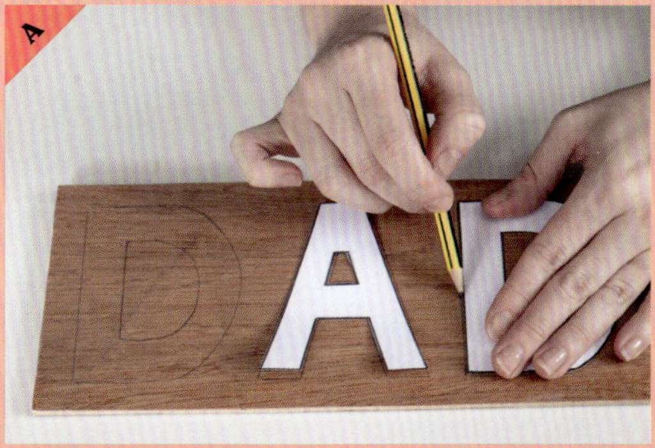

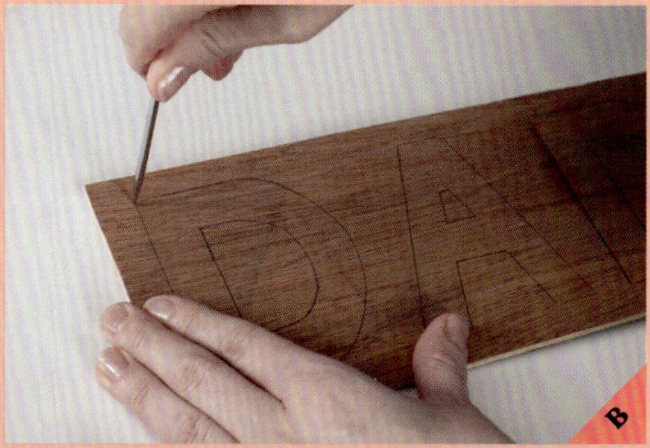

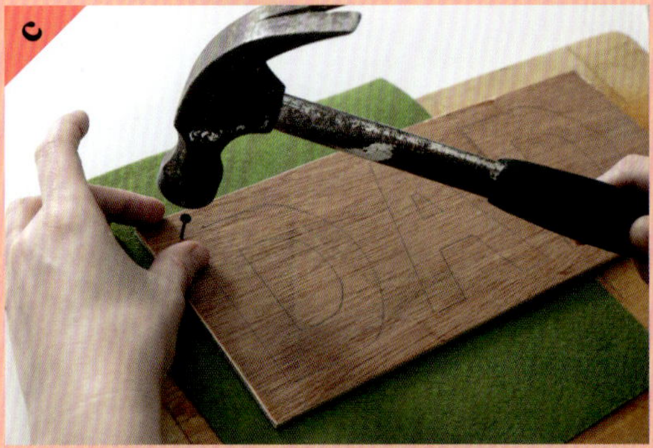

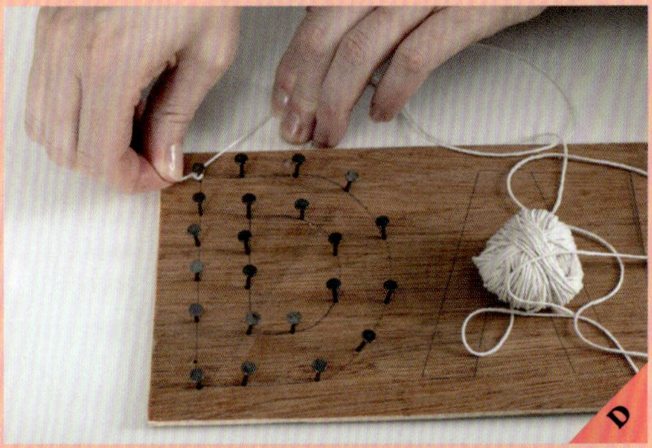

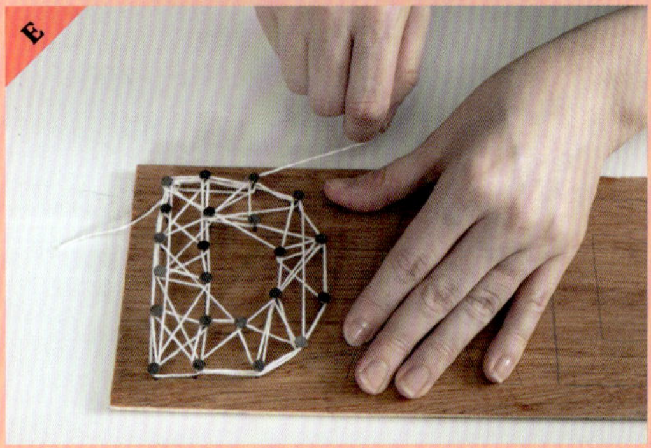

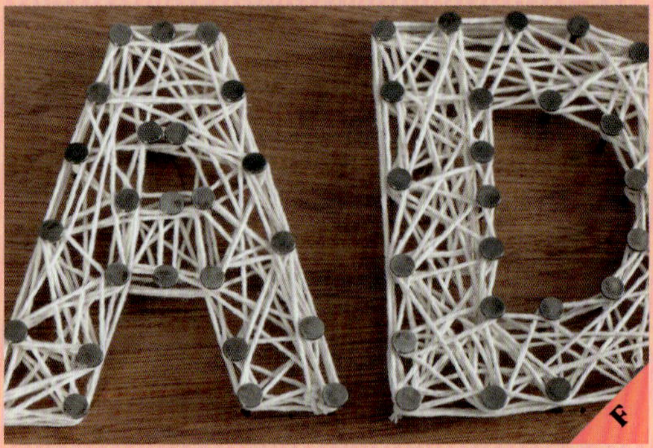

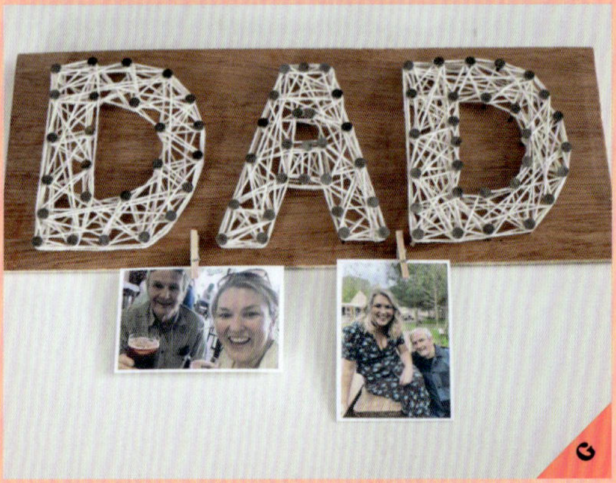

4 Place the piece of wood on a chopping board with a layer of felt or similar material in between for extra protection. Hammer a picture-hanging nail into each starter hole, ensuring the nail is secure but leaving enough height above the surface for winding string. **(C)**

5 Tie one end of the string firmly to a nail, then begin winding it around the nails to fill in the letter shape. Work randomly, keeping the string taut as you go, then tie the string in a neat knot and trim to finish. **(D and E)**

6 Repeat this process for each remaining letter. **(F)**

7 Apply wood glue or super glue to the back of the mini craft pegs and attach them along the bottom edge of the plaque. Allow the glue to set, then use the pegs to display your photos or Polaroids. **(G)**

8 Attach a length of string to the back of the plaque for hanging and check it's secure. Your personalized DAD plaque is now ready to be gifted and displayed!

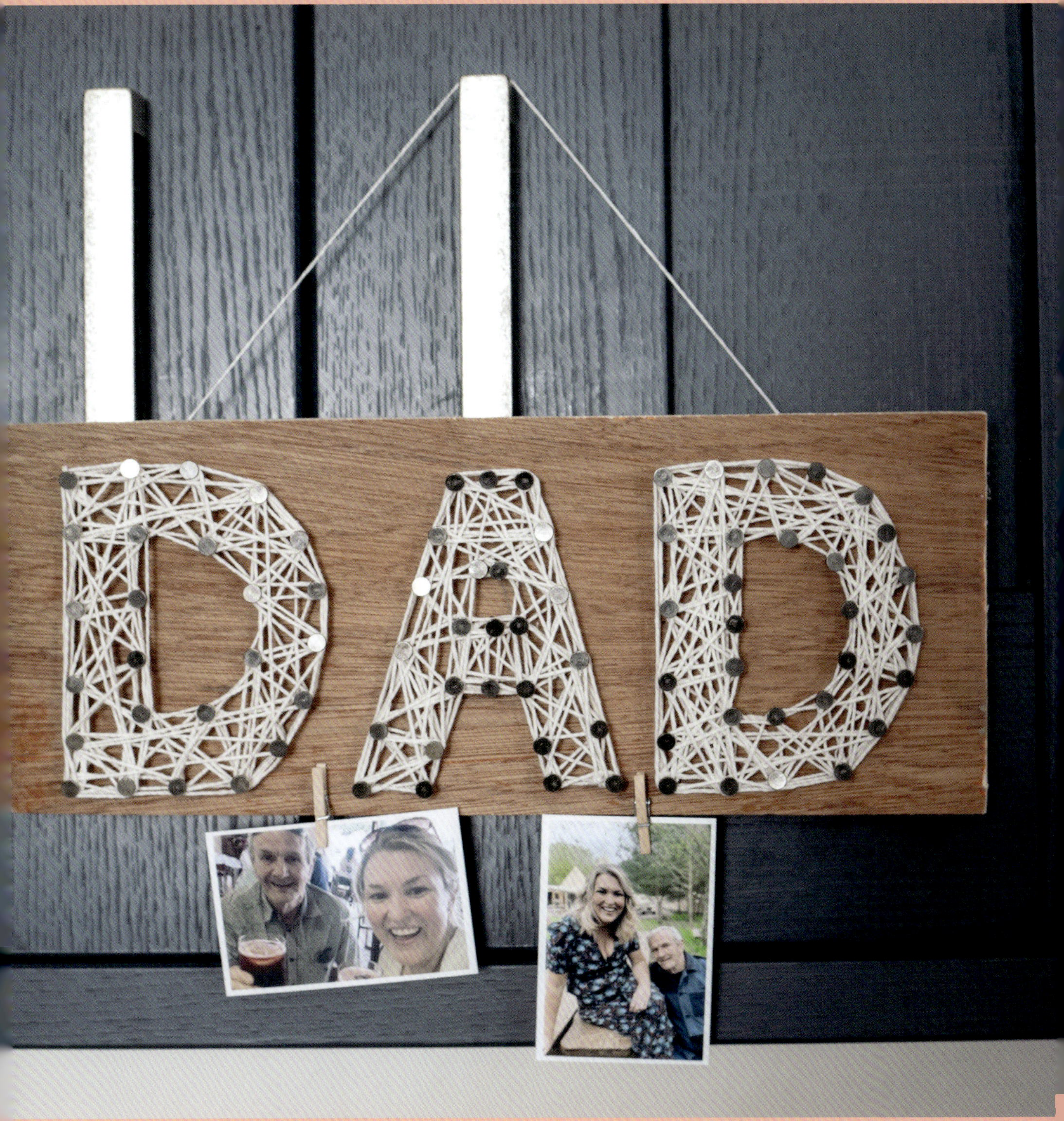
DAD

Easy

Handmade Shaving Cream

If you're looking for a quick, thoughtful gift that's both luxurious and practical, this DIY whipped shaving cream is a great option! It's super easy to make, smells amazing, and leaves skin feeling soft and nourished. The best part? You know exactly what's going into it, using just a handful of natural ingredients, although always check whether the person you plan to give this to is allergic to any of the ingredients before doing so!

TOP TIP **Add essential oils that you know your special someone will love!**

You will need:

- ½ cup shea butter
- ½ cup coconut oil
- ¼ cup grapeseed oil
- Heatproof bowl
- Saucepan (for a bain-marie)
- Spoon or spatula
- ½ tbsp bicarbonate of soda
- Essential oils
- Hand mixer or stick blender
- Glass jar (washed on a hot dishwasher cycle to sterilize)

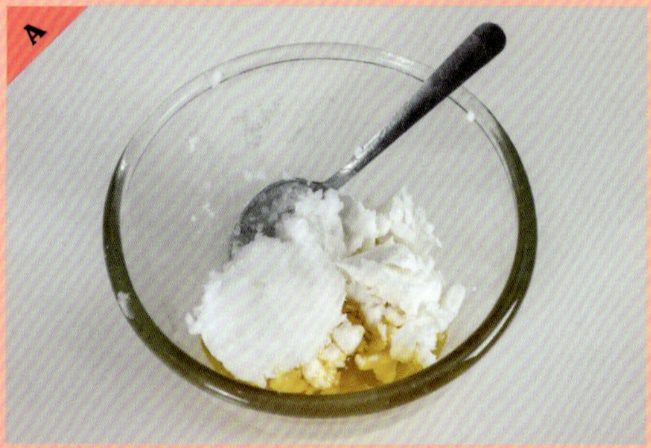

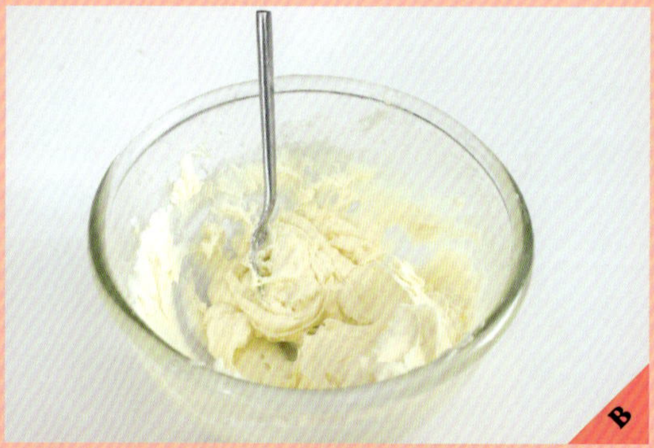

1 Add the shea butter, coconut oil and grapeseed oil into a heatproof bowl. **(A)**

2 Place the bowl over a saucepan of gently simmering water to create a bain-marie, making sure the base of the bowl does not touch the water. Melt the ingredients slowly, stirring occasionally until fully combined.

3 Add the bicarbonate of soda and a few drops of essential oils, and mix well. **(B)**

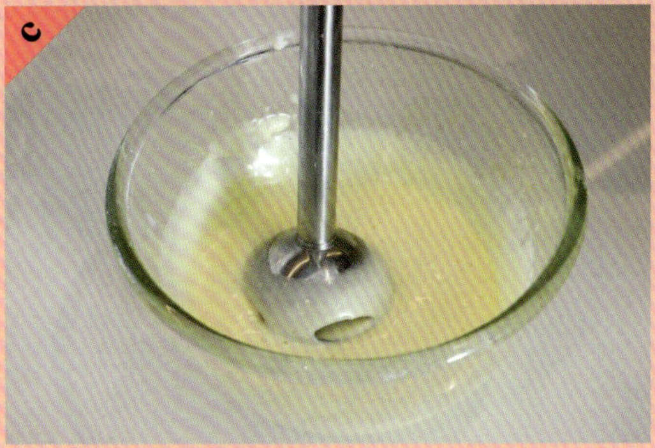

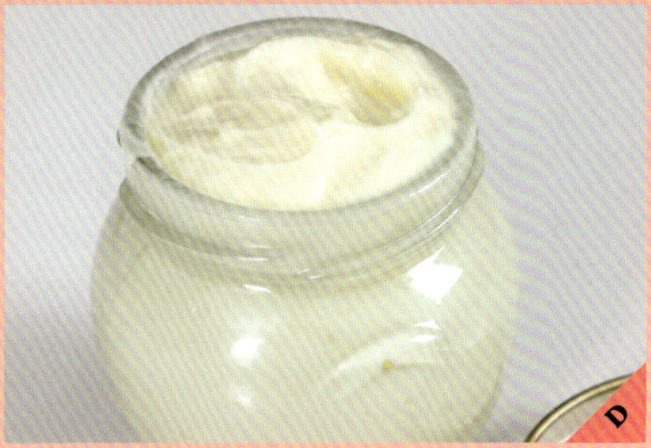

4 Remove the bowl from the heat and allow the mixture to cool slightly, then place it in the fridge for around 1 hour, or until it has firmed up but is not completely solid. This will ensure the mixture can be whipped properly.

5 Using a hand mixer or stick blender, whip the mixture until it becomes light, fluffy and smooth. **(C)**

6 Spoon the finished shaving cream into a clean glass jar, ready for gifting or use. **(D)**

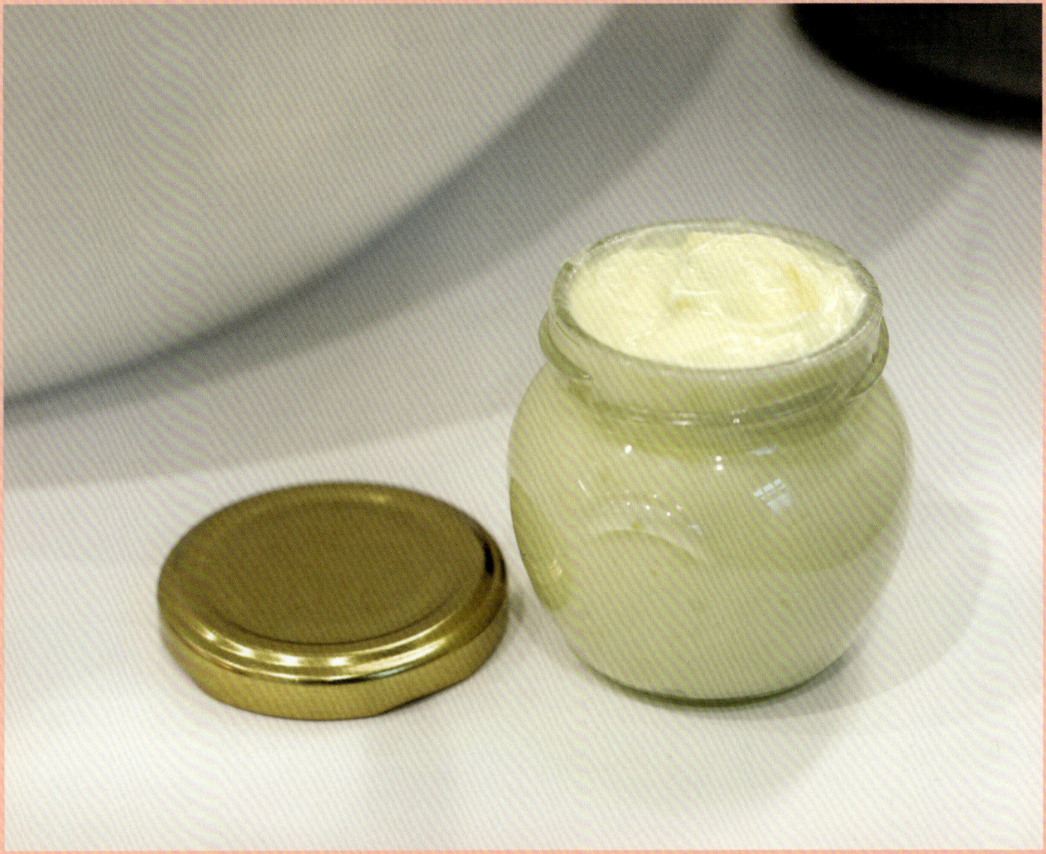

Advanced

Funky Shirt Card

Looking for a Father's Day card that really stands out? This funky shirt card is a clever design that's both fun to make and impressive to look at! Perfect for dads who appreciate a personal touch, it's a project that lets you get creative with patterns, textures and little embellishments. From folding the paper to creating a tiny hanger, every step adds a handmade element that will make your card extra special.

You will need:

- Thick patterned paper
- Ruler
- Thin craft wire
- Strong scissors or wire cutter
- Paper trimmer or scissors
- 5" × 7" white card base
- Kraft card
- Blue card
- Glue tape pen
- Black fine liner
- Small hole punch or pokey tool
- Gold thread
- Clear adhesive tape
- Wooden letters

To create the shirt:

1 Cut out a piece of patterned paper measuring 6" × 4".

2 Holding the paper in portrait orientation, fold in 1" from each long side so that both folded edges meet neatly in the centre. **(A)**

3 On one of the ends, fold the top edge back on itself by ½" to create the collar, then fold each of the top corners inwards around ½" down the piece of paper to create the collar shape. **(B)**

4 At the bottom end of the piece, fold out each of the bottom corners as shown – this will create the sleeves. **(C)**

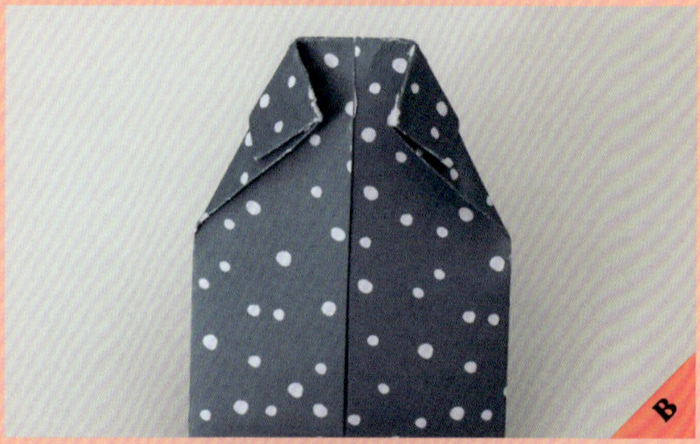
B

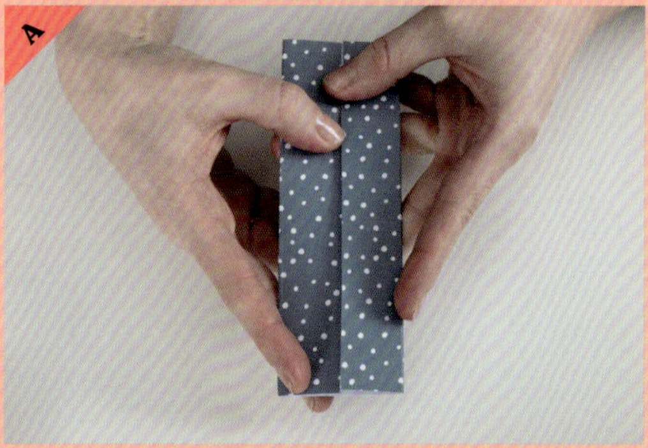
A

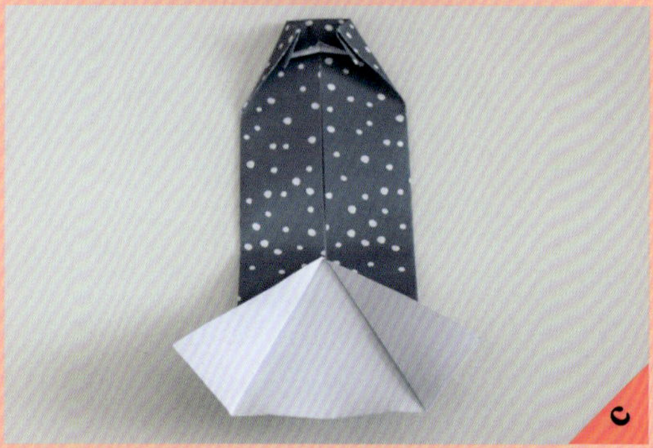
C

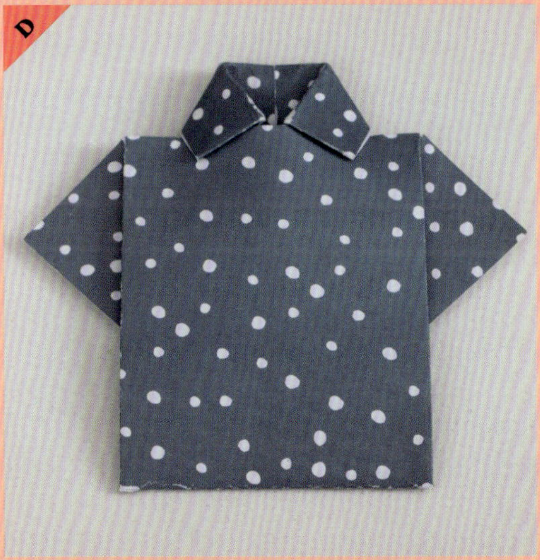

5 Fold the bottom section up and tuck it under the collar you created in step 3 to complete the shirt shape. **(D)**

6 To create the shirt hanger, cut a short length of thin craft wire and bend both ends upwards. **(E)**

7 Bend one end over to form the hook, leaving a short straight section to form the body of the hanger. **(F)**

8 Twist the remaining wire around the neck of the hooked end to secure it. **(G)**

9 Place the finished shirt on to the hanger and set aside while you make the card base.

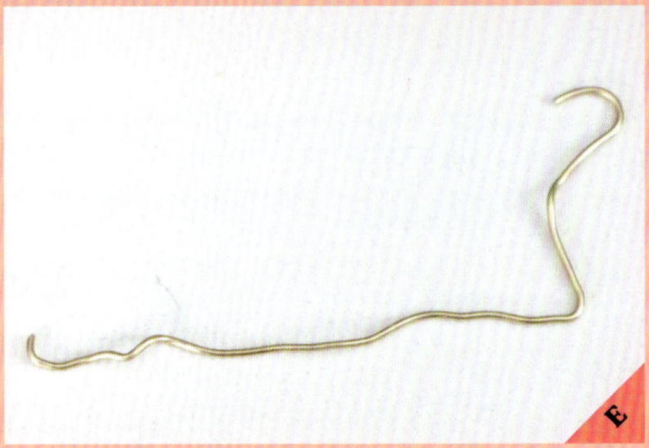

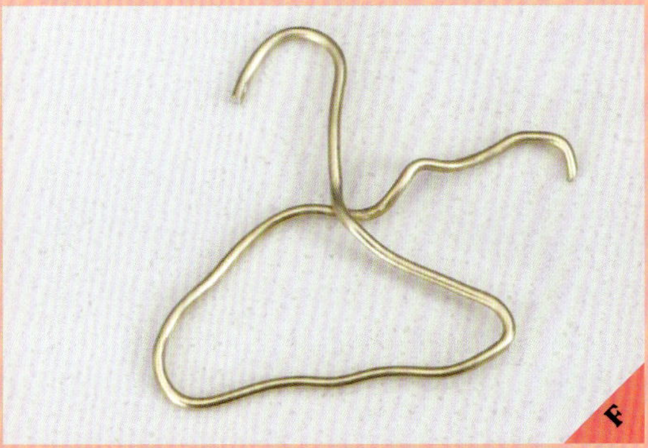

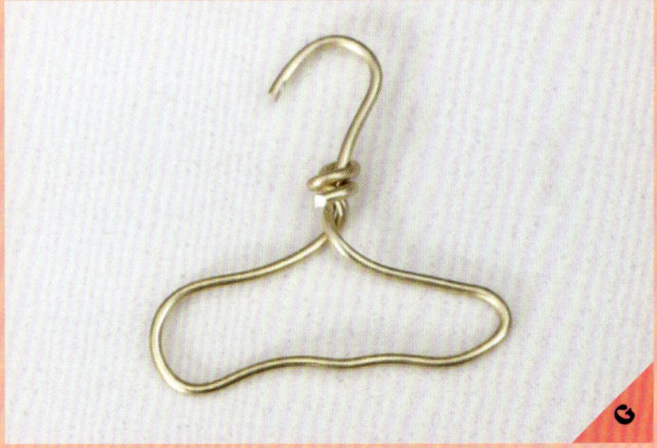

TOP TIP **Add tiny buttons or gems, washi tape stripes, or even a mini tie to personalize the shirt!**

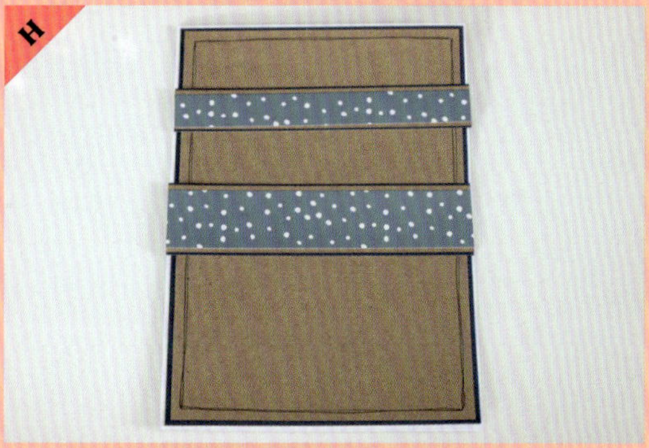

To create the card base:

1 Take the 5″ × 7″ white card base and mat it with blue card measuring 4⅞″ × 6⅞″.

2 Cut a piece of Kraft card measuring 4¾ × 6¾″ and layer it on top of the blue mat.

3 Use a black fine liner to sketch a border around the edge of the card.

4 Mat and layer two strips of patterned paper on to blue and Kraft card and adhere them to the top two thirds of the card front. **(H)**

5 To prepare the layered panel, cut a piece of white card measuring 3⅜″ × 4⅝″, a piece of Kraft card measuring 3¼″ × 4½″, a piece of blue card measuring 3⅛″ × 4⅜″ and a piece of white card measuring 3″ × 4¼″. **(I)**

6 Use a black fine liner to sketch a border around the smallest piece of white card.

7 Layer and adhere the pieces together with a glue tape pen.

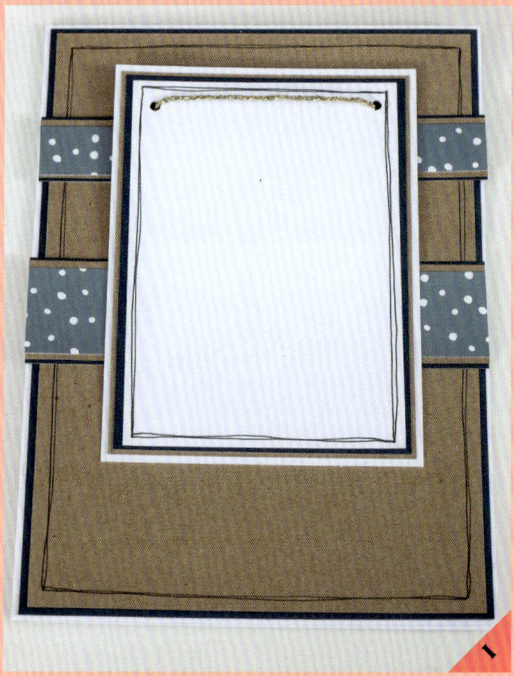

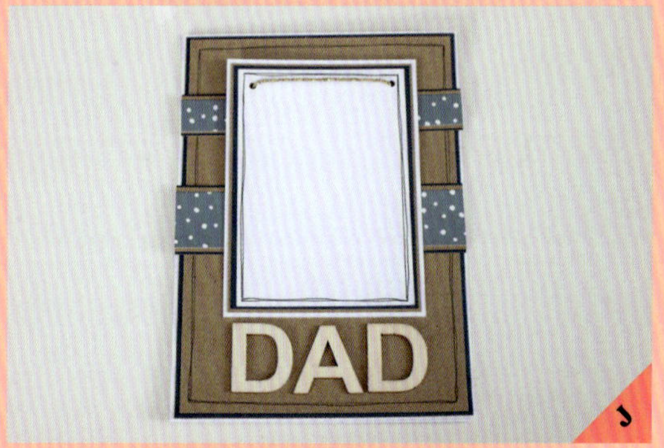

8 Punch a hole on either side of the top of the layered panel and thread through a piece of gold thread, securing it with clear adhesive tape on the back.

9 Add wooden letters to spell out 'DAD', or add a sentiment to the bottom of the card. **(J)**

10 Complete the card by hanging the shirt on the gold thread.

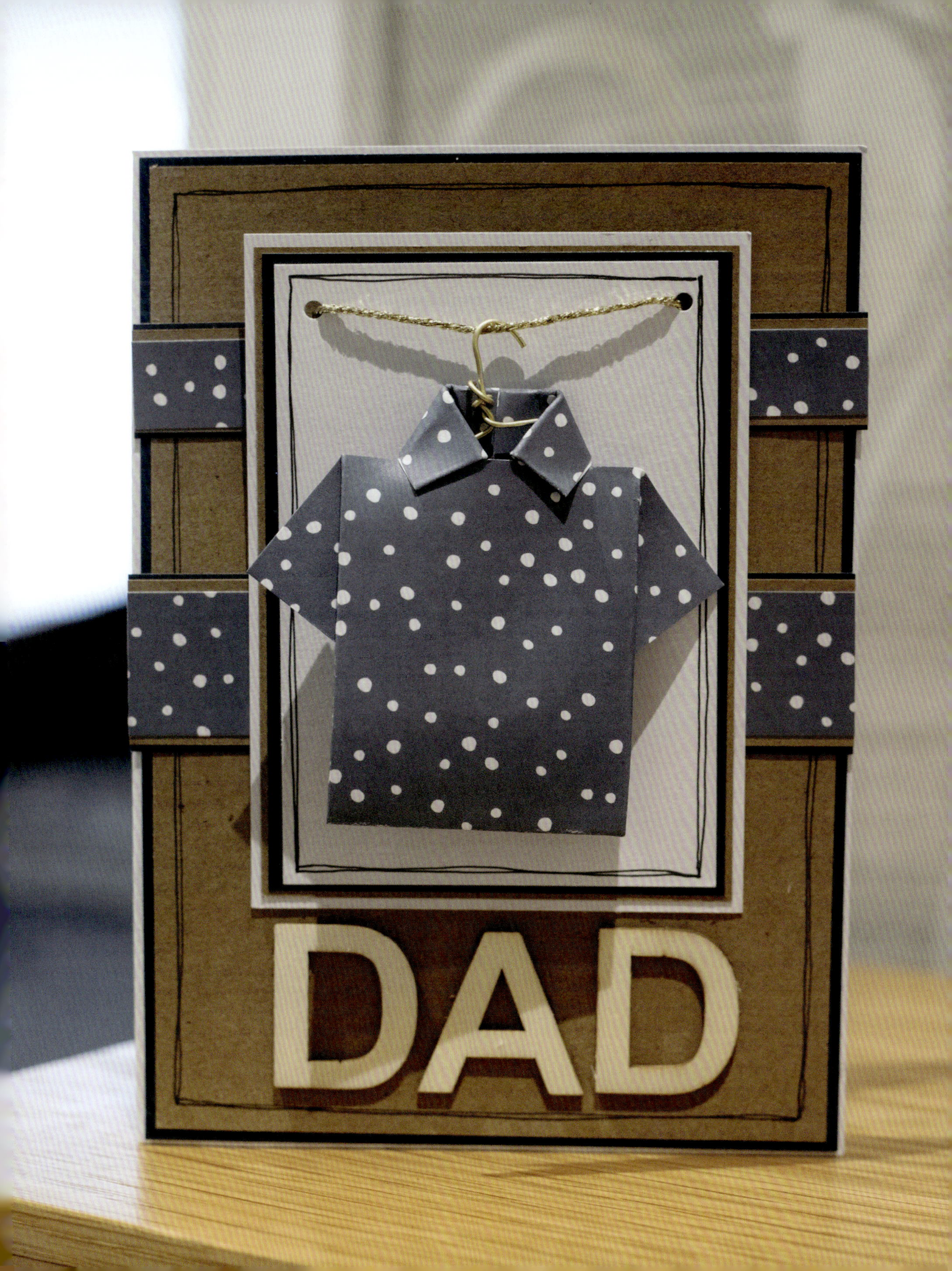
DAD

Easy

Shirt Bag

This shirt-style gift bag is a simple but effective way to add extra flair to your gift-giving. With just a few cuts and folds, you can transform an ordinary gift bag into something playful and personal – perfect for Father's Day or whenever you choose to celebrate a special man in your life. It's guaranteed to put a smile on his face before he even opens the gift!

You will need:

- Paper gift bag
- Ruler
- Scissors
- Gift
- Glue tape pen
- Glue gun
- Ribbon

TOP TIP **Choose a gift bag in a bold pattern or colour that suits the occasion. This will help the folded 'shirt sleeves' stand out. You can mix and match ribbon colours for added personality.**

1 Take the gift bag and, using a ruler as a guide, make a horizontal cut 1" down on each side, stopping level with the handles. **(A)**

2 Gently fold out the side sections underneath these strips at an angle to create the sleeve effect. **(B)**

3 Place your gift inside the bag at this stage, as the opening will be sealed once the collar is formed.

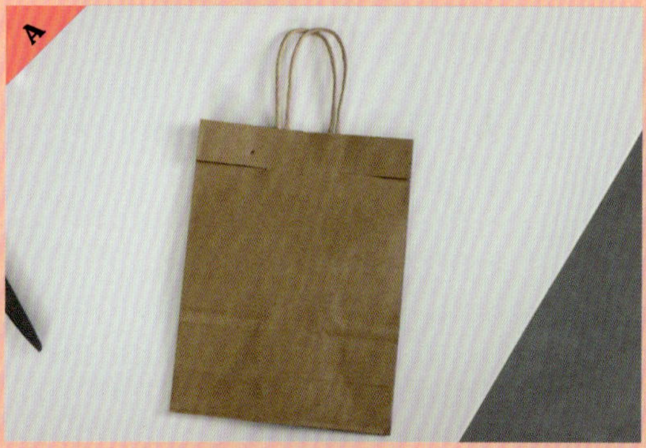

4 Fold down one of the top strips at an angle to create one side of the shirt collar, then secure it in place using a tape pen or glue gun. **(C)**

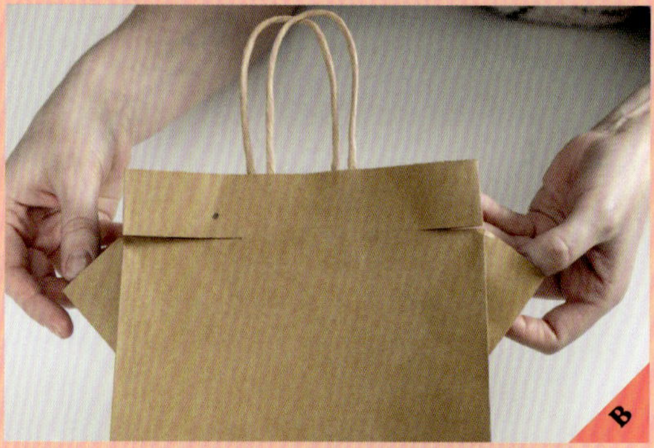

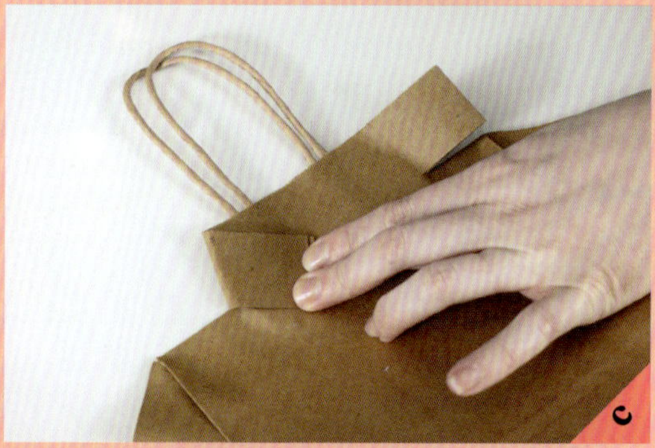

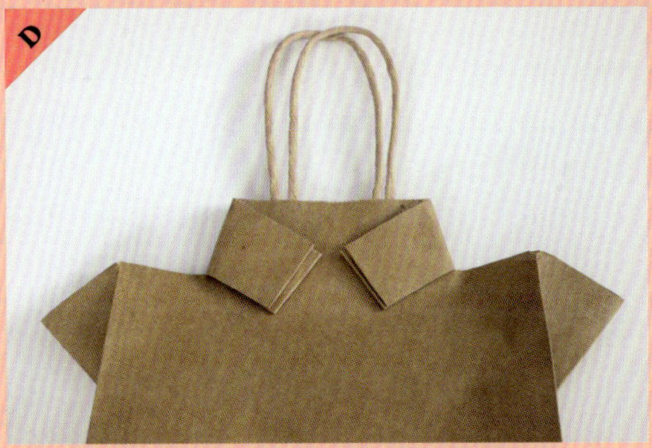

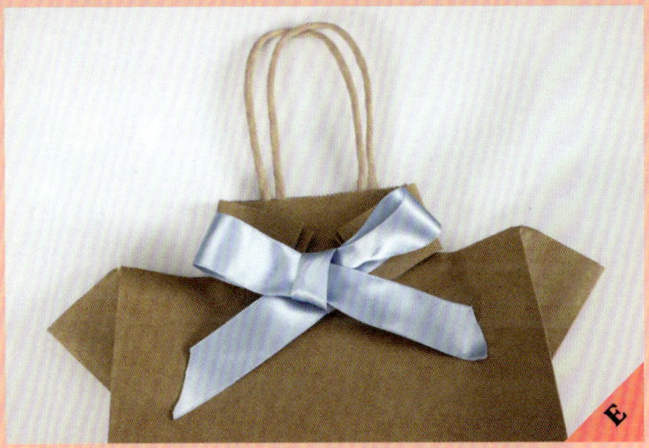

5 Repeat the previous step on the opposite side to complete the collar shape. **(D)**

6 Tie a bow in a length of ribbon and use a small amount of hot glue to secure it just below the collar on the front of the bag. Allow the glue to cool fully before handling. **(E)**

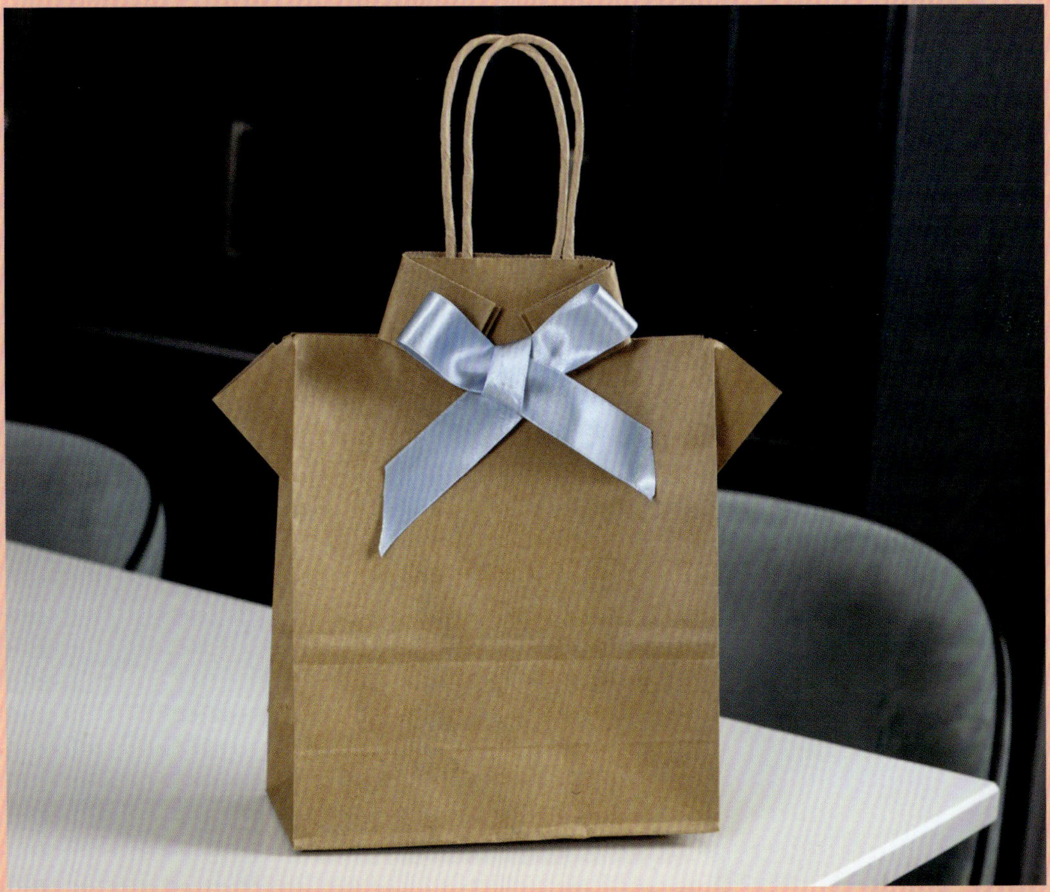

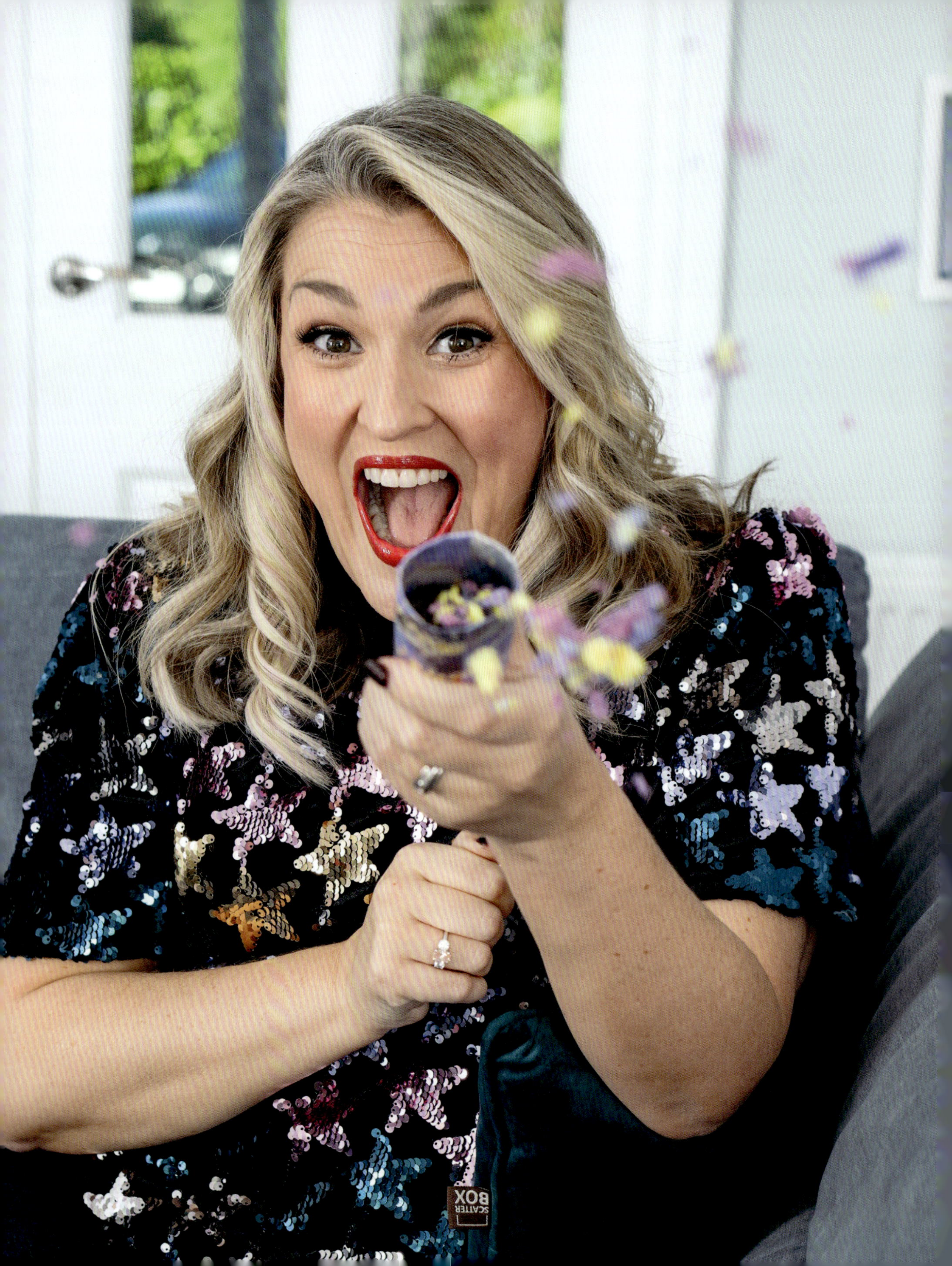
SCATTER BOX

Congratulations!

Well Done!

Graduation

Passed Driving Test

Intermediate

3D Star Card

This gorgeous 3D congratulations card is perfect for celebrating life's special moments, whether it's exam success, a new job, an engagement, or any achievement worth shouting about.

Using simple scoring and folding techniques, you'll create a beautifully sculpted star that really stands proud of the card. It looks incredibly impressive yet is very achievable, making this a design you'll return to whenever you need a card that says 'well done' in style.

You will need:

- 6" × 6" card base
- Mirror-finish purple card
- Scissors
- Scoring tool
- Ruler or scoring board
- Watercolour card
- Shimmer watercolour palette or ink pads
- Water
- Medium-sized paintbrush
- Glue tape pen
- Glue gun
- Embossed label maker, or pen

1 Cut a five-pointed star measuring approximately 4" wide from the mirror-finish purple card. **(A)**

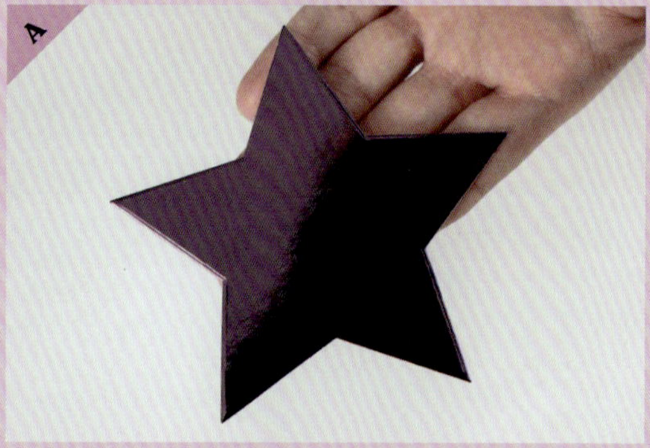

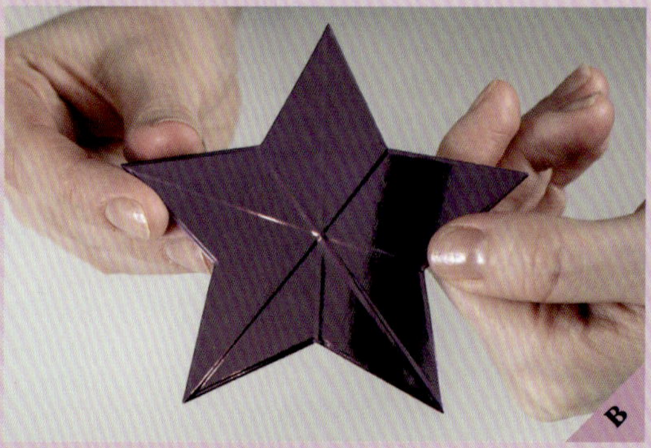

2 Using a scoring tool and ruler, score from each point straight across the star to the opposite edge, creating five score lines in total. **(B)**

3 Fold all of the score lines. The folds running from each point towards the centre should be mountain folds, while the folds between the points should be valley folds, creating the 3D star shape. **(C)**

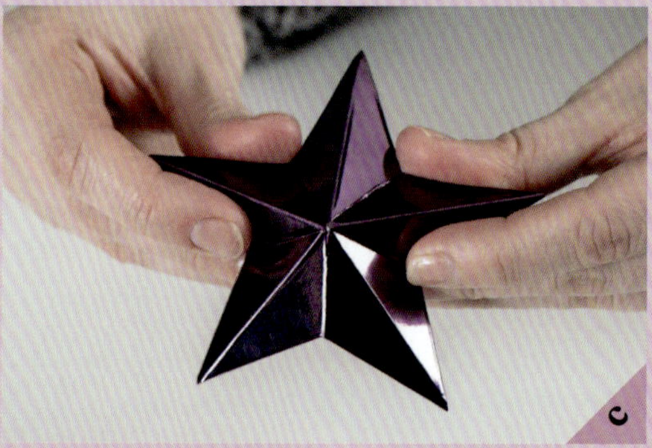

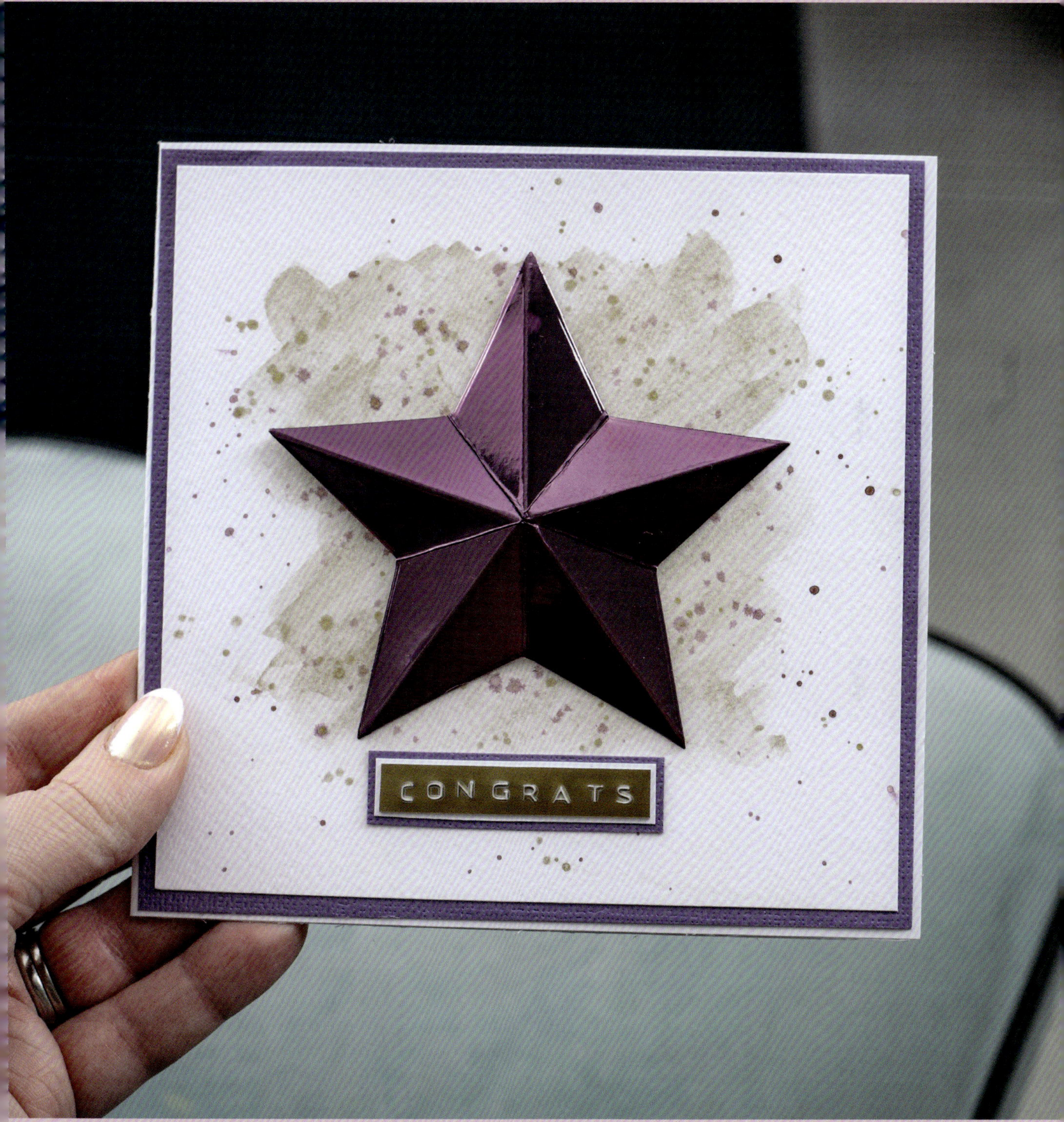
CONGRATS

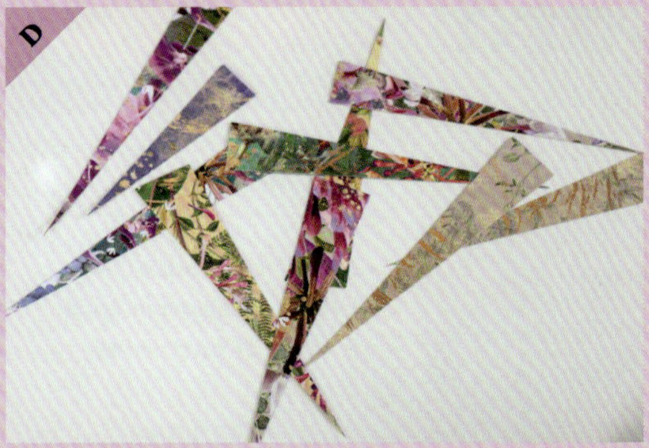

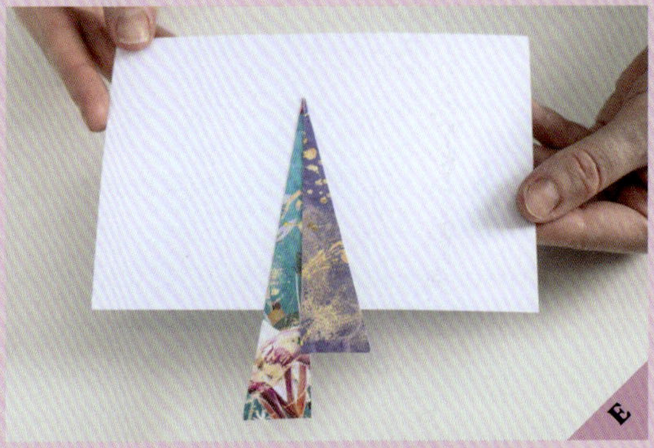

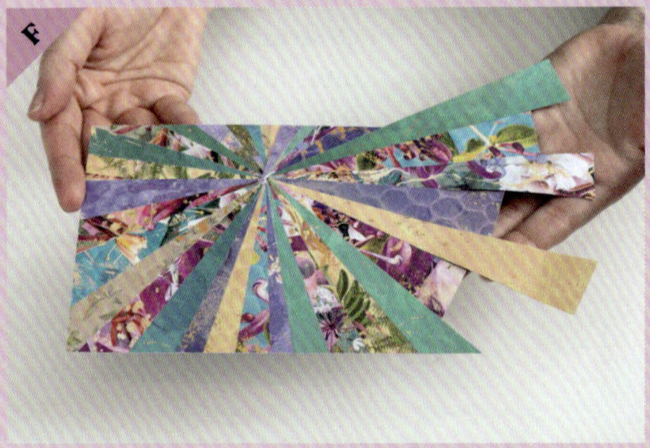

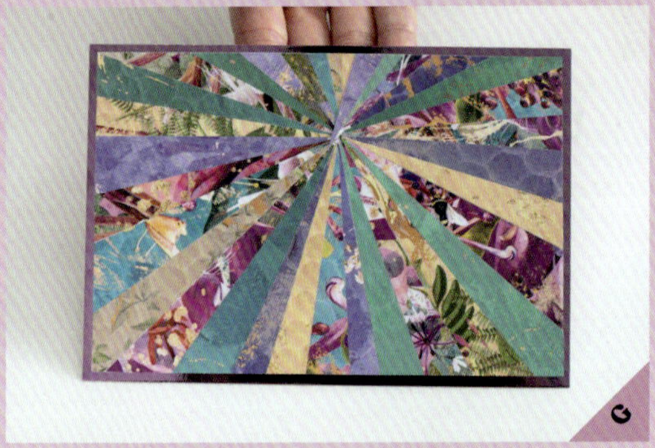

4 Repeat steps 2–3 until you have a good selection of paper strips ready to use. **(D)**

5 Using a tape pen or other adhesive, glue the first few patterned paper pieces on to the card, positioning them slightly off centre to add interest. **(E)**

6 Continue working around the card, gluing each strip into place and slightly overlapping the previous pieces until the card front is completely covered. Trim away any excess paper from the edges. **(F)**

7 Cut a piece of purple card measuring 4¾" × 6¾" and layer the patterned card front on top. **(G)**

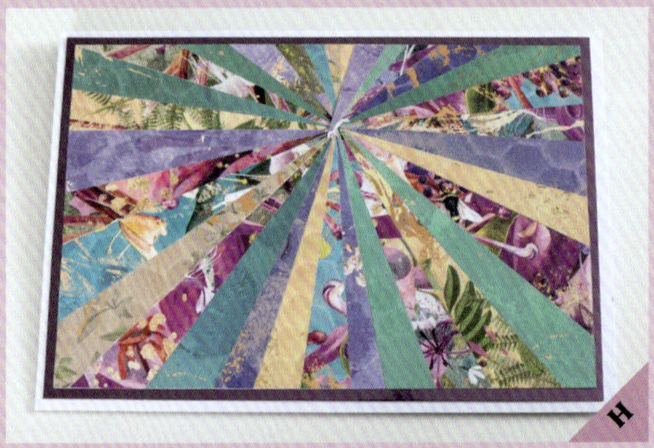

8 Adhere the layered panel on to the 5" × 7" card base. **(H)**

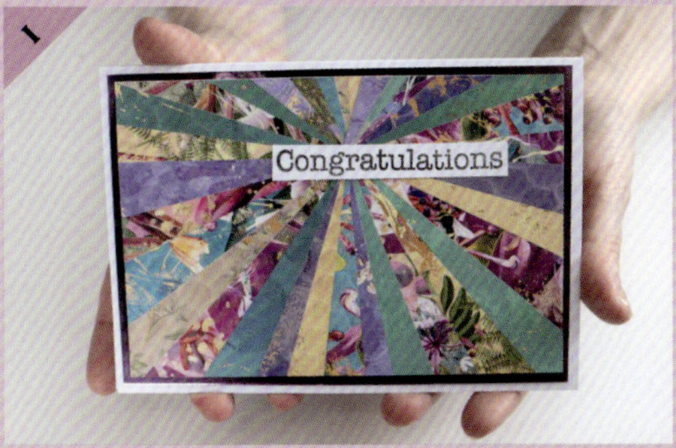

9 Finish the front of the card with a handwritten or stamped 'Congratulations' sentiment on a piece of card measuring 1″ × 3⅜″. **(I)**

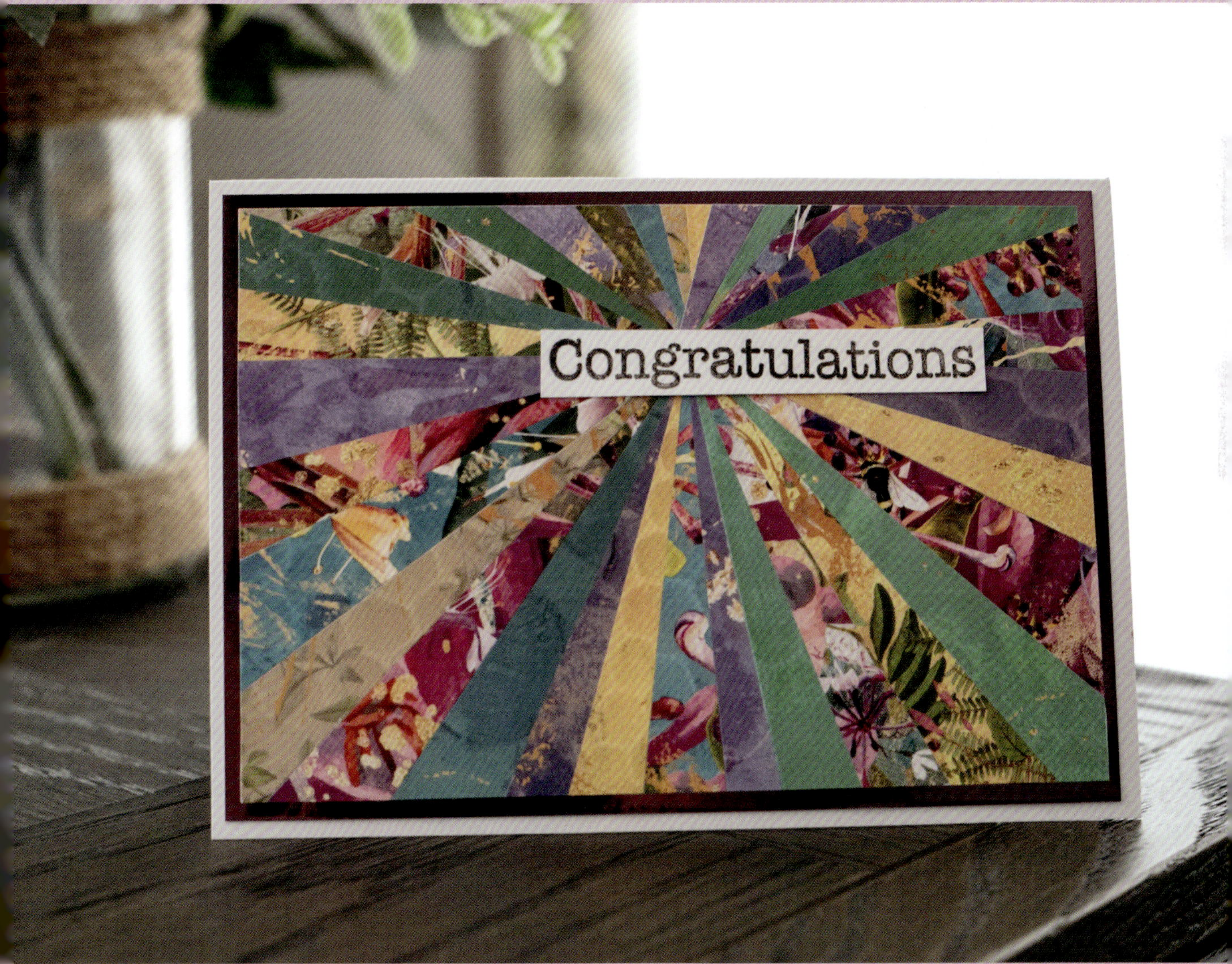

Intermediate

Mortarboard Card

This graduation cap card is such a brilliant way to mark a huge milestone. With just a few well-placed score lines, a flat piece of card is transformed into a bold, dimensional design that looks far more complicated than it actually is. It's ideal for celebrating graduations and achievements, and has plenty of scope for personalization.

TOP TIP **Combine this card with a gift card in the envelope in the next craft to really spoil your graduate!**

You will need:

- Black and white card
- Ruler
- Scoring tool
- Scissors or paper trimmer
- Small circular template
- Craft glue or glue tape pen
- Gold tassel

1. Take a piece of black card measuring 10" × 4". **(A)**
2. Using a ruler and a scoring tool, mark and score at 2", 4" and 6" from the top edge.
3. Score a connecting line across the 4" marks to create a cross shape.
4. Cut away the two triangular shapes on either side of the top section, as shown. **(B)**
5. Fold and burnish along all of the score lines so the card forms a square positioned on the diagonal, resembling a graduation cap shape. **(C)**

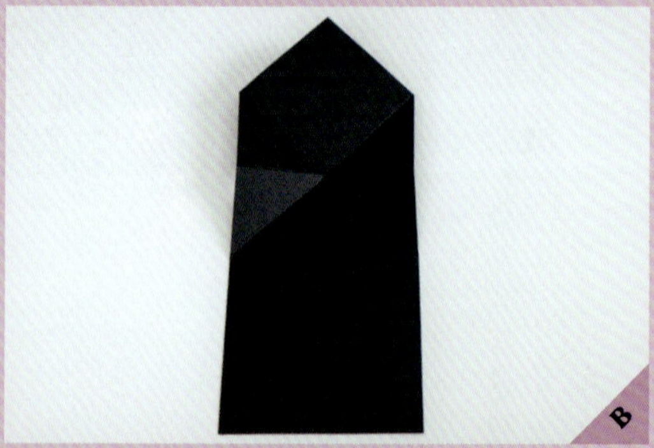

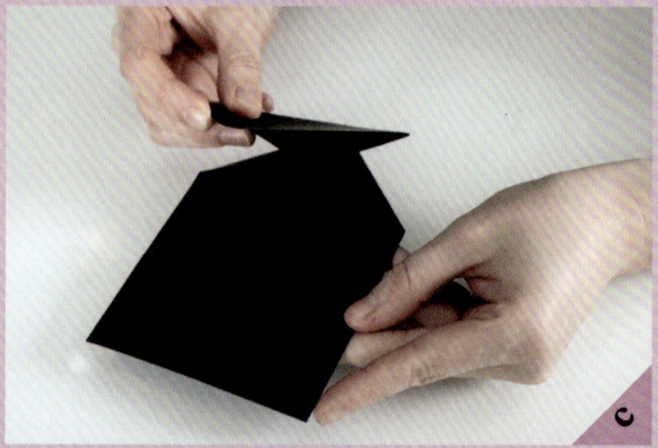

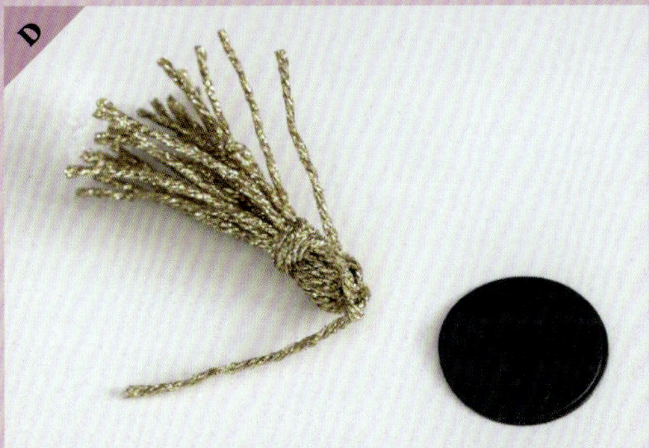

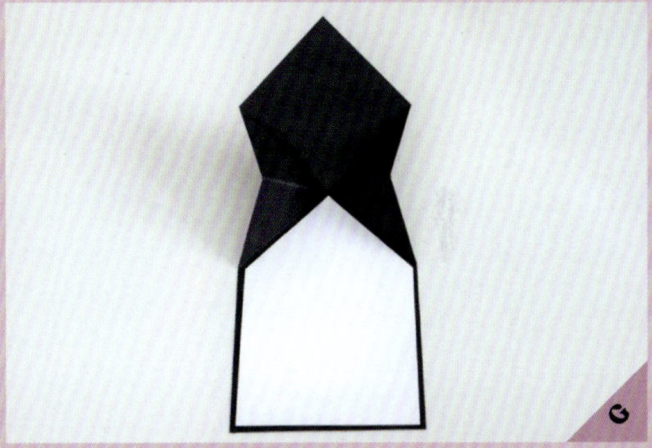

6 Cut a small circle from black card using a circular template. **(D)**

7 Cut a piece of white card measuring 5¾" × 3¾". **(E)**

8 Mark the halfway point along the top edge and the two side points, using the black card base as a guide, then trim away as required to shape the panel. **(F)**

9 Position this piece on the inside of the card so there is an even black border visible all around, then adhere it into place. **(G)**

10 Attach a tassel at the centre point of the cap, allowing it to hang over the edge.

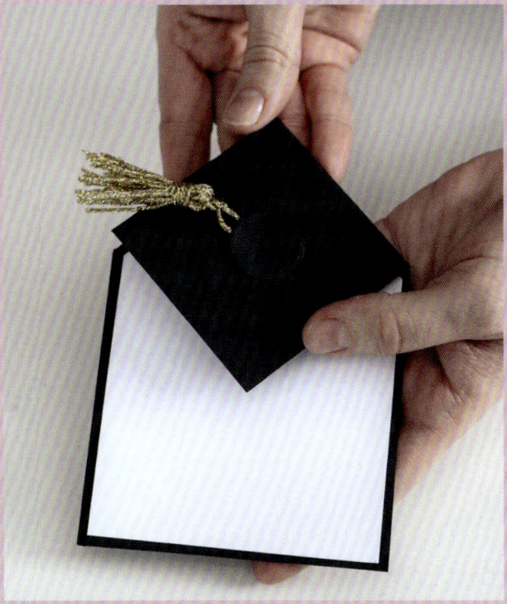

11 Cover the glued area with the black card circle to conceal the adhesive and finish your mortarboard card!

Intermediate

Mortarboard Envelope

This graduation-themed envelope is part card, part keepsake. The small pocket is ideal for holding a gift card, some cash or a voucher, along with a personal message for your graduate. With just a few folds and a tassel detail, you can create something that's fun, thoughtful and guaranteed to stand out on their big day.

TOP TIP **You can use this folding technique to create envelope designs for other occasions, simply by changing the colours and embellishments.**

You will need:

- A4 sheet black card
- Scissors or paper trimmer
- Ruler
- Scoring tool
- Black and white card
- Glue gun
- Gold tassel
- Small circular template

1 Trim the A4 black card to 11″ × 5½″. Place it in front of you in landscape orientation.

2 Using a ruler and scoring tool, score a vertical line at 5½″.

3 Make marks at 2¾″ and 8¼″ along the top edge, then repeat along the bottom edge.

4 Join these marks with score lines so they intersect across the central 5½″ score line, creating an X shape.

5 Turn the card to portrait orientation and mark 2¾″ in along the top and bottom edges.

6 Score diagonal lines from these points to the existing score lines, as shown. **(A)**

7 Fold the two bottom corners upwards along the score lines. **(B)**

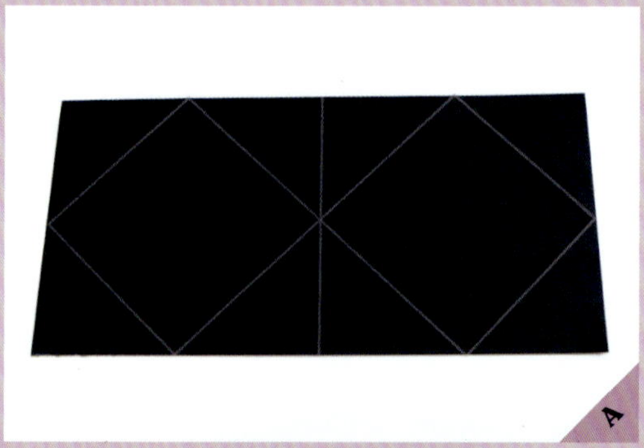
A

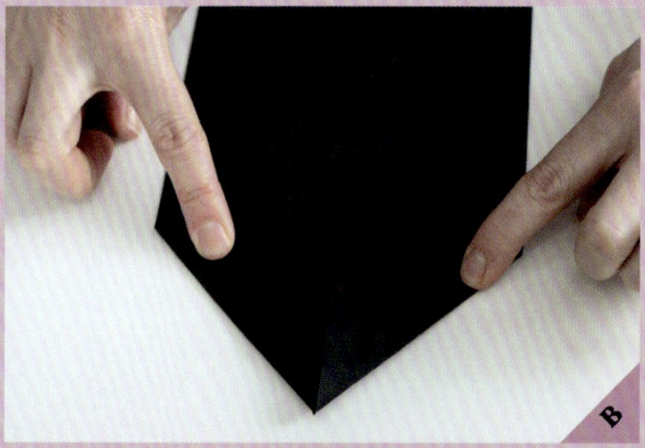
B

C

D

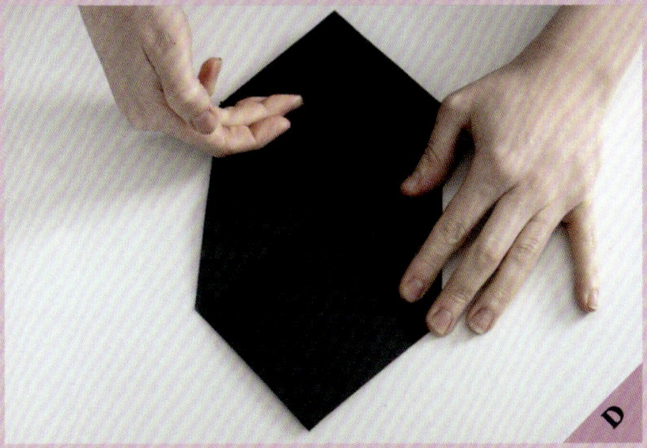

E

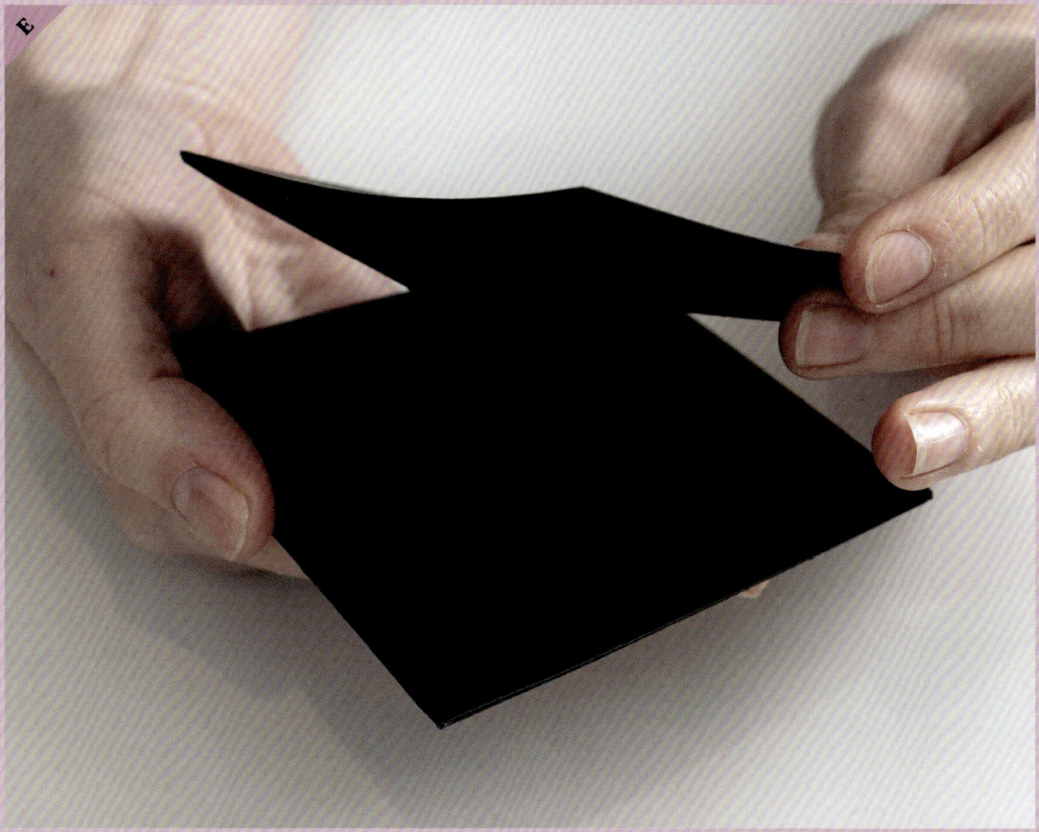

8 Cut a piece of black card measuring 3⅞" × 3⅞", then cut in half diagonally. Adhere one of these pieces over the folded corners to create a pocket. **(C)**

9 At the opposite end of the card, trim away the two corner triangles. **(D)**

10 Fold and burnish all the score lines so the card forms a square envelope shape. **(E)**

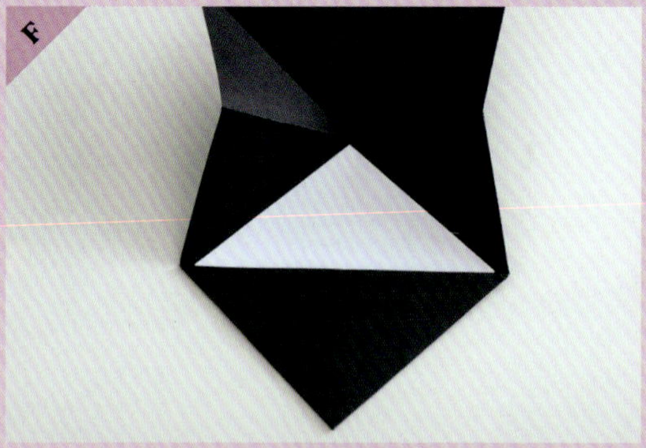

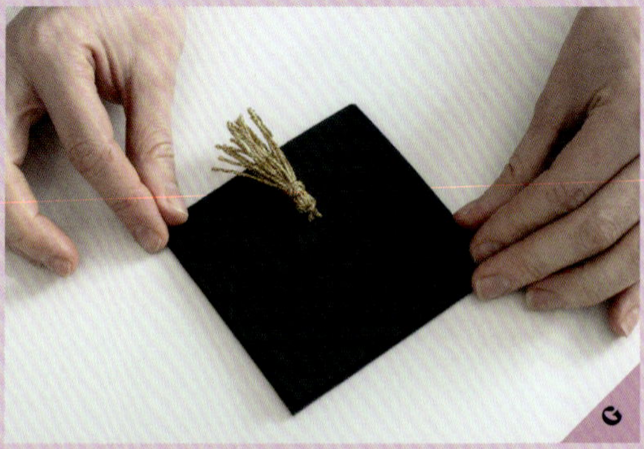

11 Cut a piece of white card measuring 3½" × 3½" and place it inside the pocket. You can write a message on this if you wish. **(F)**

12 Finish by gluing a gold tassel and a small circle of black card in place, to create the top of your mortarboard. **(G)**

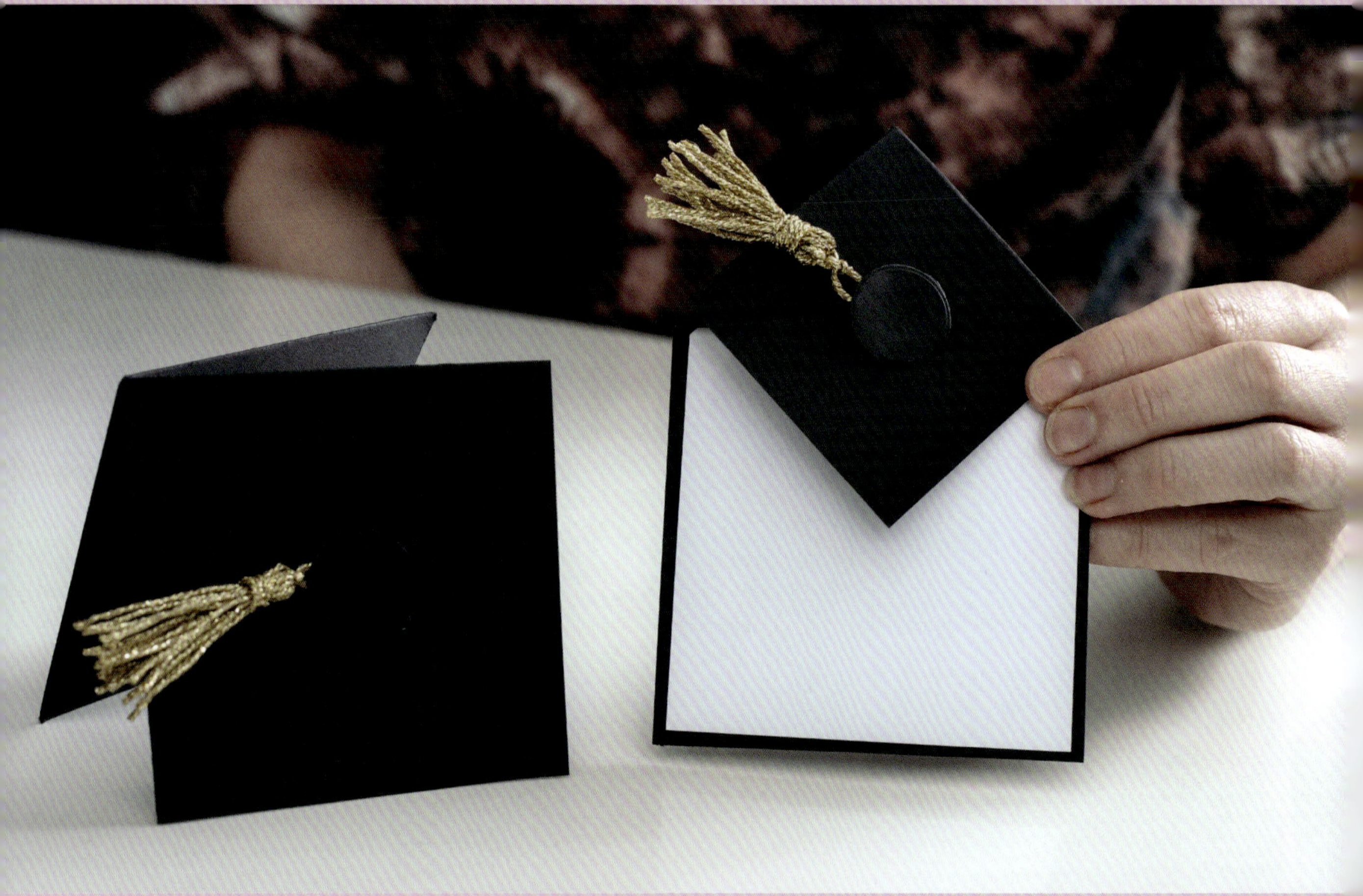

Advanced

Macramé Key Wristlet

This handmade macramé key wristlet is practical, stylish, and makes a thoughtful gift for someone who's just passed their driving test. Not only will it keep their keys safe and easily accessible, but it's also a lovely way to mark this exciting achievement with a personal, handcrafted gift!

You will need:

- Macramé cord
- Ruler or tape measure
- Scissors
- D-ring keyring
- Blu Tack
- Glue gun
- Alphabet beads
- Clear nylon thread

1 Cut one piece of cord measuring 36" and two pieces measuring 84".

2 Take the 36" cord and attach it to the D-ring using a Lark's Head knot. To do this, fold the cord in half, place the folded loop under the ring, then thread the loose ends through the loop and pull tight. **(A)**

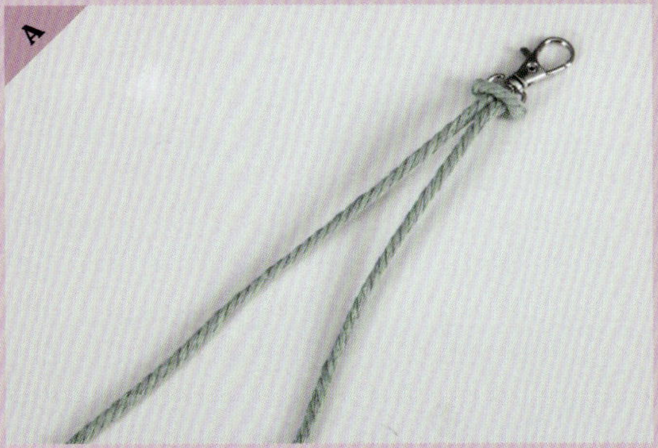

A

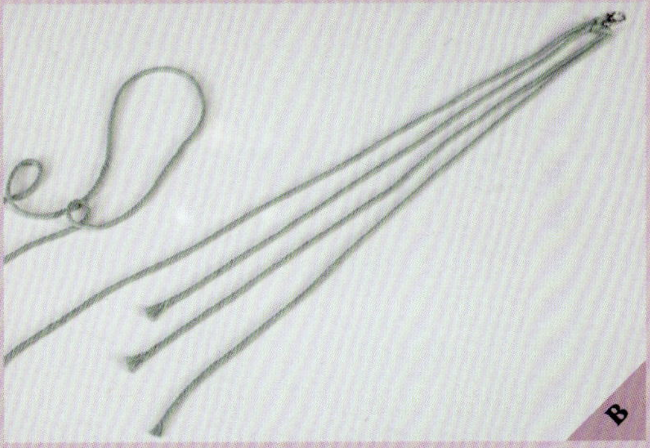

B

3 Take one 84" cord. Line up one end with one side of the cords already attached to the D-ring, then fold it over the ring and secure it with another Lark's Head knot. Ensure the shorter tail sits on the inside, next to the first cord. **(B)**

4 Repeat the previous step with the second 84" cord, again positioning the shorter tail on the inside. You should now have six cords hanging from the D-ring. You will be working with cords 1 and 6 only. **(C)**

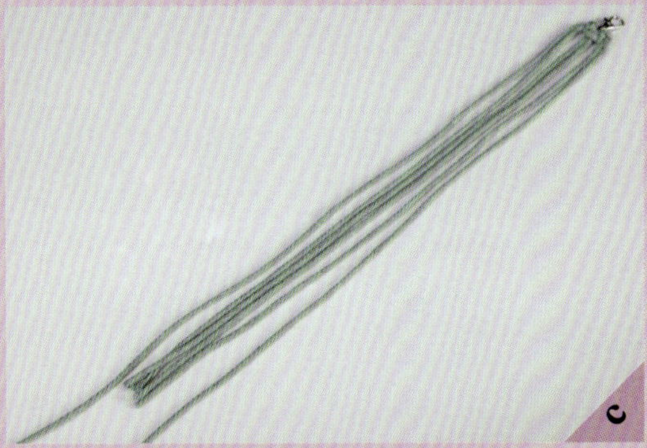

C

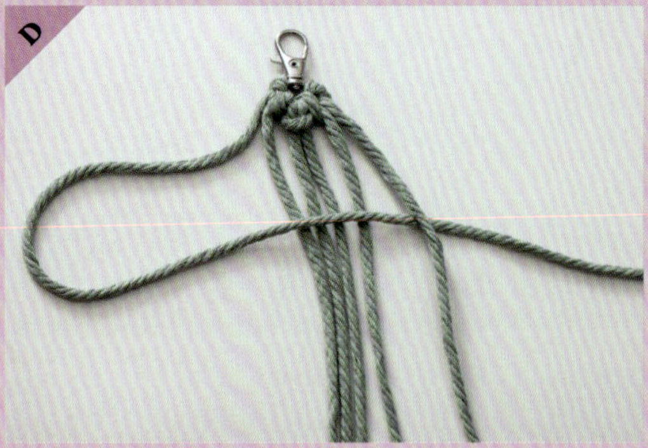

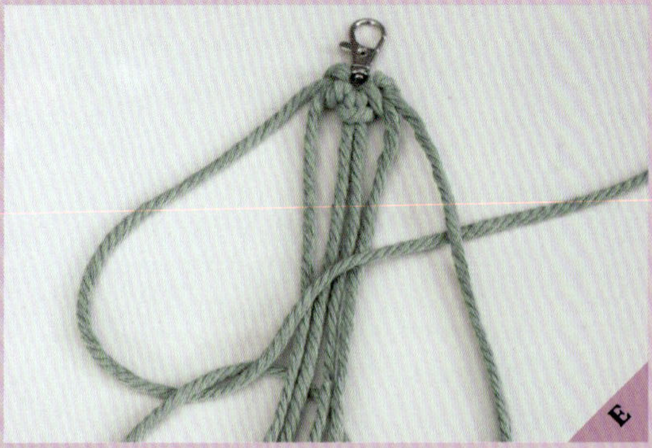

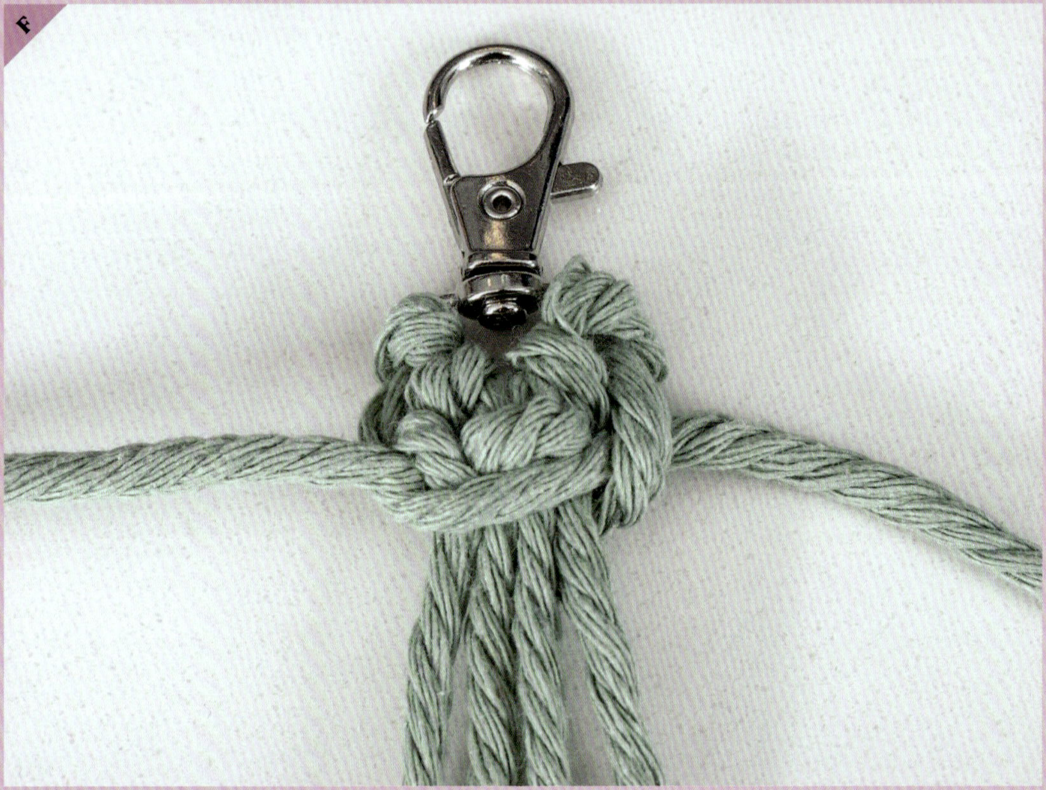

5 Secure the D-ring to your work surface with some Blu Tack. Take cord 1 (far left) and cross it over the four centre cords.

6 Take cord 6 (far right) and place it over cord 1, forming a shape similar to the number 4. **(D)**

7 Bring cord 6 behind the four centre cords and up through the loop on the left. **(E)**

8 Pull both cords to tighten the knot. **(F)**

9 Repeat this knot, always starting from the left-hand side to create a continuous spiral twist.

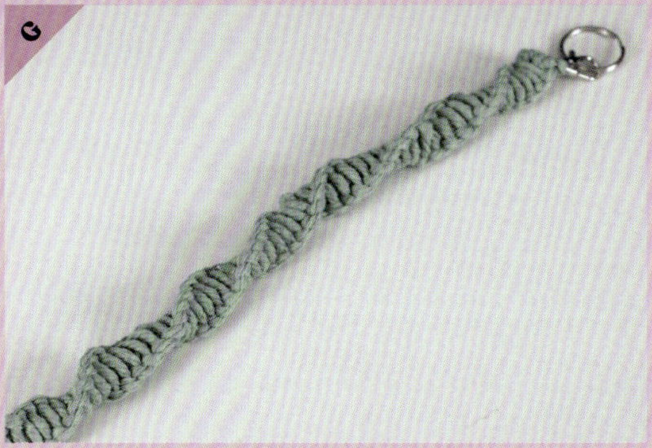

10 Continue knotting until you reach the desired length for the wristlet. **(G)**

11 Fold the finished knotted section back up towards the D-ring to form a loop, aligning the end with the cords at the top. Apply hot glue along the inside of the folded section and press it firmly in place to secure the wristlet shape. **(H)**

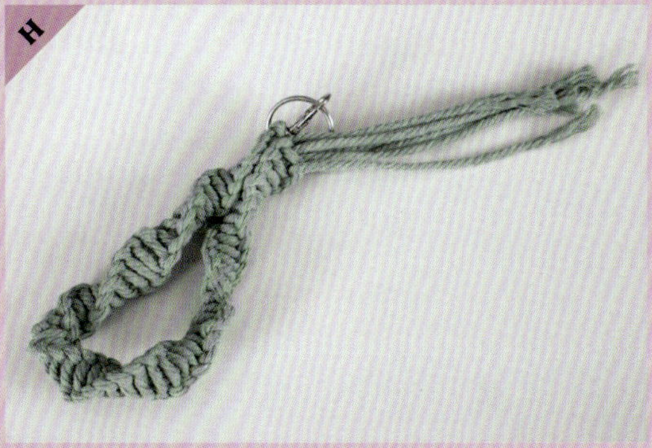

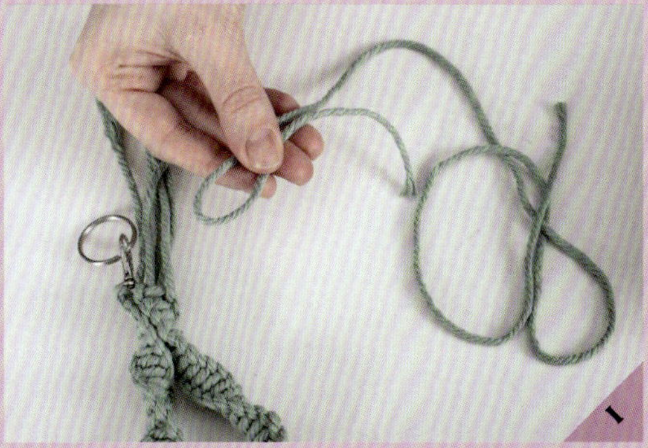

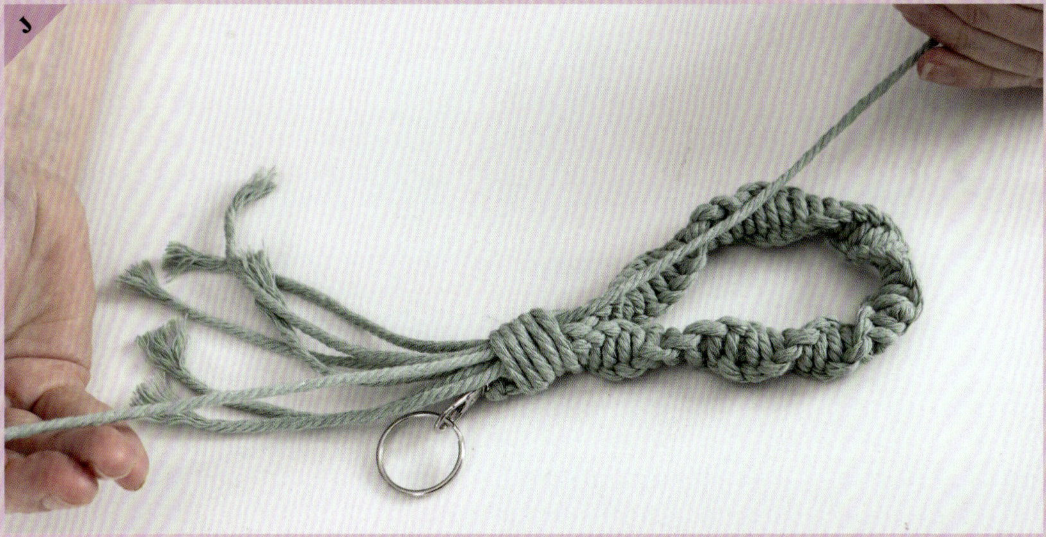

12 For a neat finish, take another length of cord and form a loop in one end. **(I)**

13 Wrap the rest of the length of cord around the joined section, holding the loop in place from the previous step. Once the cord has been wound around a few times, take the loose end and feed it through the loop to neaten. **(J)**

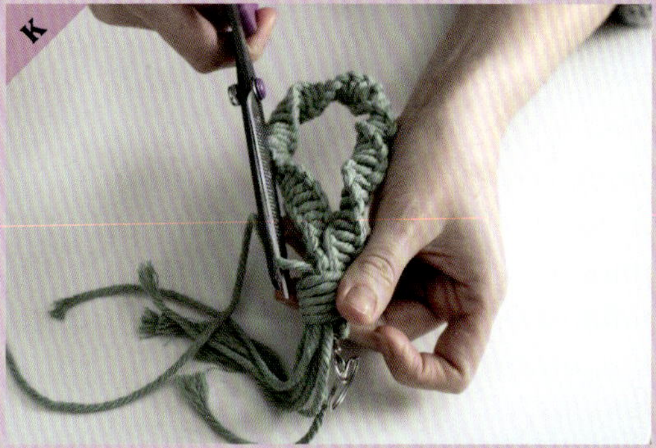

14 Trim away any excess. **(K)**

15 Thread some alphabet beads on to a length of clear nylon to create a message of your choice, and attach to the keyring at one end. Tie a knot in the other end to stop any of the letters from escaping.

TOP TIP Fix some Blu Tack to your work surface and secure the D-ring in place. This will prevent movement while you're weaving the cords and help keep your work neat and even.

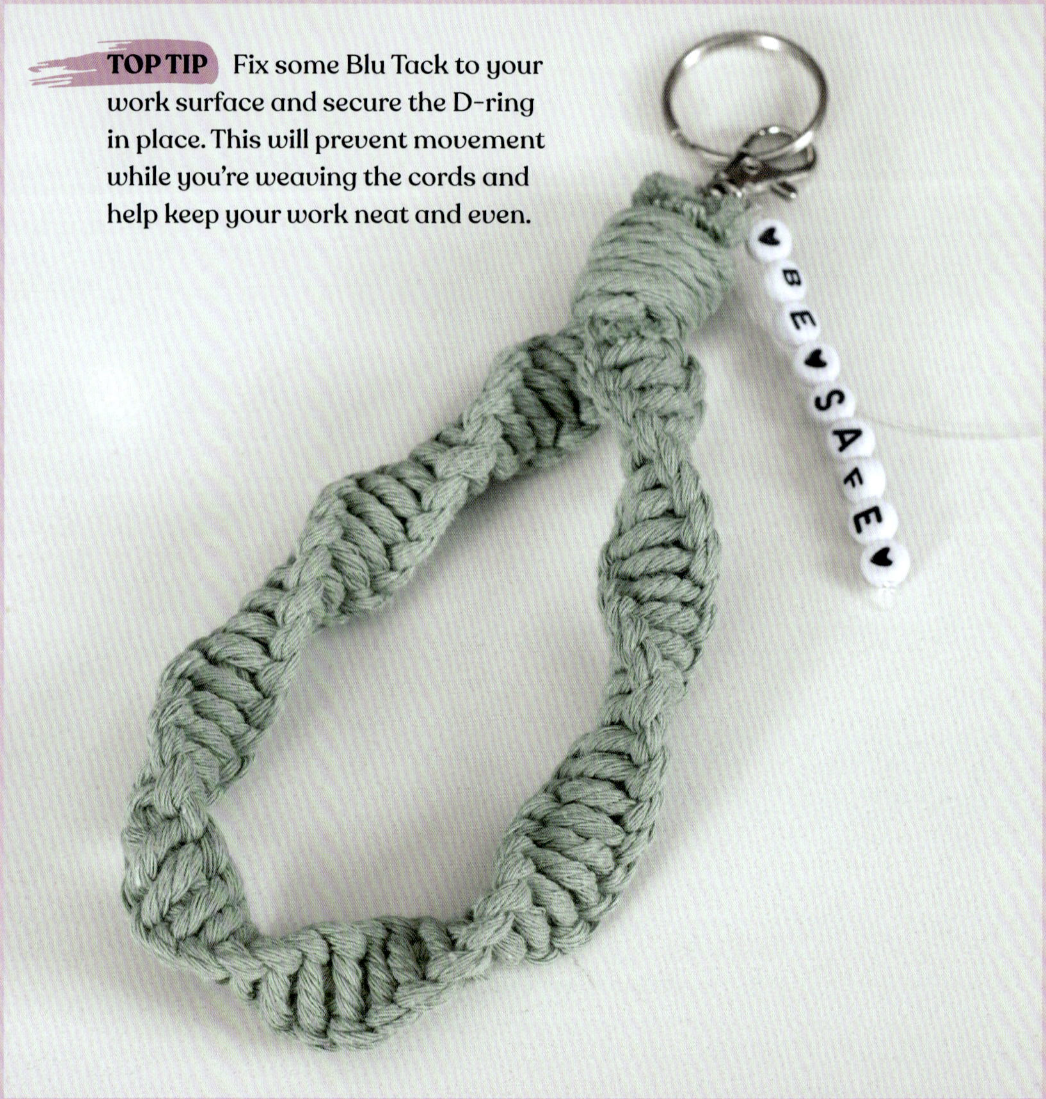

Intermediate

Traffic Light Card

Celebrate a big milestone with this fun and interactive traffic light tri-fold card, perfect for someone who's just passed their driving test. It's a fantastic way to say 'well done' in a creative, handmade way that they'll always remember. It looks oh so clever but is also very satisfying to put together, and once you've made one, you'll be thinking of all the other colour combinations and occasions you could use the design for.

TOP TIP **If you're die-cutting individual letters for your card front, using tweezers can make placement easier and more precise.**

You will need:

- Black, green, orange and red card
- Pencil
- Ruler
- Scissors
- Craft glue
- Dies and die-cutting machine
- Silver gel pen
- Black pen or marker
- Tweezers (optional)
- Foam pads
- Decorative stars

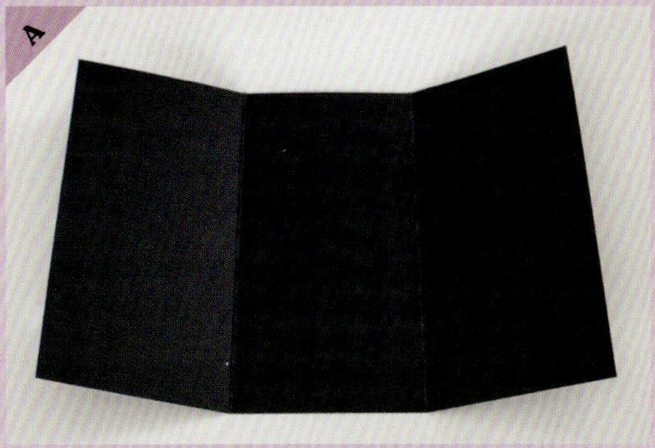
A

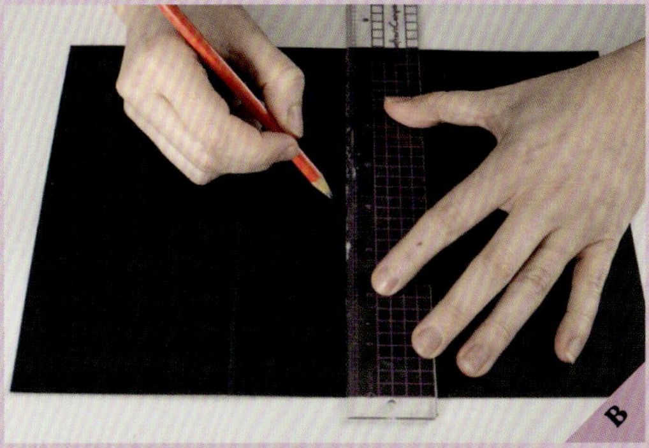
B

1 Create a tri-fold card from an A4 sheet of black card by dividing it into three equal panels. **(A)**

2 Find the centre of the middle panel and draw a circle measuring approximately 1¾" in diameter. **(B)**

3 Draw two additional circles identical in size, one above and one below the first, spacing them evenly. **(C)**

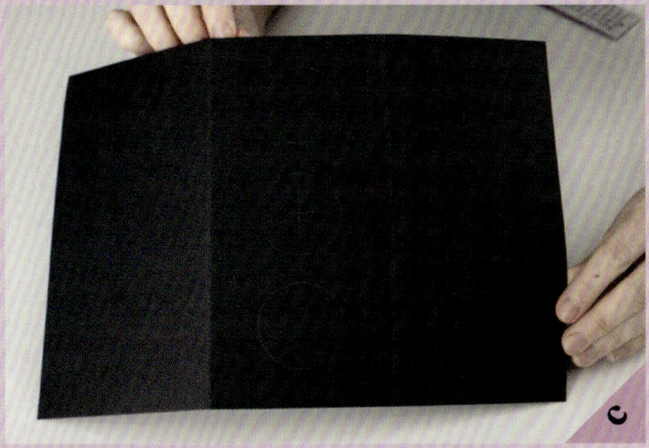
C

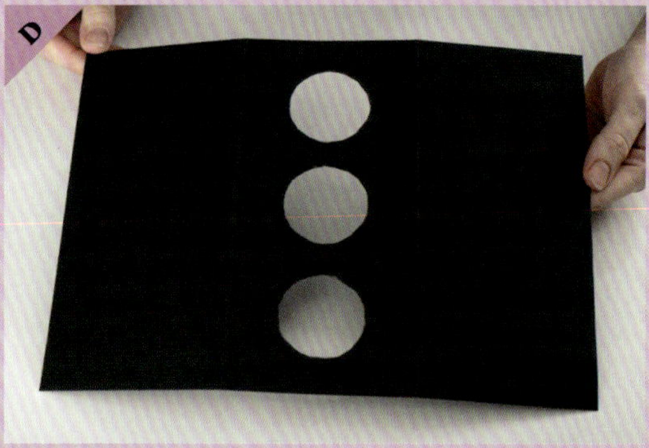

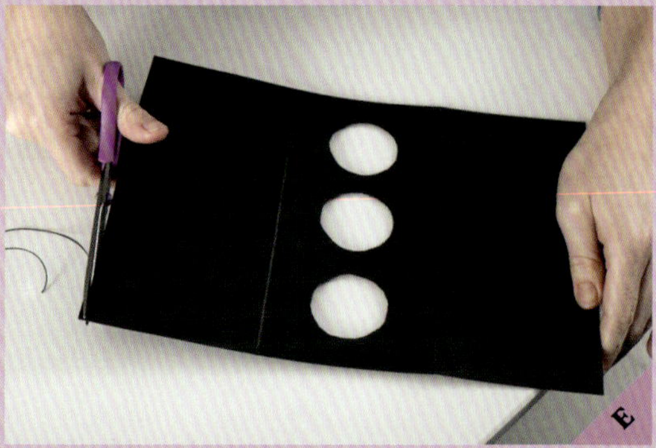

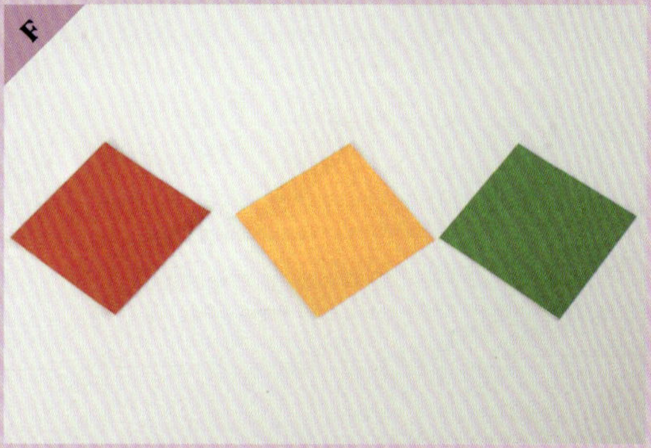

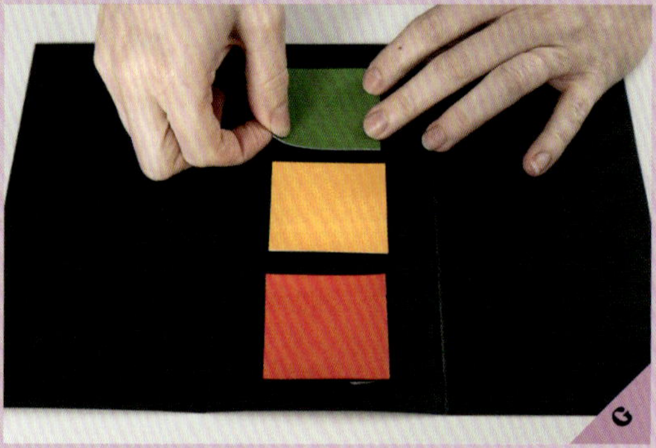

4 Carefully cut out all three circles to create apertures. **(D)**

5 Trim a small sliver from the right-hand panel so the card folds more easily. **(E)**

6 Cut three squares of red, green and orange card, each large enough to fully cover one circle aperture. **(F)**

7 Adhere the coloured squares to the central panel of the card, positioning them behind the apertures. **(G)**

8 Cut a narrow strip of black card and add die-cut letters to spell 'CONGRATS', or write the word using a silver gel pen. **(H)**

9 Secure this strip above the coloured squares so it peeks out from the top. **(I)**

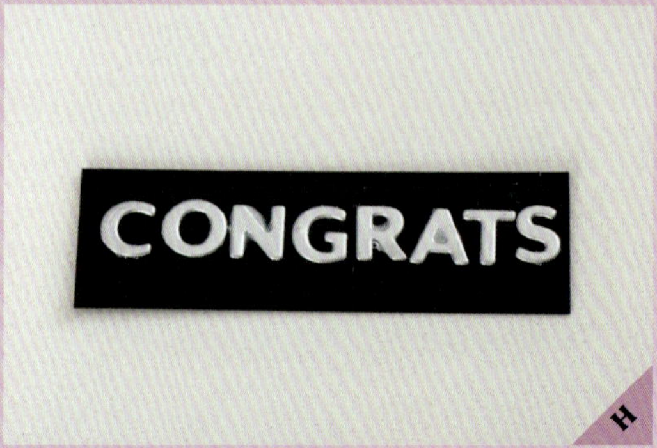

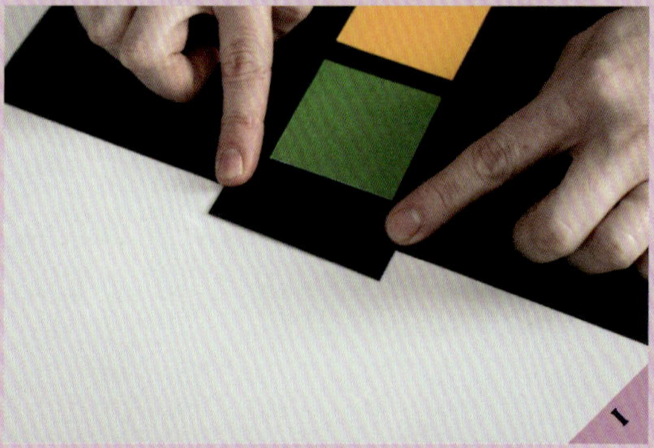

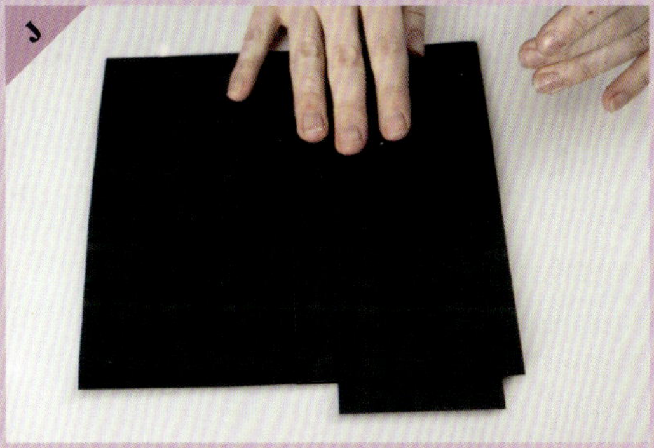

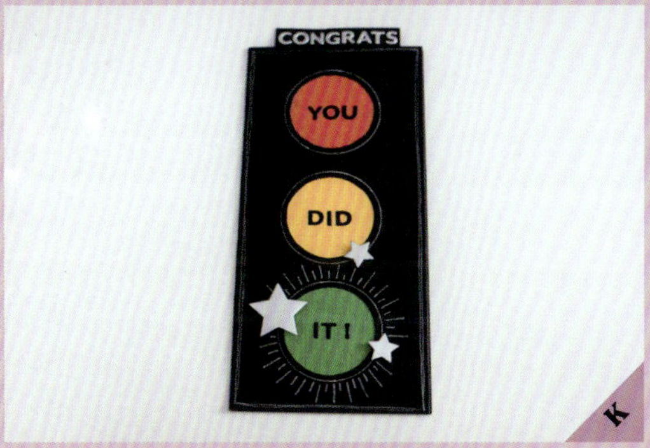

10 Fold over the trimmed panel from step 5 (this will be on the left when viewing the back of the card) and adhere it into place. **(J)**

11 Die-cut, stamp or write 'YOU DID IT' in black letters and adhere one word to the centre of each circle.

12 Finish by adding decorative stars to the card front using foam pads, and add extra detailing around the outer edges of the card with a silver gel pen. **(K)**

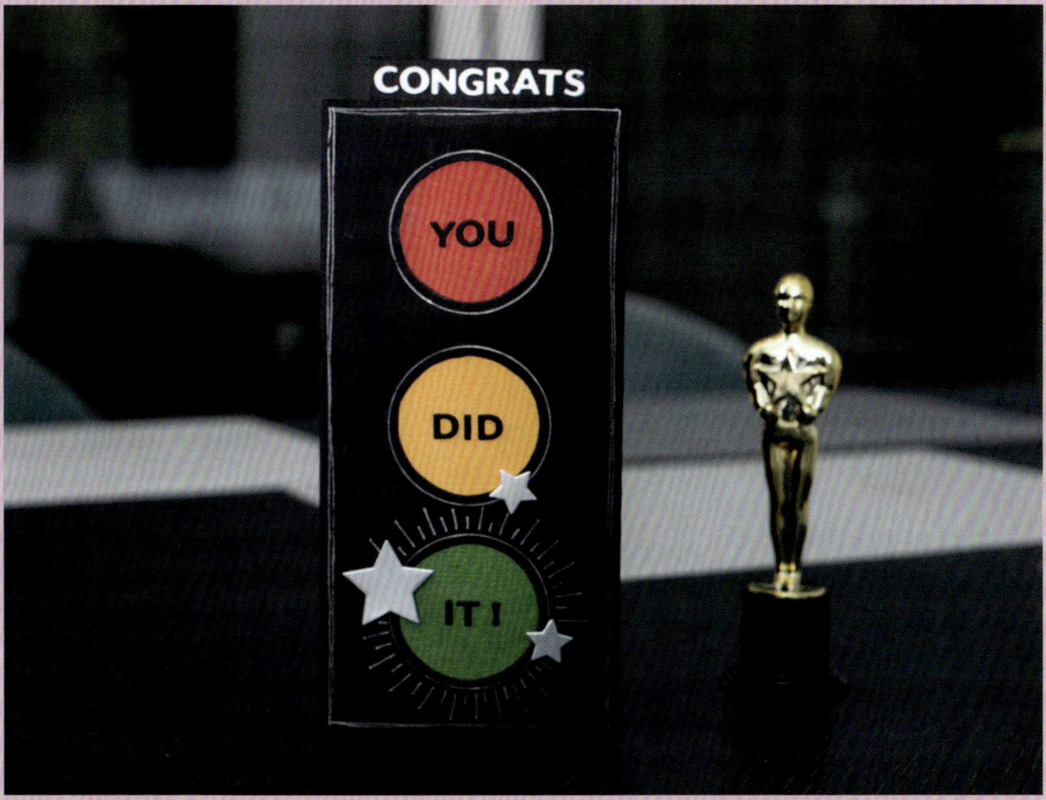

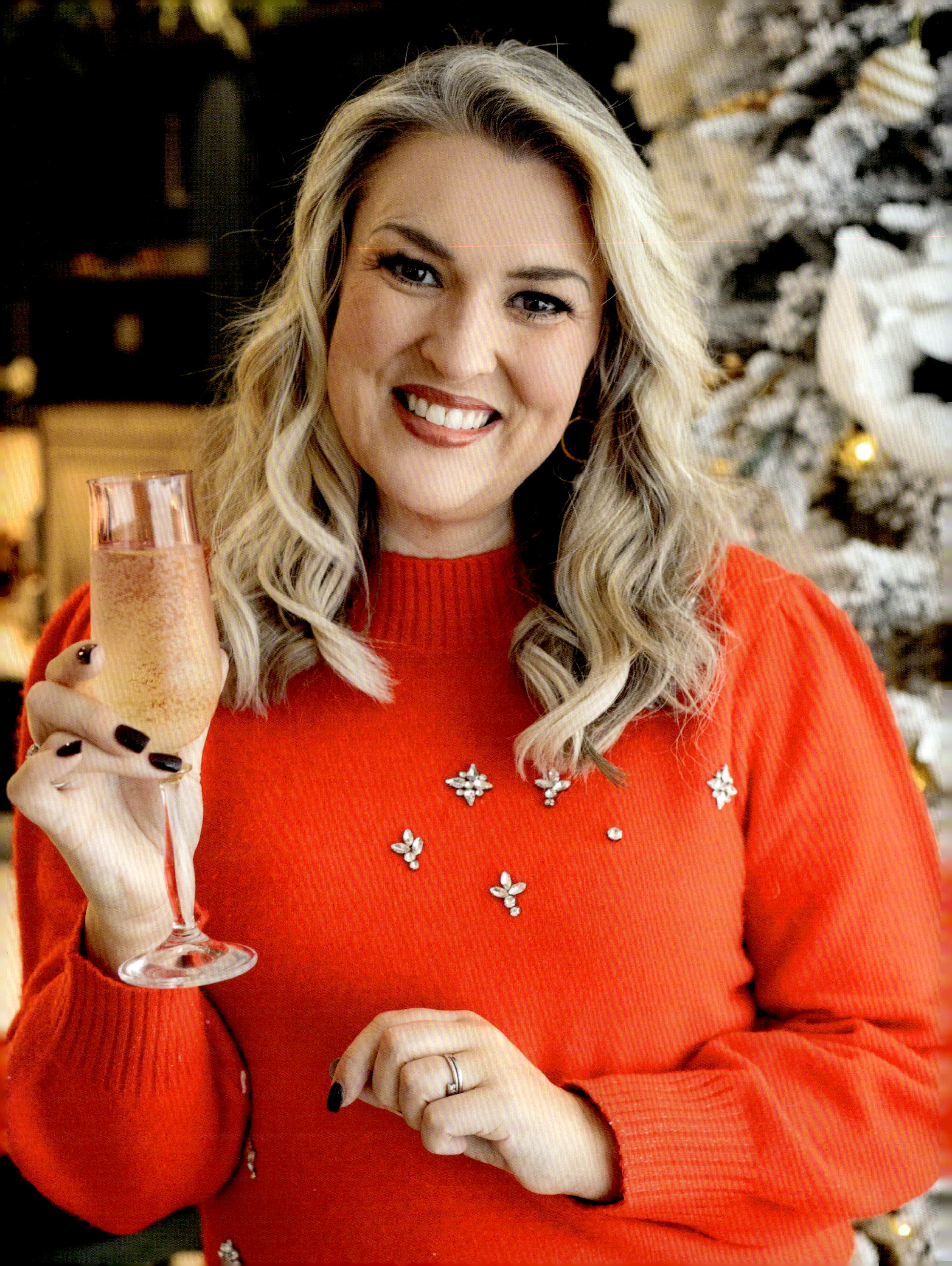

Celebrations

Christmas

New Year

Easter

Halloween

Intermediate

Bauble Card

If nothing else, Christmas crafting should be all about having fun, and this project delivers exactly that. Using simple shapes alongside colour, sparkle and plenty of festive flair, you can create a stunning card front that looks super eye-catching yet is surprisingly easy to make.

One of the best things about this design is how versatile it is once you've mastered the technique. By switching up the shapes or colours, you can easily adapt it for different occasions. So don't worry about being overly precise here. Enjoy the process, let the shimmer do the hard work, and embrace the fact that every card will turn out beautifully unique!

You will need:

- Kraft card
- Mirror card
- Washi tape
- Circular template (e.g. a glass or cup)
- Pencil
- Small and medium-sized paintbrushes
- Shimmer watercolour palette
- Water
- Glue pen
- Gilding flakes
- Kitchen paper towel
- Glue tape pen

A

B

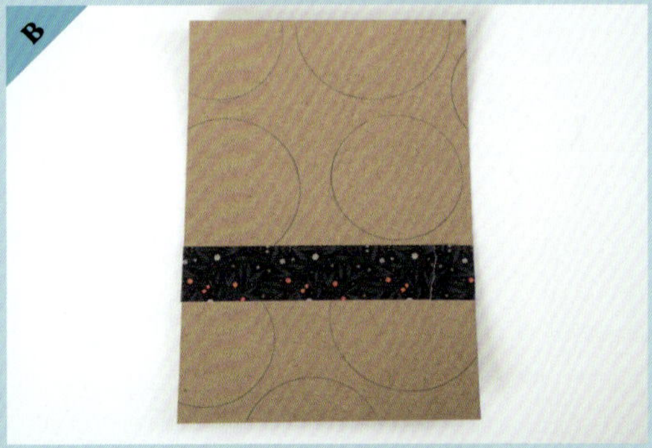

TOP TIP **Try swapping the bauble shapes for festive presents or crackers!**

1 Cut a panel of card for the card front. This can be any size you wish; the example shown measures 4¼" × 6¼". **(A)**

2 Use washi tape to mask off a section across the bottom third of the panel.

3 Take a circular object, such as the base of a glass or cup, and draw multiple circles on to the card front to create the baubles. You can use two different-sized objects to create depth and variety. **(B)**

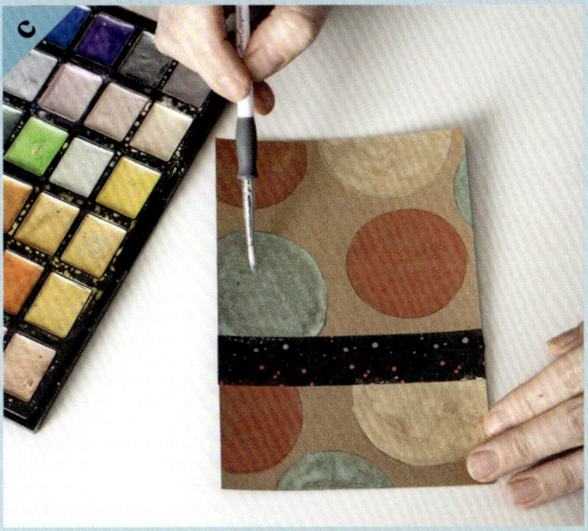

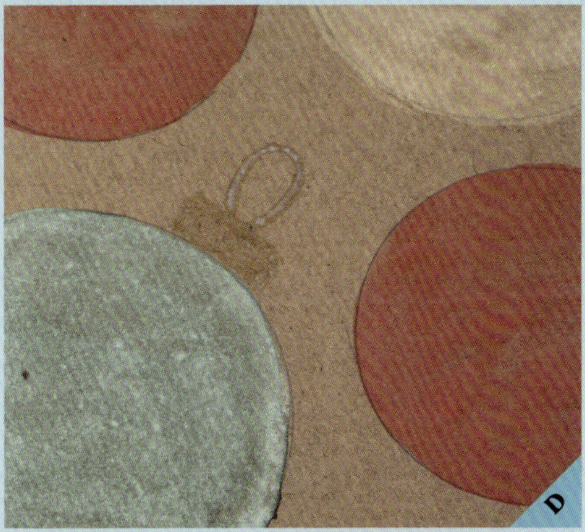

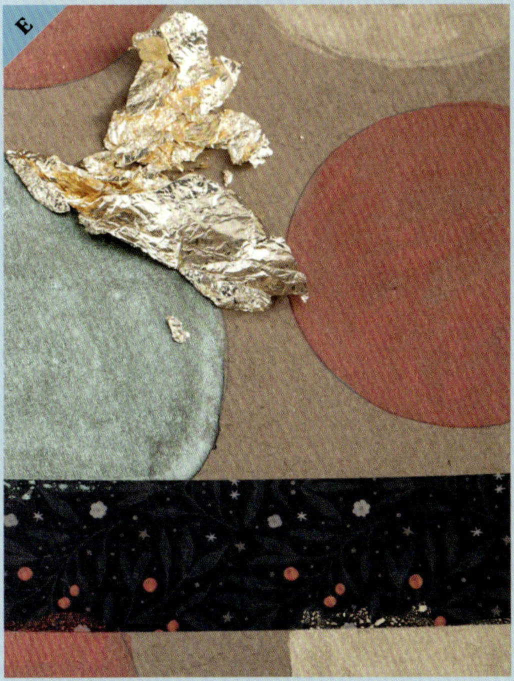

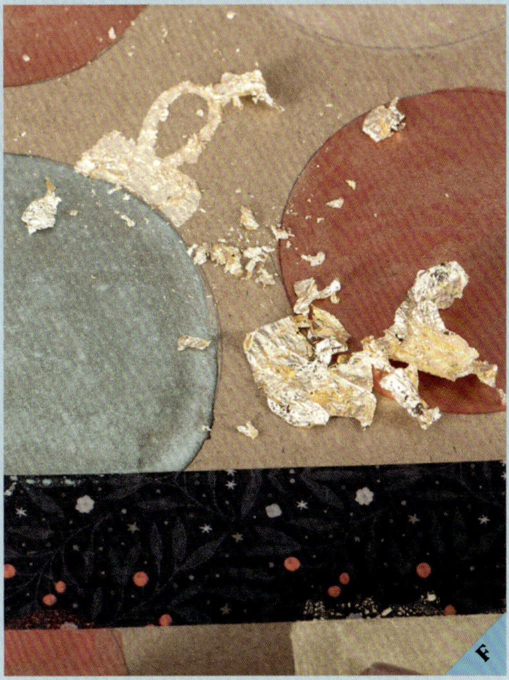

4 Using a paintbrush and shimmer watercolour paints, colour in each bauble then set the panel aside to dry completely. **(C)**

5 Once dry, use a glue pen to draw the bauble tops and add any decorative details. **(D)**

6 When the glue becomes tacky, sprinkle gilding flakes over the glued areas. **(E)**

7 Use a sheet of kitchen paper to rub away any excess and return it to the tub. **(F)**

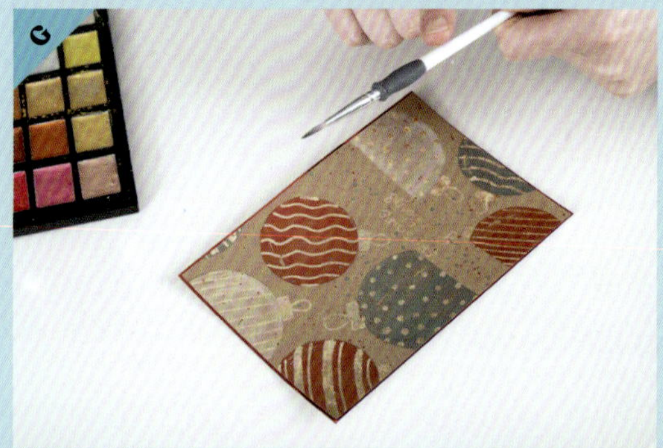

8 Carefully remove the washi tape and add a sentiment to the card front using the same glue and gilding flakes technique.

9 Finish with a spattering of shimmer paint across the panel, then adhere it to a 4½" × 6½" piece of mirror card and 5" × 7" card base. **(G)**

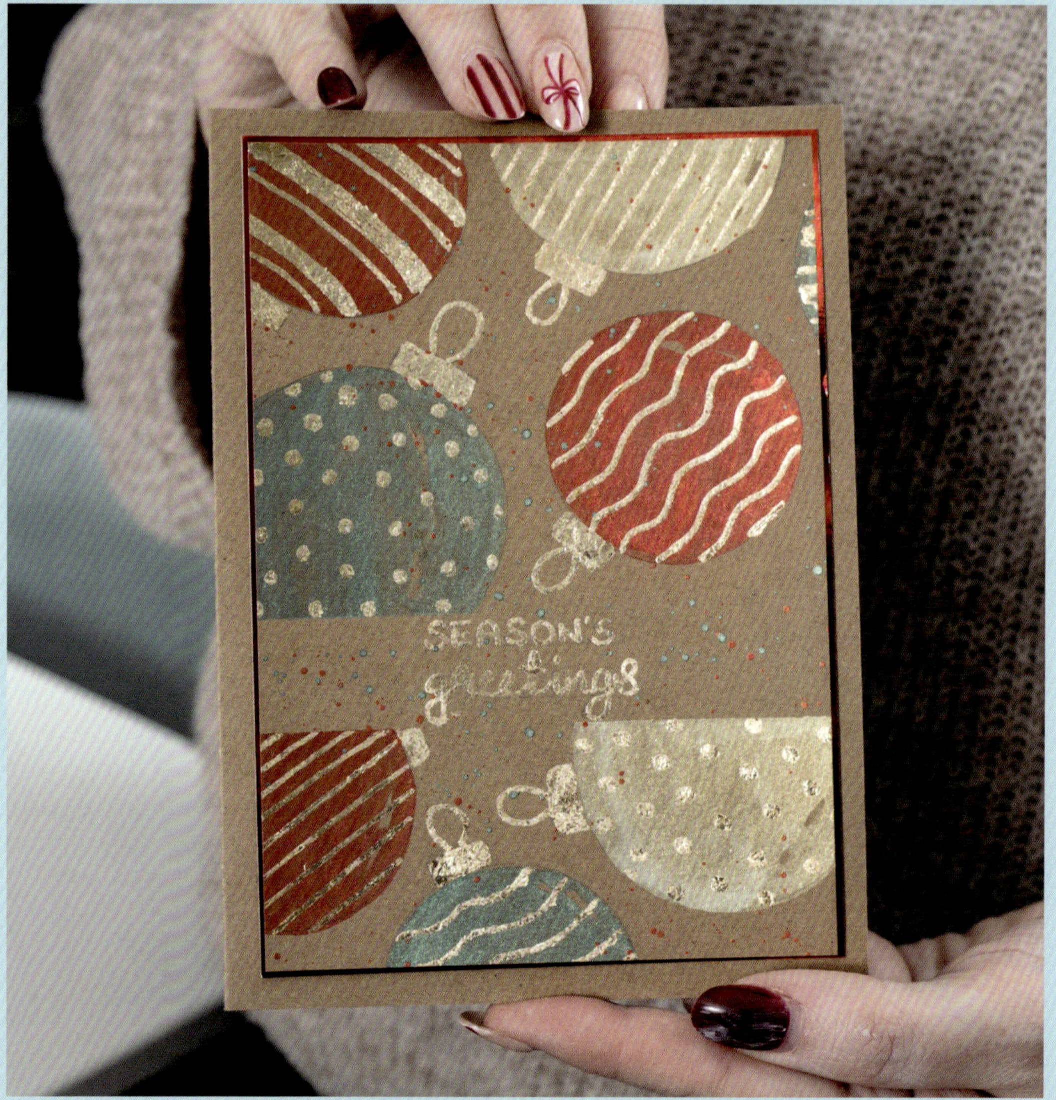

Intermediate

Sewn Christmas Card

This hand-stitched Christmas tree card is such a beautiful way to slow down, get creative and add an extra touch of magic to your festive makes. Once you've made one, you may find yourself stitching a whole stack to send out this Christmas – they're perfect for gifting to friends and family.

You will need:

- 6" x 4" Kraft card base (or cut from your own cardstock)
- Pencil
- Ruler
- Pokey tool (or other sharp implement)
- Sponge (or other soft surface)
- Eraser
- Needle
- Thread or wool
- Scissors
- Gold beads
- Glue tape pen or adhesive
- Star embellishment

1 If you don't have a pre-cut 6" × 4" card base, cut one from some cardstock.

2 Using a pencil and ruler, draw a Christmas tree template on to a piece of card. In this example, the tree measures approximately 4½" tall with a base width of 2½".

3 Measure ½" intervals along the two long sides of the tree shape and mark them lightly with a pencil. **(A)**

4 Using a pokey tool or other sharp implement, carefully make a hole at each marked point. Place a sponge or other soft surface underneath the card while doing this, to protect your work surface and prevent injury. These holes will be used for stitching.

TOP TIP You can use this sewn technique for a wide range of card and gift tag designs. Try stars, presents, baubles and more!

A

5 Use an eraser to remove all pencil lines.

6 Thread your needle with wool or thread, cut the thread from the ball and knot the free end.

7 Starting at the bottom of the tree, push the needle through from the back of the card to the front.

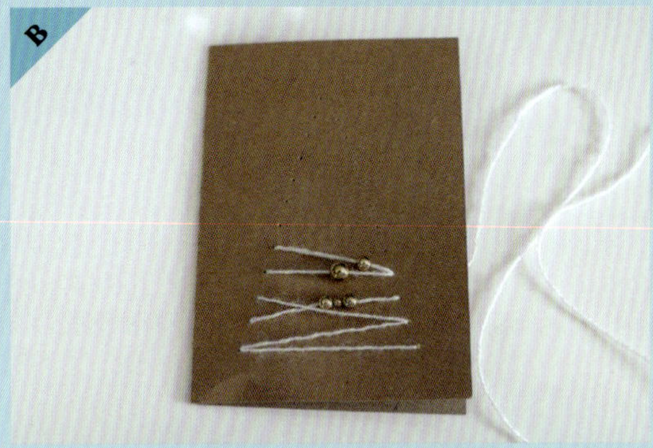

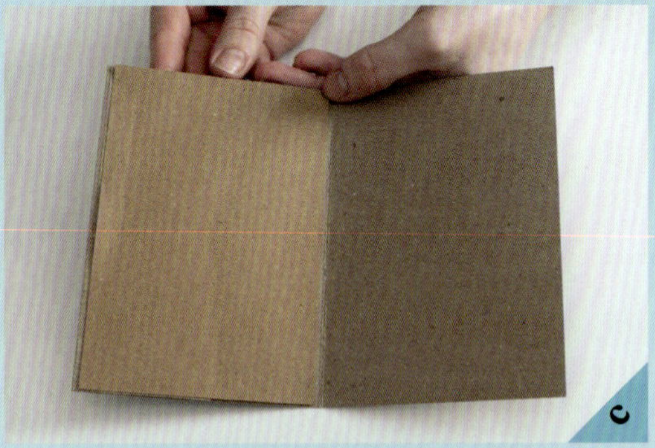

8 Continue stitching up the tree, adding gold beads as you go and passing the needle through the corresponding hole on the opposite side, in a zigzag, to complete each stitch. **(B)**

9 Once the tree is complete, tie off the thread securely at the back of the card front and trim away any excess.

10 To neaten the inside of the card, cut a piece of Kraft card slightly smaller than the card front and secure it in place using a tape pen or adhesive. **(C)**

11 Add a golden star to the top of the tree to finish.

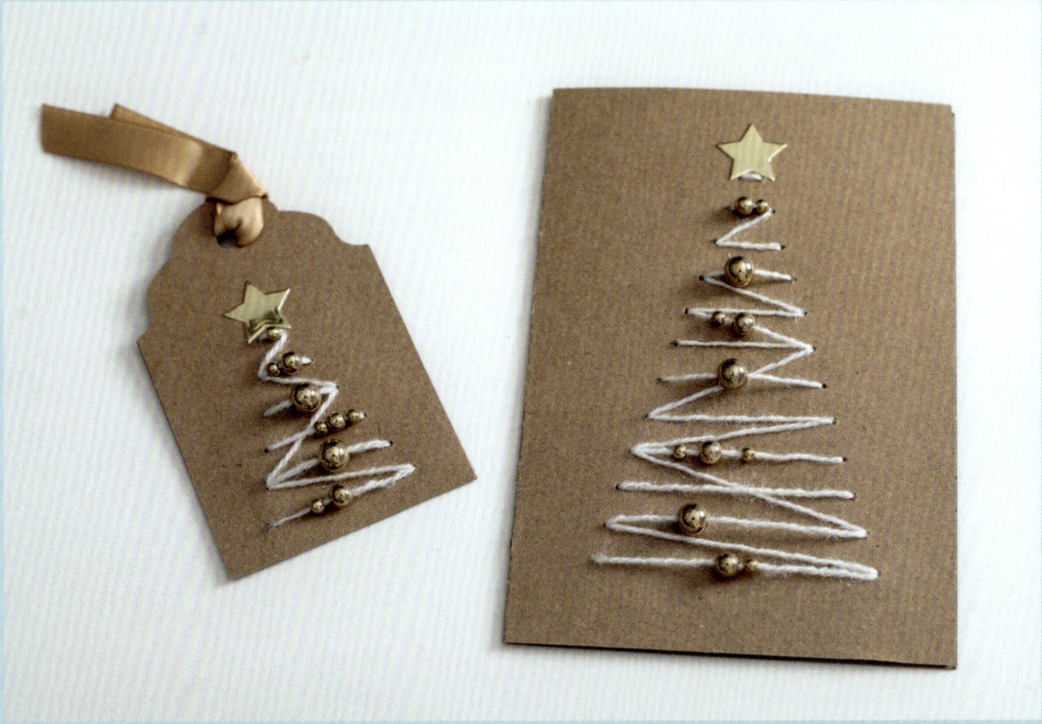

Easy

Gonk Tag

This project is festive, fun and perfect for adding a handmade touch to your Christmas wrapping. With a bit of patterned paper, some fluffy faux fur and a simple wooden bead, you can create the cutest character that will instantly raise a smile. These tags are ideal for using up stash scraps, brilliant for crafting with older kids, and make any gift look extra special before it's even opened.

TOP TIP **This little character would also work beautifully on the front of a Christmas card.**

You will need:

- Kraft card
- Die and die-cutting machine (optional)
- Pencil
- Ruler
- Scissors or paper trimmer
- Hole punch (if not using a die-cutting machine)
- Glue gun
- Faux fur fabric trim
- Patterned paper
- Coloured card
- Foam pads
- Wooden bead
- Ribbon

1 Create a tag using a die and die-cutting machine, or cut a piece of Kraft card down to your desired tag size. If cutting by hand, punch a hole at the top of the tag for threading ribbon later. **(A)**

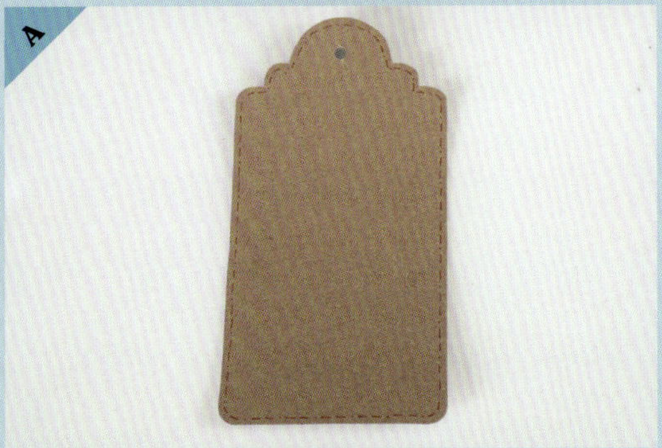

2 Apply a line of hot glue to the lower section of the tag and press a piece of faux fur trim into place. **(B)**

3 Cut a rectangle of patterned paper. Use a ruler and pencil to draw a triangle shape for the hat and cut it out. **(C)**

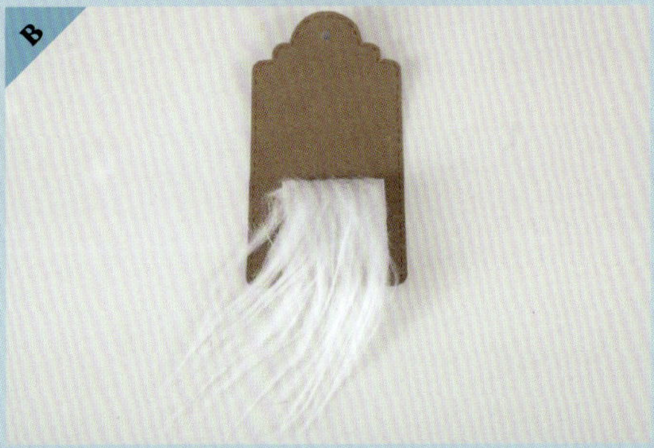

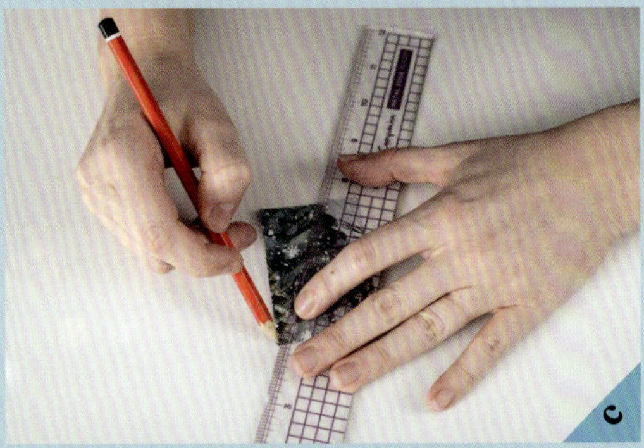

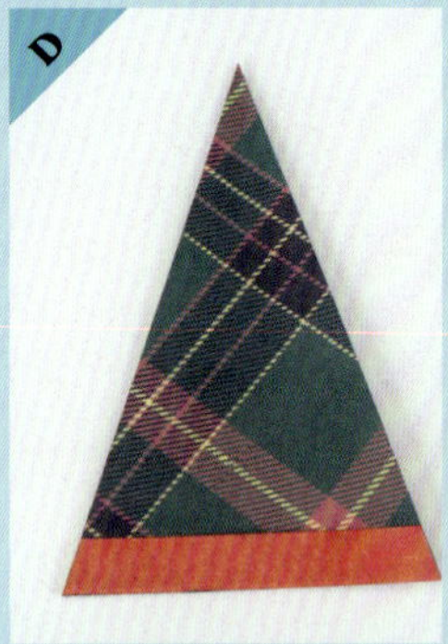

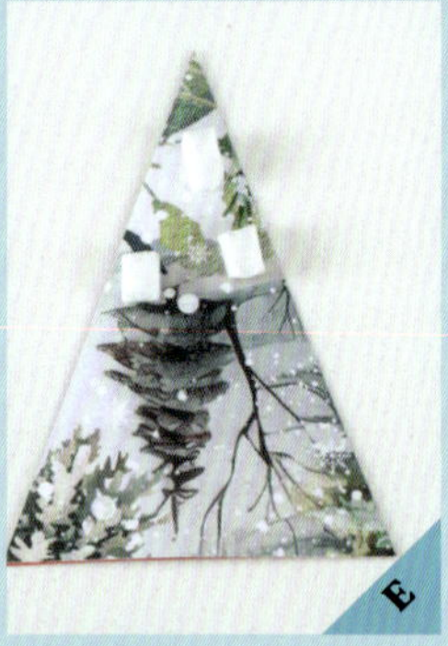

4 Cut a narrow strip of paper or card in a complementary colour to fit along the bottom edge of the triangle to create a hat trim. Glue it into place. **(D)**

5 Attach foam pads to the back of the triangle. **(E)**

6 Remove the backing from the foam pads and adhere the triangle to the tag, positioning it just above the faux fur trim. **(F)**

7 Apply a small dab of hot glue to a wooden bead and secure it below the hat to form the gonk's nose. **(G)**

8 Set the tag aside to dry completely, then trim the faux fur to shape the beard if needed. **(H)**

9 Thread ribbon through the hole at the top of the tag to finish. **(I)**

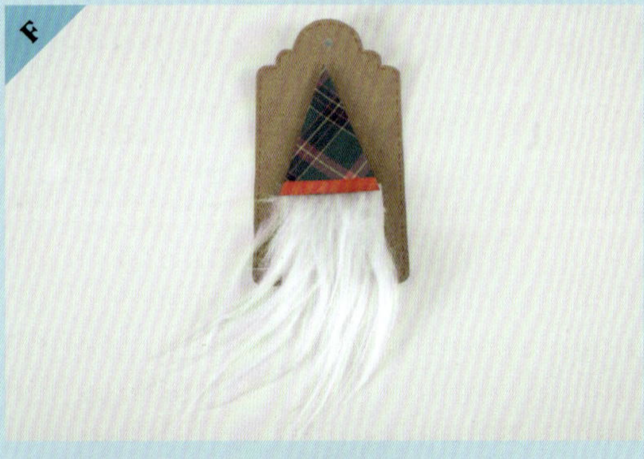

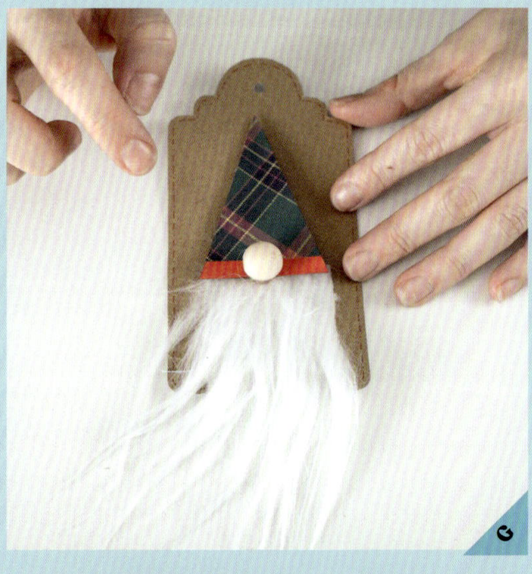

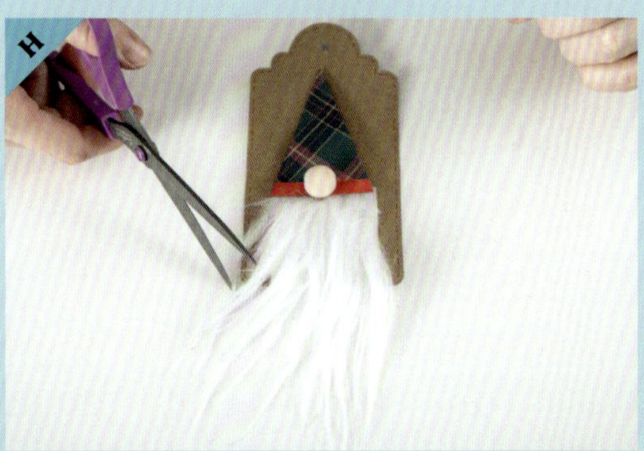

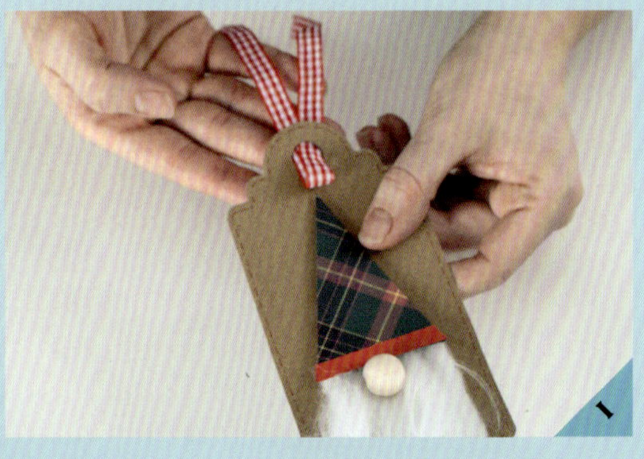

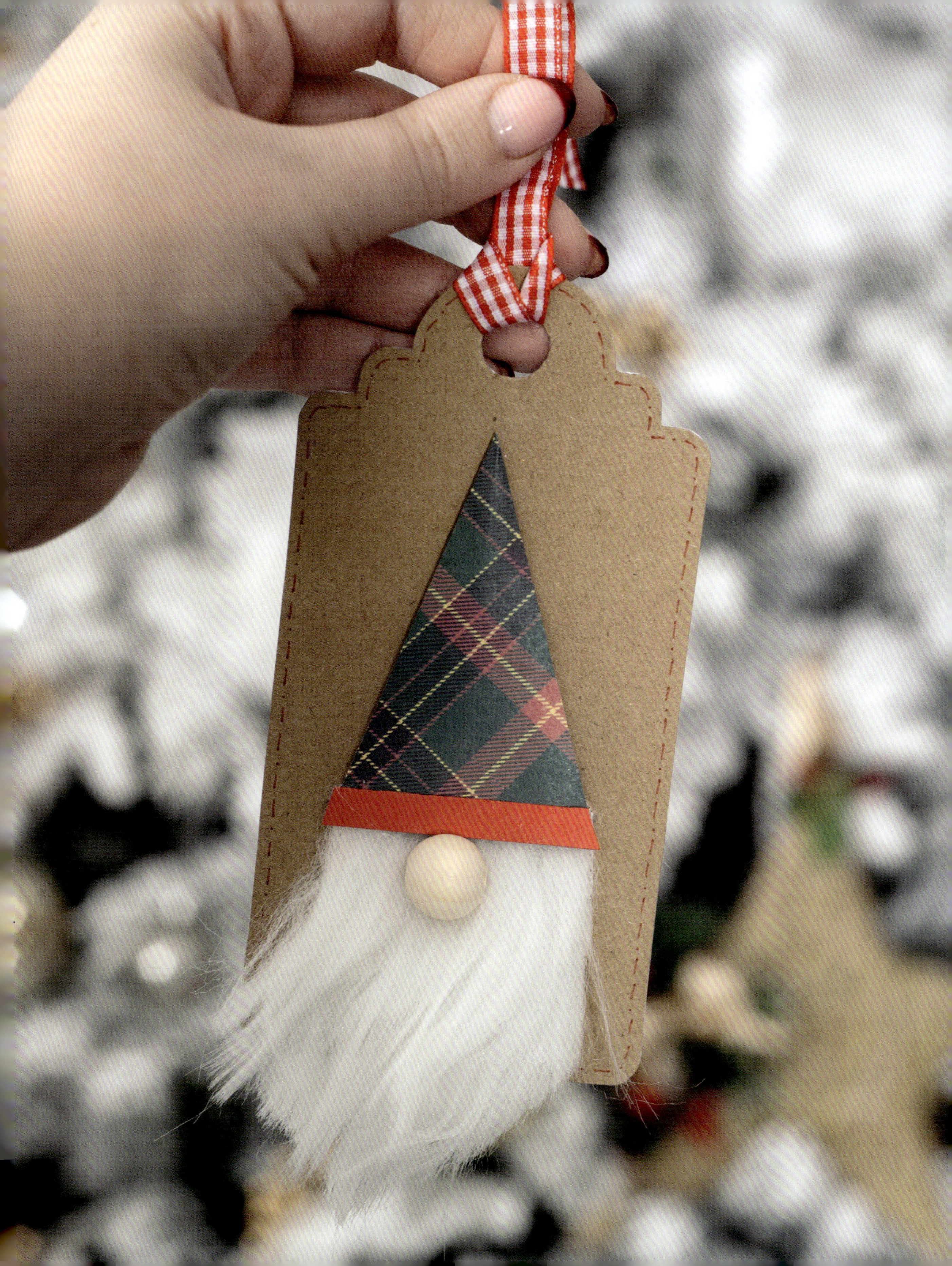

Easy

Clay Gift Tags

Clay gift tags are such a simple and effective way to add a personal touch to gifts, decorations or home décor. Using air-dry clay means there's no need for any special equipment, and you can create beautiful, bespoke tags with just a few basic tools.

This project is wonderfully hands-on and gives you plenty of freedom to experiment with shapes, textures and personalized messages. Whether you stamp names or festive words, or press natural foliage into the surface for extra detail, every tag will be completely unique.

You will need:

- Air-dry clay
- Rolling pin
- Ruler
- Sharp knife
- Cookie cutters (optional)
- Alphabet cookie stamps
- Pokey tool or pencil
- White paint
- Small paintbrush
- Ribbon or twine

1 Cut off a piece of air-dry clay and roll it out evenly using a rolling pin. Avoid rolling the clay too thin, as this can cause it to curl while drying. **(A)**

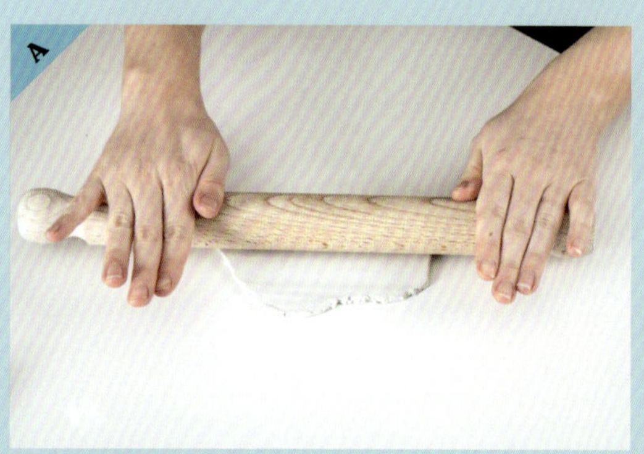

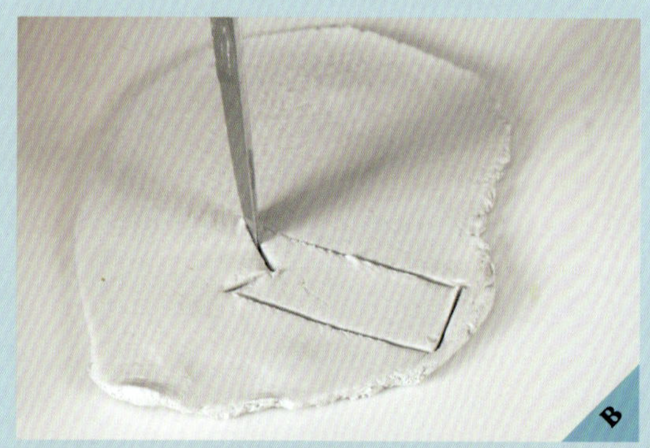

2 Using a ruler and a sharp knife, cut the clay into your desired tag shapes. Alternatively, you can use cookie cutters if you'd like a variety of shapes and sizes. **(B)**

3 Personalize each tag by pressing alphabet cookie stamps into the clay. You can also press foliage or other textured items into the surface for added interest. **(C)**

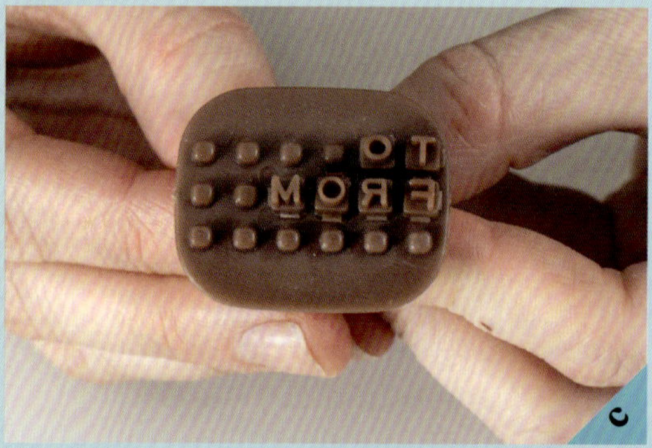

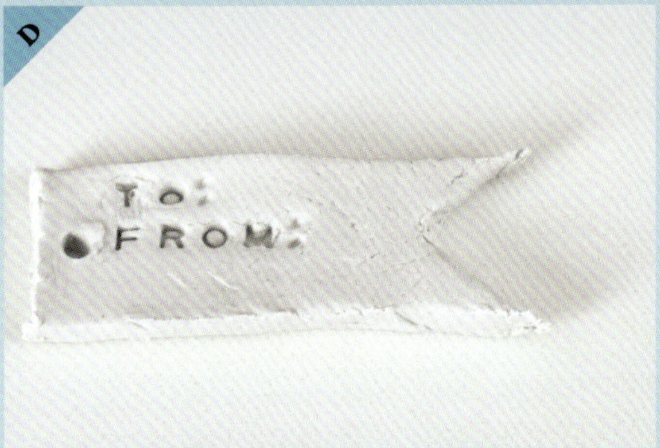

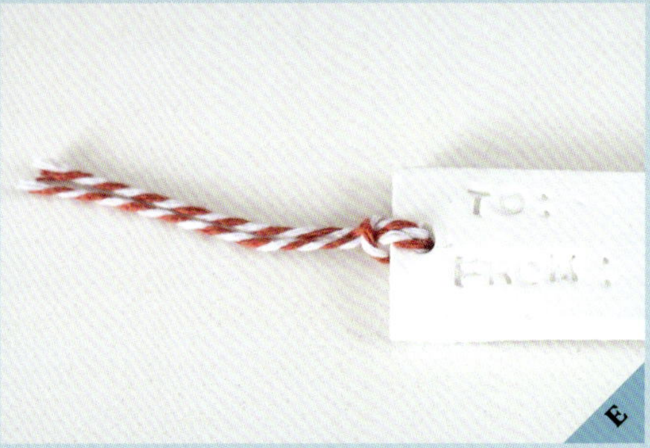

4 Once you're happy with the design, use a pokey tool or pencil to carefully make a hole in each tag for threading ribbon or twine later. **(D)**

5 Set the tags aside on a flat surface and allow them to air-dry completely. This will take approximately 24–48 hours, depending on the thickness of the clay.

6 Once fully dry, paint the tags with white paint using a clean paintbrush, then allow the paint to dry thoroughly.

7 Thread a length of ribbon or twine through the hole in each tag to finish, then add them to your gifts! **(E)**

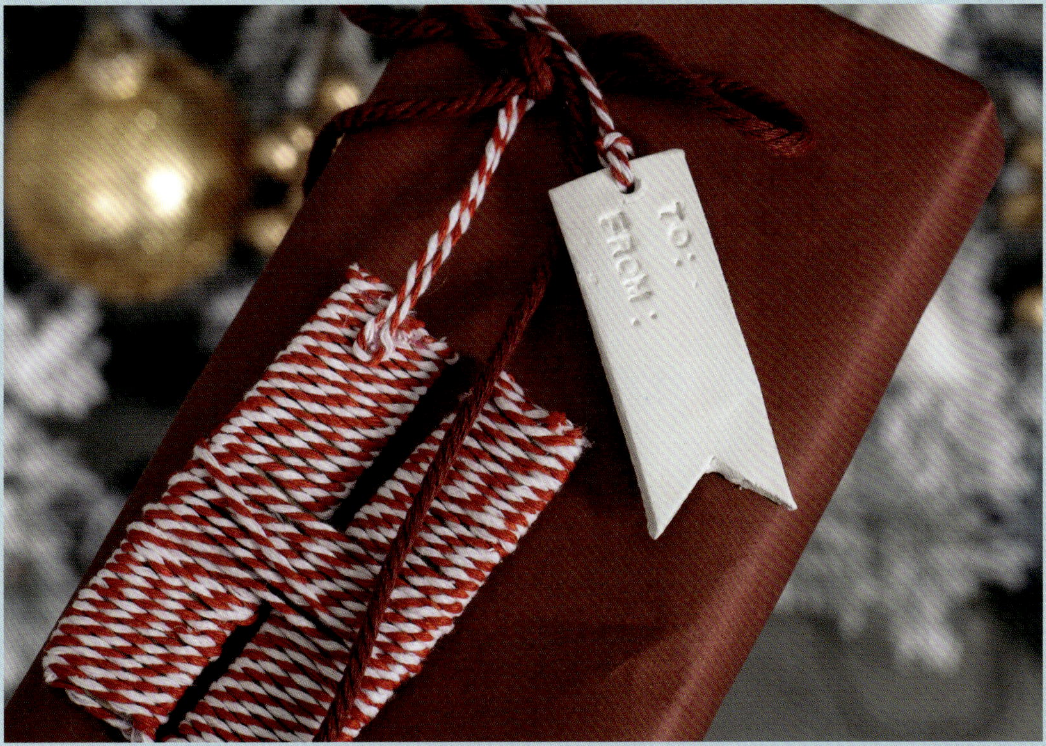

Easy

Découpage Baubles

One of my favourite things about crafting is giving new life to existing items, and these découpage baubles are a fantastic way to do just that. Using pieces you may already have at home, you can create elegant tree decorations with a luxurious, handcrafted feel. Simply choose a napkin design that suits your festive theme and let's get started!

You will need:

- Baubles
- White acrylic paint or white gesso
- Medium-sized paintbrushes
- Scissors
- Paper napkins
- Mod Podge
- Craft glue
- Gold glitter or glitter glue pen (optional)

1 Ensure the surface of your bauble is completely clean and dry. **(A)**

2 To create a base, apply an even coat of white paint or gesso over the surface of the bauble, then set it aside to dry fully. **(B)**

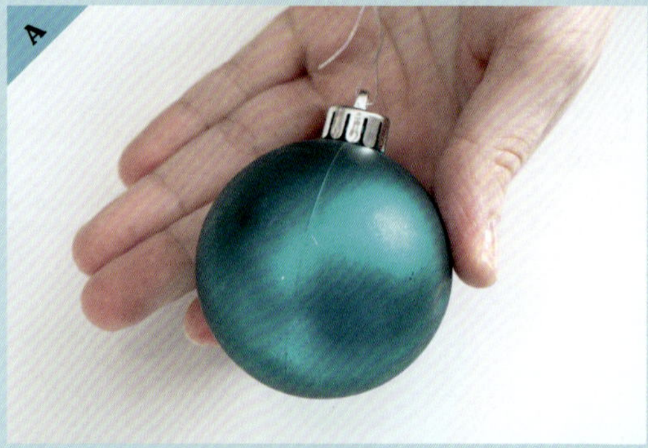
A

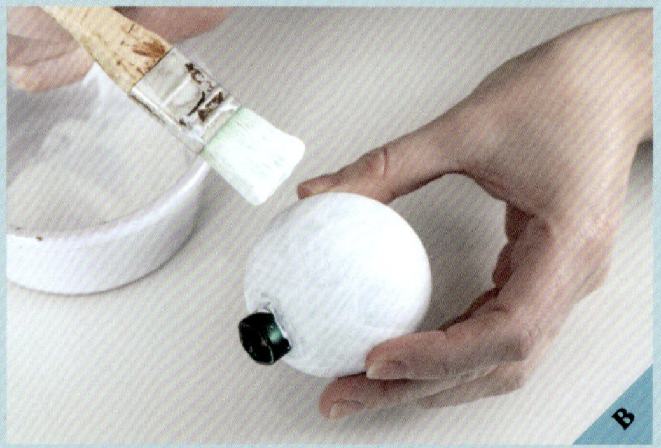
B

3 Apply a second coat of paint if needed for an opaque finish.

4 While the paint is drying, cut out the napkin elements you plan to use. Carefully separate the layers of the napkin, keeping only the thin, patterned top layer. **(C)**

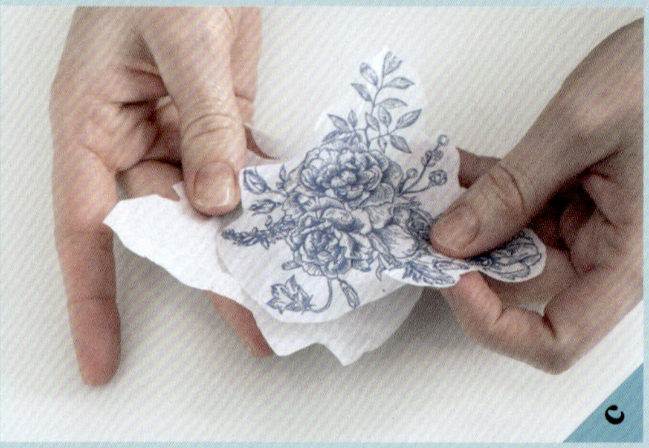
C

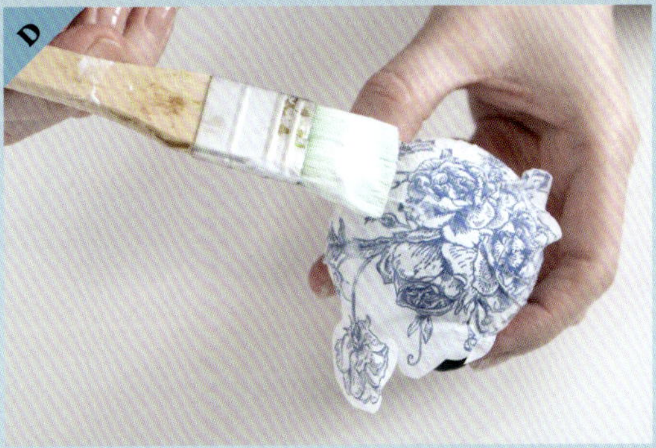

D

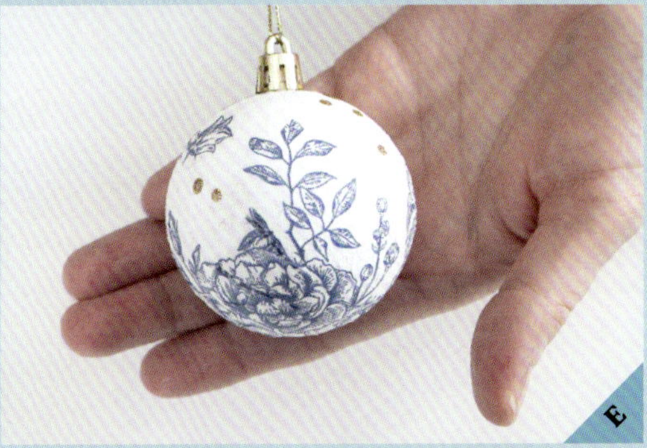

E

5 Using a clean paintbrush, apply a thin layer of Mod Podge to a small area of the bauble. Gently place a napkin piece on to the glued area and smooth it carefully to remove any creases or air bubbles.

6 Apply a thin layer of Mod Podge over the top to seal the napkin in place. **(D)**

7 Repeat the previous two steps until you're happy with the design and coverage. It's fine to leave some of the white base showing through for a lighter, layered look.

8 Set the bauble aside to dry completely.

9 Once dry, add small dabs of glue across the surface of the bauble and sprinkle with glitter, or use a glitter glue pen for added sparkle! **(E)**

TOP TIP **Use only a small amount of Mod Podge at a time. Applying too much can cause the delicate napkin layer to tear.**

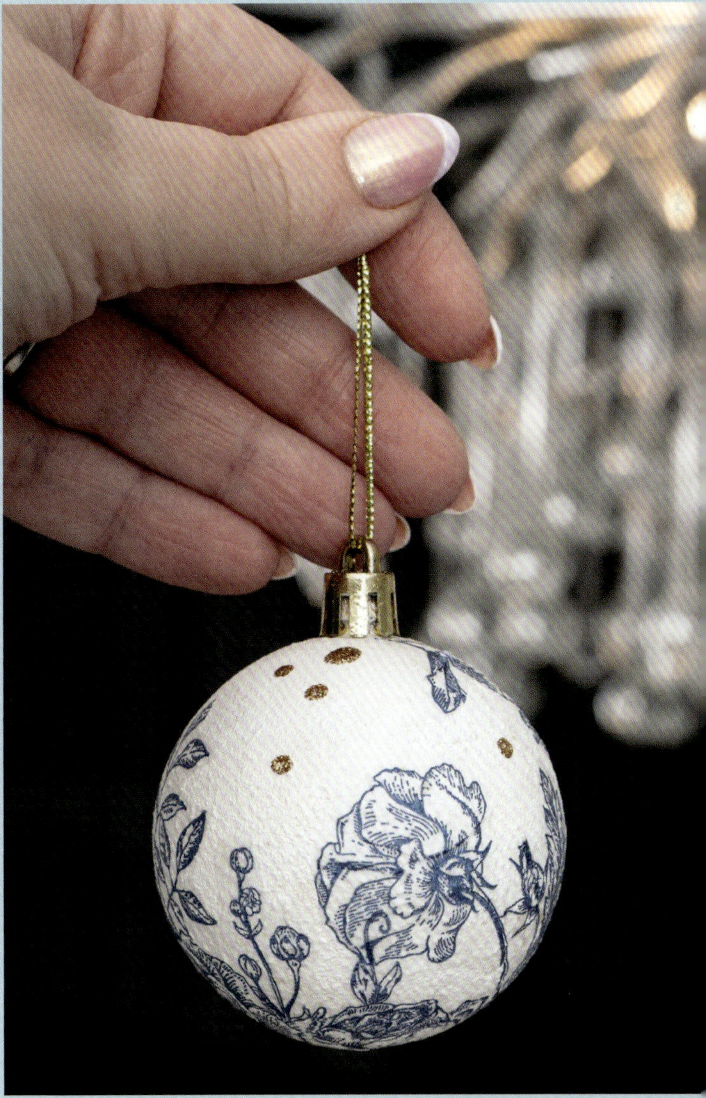

Intermediate

3D Snowflake

This beautiful 3D snowflake is one of those crafts that looks far more complicated than it actually is! With just a few simple folds, careful cuts and a little glue, you'll transform flat paper into a striking dimensional decoration that's perfect for festive displays.

Whether you're crafting with the kids, decorating your home, or enjoying some creative 'me time', this project proves that you don't need fancy materials to achieve a professional-looking finish. So grab your paper, trust the process and enjoy watching the snowflake take shape.

You will need:

- Patterned paper
- Ruler
- Pencil
- Scissors
- Glue gun
- Gem embellishment

1 Cut six squares of patterned paper, each measuring 6″ × 6″. **(A)**

2 Take one square and fold it in half diagonally to form a triangle. **(B)**

3 Along the left-hand, unfolded edge, measure and lightly mark 1″ Intervals with a ruler and pencil.

4 From each mark, draw a straight line towards the folded edge, stopping approximately ¼″ from the fold. **(C)**

5 Carefully cut along each drawn line, taking care not to cut through the folded edge.

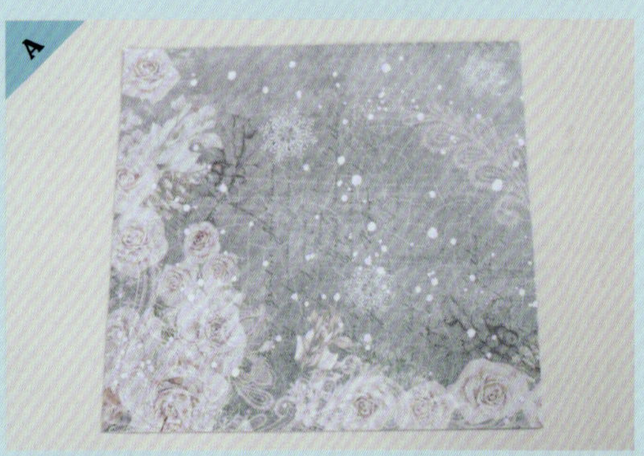
A

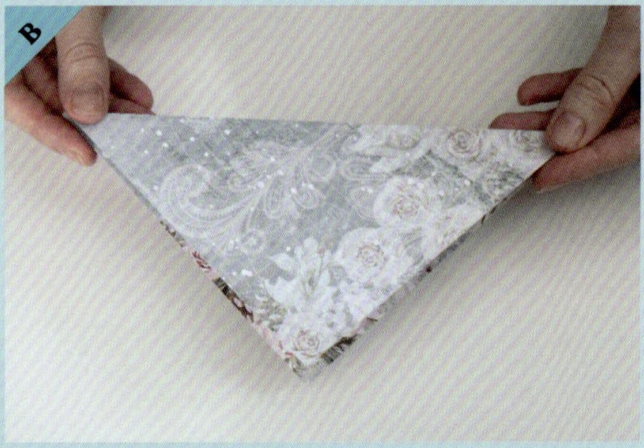
B

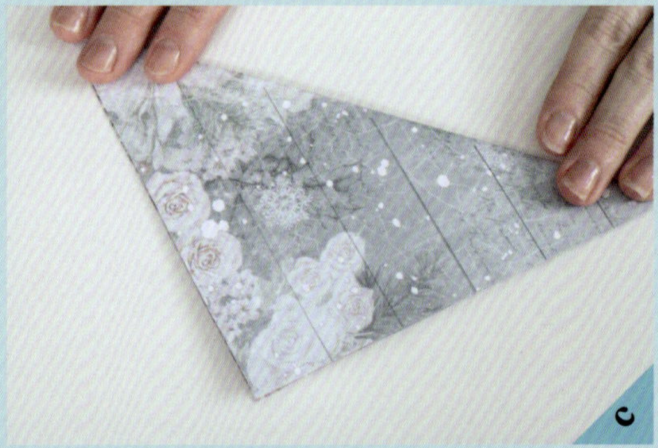
C

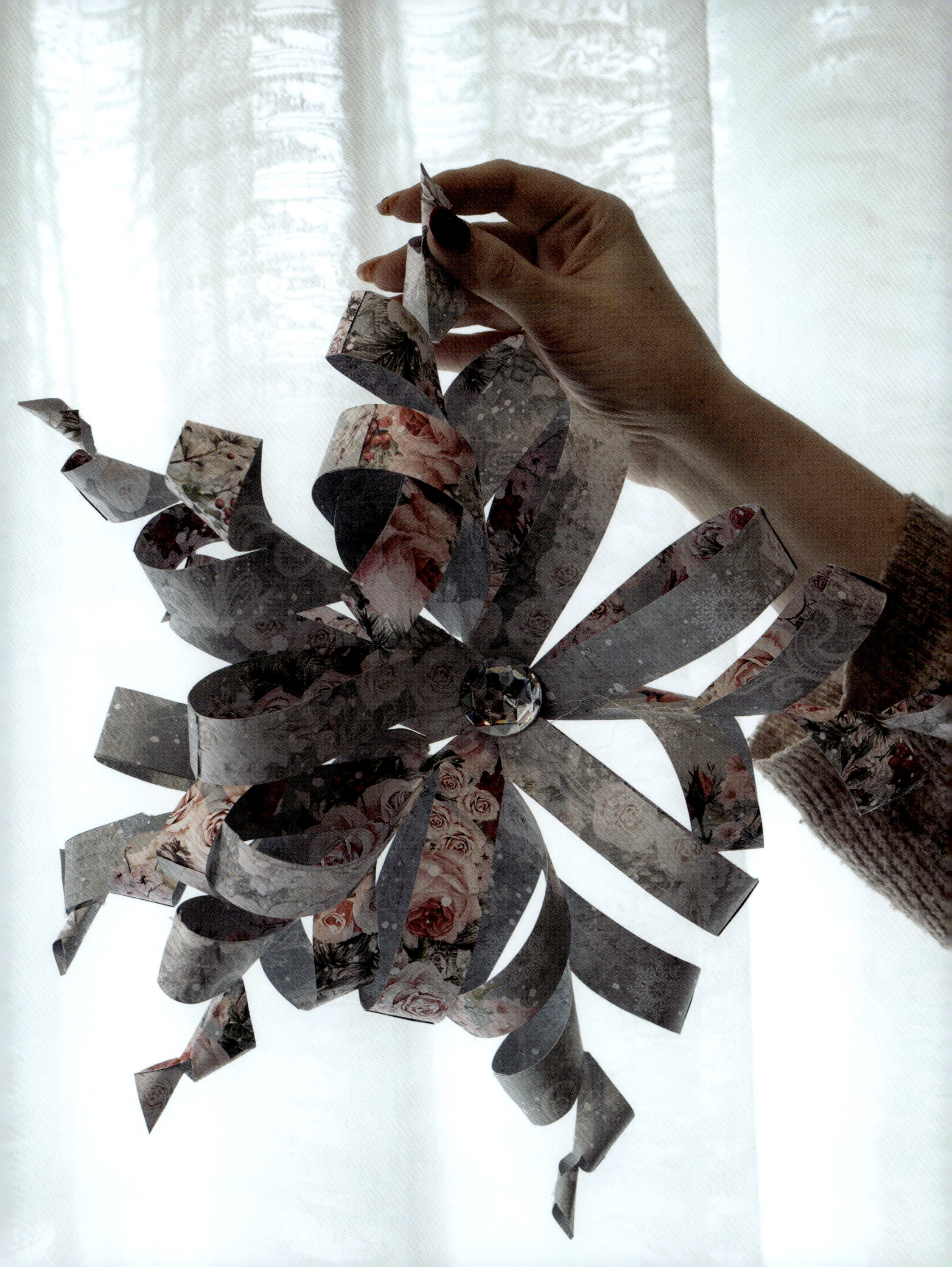

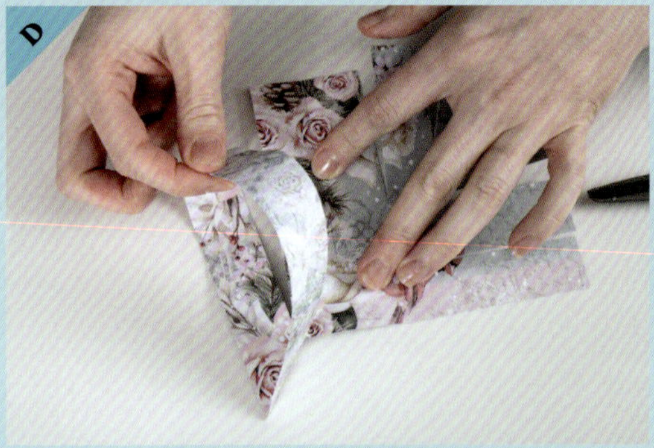

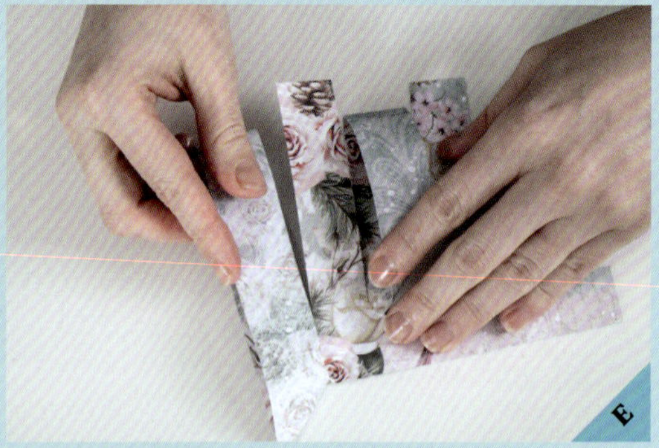

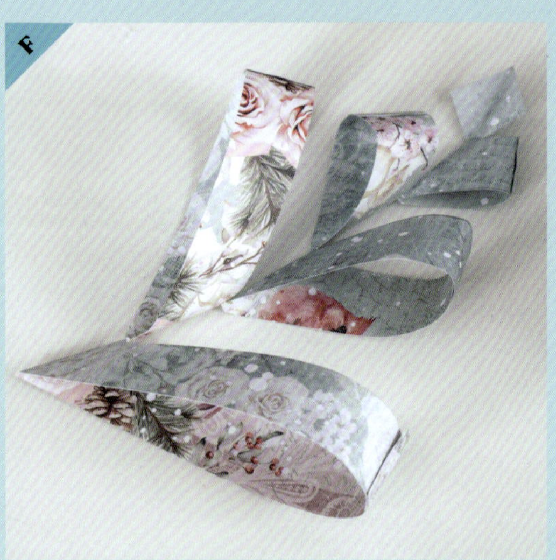

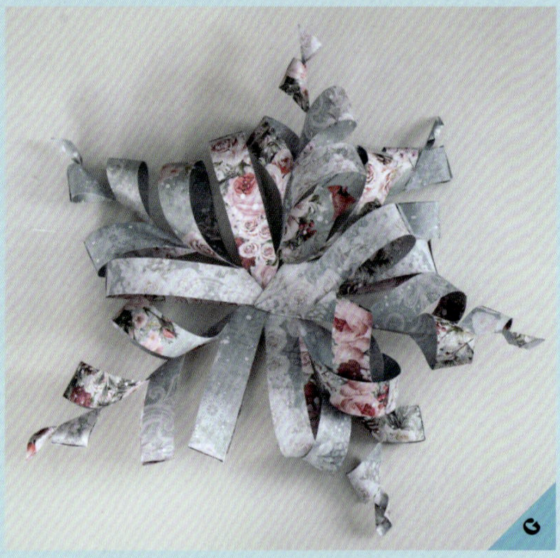

6 Open the paper out flat, positioning it so the square sits diagonally. Take the two bottom strips and glue them together to form a loop on one side. **(D)**

7 Skip the next two strips, then glue the following two strips together on the same side. **(E)**

8 Continue gluing every other pair of strips. Once complete, flip the paper over and repeat the process on the opposite side to form more loops. **(F)**

9 Repeat steps 2–8 with the remaining five paper squares.

10 Glue all six finished sections together to form one complete snowflake. **(G)**

11 Use the glue gun to secure a gem embellishment in the centre of the snowflake to finish.

TOP TIP **You can decorate the centre of your snowflake in lots of different ways. Try gems, glitter, or any small embellishments you have to hand.**

Easy

Party Hats

Bring a little sparkle and fun to your New Year celebrations with these handmade paper party hats! They're festive, fun and completely customizable, so you can choose the colours, patterns and embellishments that match your party theme. This project is quick to make, incredibly satisfying, and perfect for crafting with friends, family, or even solo.

You will need:

- Quality patterned paper
- Large circular template (e.g. dinner plate)
- Mirror card
- Ruler
- Pencil
- Scissors
- Glue gun
- Tassel
- Hole punch
- Gold elastic

1 Take a 12″ × 12″ piece of quality patterned paper.

2 Draw around a large circular object, such as a dinner plate, for a symmetrical shape. Cut out the circle and cut it in half. **(A)**

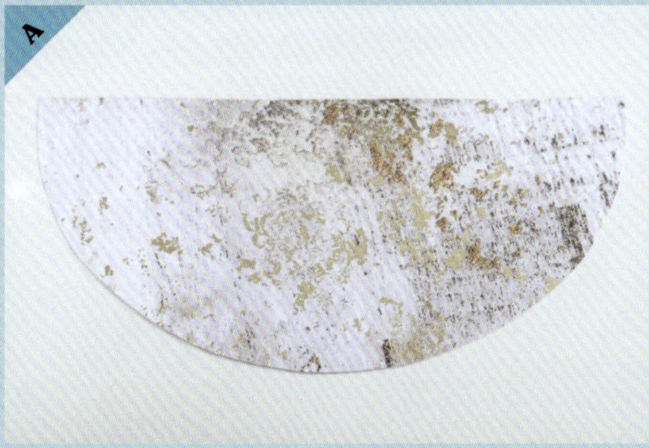

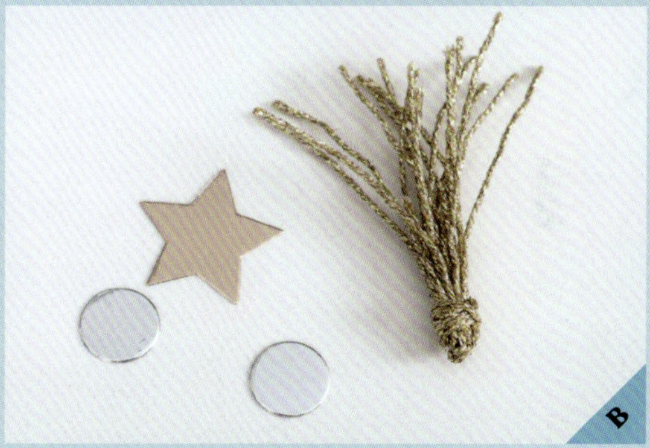

3 Use some scissors to trim away ¼″ from the semi-circle.

4 Create some decorative elements for the hat from some mirror card. Alternatively, you can purchase some ready-made alternatives. **(B)**

5 Use a glue gun to adhere the elements to the party hat. **(C)**

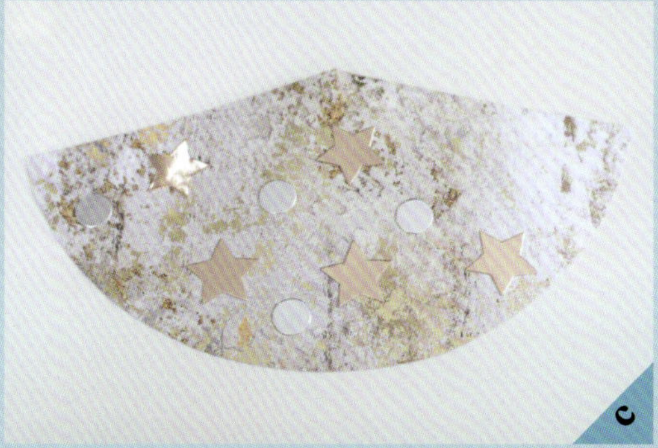

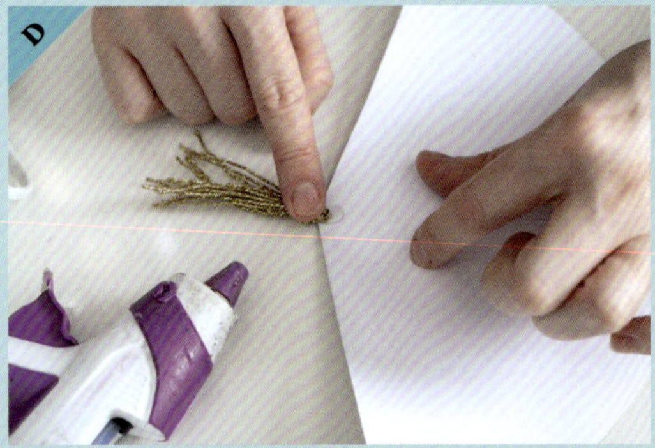

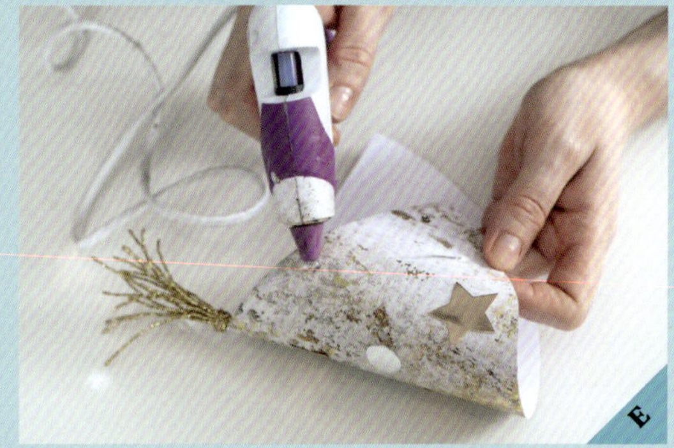

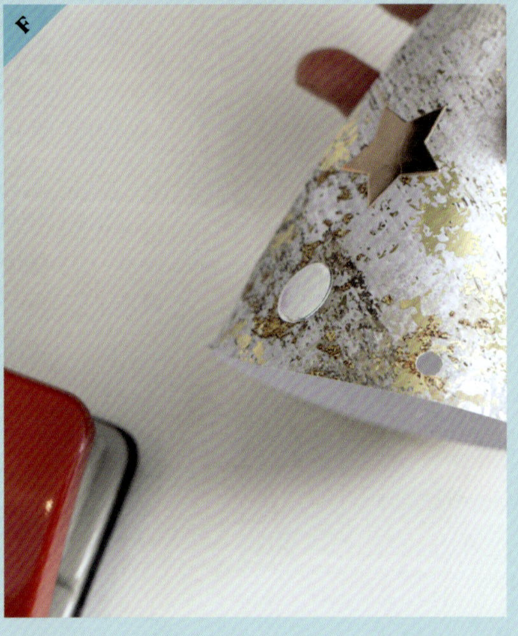

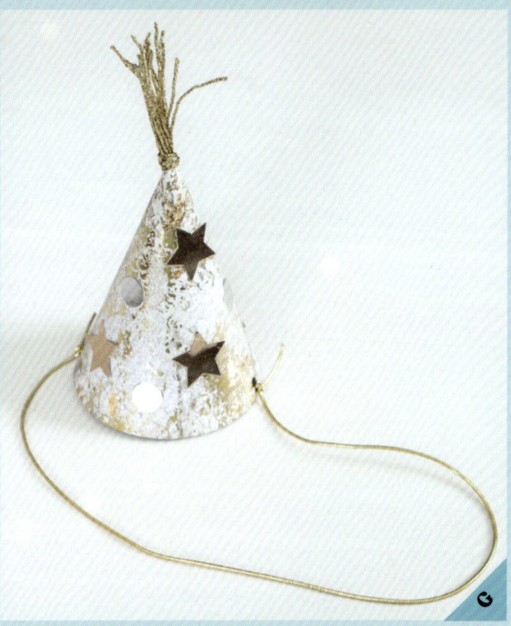

6 Turn the paper over and glue the tassel into place. **(D)**

7 Run a line of hot glue down one straight edge of the paper and adhere it to the other straight edge to create a cone shape. **(E)**

8 Punch a hole in either side of the hat for the elastic thread to pass through. **(F)**

9 Measure a length of gold elastic long enough to fit under your chin, thread it through the holes and tie a knot in either end to finish. **(G)**

TOP TIP Change up the designs on your hats so guests can choose one to suit their style. You could add wire instead of a tassel to create shooting stars, or swap in pompoms for a playful finish.

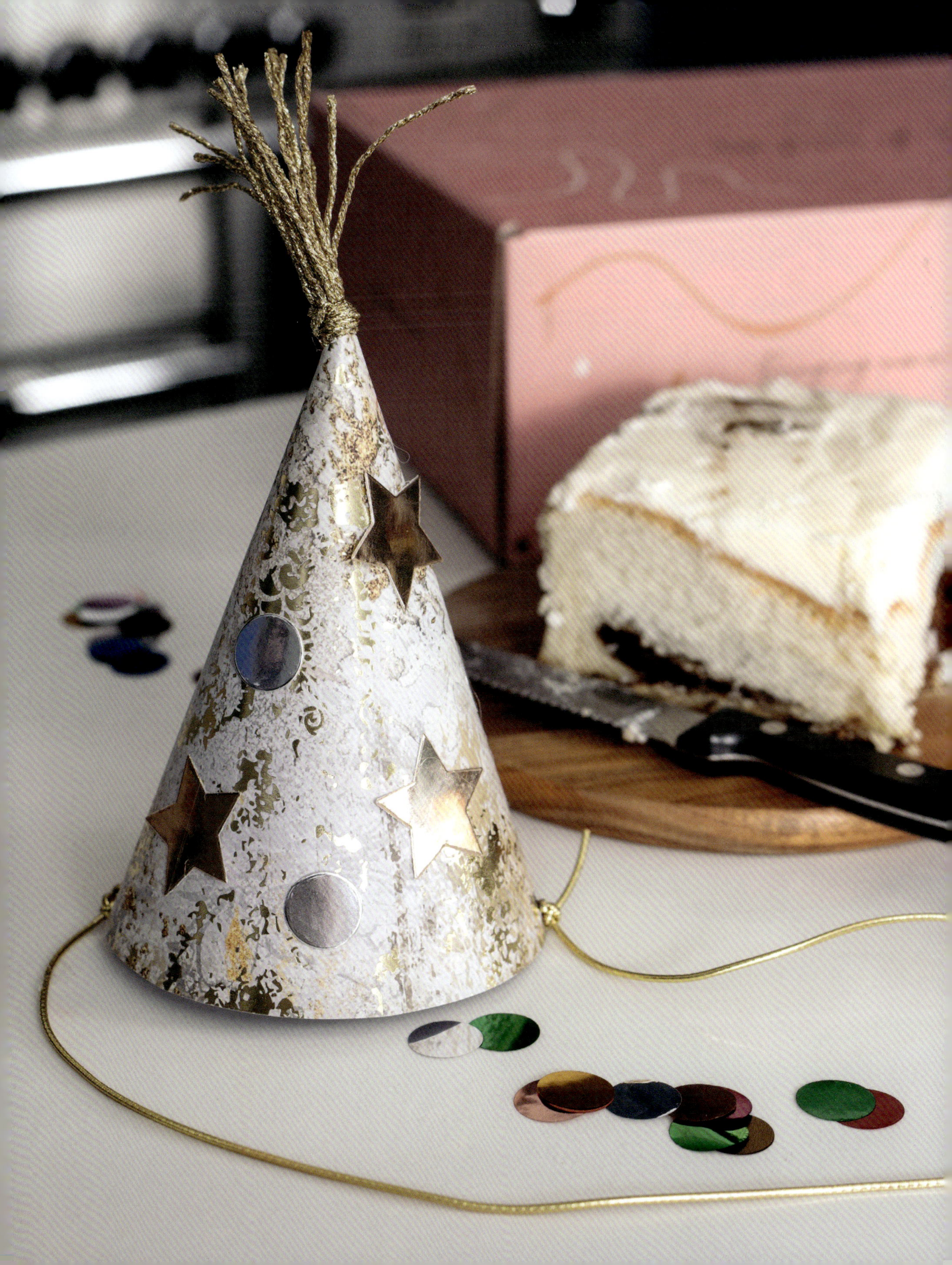

Easy

Party Poppers

If you ask me, it's the little details that really make a celebration special, and these DIY party poppers are a fun way to add that extra 'wow' factor. Quick to make and ideal for using up odds and ends that you'll already have around the house or in your craft stash, they're easy to personalize for any theme or colour scheme. Whether it's for New Year's Eve, a birthday, or just an excuse to have some fun, these poppers are guaranteed to add a burst of excitement.

You will need:

- Balloons
- Scissors
- Toilet-roll tubes
- Patterned paper
- Glue gun
- Confetti

TOP TIP **You can make your own eco-friendly confetti by cutting lightweight paper into small circles or squares.**

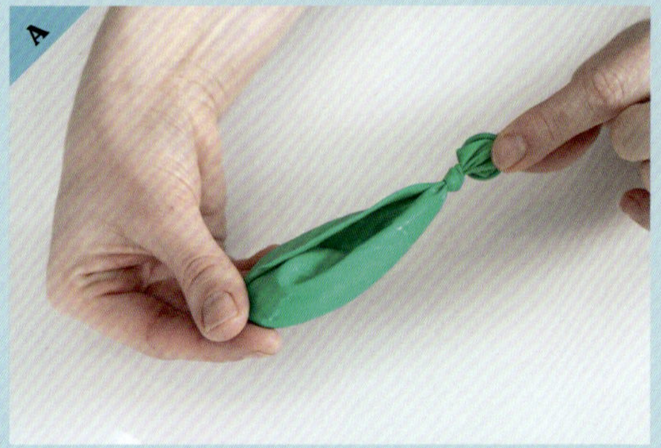

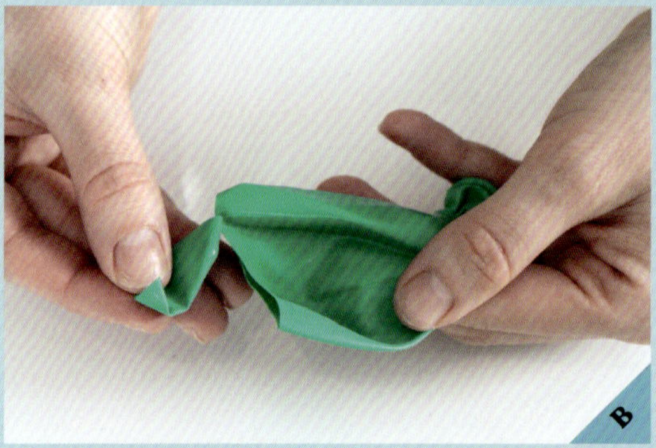

1 Take a balloon of your choice and tie a knot at the opening. **(A)**

2 Using scissors, carefully snip off the unknotted end of the balloon. **(B)**

3 Stretch the cut end of the balloon over one end of a toilet-roll tube, pulling it tight so it sits securely in place. **(C)**

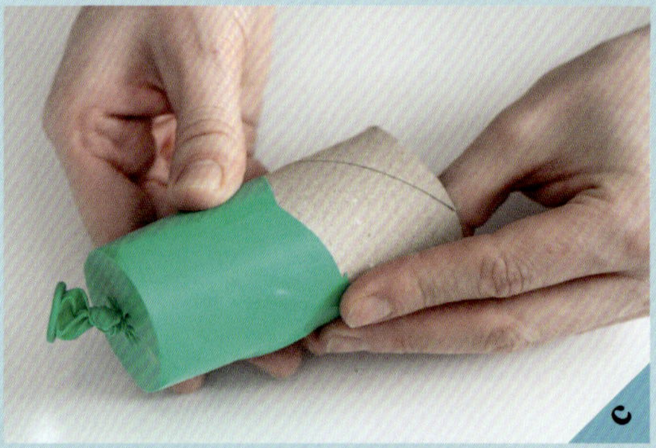

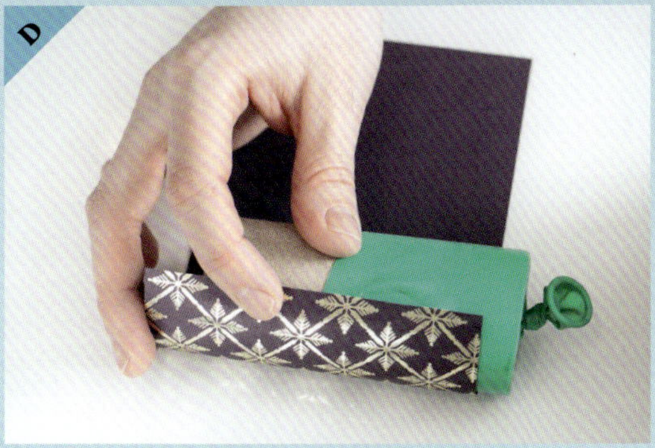

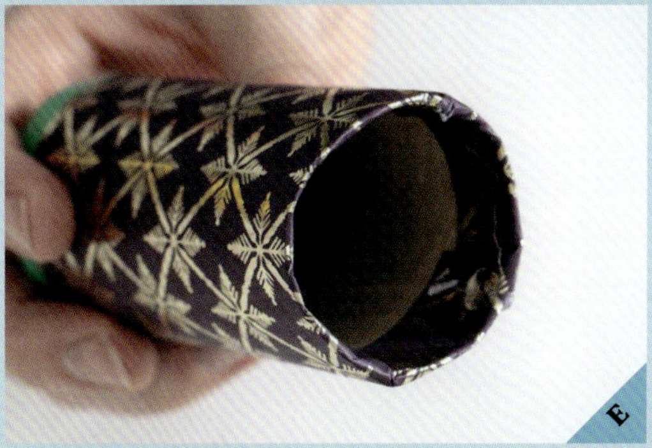

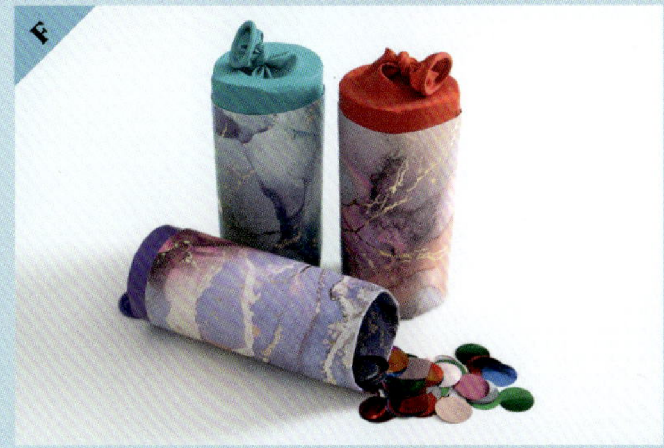

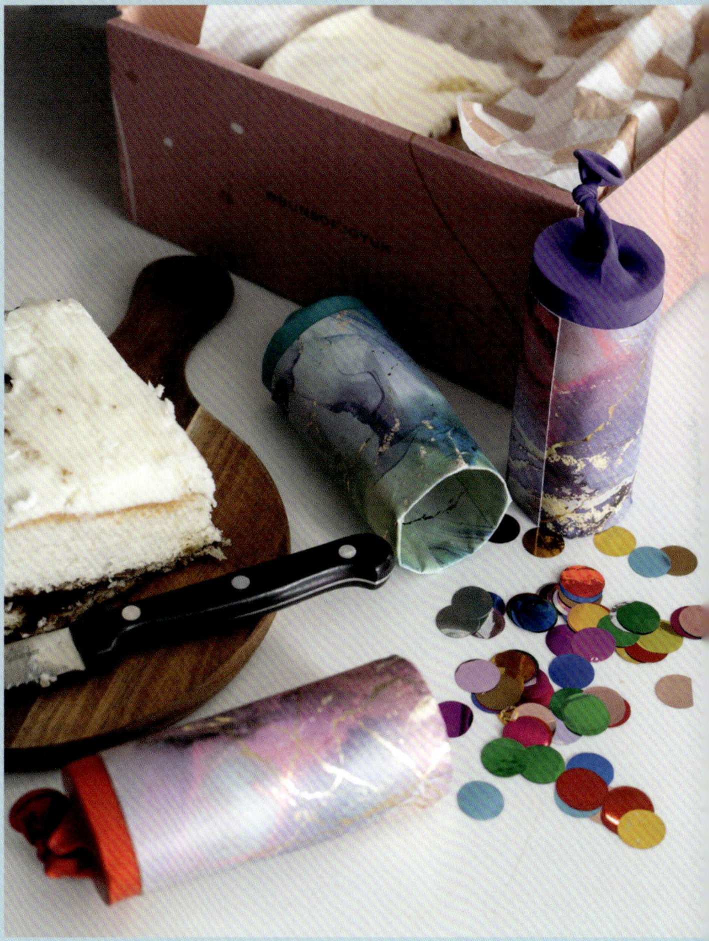

4 Cut a piece of patterned paper slightly wider than the toilet-roll tube and long enough to wrap all the way around it, allowing a little extra at one end to tuck inside for a neat finish. **(D)**

5 Run a line of hot glue down the length of the toilet-roll tube. Wrap the patterned paper around the tube and add another line of glue along the overlap to secure it firmly in place.

6 Add a small amount of hot glue just inside the open end of the tube. Tuck the excess paper inside and press it down to create a clean, tidy edge. **(E)**

7 Drop your chosen confetti into the open end of the tube to finish the party popper. **(F)**

8 To use, hold the tube firmly and pull the knotted end of the balloon to release the confetti and enjoy the surprise!

Easy

Fortune Cookies

If you're looking for a quick make that's guaranteed to raise a smile, then you are going to absolutely love these handmade fortune cookies! They're such a fun little project, ideal for parties, dinner tables, or as a personalized treat for someone special. Using just a few simple supplies, you can turn flat paper circles into adorable keepsakes in minutes.

TOP TIP **Personalize each fortune cookie with a message tailored to your guests for an extra thoughtful touch.**

You will need:

- Paper
- Ruler or circular template
- Pencil
- Scissors
- Glue gun
- Pen

1 Cut out a paper circle of your chosen size. The example shown measures 3¾" in diameter. **(A)**

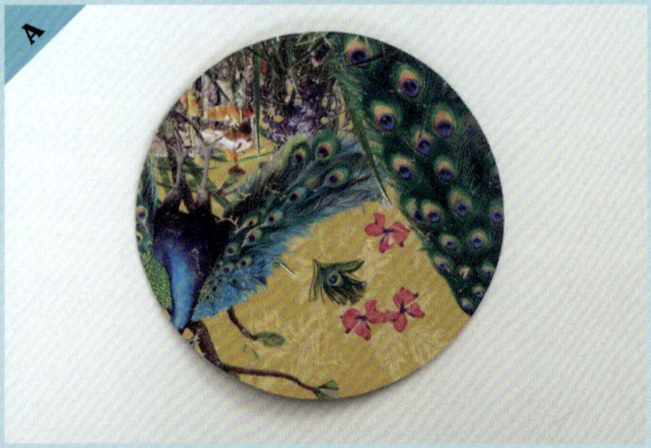
A

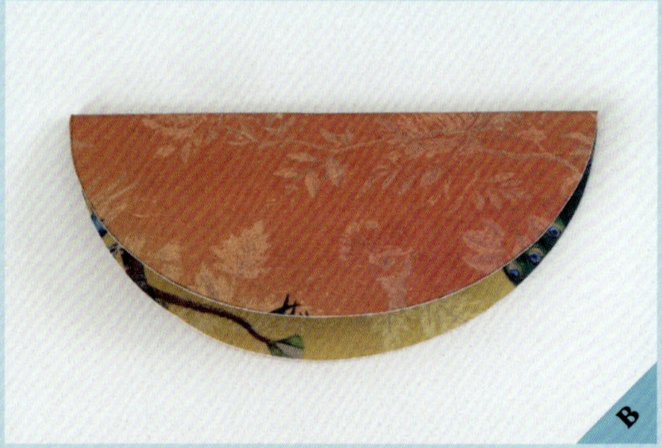
B

2 Fold the circle in half, then open it back out to create a centre crease. **(B)**

3 With the crease running vertically, bring the top and bottom edges towards the centre line. Secure them in place with a small amount of hot glue. **(C)**

4 Write your chosen fortune on to a narrow strip of paper.

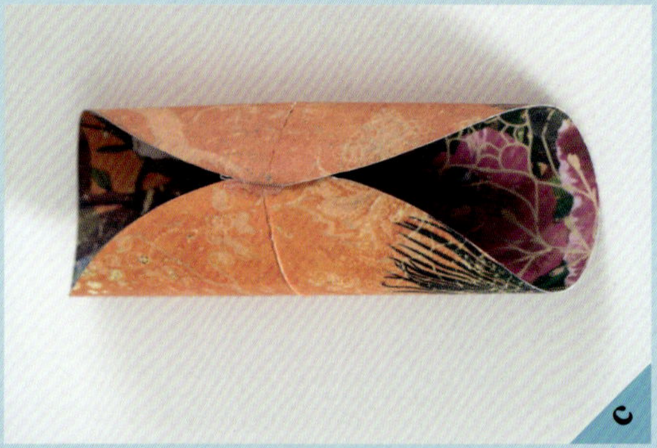
C

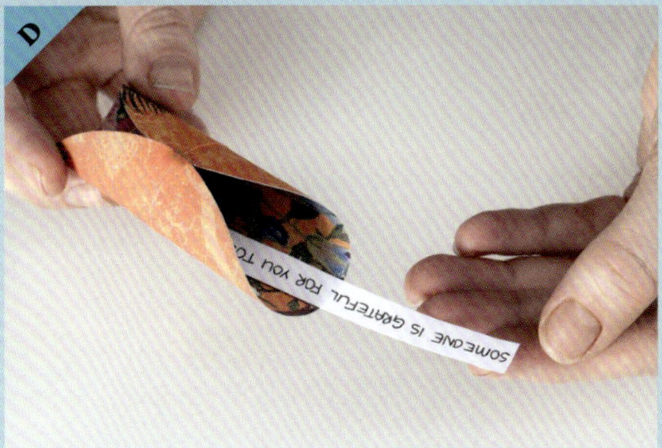

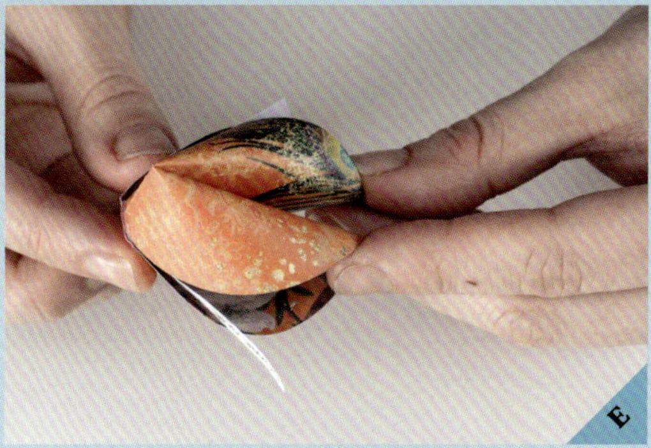

5 Place the paper strip inside the folded paper tube. **(D)**

6 Hold the two open ends of the tube and gently pull them together to form the classic fortune-cookie shape. **(E)**

7 Add a small dab of hot glue along the centre fold to hold the shape in place. **(F)**

8 Repeat steps 1–7 to create a fortune-cookie collection!

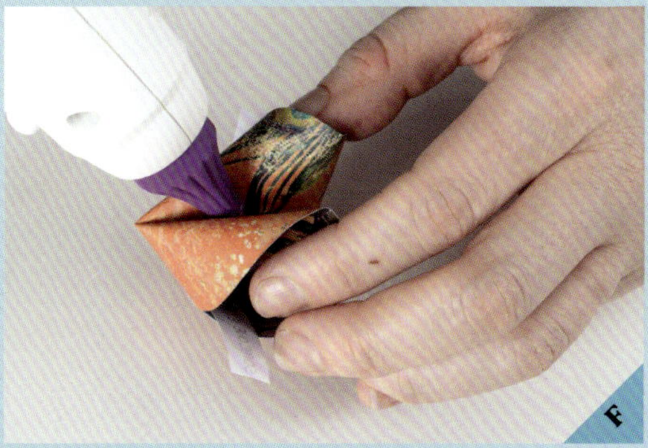

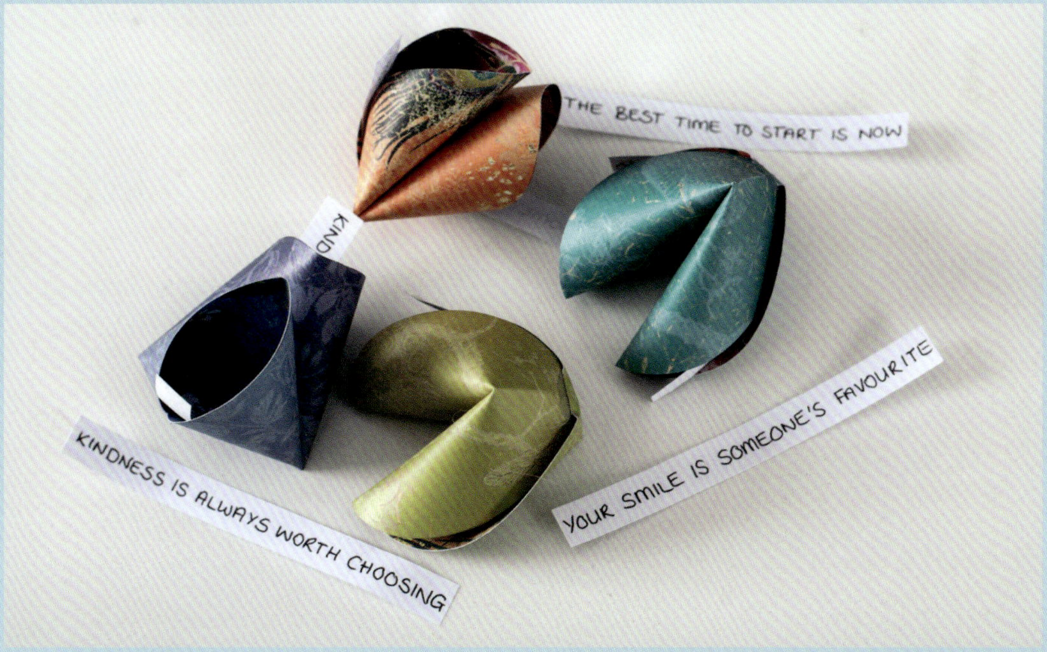

Intermediate

Paper Lanterns

Add a touch of sparkle and drama to your New Year's Eve celebrations with these 3D folded paper lanterns! They're bold, full of impact and perfect for hanging around your party space. The folding technique gives the lanterns a beautiful dimensional look that feels much more intricate than it actually is, and, once you've finished, you'll have a gorgeous, handcrafted decoration that's guaranteed to wow your guests and set the tone for a magical New Year.

TOP TIP **Why not use different coloured papers for each layer of the lantern?**

You will need:

- Patterned paper
- Pencil
- Ruler or scoring board
- Scissors or paper trimmer
- Bone folder (optional)
- Red liner double-sided tape
- Glue gun
- Gold twine
- Tassel

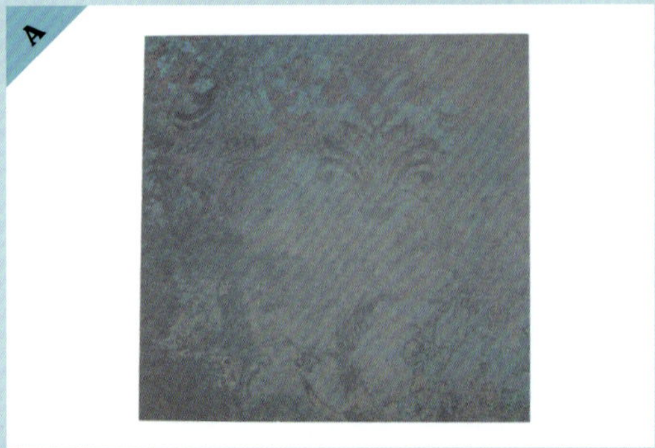

1 To create each layer, you will need four pieces of paper measuring 6" × 6". There are nine layers in total. **(A)**

2 Take one piece of paper and fold it in half. **(B)**

3 Open it out and fold it in half in the opposite direction. **(C)**

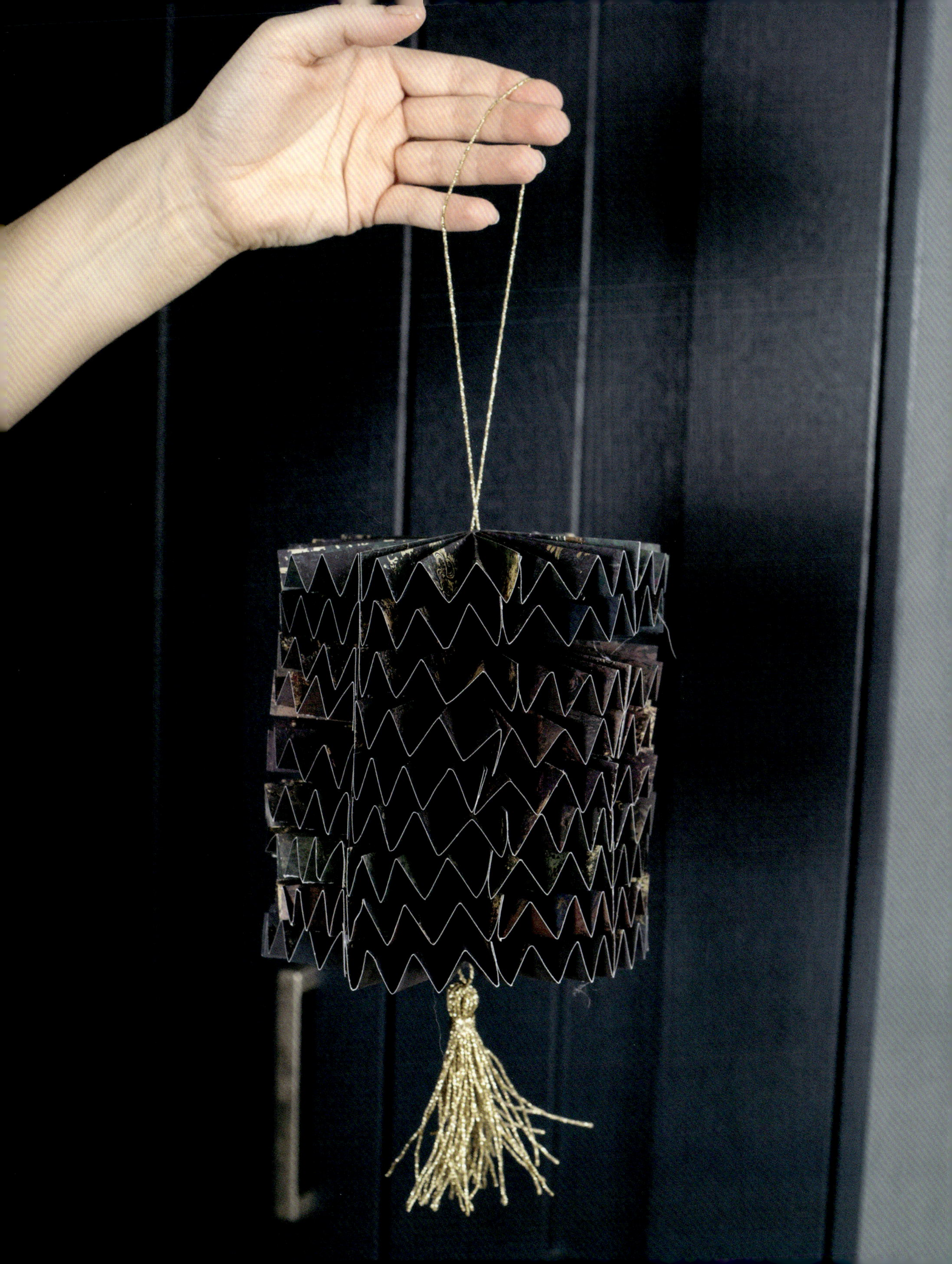

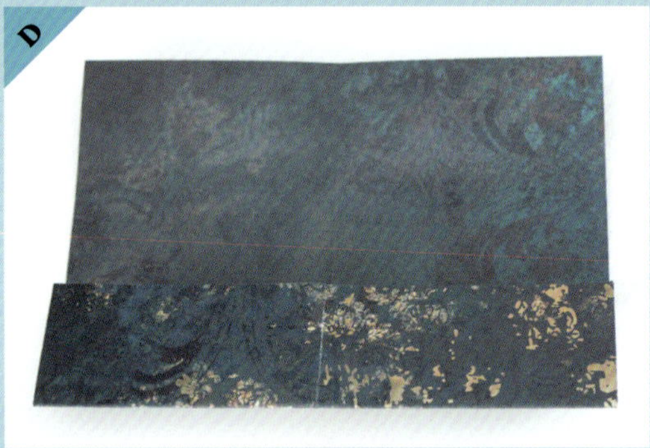

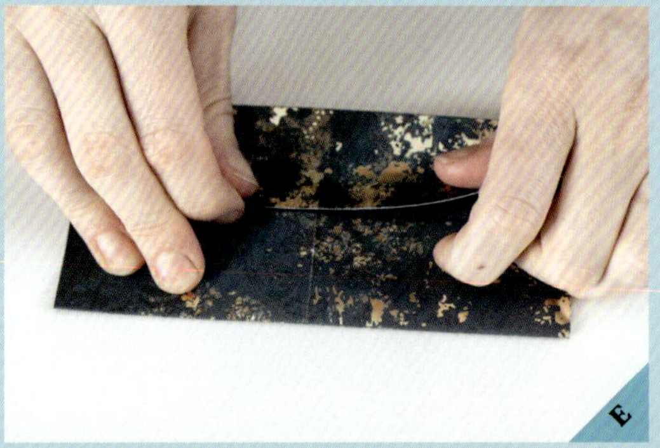

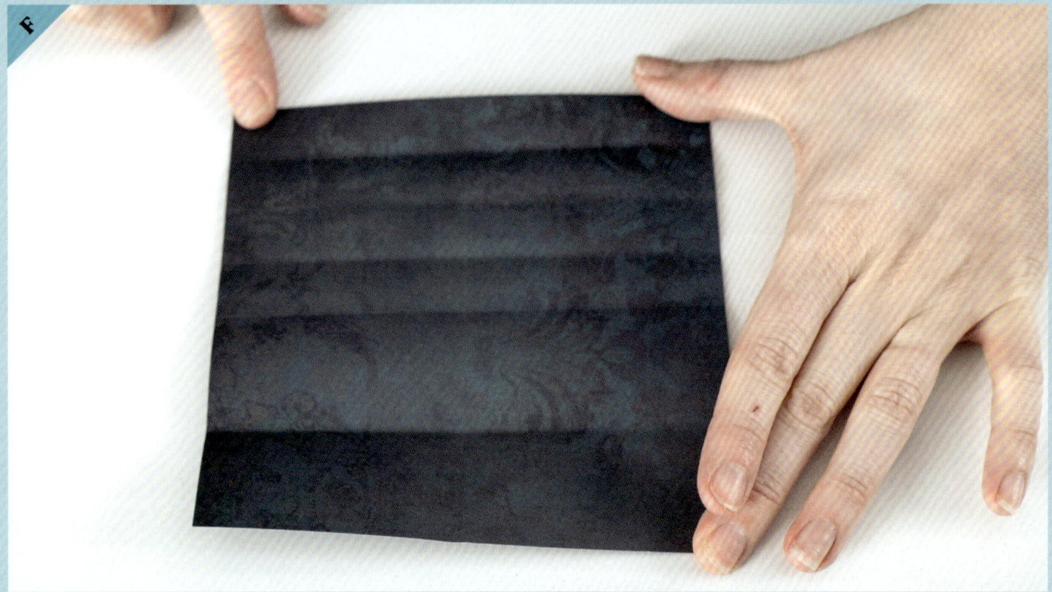

4 Open the paper out again. Fold one edge in towards the centre fold. **(D)**

5 Repeat on the other side. **(E)**

6 Lay the sheet flat. Fold the bottom edge up to the first fold line, then unfold. Fold the bottom edge up to the top horizontal fold line. **(F)**

7 Turn the sheet around. Fold the bottom edge up to the first fold line, then unfold. Fold the bottom edge up to the second fold line from the top. **(G)**

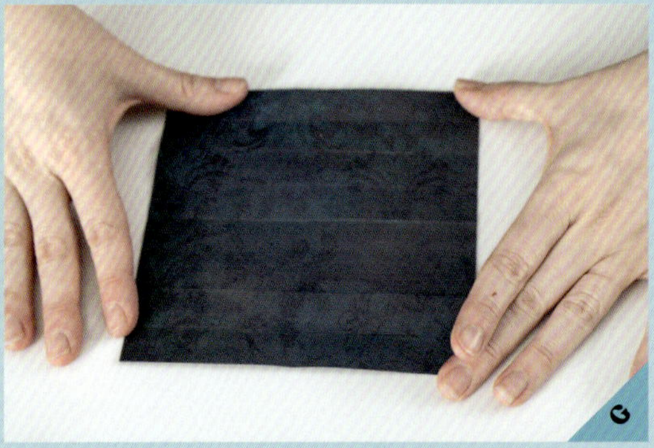

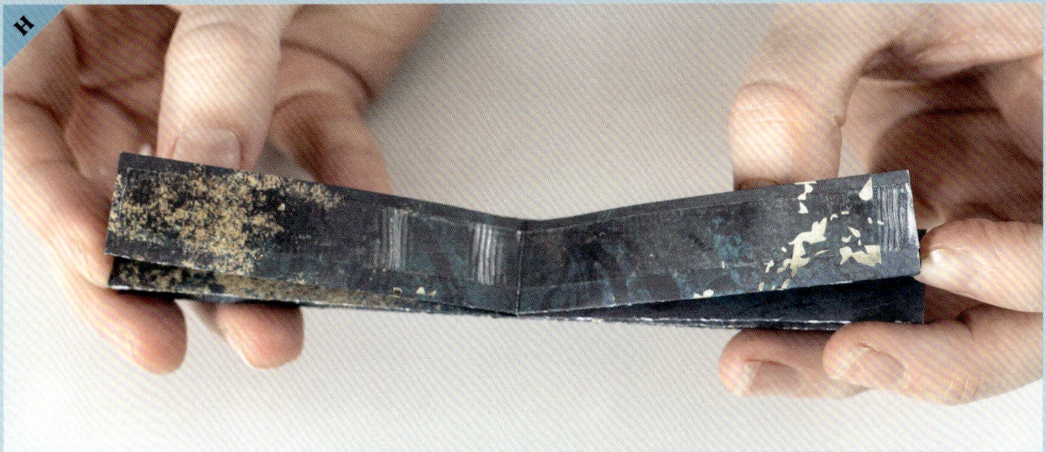

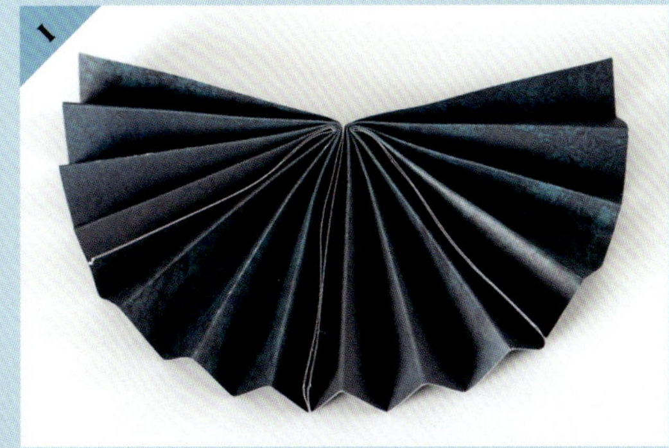

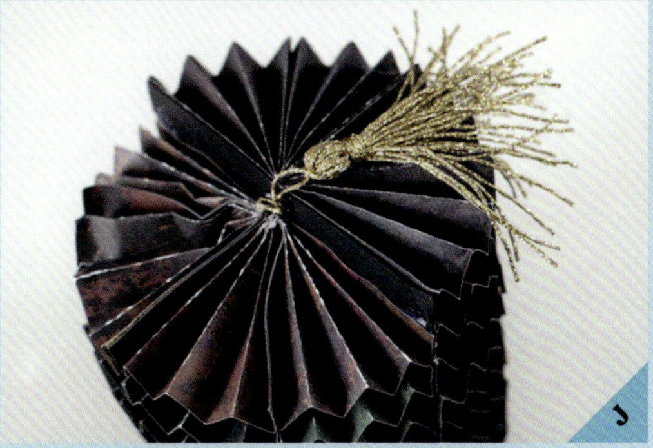

8 Create alternating valley and mountain folds along the existing creases, then fold the paper in half, apply red liner tape along the outer edge and remove the backing. **(H)**

9 Repeat the folding-and-taping process three further times so you have four completed folded pieces.

10 Join two folded sections together using the adhesive, aligning the edges carefully. **(I)**

11 Repeat the folding process with the remaining papers until you have eighteen folded half-circles in total.

12 Glue a length of gold twine to one half-circle to create a hanging loop.

13 Continue to adhere half-circles to the twine until you have nine stacked layers.

14 Flip the lantern over and repeat with the remaining pieces on the other side, pressing the joins together.

15 Before attaching the final section, glue a tassel in place, then secure the last piece to complete the lantern. **(J)**

Intermediate

Bunny Card

This has to be one of the cutest cards you'll ever make. Projects like this are a joy because they're simple, fun and guaranteed to raise a smile. This bunny card is perfect for Easter, springtime, or just as a friendly hello, and it's a great project to enjoy with the kids.

TOP TIP **Use quick-dry craft glue and allow each layer a moment to stick before moving on. This will help keep all the shapes neatly in place and make the finished bunny nice and sturdy.**

You will need:

- Orange, white, pink and green card
- Ruler
- Pencil
- Scissors
- Quick-dry craft glue (e.g. Collall Tacky Glue)
- Grey pen
- Black fine liner

1 Cut a circle measuring approximately 6″ in diameter from the orange card. Fold it in half to create the card base. **(A)**

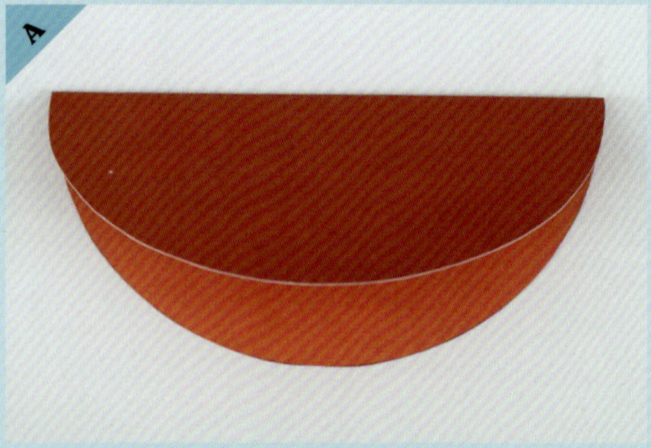

2 Cut a white circle of card measuring approximately 3″ in diameter. **(B)**

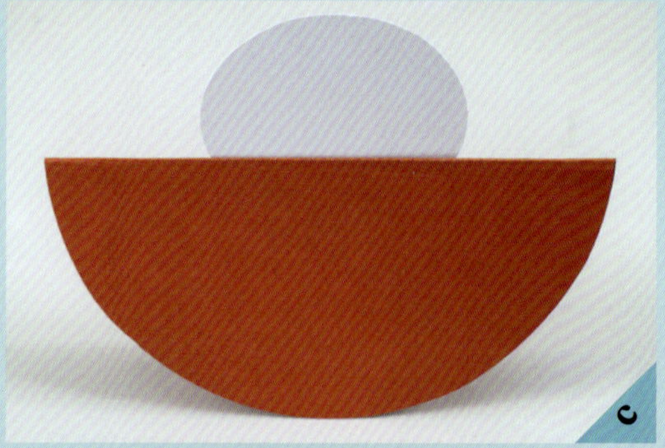

3 Glue the white circle to the back of the orange card so that roughly three-quarters is visible above the folded edge. **(C)**

4 Cut two ear shapes from white card, then cut two smaller inner-ear pieces from pink card. Glue the pink pieces on to

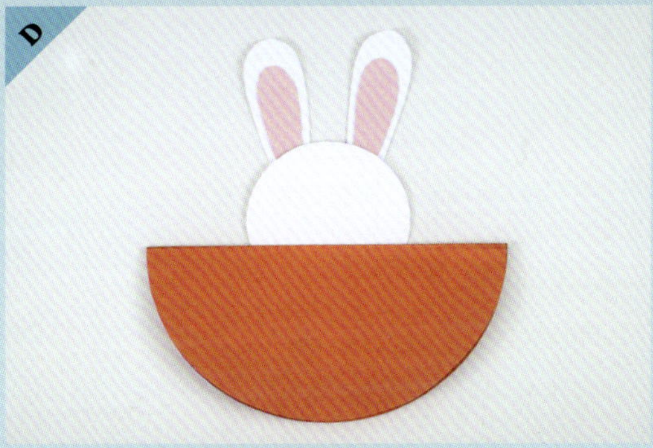

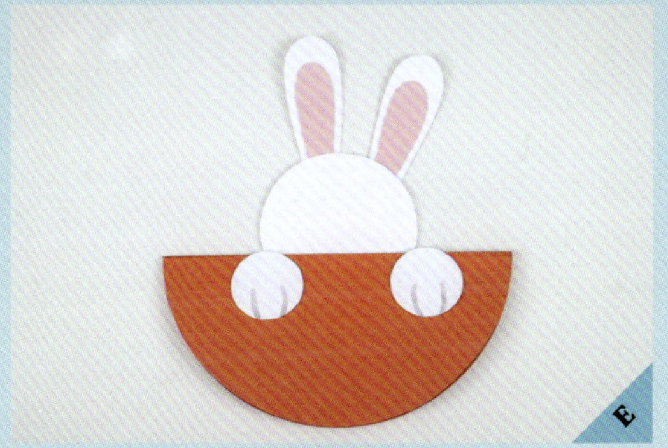

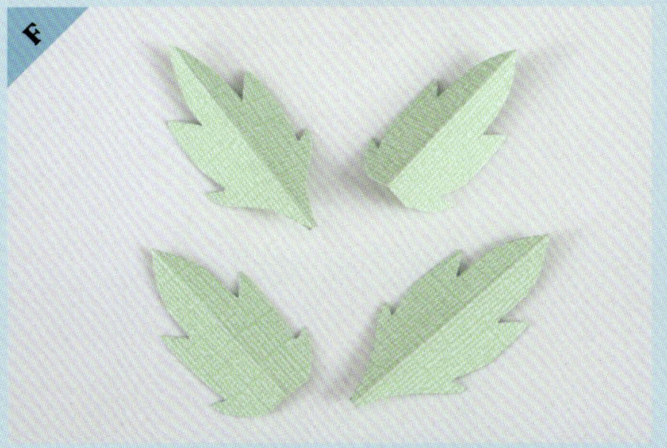

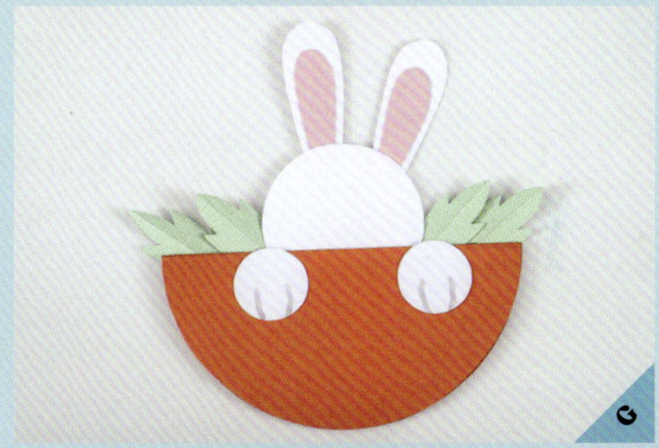

the white ears, then adhere the ears to the top of the bunny. **(D)**

5 Cut two white circles measuring 1¼" in diameter each and glue them to either side of the larger white circle on the front of the card. Add small details to turn these into the bunny's feet. **(E)**

6 Fold a piece of green card in half and draw a leaf shape along the folded edge. Cut it out to create a symmetrical leaf. Repeat to create four leaves. **(F)**

7 Glue the leaves to the back of the card so they peek out behind the bunny. **(G)**

8 Use a black fine liner to add facial details to the bunny. Allow everything to dry fully, then gently open the card to reveal your finished bunny carrot card!

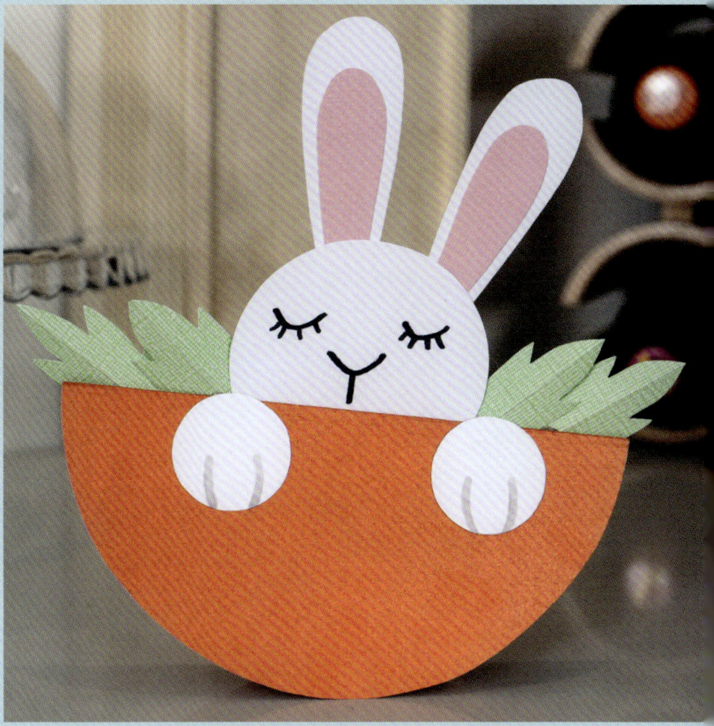

Intermediate

Easter Egg Card

This is one of those projects that looks striking but is surprisingly simple to make. By cutting an egg-shaped aperture and filling it with strips of patterned paper, you can create a bright, cheerful card that's perfect for Easter or springtime crafting.

It's also a fantastic way to use up those little paper scraps from your craft stash. Because every combination of colours and patterns is different, each finished card will be completely unique while still following the same straightforward process.

You will need:

- Paper (for egg template)
- Pencil
- Scissors
- White and green card
- Pokey tool
- Scrap pieces of patterned paper
- Glue tape pen
- Card base measuring 5⅞" × 4⅛"

1 Create a 4" egg template by folding a piece of paper in half and drawing half an egg shape along the folded edge. **(A)**

TOP TIP Try a flower, bunny or sheep shape if you're feeling adventurous!

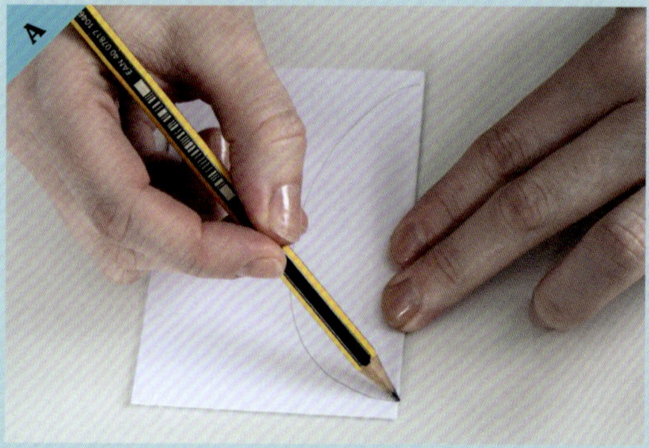

2 Cut it out and unfold it to reveal a neat, symmetrical egg shape. **(B)**

3 Use the template to draw the egg shape on to a piece of white card measuring 3¾" × 5½". For ease, use a pokey tool to create a hole in the centre of the card, then carefully cut out the egg shape to create an aperture. **(C)**

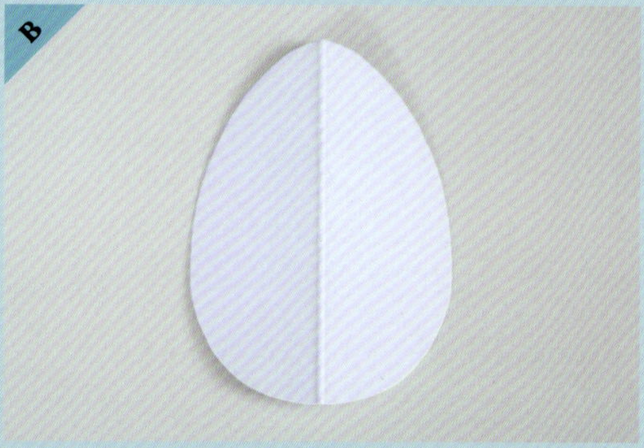

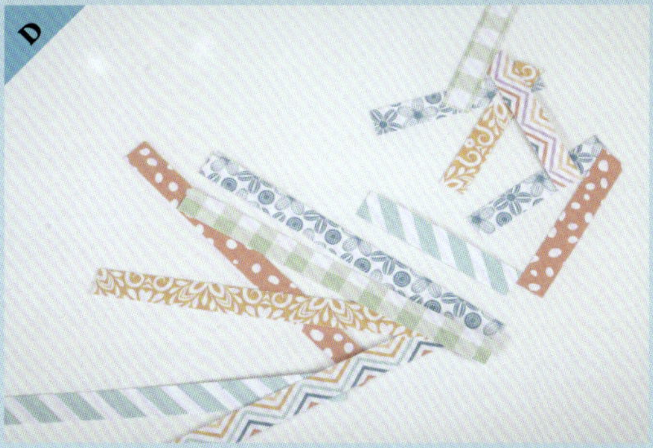

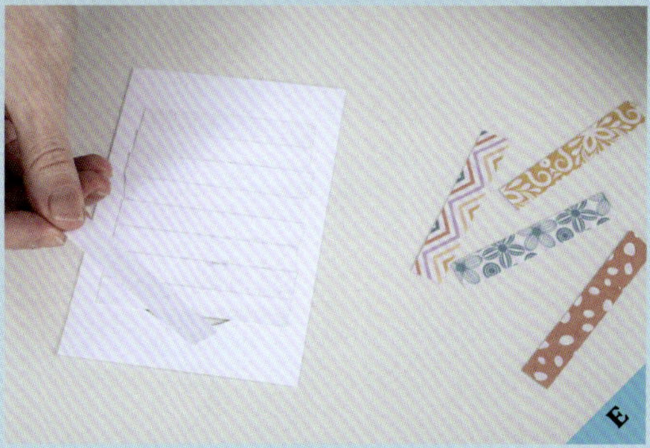

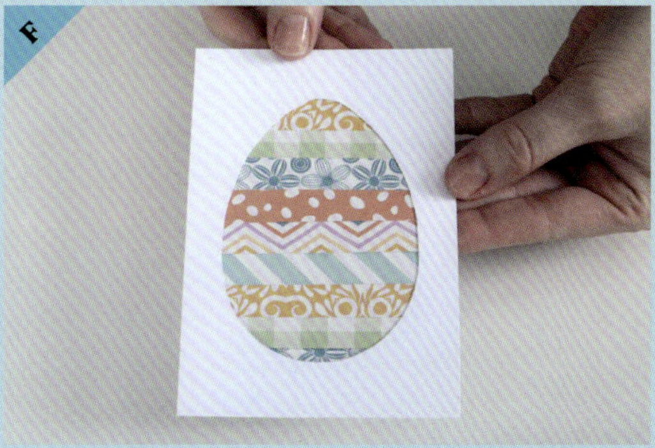

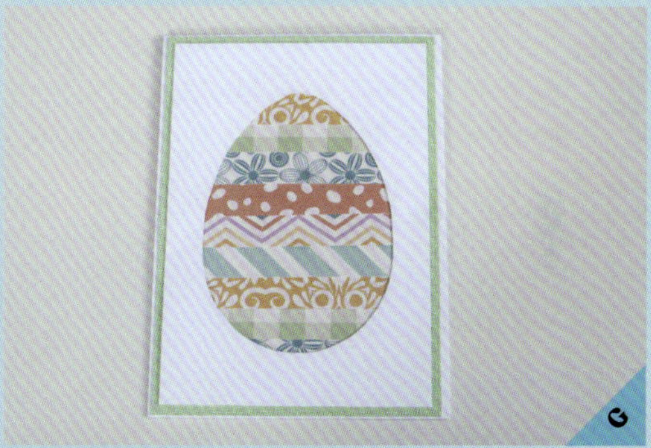

4 Cut scrap patterned paper into strips approximately ½" wide. Choose papers that suit a spring colour palette. **(D)**

5 Turn the aperture panel face down and glue the patterned paper strips across the back, slightly overlapping them, until the opening is fully covered. **(E)**

6 Turn the panel back over so the layered patterned paper shows through the egg aperture. **(F)**

7 Cut a piece of green card measuring 4" × 5¾" and adhere the aperture panel on top. Attach this layered panel to the front of the card base. **(G)**

8 Finish the card with a sentiment of your choice, if desired!

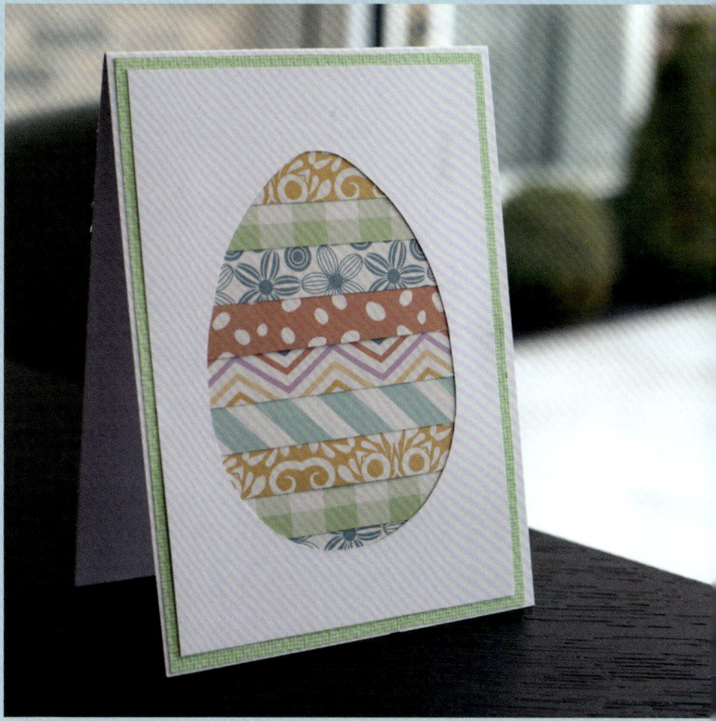

Easy

Easter Egg Bunting

Whether you're decorating for an Easter gathering or simply adding a handmade touch to your home, this bunting makes a cheerful and eye-catching display. Draped across a mantelpiece, shelf or window, it's as satisfying to make as it is to admire once finished.

TOP TIP **Before attaching the eggs to the yarn, lay them out evenly on a flat surface. This makes it easier to check spacing and ensures your bunting hangs neatly, with no eggs sitting too close together.**

You will need:

- Yarn
- Pencil
- Egg-shaped cookie cutter (optional)
- Scissors
- Patterned paper
- Coloured paper
- Glue gun

1 Cut a length of yarn to your desired bunting size and set it aside.

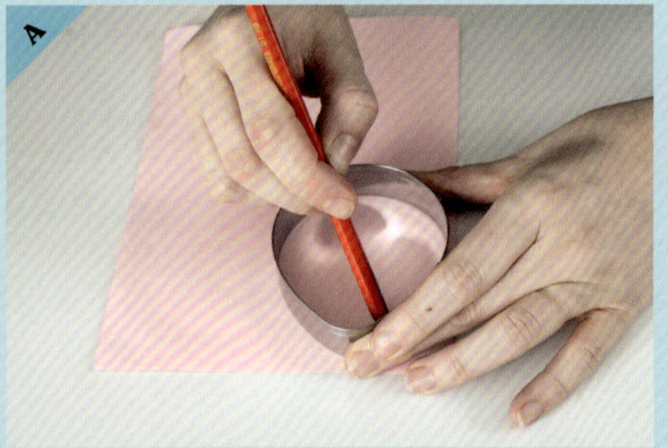

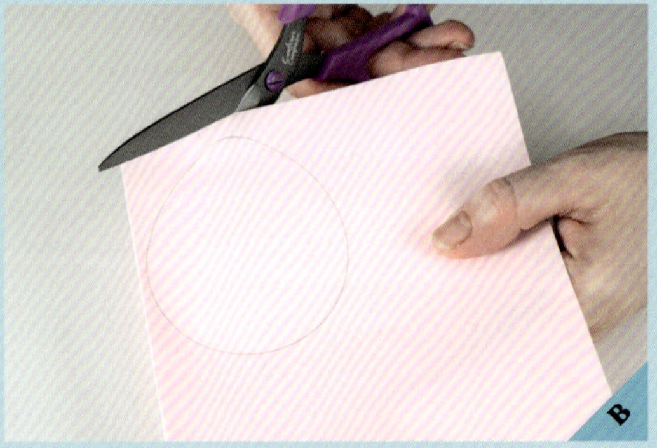

2 Draw an egg shape on to scrap paper using a pencil or tracing around an egg-shaped cookie cutter. **(A)**

3 Carefully cut out the egg shape. **(B)**

4 Fold the egg shape neatly in half lengthways. **(C)**

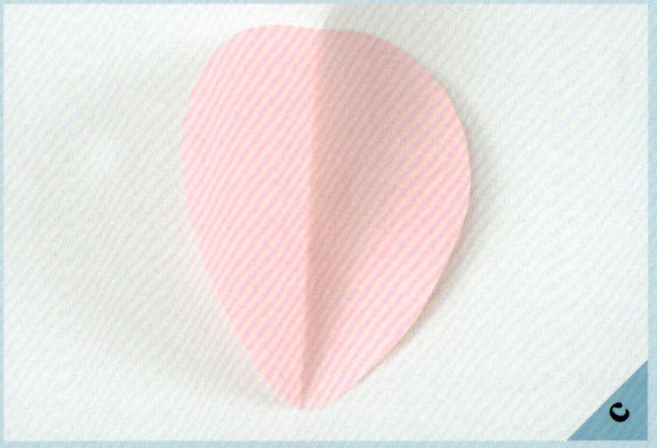

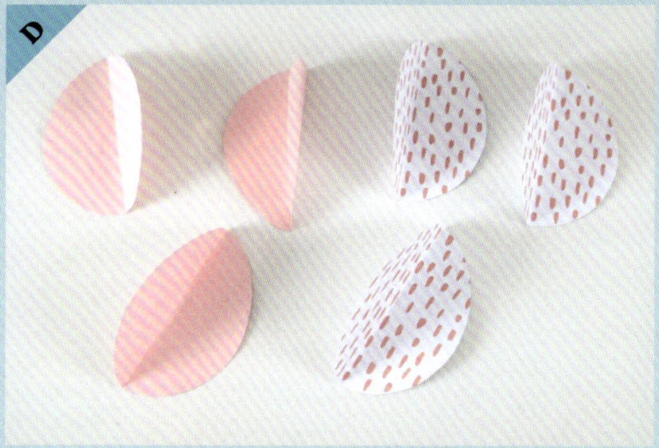

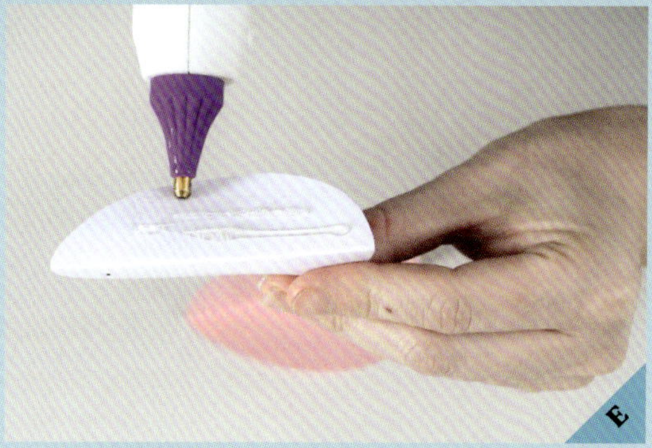

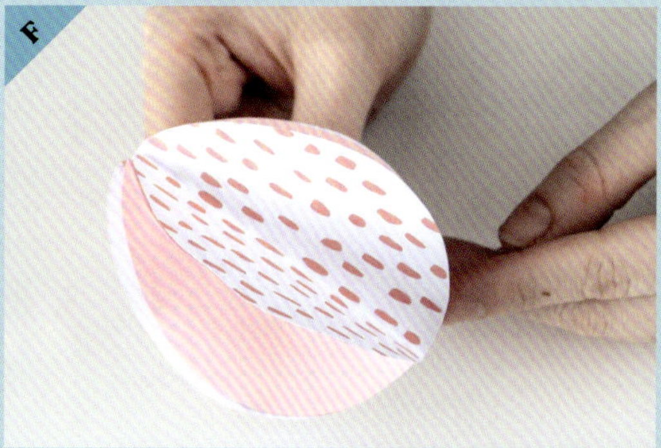

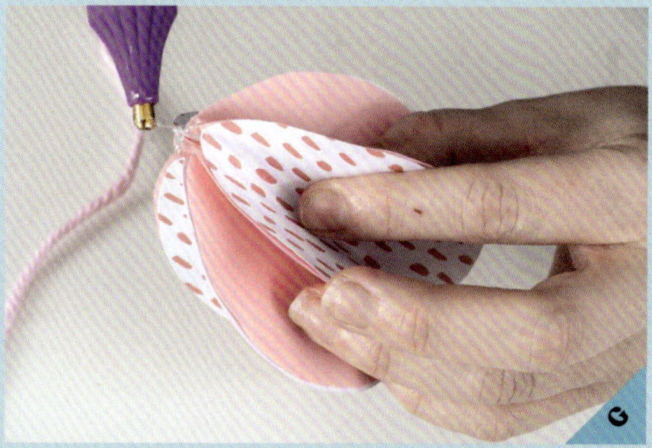

5 Repeat steps 2–4, mixing patterned and plain papers, until you have six egg shapes identical in size. **(D)**

6 Using a glue gun, glue the folded sides of the six egg shapes together, aligning the centre folds to form one complete 3D egg. **(E and F)**

7 Repeat the process to create as many eggs as needed for your bunting.

8 Set the eggs aside and allow the glue to dry completely.

9 Once dry, use the glue gun to attach the tops of the eggs evenly along the length of yarn. **(G)**

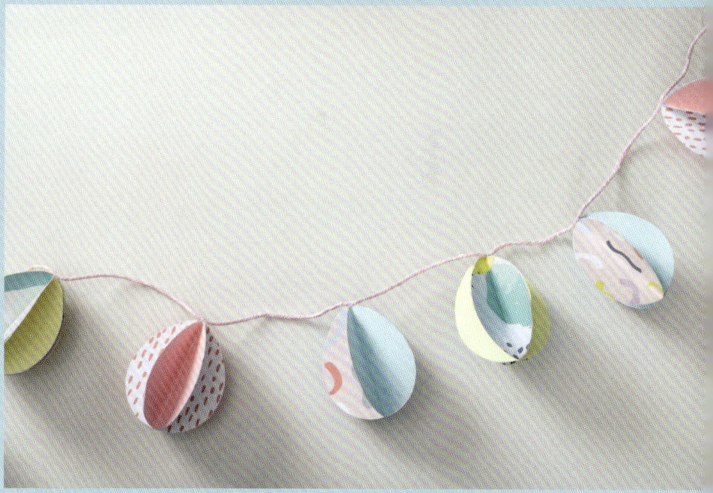

Easy

Easter Egg Planter

Easter crafting doesn't have to be complicated! With just a few sheets of toilet paper – yes, really – you can create this sweet Easter egg planter. This project is a lovely way to welcome spring on your windowsill.

TOP TIP Give the layers plenty of drying time to ensure they are sturdy.

You will need:

- Balloon
- Medium-sized jug or bowl
- Toilet roll
- Spray bottle filled with water
- Scissors
- Small plant

1 Take a balloon and blow it up to roughly 6" in diameter, then place it on top of a jug or bowl. **(A)**

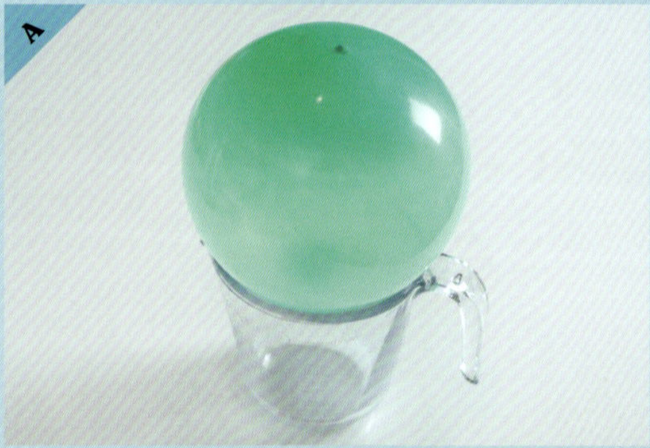

2 Rip off some sheets from the toilet roll. Place them one by one on top of the balloon, spraying each sheet with water as you go. The sheets need to be soaked through to stick properly, so make sure to spray plenty of water. **(B)**

3 Continue applying layers of toilet paper until the colour of the balloon is no longer visible through them. **(C)**

4 Leave the piece to dry for 24 hours, or until the egg shape is completely dry. Then pop and remove the balloon. **(D and E)**

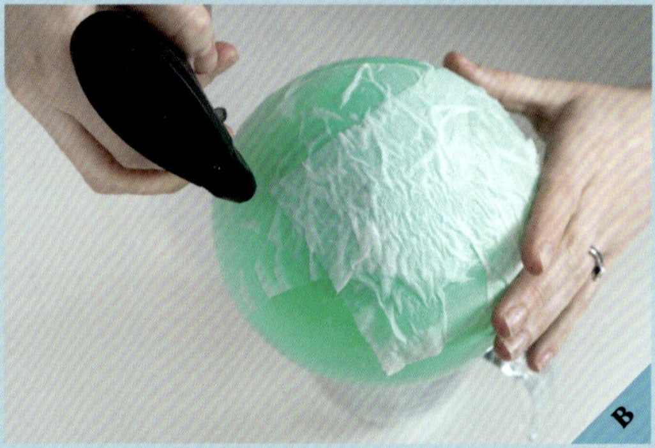

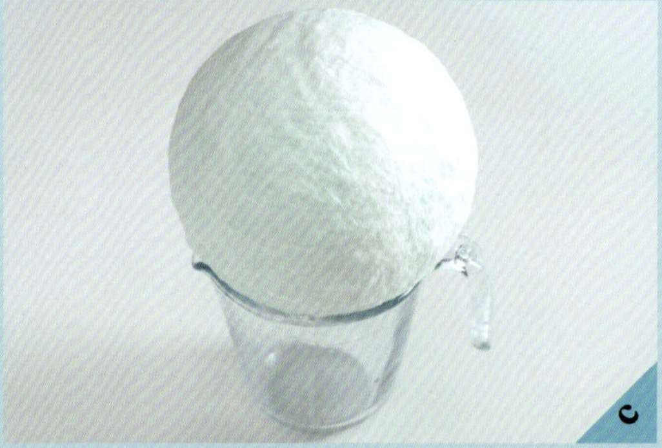

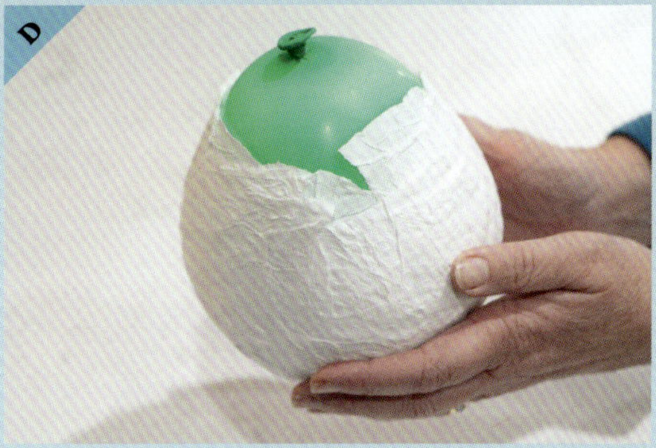

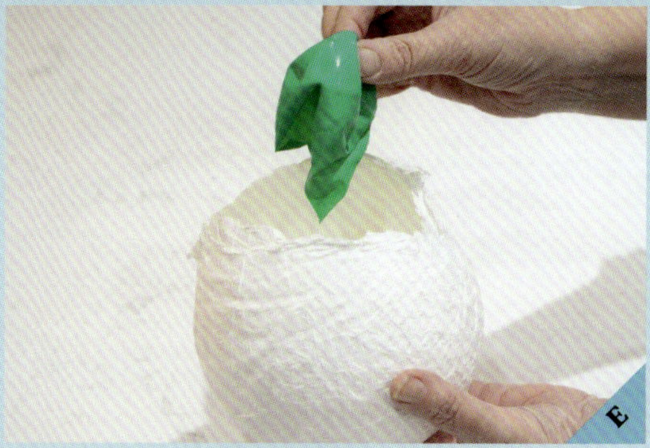

5 Snip away the edges of the egg to create a jagged edge, so that it looks like a cracked egg. **(F)**

6 Place a small plant inside the egg and display it somewhere in your home. Remember to take the plant out of the egg before watering, as the paper pot isn't waterproof!

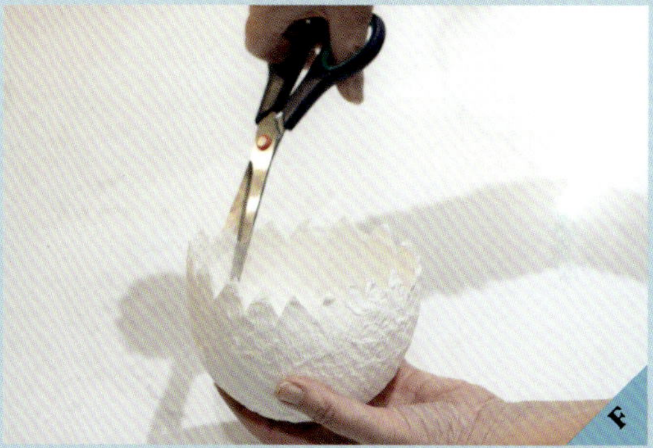

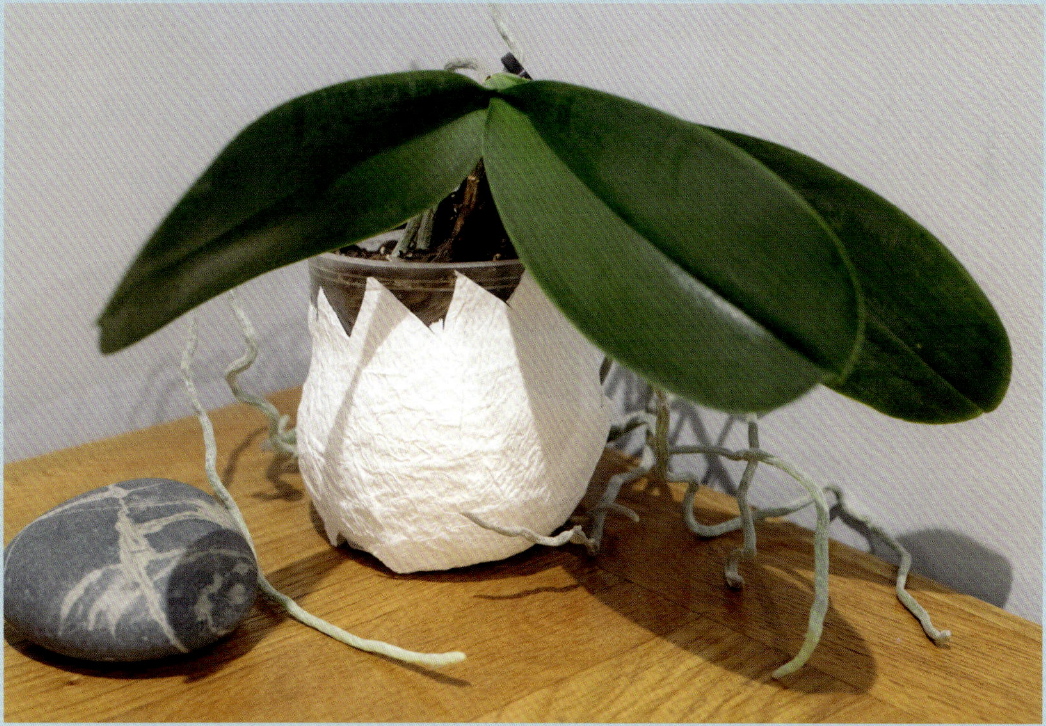

Intermediate

Macramé Bunny Ornament

If you're looking for a really special handmade touch for Easter, this project is a delightful choice. It looks beautifully intricate, but once you settle into the rhythm of the knots, it becomes a calm and enjoyable make. The finished bunny is something you'll be proud to hang up year after year.

You will need:

- Craft wire
- Egg-shaped cookie cutter (optional)
- Clear adhesive tape
- Macramé cord
- Scissors
- Wooden beads
- Miniature pompom
- Felt or card
- Glue gun

1 Take a length of craft wire and bend it into an oval shape – use an egg-shaped cookie cutter as a template if you'd like. Secure the ends of the wire together using clear adhesive tape. **(A)**

2 Cut a long length of macramé cord (around 36"). Cut it into two pieces of equal length to make it easier to work with.

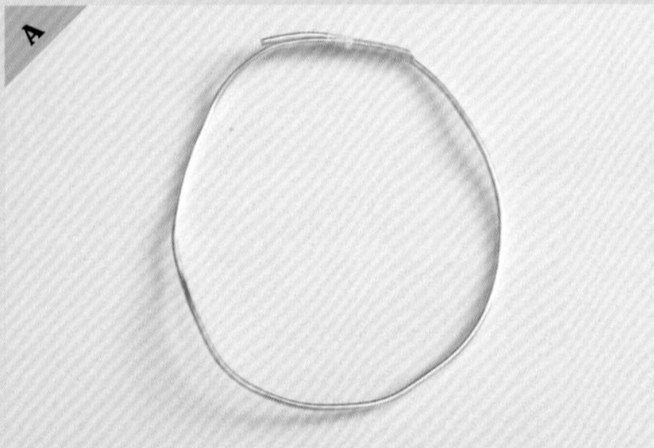
A

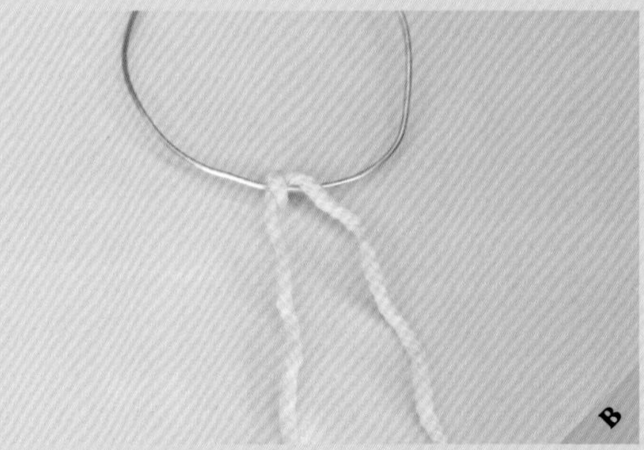
B

3 Tie one end of each cord around the wire. **(B)**

4 To create the twisted square knot, take the right-hand cord and keep it underneath the wire shape. Take the left-hand cord, loop it over and under the right-hand cord, then pull through and tighten, as shown. **(C)**

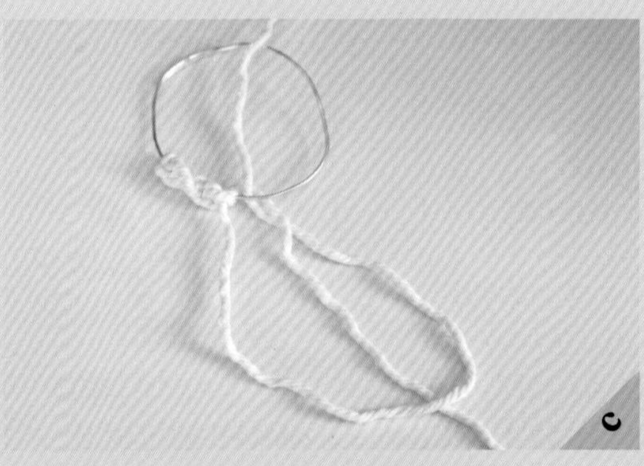
C

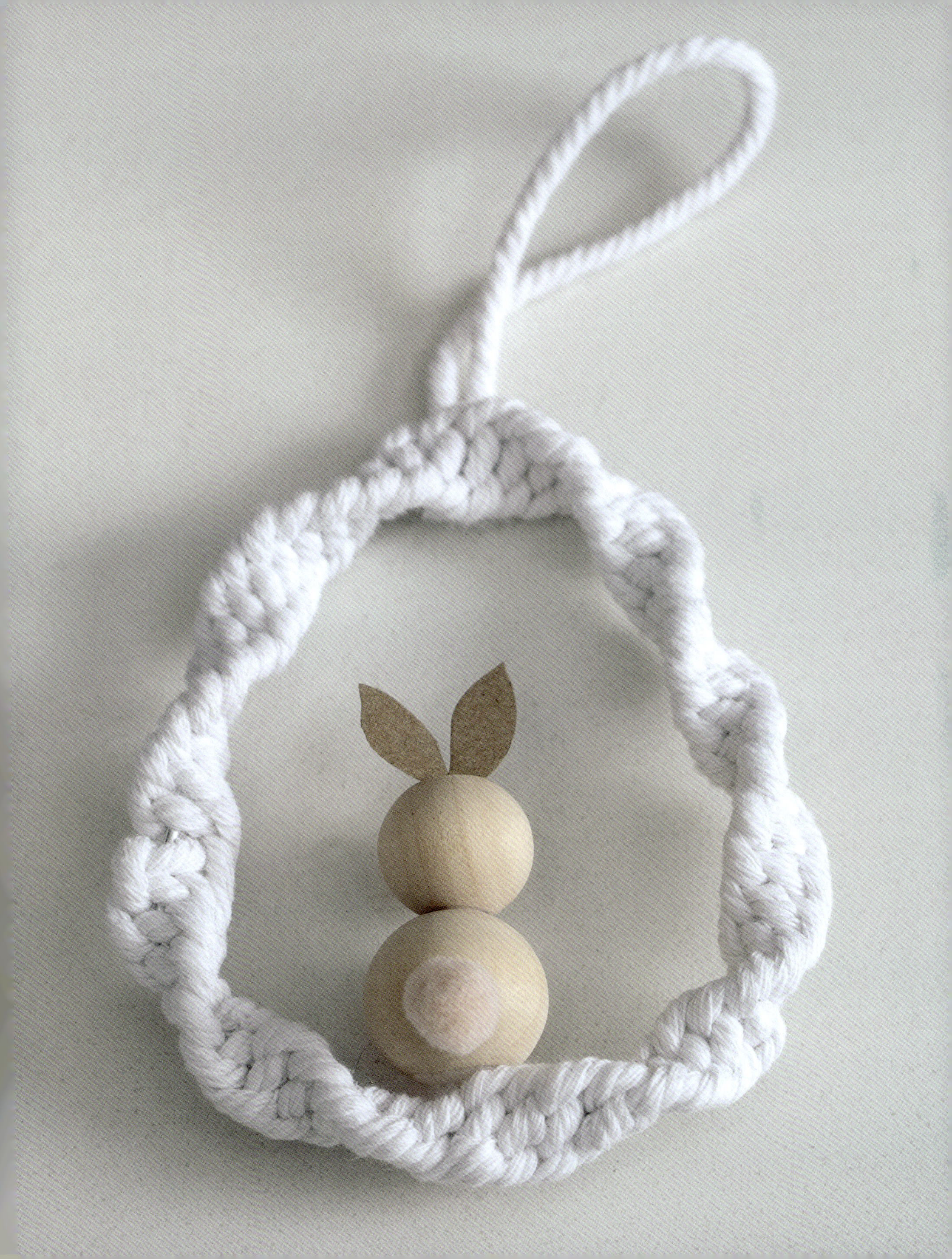

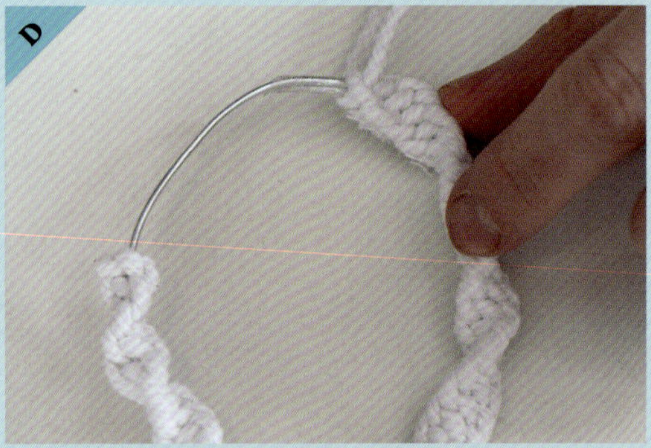

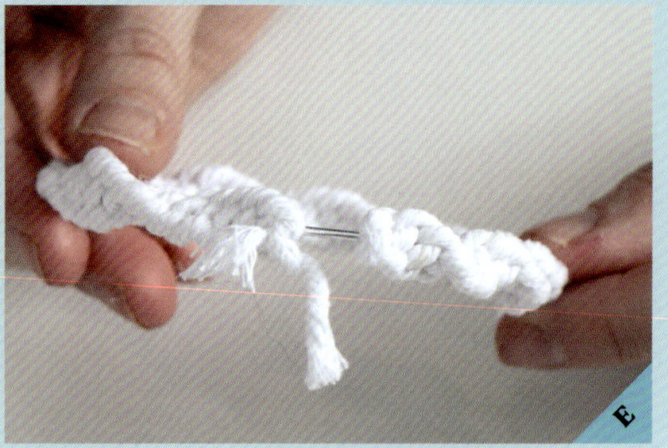

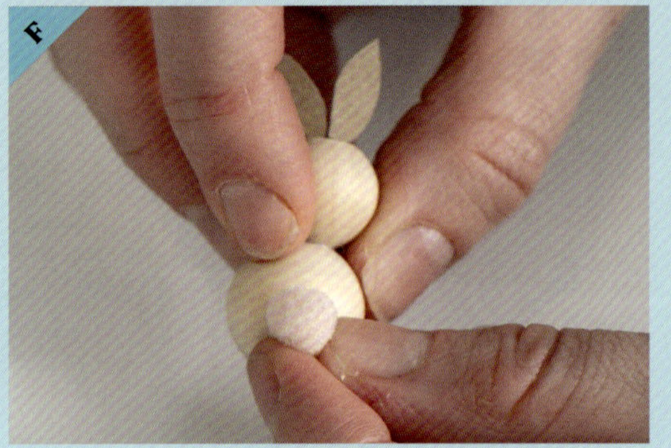

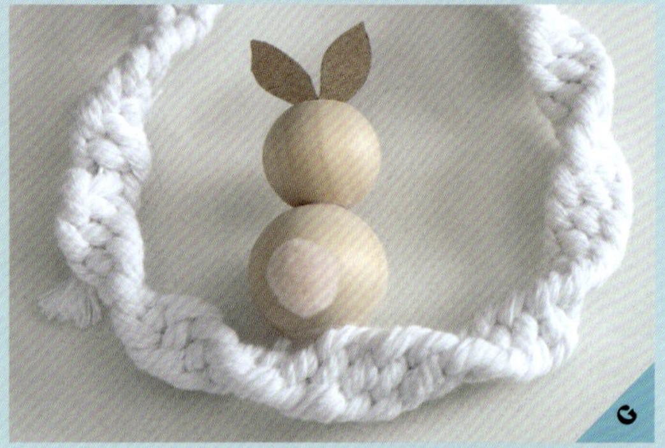

5 Continue working your way around the wire, repeating the knot until the entire shape is covered. The knots will naturally begin to twist as you go. **(D)**

6 Once the wire is fully covered, cut the macramé cord, tie it off neatly, and trim away any excess. At this stage, gently reshape the wire if needed to refine the egg shape. **(E)**

7 Create a bunny using wooden beads for the body and head, a miniature pompom for the tail, and felt or card for the ears. Secure all the pieces together using hot glue. **(F)**

8 Glue the finished bunny to the bottom of the macramé egg shape. **(G)**

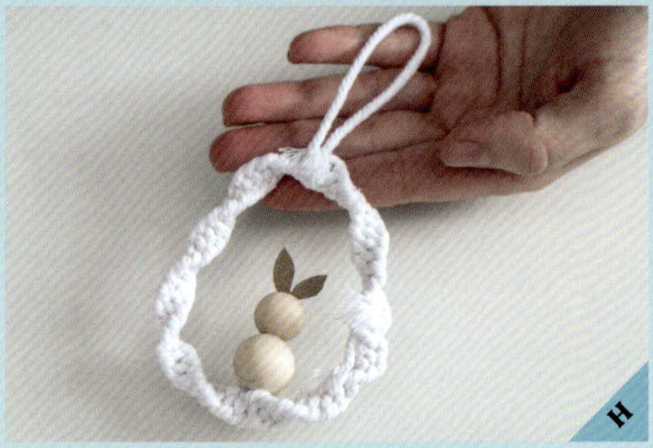

9 Finally, attach a small length of macramé cord to the top of the egg to create a hanging loop. **(H)**

TOP TIP To work out the exact length of cord you'll need, simply multiply the length of the craft wire by 3 and add 12" for safety!

Intermediate

Boo Card

Halloween cards are growing in popularity, and it's easy to see why. They're a fun way to add a playful spooky touch to your handmade card collection. This floating ghost card is a brilliant example of how a simple idea can be taken to the next level with a clever, interactive element. It's a satisfying project to make and a memorable card to give!

You will need:

- Black and white card
- Scissors
- Ruler or scoring board
- Scoring tool
- Acetate
- Glue tape pen
- Black fine liner
- Patterned paper

1 Cut two pieces of card measuring 5½″ × 4″ each. Score ½″ in from one short edge on each piece and fold along the score lines. **(A)**

2 Cut five strips of acetate measuring ½″ × 5½″ each.

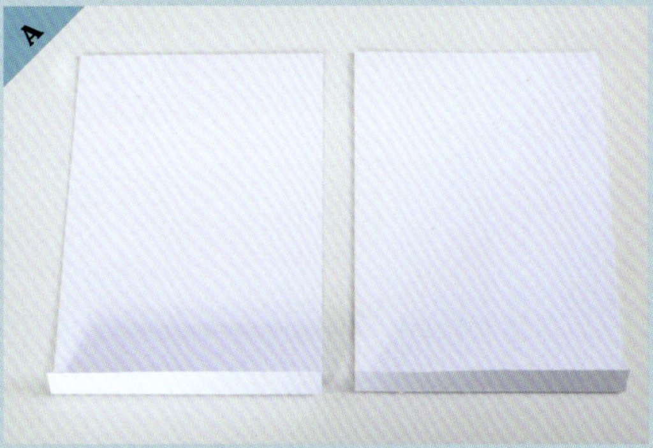

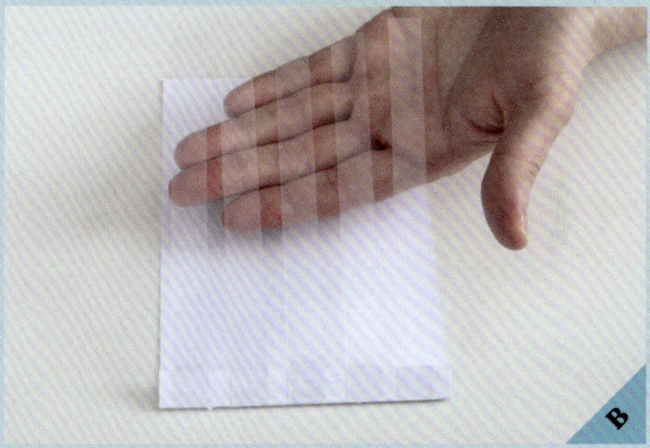

3 Adhere the acetate strips to the folded ½″ tabs on one of the card pieces, spacing them evenly. **(B)**

4 Apply adhesive to the folded ½″ tab on the second card piece, then press the two card panels together along the bottom edge so the acetate strips are sandwiched neatly in between them. **(C)**

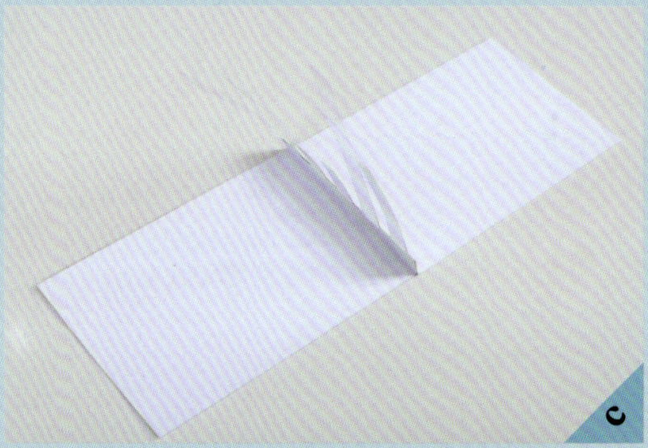

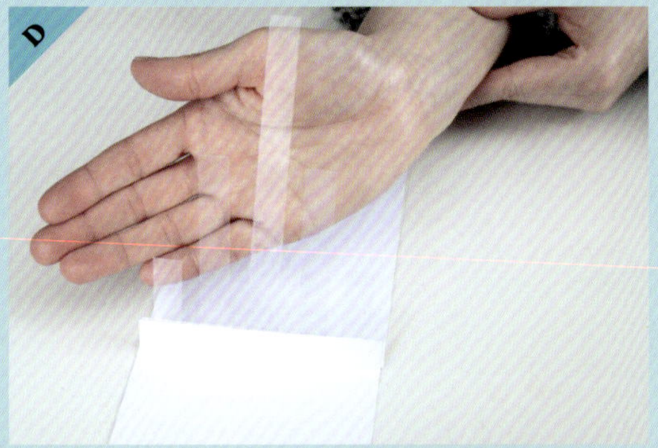

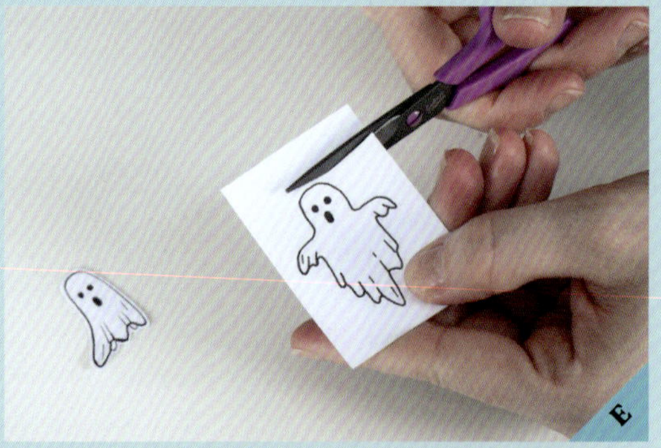

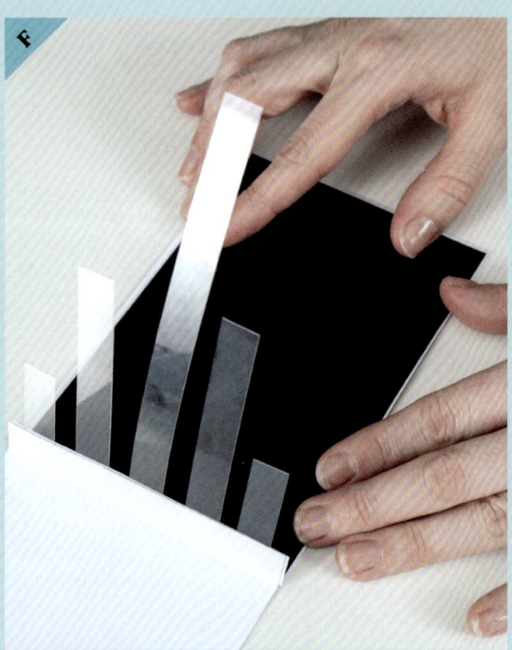

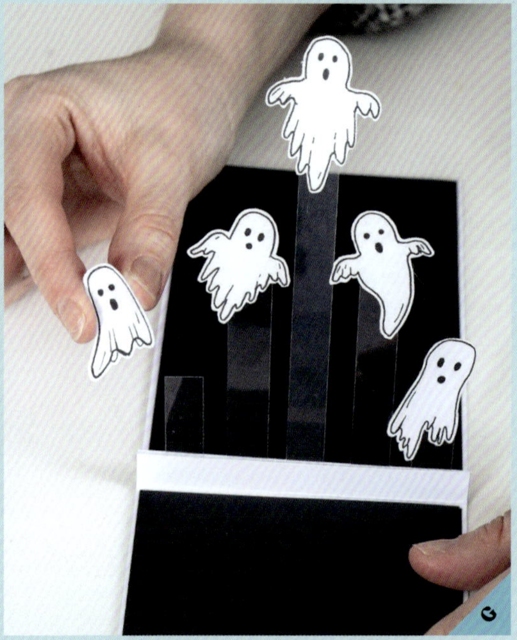

5 Trim the acetate strips to staggered heights to create a more dynamic floating effect. **(D)**

6 Draw ghost shapes on to white card and cut them out, leaving a narrow white border around each shape. **(E)**

7 Cut black mats to fit each of the white card panels and adhere them in place. **(F)**

8 Adhere the ghosts to the acetate strips so they appear to float between the two card panels. **(G)**

TOP TIP **Try using the same floating technique with other spooky characters, such as mummies, vampires or Frankenstein's monsters, to create different Halloween designs.**

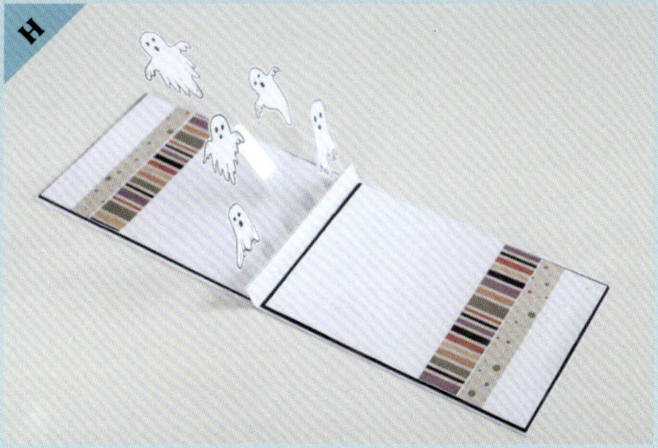

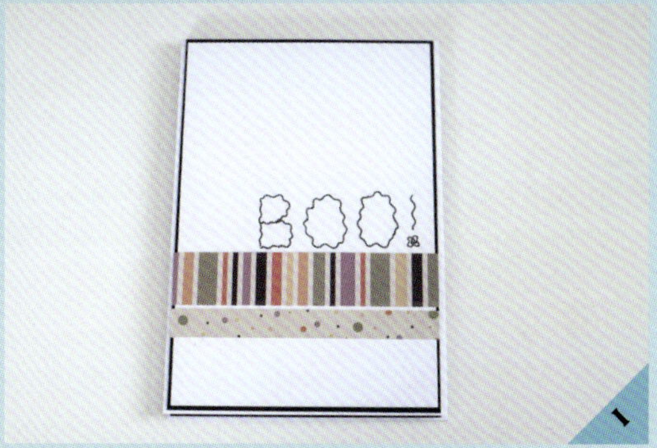

9 Add another layer of white card on to the black mats, then finish by adding narrow strips of patterned paper across either side. **(H)**

10 Finish the front of the card by adding a final mat and layer with some patterned paper and writing the word 'BOO!' using a black fine liner. **(I)**

11 Write a message on the inside to complete your design and send your spookily cute card to someone special!

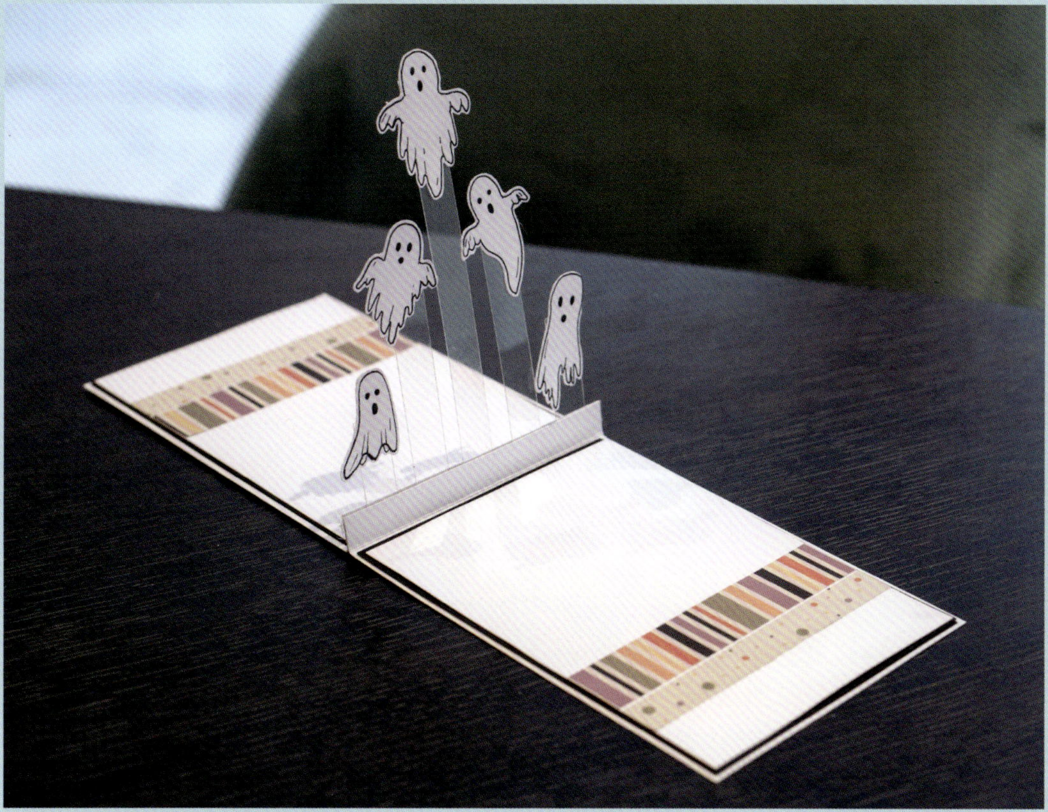

Intermediate

Bat Bunting

Add a touch of spooky fun to your Halloween celebrations with this brilliant bat bunting! These bats are not only adorable but also have a clever 3D fold that makes them really stand out. You can hang them individually or string several together to make a spooky bat garland to steal the show. The best part? This project is simple enough for crafters of all levels, making it a great one to do with kids, and only needs a few basic supplies!

TOP TIP **To save time when making a full garland, stack folded card and cut out two or three bats at once.**

You will need:

- Scrap paper
- Pencil
- Scissors
- Black, red and white card
- Ruler or scoring board
- Stapler
- Clear string or twine
- Glue
- Googly eyes
- Clear nylon thread, or string

1 Fold a piece of scrap paper in half and draw half of a bat shape, starting from the folded edge and working outwards. **(A)**

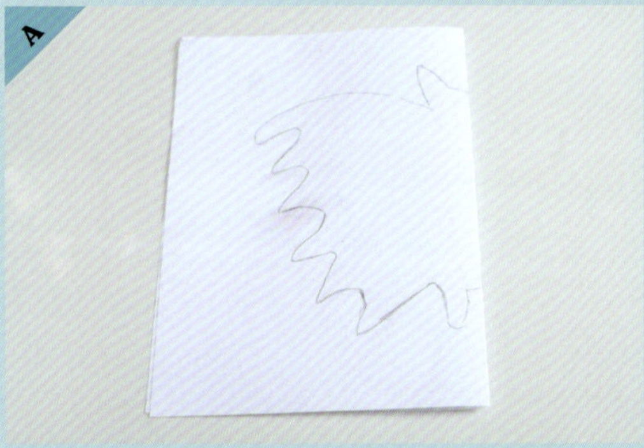

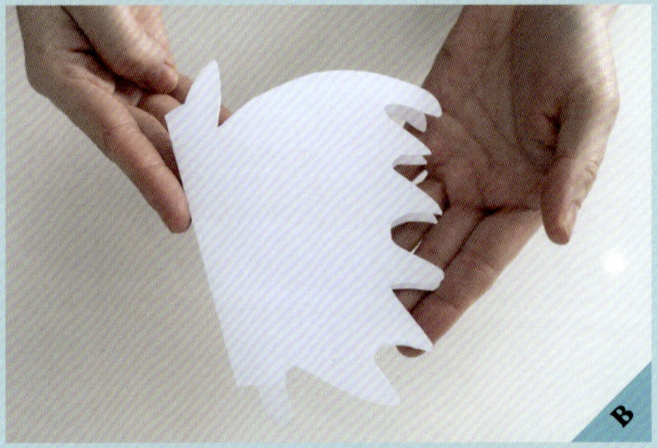

2 Cut out the shape, keeping the paper folded, to create a symmetrical bat template. **(B)**

3 Use the template to draw a bat shape on to a piece of folded black card. **(C)**

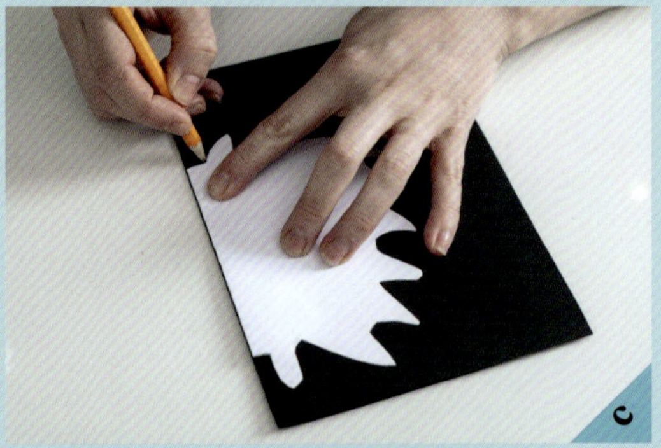

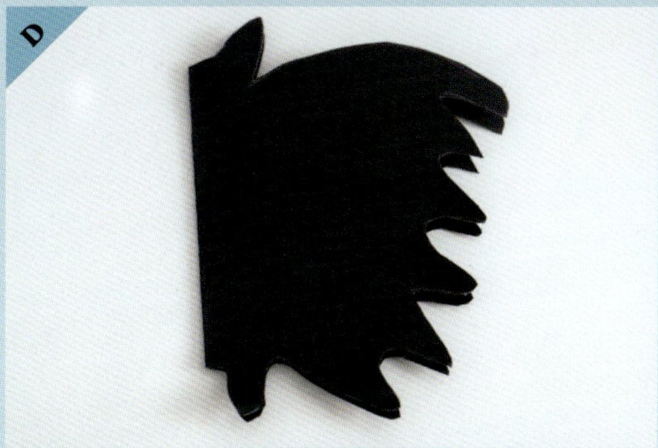

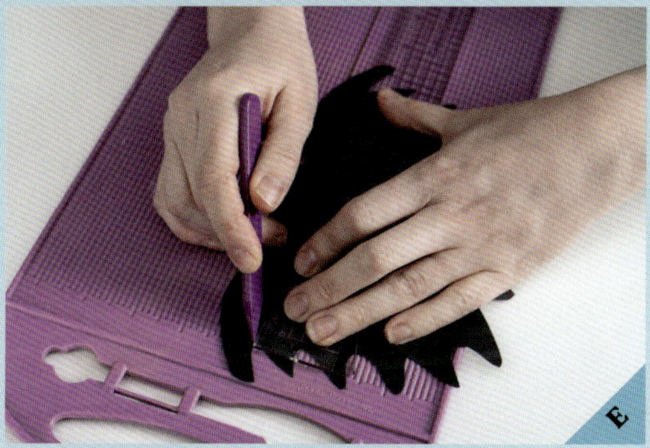

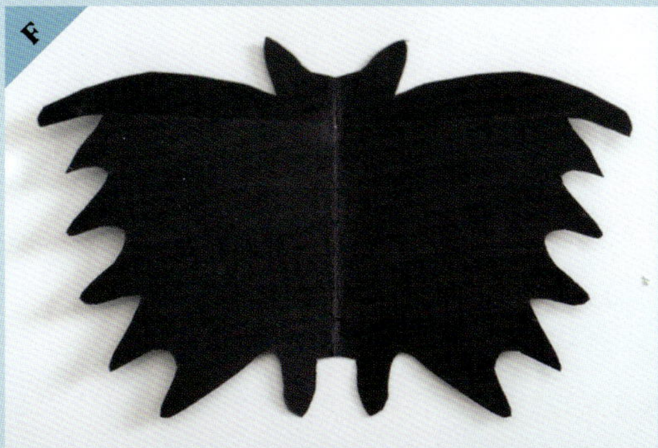

4 Cut out the bat shape from the black card, then open it out flat. **(D)**

5 Using a pencil and a ruler or scoring board, measure and mark a point 1" down from the top of the bat's head. **(E)**

6 From this point, continue marking at ½" intervals down the length of the bat. **(F)**

7 Starting at the lowest mark, create a mountain fold. Move up to the next mark and create a valley fold, alternating between mountain and valley folds as you work upwards, keeping the folds straight and even. **(G)**

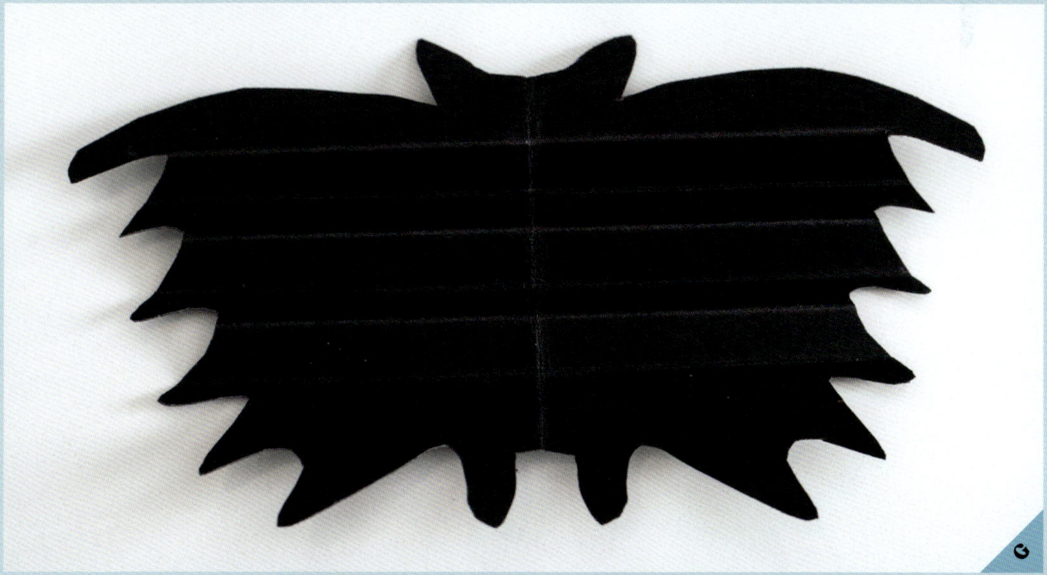

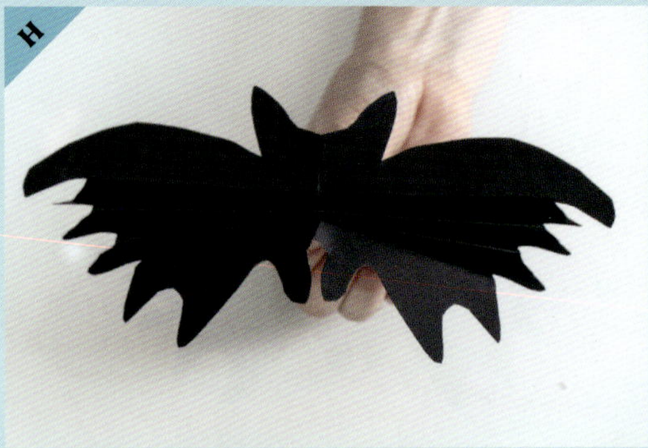
H

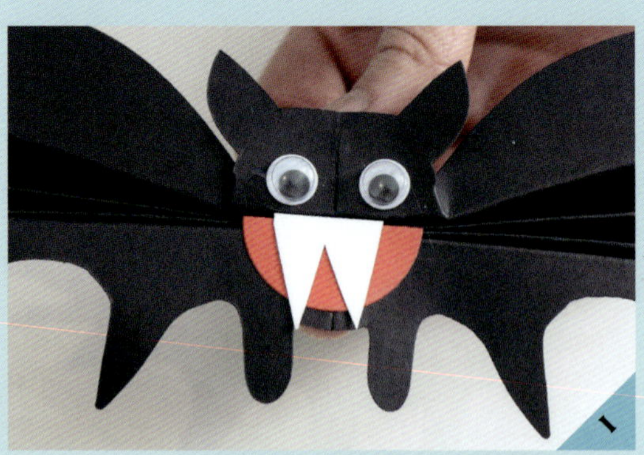
I

8 Gather the folded bat together at the centre and secure it with a staple on each side to hold the shape firmly in place. **(H)**

9 Cut a mouth and teeth from red and white card, then use glue to secure them in place, along with googly eyes, to bring your bat to life. **(I)**

10 Repeat the process to make several bats. Either attach clear nylon thread to the back of each bat to hang them as individual decorations, or glue them along a length of string to create a spooky bat bunting display!

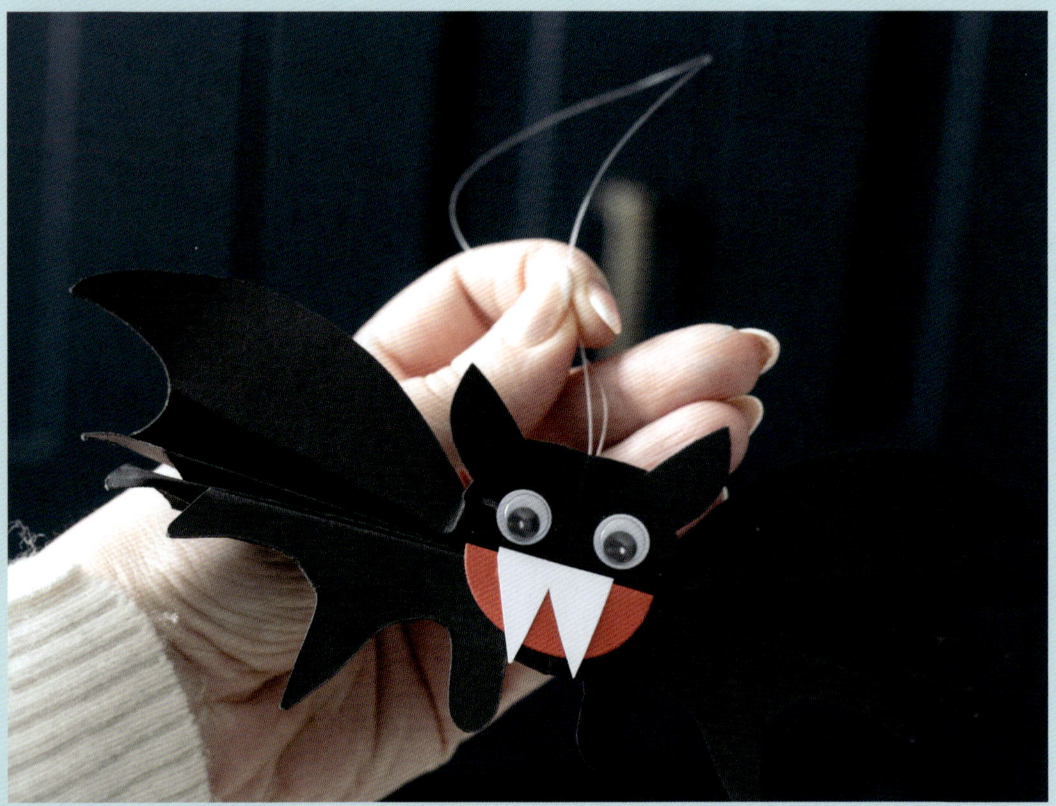

Easy

Yarn Pumpkin

Celebrate all things autumn with this adorable yarn pumpkin craft! Each pumpkin is simple and fun to make, and the perfect way to bring a cosy, seasonal touch to your home. By using soft chenille yarn and a cinnamon stick for the finishing touch, these pumpkins don't just look great, they'll smell amazing too!

TOP TIP **Make the pumpkins in a variety of sizes to create the perfect autumnal display.**

You will need:

- Packing paper
- Clear adhesive tape
- Orange chenille yarn
- Scissors
- Cinnamon stick

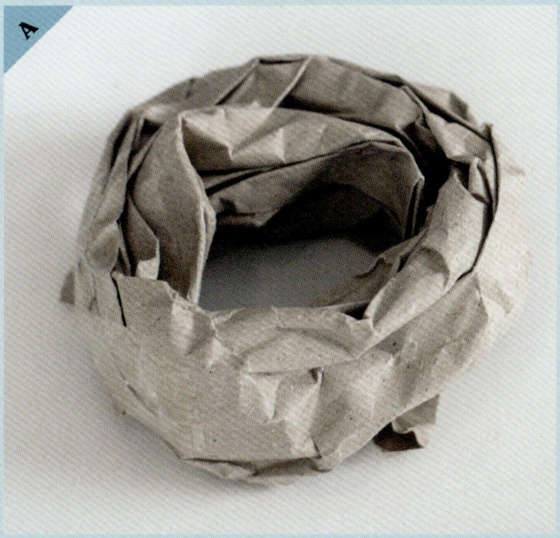

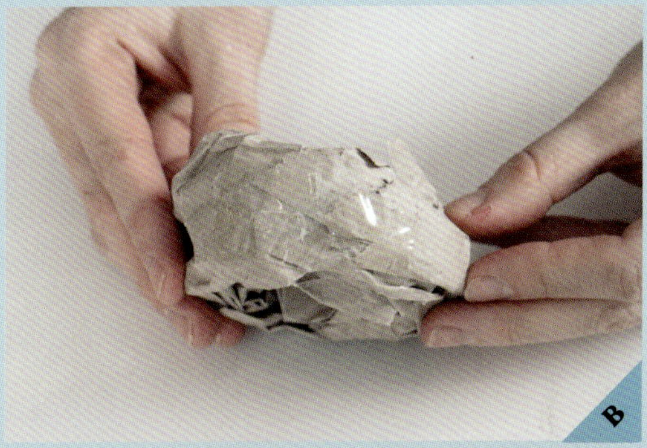

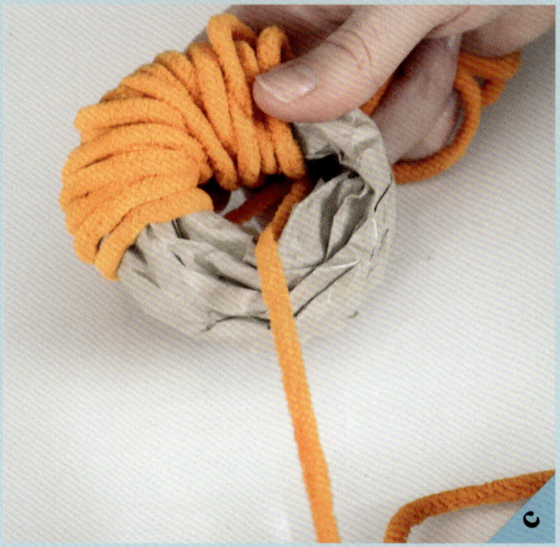

1 Take a piece of packing paper and scrunch it into a doughnut shape. **(A)**

2 Secure it in place with clear adhesive tape. **(B)**

3 Wrap the end of the yarn on to the doughnut shape and begin winding it around, pulling the yarn through the centre each time. **(C)**

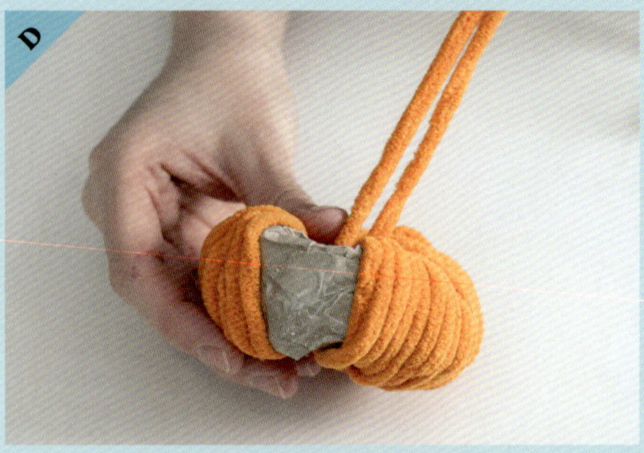

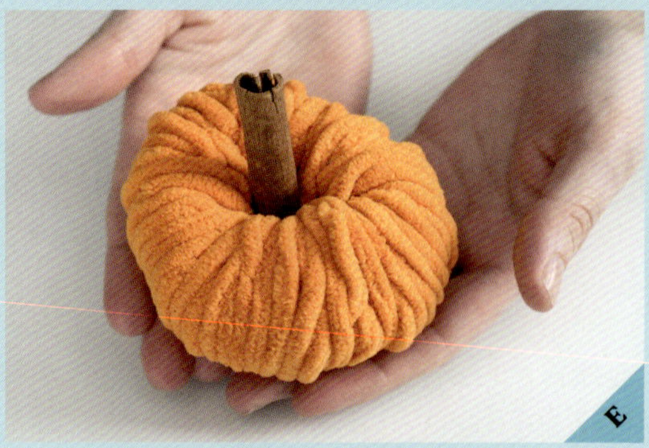

4 Continue winding until the doughnut is covered with yarn and begins to take the shape of a pumpkin. **(D)**

5 When the pumpkin is full enough, cut the yarn and tuck the end neatly into the pumpkin.

6 Finally, insert a cinnamon stick into the centre. If the pumpkin is full enough, you shouldn't need any adhesive to keep it in place. **(E)**

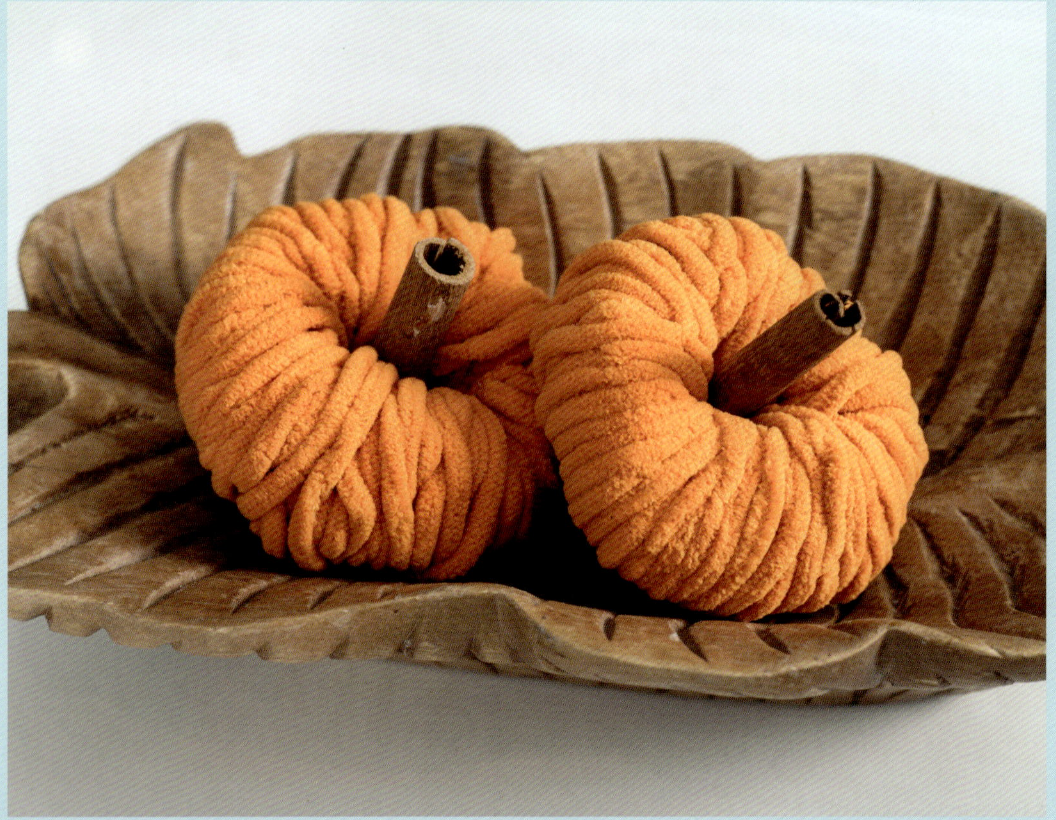

Intermediate

Monster Treat Bag

Make Halloween extra fun with these monster treat bags! They're perfect for parties, treats or a spooky surprise, and use simple scoring and folding techniques to create a characterful bag that's as cute as it is creepy. With a few finishing touches, you'll have a fun make that's great for filling with sweets. You can also use these as children's party bags, decorated to suit your chosen theme.

You will need:

- Sturdy green A4 card
- Scoring tool
- Ruler or scoring board
- Scissors
- Glue tape pen or adhesive
- Grey and black card
- Googly eyes
- Black marker
- Sweet treats

1 Take an A4 sheet of green card and place it in landscape orientation. **(A)**

2 Along the long edge, score at ¾", 4⅝", 5⅜", 6⅛ ", 10⅛", 10⅞" and 11⅝". **(B)**

TOP TIP Use the same bag construction to create a whole cast of creepy characters!

3 Along the short edge, score at 6¾".

4 Cut away the bottom-left section where the score lines intersect, then trim approximately ⅛" around the three scored sections, as shown. **(C)**

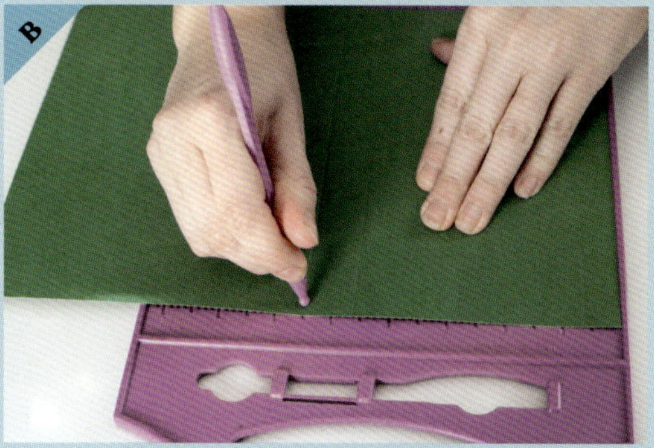

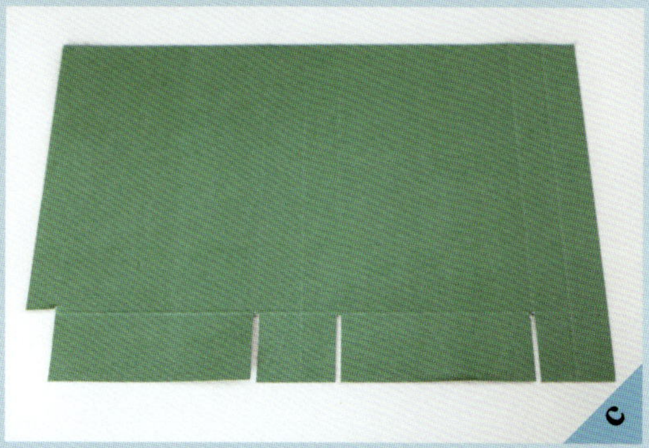

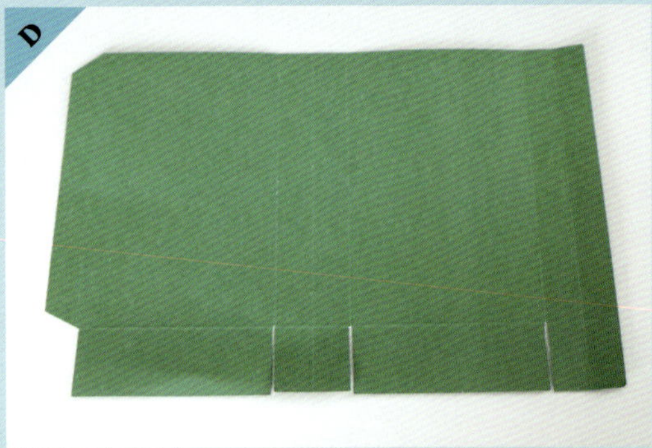

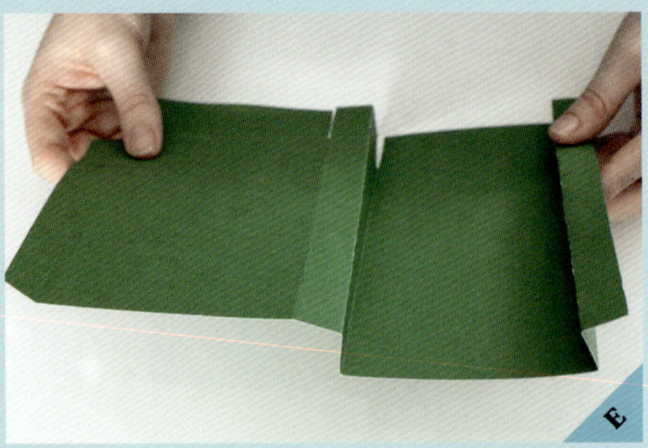

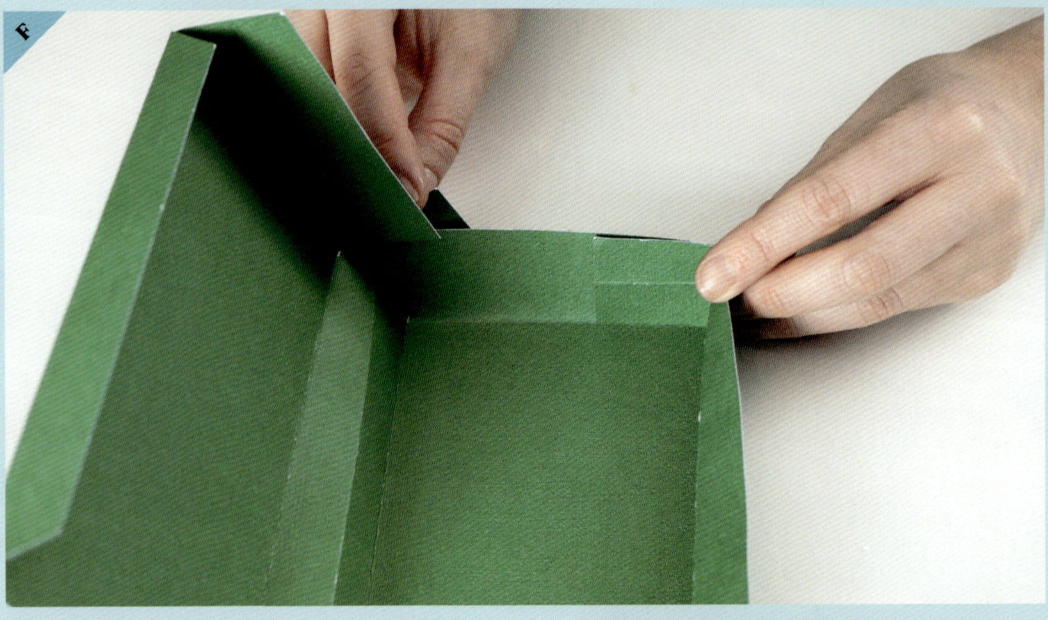

5 Cut away small diagonal sections from the top and bottom of the first scored tab. **(D)**

6 Fold and burnish along all the score lines to begin forming the bag shape. **(E)**

7 The bottom section created in step 3 will form the base of the bag. Apply glue tape or adhesive to the tabs and secure them in place. **(F)**

8 Adhere the final side tab to complete the bag's structure. **(G)**

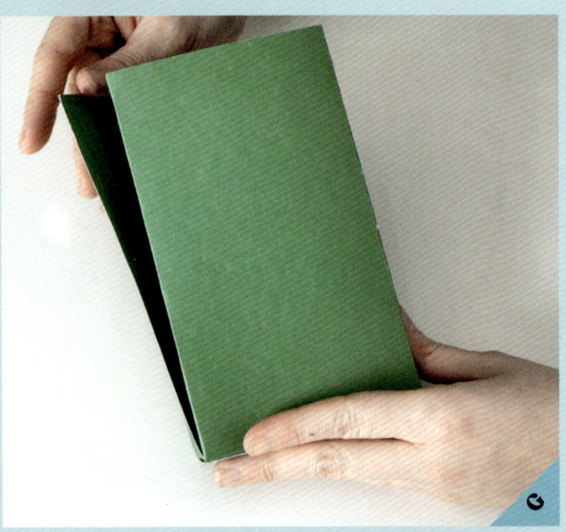

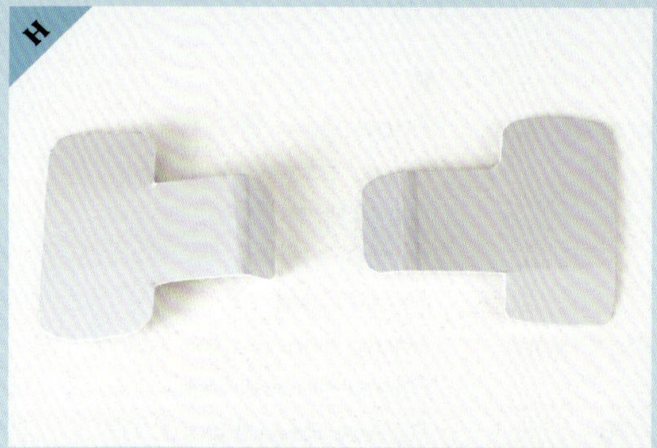

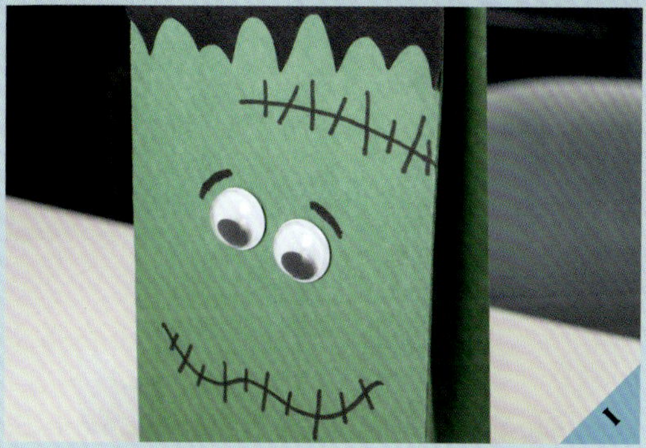

9 To create the monster's bolts, cut two T shapes from grey card, each measuring approximately 1¼", with a ¼" tab for easy attachment. Glue them to the lower sides of the bag. **(H)**

10 Cut a strip of black card to form the monster's hair and adhere it to the front of the bag.

11 Add googly eyes and draw facial details using a black marker. **(I)**

12 Fill the bag with spooky sweet treats to finish, and enjoy your freaky Frankenstein's monster!

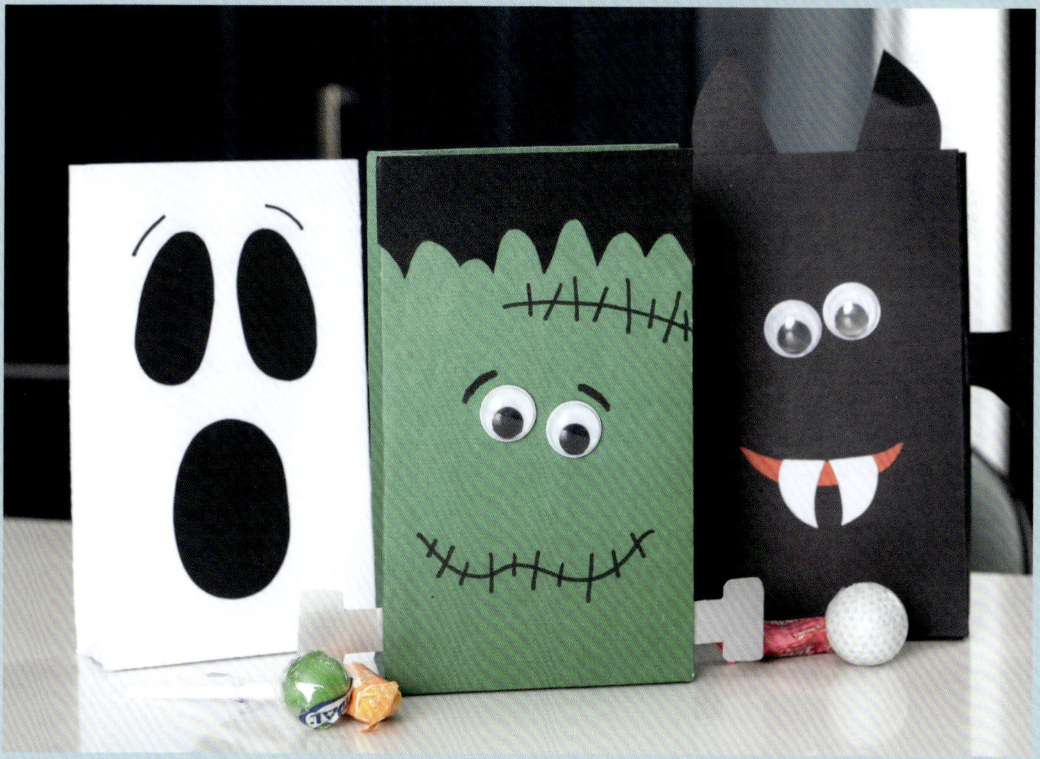